MY
BAR MITZVAH—
OY, DON'T ASK!

POP
AND MY
NIECE,
ALYSÉ

ME & MERYL STREEP
AT MY BIG
MOVIE PREMIERE
IN 2009

MOMMA IN
YOUNGER DAYS—WHAT
HAPPENED?

Praise for *Taking Woodstock*

"This book is absolutely amazing! This reviewer couldn't put It down—in fact, read it twice before writing this review. If you've ever dreamed of being at Woodstock or even if you were there, the author Elliot Tiber will take you back."

—Midwest Book Review

"Momentous . . . [a] thoroughly entertaining tale [and] very human story."

—Publishers Weekly

"Comic and creative . . . [from] the man who serendipitously brought the Woodstock Music and Arts Festival to Bethel, NY, in the summer of 1969 . . . recommended."

—Library Journal

"The true story of Elliot Tiber, hero of the original Woodstock Festival . . . [a] snapshot of America Yesterday"

—The New York Post

"Gleefully candid and often hilarious . . . the story of a middle-aged gay man challenging bigotry, intolerance and the rural peace of Upstate New York residents for the legal rights to sing, dance, and make love not war."

—Foreword Reviews

Praise for *Palm Trees on the Hudson*

"[Carries] the weight of social history.
Among a dwindling number of first-person accounts
recalling urban-American life before the great liberation
movements found their voice. Tiber has a way
with a tale . . . a surprising read for all."

–The Denver Post

"A young man's coming-of-age amid the glitzy backdrop
of mid-20th-century New York . . . a humorous tale."

–Kirkus

"Tiber's rollicking prequel to *Taking Woodstock* has all of
the prime ingredients of a madcap literary comic sendup . . .
Tiber balances belly laughs and sincere emotion . . .
readers of his previous offering will enjoy these candid
episodes of his remarkable backstory."

–Publishers Weekly

"Exceptionally well-written . . .
[a] rags-to-riches-and-back-again riveter."

–BookPleasures.com

"Thought-provoking, fun, meaningful, educational,
and historical . . . supremely fantastic writing."

–Feathered Quill Book Reviews

after woodstock

The True Story of
a Belgian Movie, an Israeli Wedding,
and a Manhattan Breakdown

ELLIOT TIBER

FOREWORD BY ANG LEE

SQUAREONE
PUBLISHERS

I have changed a few names and places here and there, mostly because my wimpy but wise publisher made me do it. I changed the names of those who lost loved ones to AIDS (many of whom may still not realize that AIDS was to blame); those who made my life a living hell by trying to screw with my mojo; and those who chose with full and treacherous intent to filch the very best creative essence from my beloved André, casting him aside when they were done. Who knows? One of the people I'm talking about might be you. Everything in this book is true, even the things that make me look less than perfect. All this being said, I'd say we now have a level playing field. Go ahead, turn the page— if you dare.

IN-HOUSE EDITOR: R.M. Bromberg
TYPESETTER: Gary A. Rosenberg
COVER DESIGN: Jeannie Tudor
COVER ART: Elliot Tiber
BACK COVER PHOTO: Calvin Ki

Square One Publishers
115 Herricks Road
Garden City Park, NY 11040
(516) 535-2010 • (877) 900-BOOK
www.SquareOnePublishers.com

Library of Congress Cataloging-in-Publication Data
Tiber, Elliot, 1935-
  After Woodstock : the true story of a Belgian movie, an Israeli wedding,
& a Manhattan breakdown / Elliot Tiber.
      pages cm
  1. Tiber, Elliot, 1935- 2. Gay men—New York (State)—Biography. 3. Authors,
American—21st century—Biography. I. Title.
  HQ75.8.T53A3 2015
  306.76'62092—dc23
  [B]
                                        2014040856

ISBN: 978-0-7570-0392-9

Printed in the United States of America

10 9 8 7 6 5 4 3 2 1

Contents

*To my sister, Renee,
who has shown me love and acceptance
in a world that remains in dire need of both.*

Acknowledgments

First, a special thanks to Ang Lee, James Schamus, and the rest of the Focus Features family for immortalizing the early period of my life in the film of my book *Taking Woodstock*. You are to be commended for serving art before commerce—always the braver and more exciting choice.

Thanks to those of you who have supported and inspired me over the years:

Alyce Finell

Adam Johnson and his doggie, Railee

Antonio Melez Pelerio

Dr. Andres Lichtenberger

Vlada Von Shatz

Alyse, Steve, and Scott Peterson

Roy Howard (R.I.P., my Woodstock brother)

Jeryl Abramson

Calvin Ki

Joan Wilen

Lydia Wilen

Sebastian Fortino

Marti Mabin

David Schnitter

Jack Blumkin, CPA

Robin and Steve Kaufman

Judy Garland

Marlon Brando

Truman Capote

Tennessee Williams

Greta Garbo

Groucho Marx

Madonna

Sammy Davis, Jr.

Claude Lombard

Anny Duperey

Michael Moriarty

Richie Havens (R.I.P., friend and singer of "Freedom")

Janis Joplin

Jimi Hendrix

Arlo Guthrie

Max Yasgur

Joseph Papp

Michael Lang

Artie Kornfeld

John Roberts

Joel Rosenman

John Morris

Stan Goldstein

Elliott Landy (the "other" Elliot at Woodstock back in '69!)

Melanie

Federico Fellini

Pier Paolo Pasolini

Harvey Milk

Roger Orcutt

Fanny Ernotte

Suzy Falk

Renee Teichberg Brisker and Yuri Brisker

Rachelle Teichberg Golden and Sam Golden

Lee Blumer

Annie Cordy

Mort Shuman

Bert Struys

Annette Insdorf

Colleen Dewhurst

Meryl Streep

Barbra Streisand

John Lennon

Peter Cromarty

Liza Minnelli

Phil Katzman

Bennett Cerf

Jacques Brel

Carol Channing

Imelda Staunton

Henry Goodman

Dick Shepard

Larry Kramer

Gay Men's Health Crisis (NYC)

Father Rodney Kirk

Richard Hunnings

Broadway Cares/Equity Fights AIDS

Polly Pen

Frank Rich

Harry Haun

John Fricke

Ron Simon of the Paley Center for Media

Simon Wiesenthal Museum of Tolerance

Madonna

Lady Gaga

The Village People (all Village People, in fact)

Michael Musto

Tony Kushner

Vikki Carr

Mart Crowley

Jodie Markell

Susana Rossberg

Dennis Bacigalupi

Billie Holiday

Martin Scorsese (he was at Woodstock, too!)

Marie Dressler

Audrey Wood

Charlie Chaplin

Andy Warhol

Salvador Dalí

Marquis de Sade

And my loving doggies: Shayna, Molly, and Woody

I want to extend a boatload of gratitude to my lawyer, Neil Burstein, Esq., for his unerring instincts, all of which have served me immeasurably over the years; his kindness and consideration, which have often kept me from getting too far adrift in this tumultuous sea called life; and his friendship, which has always put a touch of sun into my rainy-day skies.

Thanks to my publisher, Rudy Shur, for being the brother I never had—and for seeing the pivotal moments in my crazy-quilt kaleidoscope of a life before I even did.

A special thanks also to Joanne Abrams at Square One, whose editorial guidance on my previous two books did much to prepare me for what I would revisit and write and *rewrite* in this third and final memoir.

To my editor, R.M. Bromberg, I extend undying gratitude for ensuring that this speeding vehicle of a book never veered off the road too wildly as I put both my queer shoulders to the wheel.

Lastly, I want to give my heartfelt thanks to Anthony Pomes. From our very first conversation in 2006, Anthony has totally dug and understood and appreciated and championed my story—and me. Going above and beyond the realm of any PR and marketing director at any book publishing house, Anthony has been a tireless source of strength and wisdom and inspiration to me. He's a mensch, and I think of him as the good Jewish son that I never had. Which makes perfect sense, since he's Catholic!

Foreword
by Ang Lee

The movie *Taking Woodstock,* based on Elliot Tiber's first book, came out of a chance encounter at 6 AM in a San Francisco television studio. I had just finished promoting my Chinese-language film *Lust, Caution* on Jan Wahl's show on KPIX. (Because of her extravagant headwear, I will always think of Jan as the hat lady, and I am forever grateful to her for giving my film a four out of five hats rating.) On my way out, I bumped into Jan's next guest. This was Elliot Tiber, then a very vigorous seventy-something, who cornered me and thrust a copy of his new book into my hands. I am rather shy, and Elliot is a nonstop talker, and an extremely funny one, so I had no choice but to mumble something polite and take the book on my way to the airport.

The book was *Taking Woodstock,* and it really stuck with me—mostly because I was traveling to promote my film, and simply didn't get a chance to unpack. The book settled near the bottom of my suitcase. A month went by, and somewhere between Bombay and Naples, as luck would have it, a mutual friend of ours, Pat Cupo, urged me to read the book. So I did. The work came across much as Elliot himself had—as a bright, rushing stream of funny stories.

Lust, Caution had been a dark and difficult film for me, so *Taking Woodstock* came at exactly the right moment. It was full of light, love, and laughs, a memoir about the last days of American innocence. And strangely enough, it also fit in with the movie I had just made: both were coming-of-age stories, a genre that I have continued to explore with *Life of Pi* and my current project.

I had a great time making *Taking Woodstock* and getting to know Elliot a little better. And I am very proud of the film, even if it wasn't always understood by viewers and critics. "Woodstock" makes people think of the concert and the music, but that really was not the point of my film. What *Taking Woodstock* offers is the experience of actually being at the festival—the wonderfully confusing, messy, and transforming journey (and trip) that took place far from the stage.

The book you now hold in your hands is a continuation of *Taking Woodstock*. It chronicles the events that brought Elliot from the quiet aftermath of the festival in 1969 to that morning TV show where I first saw him. It is by turns a brave, hilarious, mortifying, and heartbreaking story. In this new book, we get to see Elliot Tiber just as he has always been—a gay man who has been unafraid to stand up for who he is. This is a man who lived through the Stonewall riots, the AIDS crisis, and the slow but steady legalization of gay marriage in the United States. But much of what makes Elliot's story *after* Woodstock so pure and compelling can be found in the figure of Elliot's longtime lover, the late Belgian actor and director André Ernotte.

As presented by Elliot in the pages that follow, André stands as a gentle, brilliant, and often flawed counterpoint to Elliot. Without the love and respect that he received from André, Elliot might never have become the unapologetically free and confident man I met all those years later. We watch in this book as life with André helps Elliot become a better writer, a better brother, a better friend, and a better son to a mother whom he never truly understands.

At the same time, we also see through the prism of this decades-long relationship all that can rock and ruin your sense of identity and self-worth, and everything that happens whenever you let the outside world too close to the hidden comfort of your dreams. We witness how perilously close both Elliot and André come to that terribly harmful place within—the dangerous terrain that all artists, gay or straight, must navigate during the creative process. Here, in *After Woodstock,* I feel that Elliot Tiber has both depicted and transcended that terrain masterfully. I remain proud to have already shared one of Elliot's real-life stories with the world, and I hope that the world will embrace these new stories as well.

—Ang Lee

Getting older is no problem.
You just have to live long enough.

–Groucho Marx

1

Escape
from White Lake

The early afternoon sun blazed in the September sky, shining like a single spotlight on me. Barbra Streisand serenaded me through the speakers of my portable cassette player. I was headed west from New York in my brand-new maroon 1969 Cadillac Eldorado, flying by the gas stations and vile diners that dotted Route I-80, and leaving my largely miserable past behind. For the first time in my thirty-four years schlepping around the planet, I was free—physically, mentally, and financially free.

I was escaping the life forced on me by my chronically unhappy parents. I'd seen freedom before only briefly, changing my name from Elliot Teichberg to the less Jewish-sounding Elliot Tiber and working as an ultra-chic interior designer in Manhattan. But when my parents told me they were opening a motel in upstate New York, this secretly gay Brooklyn-bred yeshiva boy had done the right thing and moved to the backwoods to help.

The El Monaco motel had been a miserable failure, the worst investment in the history of the universe. Nobody in his right mind would have invested a penny in this shambles of a resort—and yet I had been sucked into this black hole by my parents, working there as equal parts slave, toilet cleaner, lawn mower, and promoter.

By the start of 1969, our fourteenth year polluting the world of tourism, all we'd had left to keep the motel from going into foreclosure were the remnants of my savings as an interior decorator. I had done everything I could to bring business to the El Monaco. I had even become president of the local chamber of commerce in the hopes that something would happen. And then, something *had* happened—something just short of a miracle.

As the president of the Bethel Chamber of Commerce, I had had the authority to issue licenses for outdoor music festivals. So when I read in the local paper that the Woodstock Ventures people had lost their permit to hold a concert in Wallkill, about fifty miles away, I made a call. I introduced myself to Woodstock mastermind Mike Lang and said I could provide them with a permit to hold their festival on my fifteen acres of glorious Borscht Belt swampland. That didn't quite work out as planned. But three weeks later, on Max Yasgur's farm, our world changed. The Woodstock festival was a massive success. And for the first time in our crummy motel's existence, we were making more money than we could count, renting out the entire motel to Woodstock Ventures staffers and festival-goers.

When the music ended, the nearly one million hippies had left the White Lake area almost as swiftly as they had arrived. Soon enough, the town had gone back to its dull and boring rhythms. In the wake of the festival, there remained only mud. Heavy rains had started to fall during the middle of the concert festival, turning the whole area into what looked like a giant pit of my mother's *cholent*—a barely edible brown stew that tended to harden in your bowels and stay there for weeks. There were miles of mud. It was in the front office of the motel, on the floors and walls, and in nearly all the rooms. Where there had once been green lawns, there now stood a mud-soaked combat zone.

My parents and I scooted and slipped around in it as we worked to restore a sense of order to our property and to our lives. By the time the festival was over, we were not only debt-free, but we were finally rich, at least by our definition. We were bone-weary as usual, but things were different now. We finally had something to show for our work—money! One night I locked myself into the motel room farthest from my parents, and calmly began to count through and smooth out the crumpled dollar bills that I had been stuffing into a black garbage bag over the past weeks. To my amazement, all the ones and fives and tens I had accumulated in the previous weeks added up to a little more than fifty thousand dollars!

And I knew just what I was going to do with it. Right before Woodstock, I had gotten a call from my friend Felix Fligelman, who had wanted to know if I was interested in moving to Los Angeles with our mutual friend Jerry

Plotznik. Felix was practically singing into the phone: "It's L. . . A, Elliot! That's where it's all happenin', baby! Plus, the drug scene is totally cooler in LA than back here in the city. Fewer narcs, wider selection, better prices." At the time, with financial ruin seemingly around the corner, it had seemed inconceivable. It had taken all my strength to suppress what I was thinking at that moment: *Fuck yes! Swing by the motel, and roll the car window down far enough for me to jump right in!*

Over the summer, Felix had sent me a postcard with the familiar image of the Hollywood sign and his new phone number written on it. I had taped that wonderful Hollywood postcard to my wall to remind myself that life—and opportunities—existed beyond White Lake. I was an artist, I was gay, and I had always loved the movies. The things that sustained me were totally out of whack with the values of rural White Lake. Sitting there in the aftermath of Woodstock with that pile of cash before me, my plan was crystal clear: I would move to California and become a movie set decorator.

It hadn't been easy to tell my parents that I was going. I knew I'd have to fight to keep my money away from Momma. She wasn't going to let me go so easily, either. Thankfully, my father stepped up. He insisted that she give me what was rightfully mine. For the first time that I could recall, he stood up to my mother and made her take heed. "Sonia, give Elli the money, and not another word!" he said, loud enough to make his point. Having spent nearly all of his life under Momma's thumb, it was a joy to see how the spirit of the concert had finally allowed him to grow a pair of assertive Jewish balls.

And so I got ready to leave White Lake. On that Monday morning in late September, my parents had stood in the driveway outside our motel office, watching me as I packed the trunk of my new Cadillac with my art portfolio, suitcase, and, of course, the duffel bag. Filled with all my cash, plus an additional five hundred bucks that my father had smuggled away from my mother, my duffel bag held what was probably the greatest stash in Teichberg history—only God and Momma knew where she had hidden her own cut of the money.

My father had had other gifts for me, too. There was a shopping bag of dry sandwiches made on rye bread and pints of Momma's grease-laden chicken soup. I tossed these culinary inedibles into the trash at the first rest stop I visited. But he'd also given me a bundle of AAA road maps. Pop knew his only

1955. A hovel grows in White Lake. My mother (the sumo wrestler on the left) and my baby sister Renee (the hotsy-totsy calendar girl on the right) in front of what was to become our dread El Monaco motel.

1969. Portrait of the artist as a young stud. Taken a few months before my life changed as a result of the Stonewall Riots and the Woodstock festival.

son well enough to realize that I had practically no sense of direction. I had made more than a few wrong turns on Route 17B when I first started coming up to White Lake to work in "motel hell." So the map set was a thoughtful present indeed. Pop had even gone through the maps and highlighted various motels where I could stay on the way to LA. These carefully marked maps gave me a feeling of security.

Once I had finished packing up the car, I had turned and looked at Pop and Momma. There was an awkward silence; my father's eyes met mine but my mother looked away. Affectionate gestures were not common in the Teichberg family. To be sure, there had been countless occasions over the years when I had had a strong desire to hug my three sisters—Rachelle, Goldie, and Renee—or even to hug those crazy Hebrew-hewn lunatics who brought me into this world. But my parents' inability to publicly demonstrate affection kept us all in a freeze-out when we most needed a warm embrace.

Getting ready to leave, I hadn't expected this occasion to be different from any that had come before. I was half-wrong. Pop's eyes welled up with tears as he shook my hand. Working together that summer, he and I had established a stronger bond than we had ever had before. Momma's response was not a surprise. She knew that this was the escape I had dreamed of over the years, and she wasn't going to wish me luck. With words so caustic they would have burned through a bank vault door, she spat: "I know you. You'll drive off in that fency-schmency Cadillac and waste every penny! What, you think you'll find something better out there? I'm telling you now, when you lose all your money, Elli, don't think we're going to give you more! Don't let your *meshuggeneh* friends take it away from you. Go, already. Go!" She turned and marched back into the office. Her final admonition, delivered with the thunderous force of a thousand drunk rabbis, was: "Remember, Eliyahu—a Jewish boy needs his Momma!"

Her ominous pronouncement couldn't take away my good mood on that morning, though. I must have looked positively deranged as I cruised along, singing and smiling and laughing with Barbra, and sometimes Janis Joplin and Joan Baez, too. I drove for the next thirty hours straight, stopping only for gas and chocolate bars. I was running on the sheer adrenaline rush of escape—the heady knowledge that I was no longer shackled to my parents and the wretched El Monaco motel. I knew better than to have any marijuana in the car, in case I happened to get pulled over. I felt naturally high just knowing that I was driving toward a better future, a future on my own terms. With every mile I drove, I was that much closer to reinventing myself, and that much closer to starting a new life in a place I had fantasized about since I was a kid.

The old me might have been fearful that the Teichberg Curse—a malicious family spell that had hung on me for years like soiled laundry—would have me back in White Lake within a week. But that magical three-day-long concert, with its spontaneous family of hippies, had finally banished the curse. At least that's what I believed in my heart.

A few miles shy of the Indiana state line, I pulled up at a rest stop and phoned my father from a motel he'd highlighted on the map. He was very happy to hear from me, and reported that the town was swiftly turning back into what it had always been—a cemetery with vacancies. Pop told me that Momma was going about the motel as if it were just another season. As I dropped some more coins into the pay phone, I heard Momma yelling in the background. Pop said, "Elli, your mother, she wants to speak to you. We'll talk again soon."

True to form, Momma took the phone and immediately began to nag me about joining a local Jewish center the minute I got to California. She assured me that this was how I would find the "nice Jewish girl" that I was always supposed to marry. That way, she argued, I would finally be able to give her nineteen grandchildren and a special laminated membership card from B'nai B'rith International. Talk about your old and familiar—if I weren't already gay, this constant pressure from Momma to marry and make a little shtetl of Teichbergs would have been enough to send me racing either to a suicide society or to the nearest friendly gay bar.

When the operator finally broke in and said, "Please deposit another twenty-five cents." I quickly blurted out, "Sorry, Mom, don't have any more change. Gotta go! Bye!" Then I hung up the phone and got back on the road but fast, resolving always to use pay phones to call home in the future. Leave it to Momma to give me that familiar feeling of not being good enough.

The monotony of driving hundreds of miles a day was starting to make my mind wander a bit. I was glad that I had had the foresight to bring my own portable cassette deck with me. True to my training as an interior decorator, I intended to design the musical soundtrack to suit the places I passed. Over those long stretches of highway, the music of Judy Garland kept me thinking about the yellow brick road that had brought her character, Dorothy, all the way from Kansas to the magical land of Oz. I hadn't listened so intensely to Judy's music since a little over a year before, when my life came together with Ms. Garland's ever so briefly.

By the spring of 1968, I had reached the absolute top of my game as an interior designer. I had almost become a fixture in elegant Sutton Place and Park Avenue in Manhattan, and they knew me on Long Island, too. In mid-April, I had been given carte blanche to organize an extravagant birthday party for a big-shot mob boss on a Hudson River cruise boat. One of the party's guests of honor was none other than my beloved idol, Judy Garland. Though she appeared frail and rather out of it, Judy had agreed to perform a few songs. She sang "Over the Rainbow," which sent me over the moon. Later that night, a fight broke out and total anarchy ensued. People even tossed my rented palm trees overboard as the boat passed the Statue of Liberty. In the midst of the chaos, I suddenly found myself face to face with Judy herself. We talked for only a few minutes, but she had some beautifully eccentric yet heartfelt things to say about what it meant to have a home. Those moments with Judy provided me with much-needed proof that a happier life awaited me over the rainbow—a destination that I had come to realize might be waiting for me in California.

After a night's rest at another motel circled on the map, I was back on the highway, driving toward Illinois. As I drove past innumerable towns, road signs, and highway motels, I grew increasingly eager to get to Chicago, the midpoint of my trip. Occasionally, I switched on the car radio in hopes that I might catch some mention of the big hippie hoopla that had rocked my world less than a month earlier. From July to mid-August, the media had been filled with stories about Woodstock. Now, as I zoomed along in the car, there was absolutely nothing about the concert on the air. What *was* on the air was the Beatles' new album, *Abbey Road*. As I drove, I listened to the album's first single, "Come Together." The lyrics reminded me warmly of the Woodstock experience, but nobody on the radio seemed to make this connection.

Then, as Petula Clark trumpeted the many pleasures of "Downtown" through my cassette player, the Chicago skyline suddenly exploded into view. I had never driven to Illinois before, though I'd flown in many times on shopping trips to buy furniture and fabric during my interior design career. During my stays in the Windy City, I had come to know where the few gay bars were located. In New York, my friends Jerry and Felix had introduced me to the Mattachine Society, an early gay rights organization with local chapters nationwide. The Mattachine Society had told us all that there was strength in numbers, and that together we could fight the marginalization and harassment we suffered as gay men. It planted the first seeds of the Stonewall Riots, and had introduced me to the idea of gay pride. What stayed with me more than speeches or leaflets, however, was the feeling of closeness that we shared when we got together. Through the Mattachine Society, I got to meet people like me, people who lived throughout the country and shared my fears and concerns and interests. And, of course, the Mattachine had been a good place to pick up tips about gay hot spots outside of New York.

It had been through a Mattachine contact that I had learned about the leather scene in Chicago back in 1967. As I drove through the city streets, my mind drifted back to the last time I'd visited. After taking care of some appointments with various vendors during the day, I had bought a full new outfit at a leather shop—pants, jacket, boots, and police cuffs—and gone out to a club that my friend had recommended. It was a large, seedy bar underneath the elevated trains, painted black inside and featuring a large poster of Marlon Brando on his motorcycle from *The Wild One*. At the club, I'd been picked up by a six foot six muscular black man dressed in a leather policeman outfit. Thor was his name, and he'd taken me back to his place in his car, which turned out to be a black hearse. The sex had been rough and fiery, just the way I liked it.

Energized by these memories of Thor, I was about to steer my Eldorado in the direction of the hotel where I had stayed in 1967, when I was hit by a second thought. I was sitting in a brand-new Cadillac with upwards of fifty thousand dollars in cash stuffed behind a spare tire in the trunk. If I checked into a hotel and put the money in their safe, there was no way I could be sure that someone wouldn't steal it. If I left the money in the Cadillac, somebody could steal the car *and* my stash. Neither option seemed ideal.

Suddenly, I realized that my newfound freedom came with a lot more responsibility than I had expected. It also required a healthy dose of paranoia. So I decided to head west out of Chicago and keep to the relative safety of the interstate highway. The erotic memories of my one-night stand with mighty Thor would have to sustain me through the drive. Until I reached Felix and Jerry in Los Angeles and could get my loot locked up inside a safe deposit box, that duffel bag of cash would be my only sleeping companion. *Who knows?* I thought, *perhaps Momma really put a Jewish voodoo hex on me and the money the night before I left.*

❁   ❁   ❁

I hoped to get to California by Sunday. On the highways taking me further west, I saw signs advertising the joys of various local tourist attractions, miles of corn and wheat fields, and stray whiskey bottles, soda and beer cans, and less-than-fabulous bits of garbage littering the sides of the road. The long drive was really beginning to weigh on me. I barreled through the Midwest like a man with his pubic hair on fire. Now I was doing between eighty and ninety miles per hour, blowing through Missouri and then Kansas, where I couldn't suppress thoughts of Dorothy Gale and Auntie Em from *The Wizard of Oz*. I hunkered down at a little motel in Kansas on Friday night and called Pop on the pay phone outside the motel office to let him know where I was and how I was doing. He told me that they had rented out three rooms at the motel. That kind of occupancy would have felt like winning the lottery for us only a year before; now, it made me miss the Woodstock weeks that much more. I could tell that Pop was sad to lose all the frenetic energy and youthful spirit surrounding the event—and especially sad to lose me.

On Saturday morning, I drove into Oklahoma on Route 66 only a few hours after dawn, listening to the original 1943 cast recording of Rodgers and Hammerstein's musical *Oklahoma!*. I figured if I kept to my schedule, I would be with Jerry and Felix in time to catch the *Ed Sullivan Show* on TV, sitting pretty with a banana daiquiri in one hand and a mammoth joint in the other.

And then there was Texas, hot and dry. Driving through Texas was like eating an entire box of *matzoh* without having so much as a glass of water to drink, let alone the obligatory glass of thick, kosher Manischewitz wine. I had not expected to see an infinite desert on the landscape, pierced only here and there with gas stations and a handful of ranch houses set far off from the highway. How anyone would want to live in a place that looked like Mars or a cratered moonscape was beyond me. Having heard that the Texas Highway Patrol were none too friendly, I made sure to keep my speed under sixty-five miles per hour.

I had been driving on the highway for several hours. It was a straight run through the middle of nowhere. The road was relatively empty, precisely the kind of place where you would never want your car to break down. It was about midday—high noon—when I saw it. At first it appeared as a small dot in my rearview mirror, growing larger and moving toward me at a very fast pace. Within a minute or so, the dot had turned into a vehicle with a pair of red flashing lights. The police car kept following me at the same speed to which I had now guiltily slowed down the Cadillac. I wondered whether he was flashing his lights for me. A quick glance at the road before and behind me cinched it: ours were the only two cars on the road for miles. I pulled off the highway and into the dirt, and the police car rolled up directly behind me, as if it were hitched to the back of my car by a heavy chain.

As I stopped the car, I cautiously rolled down the window. In my rearview mirror, I saw the officer open the door of his vehicle and step outside. He was really big, and I was really nervous. As he approached, I could see he wasn't a happy man. He walked over to my window and looked down at me suspiciously, keeping one hand steady on the butt of his revolver.

"Boy, let me see your driver's license," he said with as heavy a Texas accent as I had ever heard. Without saying a word, I pulled the license from my wallet and handed it to him.

"Who does this here vehicle belong to?" he asked.

"It belongs to me, sir—officer—sir," I managed to blurt out. He looked up from my license long and slow, smiling faintly in a way that reminded me a bit of Thor from Chicago.

"Now then, where's a long-haired hippie like you goin' to git the money to buy a nice new Cadillac like this?" he asked, with all the pleasure of a cat playing with a mouse—me being the mouse.

I had totally forgotten that I must have looked like some spaced-out hippie vagrant with my longish hair, beard stubble, and sweaty pea-green T-shirt. "You git out of the car now, boy," he said, as he ordered me to place my hands on the side of the "VEE-hick-uhl."

I was trembling like a leaf. It took everything inside of me to string together a single sentence. I said simply, "I am a college professor." This unexpected statement made him even more suspicious. "Keep your hands up on that thar automobile, son," he said in that same slow drawl, heading back to his car to make a call on his police radio. He was on the call for what was probably only five minutes. To me, it felt like five hours. I remembered thinking that Texas must operate on a different time continuum than the rest of the planet. Having established that I was neither a murderer nor a thief, he came back over to me and squinted in my face. We stood there for a few seconds, just staring at each other. His stare was filled with more power and menace than mine, which resembled the disoriented gaze of a deer caught in front of a headlight.

"I tell ya," he finally said through a tight little laugh, "we here in Texas don't take too kindly to you long-hair hippie types. No sir-ree!" I was standing face to face with a person who represented everyone who had ever judged others based only on their appearances—a person who was fully capable of doing anything he wished to me there in the middle of sun-soaked Texas. All those times when my friends or I had been stopped or threatened because we were gay, we had been powerless to fight back. For that one night back in June at the Stonewall Inn, we had stood united. Here in the burning-hot emptiness of the Texas desert, though, I was alone and scared. I had a lot I wanted to say to this guy, but I knew he would probably enjoy taking a pipe to the back of my head in some dusty jail cell if I gave him cause for arrest. Instead, I looked at him meekly and asked if I was free to go.

He waved me off with his left hand, his right hand frozen on top of his revolver. It occurred to me that this man could very well pull out his gun and shoot me dead on the side of the road. As I lifted my hands away from the car and moved toward the driver's side door, he stopped me. I looked at him, and he held out my license. "You don't want to forget this now, son," he said. "A young man can get into a heap of trouble around here if he can't prove who he is, y'know."

I thanked him, got in the car, and drove off very slowly, with both hands firmly wrapped around the steering wheel. As I pulled away, I could see his face in the rearview mirror, a twisted look of disappointment appearing on it for not being able to throw me into jail.

The experience jangled my nerves, and I made it my mission to get the hell out of Texas by nightfall. That evening, cooped up in yet another motel just inside New Mexico, I wanted more than anything to get to California— farther still from the emotional jails of Momma and the physical jails of Texas, and closer to the land of silver-screen dreams.

2

Ḩooray
for Ḩollywood!

I awoke from a fitful sleep with a jolt. The rusted steel clock on the bedside table clanged its alarm so loudly that I almost fell out of bed in my scramble to silence it. It was a quarter to five on Sunday morning, and I was worried the alarm would somehow wake everyone else in the motel, even though I had counted only four other cars in the lot when I checked in the night before. My paranoia-fueled exodus out of Texas had taken nearly seven hours, including a quick stop at a service station for gas, candy bars, and trip to a bathroom that, by the looks of it, must have been used by some roadside chainsaw killer to clean up his equipment.

With the difference in time zones, it had been too late for me to call my parents when I arrived at this motel just off the highway in Santa Clara, New Mexico. What I had needed was rest, but I had wound up tossing and turning most of the night. My cash-stuffed duffel bag had hardly gotten any sleep either, as I had kept knocking it from the bed down to the shag carpet floor. Every time I reached down in the darkness of the room to scoop up the bag, I felt anxious and instantly thought of my encounter with that cop in Texas. First, I had been scared. Then I had gotten pissed off. Ultimately, though, I was bummed out. That cop had taken away many of the good vibes I had had when I'd set off on this road trip. During the festival, a New York state cop had been kind enough to give me a ride on his motorcycle from the motel over to the concert site—and he was cute, to boot. The cop in Texas, on the other hand, had been arbitrarily cruel and seemed more interested in intimidating me than he'd been in keeping the highways safe. What a difference a state makes.

Getting ready to go, I went through what had become a sort of ritual on the trip. I brought the duffel bag into the bathroom with me and placed it midway between the shower and the door. While cleaning up in the shower, I left the curtain open just enough so that the bag was always within view. That way, I figured I could see the motel clerk in action if he tried to make off with my cash. Thinking back, I am not sure how a wet, naked man armed only with a bar of soap would stop someone from stealing his nest egg, but logic didn't seem to play a role in my thinking at that point.

Once I toweled off, I splashed my face with cold water, brushed my teeth, put on some deodorant, got on my jeans—which by now needed a washing—and slipped on another T-shirt. I was finally on the last leg of my trip, and all I could think was that by the end of this day I was going to be in Los Angeles. So by 5:30 that morning, I was ready. I headed out on Route 66 as the sun was starting to rise. *This is it,* I told myself. Today, it was Hollywood or bust for Elliot Tiber. If the car broke down, I would get a bicycle. And if the bike got busted, I would sling the duffel bag over my shoulder and run the rest of the way.

I was really looking forward to meeting up with Felix and Jerry. Gay like me, Felix and Jerry were both former playmates of mine from when I had lived in Bensonhurst. I had first met Felix when we were students at Brooklyn College in the early 1950s. He had a bright smile and an even brighter spirit. Felix thought he looked like the actor Burt Lancaster. He was a handsome guy, but any spell he might have cast was immediately broken whenever he opened his mouth. He sounded like a cross between Bette Davis and a city bus horn. Nor was he the brightest bulb in the box. Whatever Felix lacked in common sense, though, he more than made up for with his good nature and kind heart.

Jerry had been introduced to me by my kid sister Renee. Renee and Jerry had attended Brooklyn College together several years after Felix and I had gone through. Blessed with Tony-Curtis-like good looks, Jerry considered himself to be Renee's steady boyfriend. Renee did not see things that way. Regardless, he would announce to anyone within earshot that he and Renee were engaged and planning to rent out the Flatbush Jewish Center for a *glatt* kosher wedding. Renee's reaction was usually to say that he had inhaled too many mind-altering fumes in the college's chemistry labs—a claim that probably had some truth to it.

I had discovered that Jerry played on the same team as Felix and I did one night at Renee's apartment in Brooklyn. We all had had a bit too much to drink, and Jerry and I found ourselves making out on the living room couch after Renee had gone to bed. He kept telling me he wasn't gay, and that I was just a handy substitute for those sexual urges he felt toward Renee. I pretended that I was having a potent sexual liaison with Tony Curtis. Some definitely like it hot! When I told my sister a few days later what had happened, she was actually relieved. "Now maybe he'll give up on all that silly wedding business," she said, giggling. Soon after, Jerry figured out he was gay; he and Renee remained friends after he agreed to break off their imaginary engagement.

Where Felix was only handsome, Jerry had both good looks and brains. He was exceptionally book smart, having graduated college with a major in chemistry and a minor in economics. At some point in the mid-1960s, Felix and Jerry had become a couple. Even though he was younger, Jerry had always came across as being older and wiser than Felix on most levels. Their romantic partnership didn't last, but their business partnership did. By early 1968, they began to work up a scheme to become real-estate moguls out in Hollywood—hence the move to LA. I would learn soon enough what they had been up to in California.

By dusk, I knew I was close to Los Angeles because of the enormous traffic-clogged freeways—and because of the palm trees. They seemed to be everywhere, lining the sides of the highways. My heart began to pound with anticipation. As I left Route 66 and turned onto the Hollywood Freeway, it wasn't too long before I saw what I had been waiting to see. It was my personal Holy Grail, the legendary Hollywood sign, standing proudly atop Mount Lee in all its tall, white-lettered splendor. Okay, so the letters weren't exactly straight; well, neither was I. Forgetting about the nearly seven days on the road and that cop in Texas, I felt like I had been magically transported into that colorful postcard I had gotten from Felix earlier that summer.

"I made it! I'm here!" I shouted to nobody in particular. As I made my way off the highway, I put on the cassette I had been saving for this exact moment. It was the great Broadway star Ethel Merman singing "There's No Business Like Show Business." I sang every word of the song along with Ethel, wearing a grin on my face so big it could have lit up the entire city.

❀   ❀   ❀

"Elliot! Hey, what's shakin'? Where the hell are you, man?" shouted Felix. I was calling him from a pay phone outside an International House of Pancakes just off Hollywood Boulevard. I told him that I had arrived and needed to confirm with him the address of their house.

"No problem, El," he responded. "Take the boulevard heading east of Eden until you see Hillhurst on your left. Make the turn and then drive on until you see us!"

"Um, it's dark out, Felix," I said, thinking that he sounded a little spaced out. "Which side of the road are you on?"

"Don't worry, Elliot," Felix said quickly, as I heard him fumble with the phone a bit. "Hold on a sec—hey, Jerry?" he shouted away from the phone receiver.

A few seconds later, Jerry came to the phone. "So you're here, Elli baby?!" he teased. "Listen, drive up Hillhurst like Felix said and we'll be standing in front of the mansion gate waving flashlights—dig?" I dug.

I turned left on Hillhurst Avenue as instructed, but any new town is always a little tough to traverse at night, especially with my sense of direction. And if you've ever taken the wrong road while cruising around those poorly lit towns that border Hollywood, you know that you're lucky if you don't accidentally drop down the side of a steep canyon. Just as I was starting to get a little anxious, I spotted two beams of light on the right side of the road. They darted frantically back and forth, like searchlights at a movie premiere. Given the scope of my show-biz dreams, I took this to be a very good sign.

As I got closer, I saw Felix and Jerry standing at the foot of the driveway, giving me the Hollywood treatment upon my arrival. After I put the Cadillac in park, they practically yanked my car door open and smothered me with kisses and hugs. This happy hug fest was the first physical contact I had had since my father shook my hand and said goodbye in White Lake. We were like three blind mice that had finally found each other again.

"Holy shit, it's great to see you, man!" shouted Felix.

I had arrived. I drove carefully through the iron entry gates, and my headlights caught a lawn as massive as the Pacific Ocean leading up to the mansion. There were two cars in the lot. One was a big stretch limousine, which I learned the next day belonged to Jerry, and the other was a red BMW convertible that belonged to Felix. I parked and headed on up to the house, duffel bag in hand.

Once inside the foyer, which was dimly lit by a big glass chandelier with only about half of its bulbs working, I was able to see Felix and Jerry a little more clearly. They were tanner and a bit chunkier than they had been back in New York. They were excited to tell me that the mansion had once belonged to Marie Dressler, a popular Oscar-winning silent film actress who had passed away in the 1930s. As a big film buff, I knew who Marie Dressler was and was honored to be staying in a house that had probably once counted Charlie Chaplin as a dinner guest.

At first glance, I could see that the house was typical of early Hollywood's opulence. Jerry explained that he and Felix had bought the house and its grounds for the huge bargain of fifty-seven thousand dollars. They were able to get this price for several reasons. For one thing, the former owners had declared bankruptcy five years before, and after several years of litigation the property had finally reverted back to the bank—which meant the bank was stuck paying the property taxes. For another, the mansion was located in Los Feliz; by the time the bank had taken ownership, the area had fallen out of fashion among the showbiz set and seen an increase in crime. And lastly, as Jerry put it, he and Felix were two suckers who were willing to put down 10 percent. The rest had been history.

Jerry had mastered the art of real estate property management back in New York. Felix had grown in charm and confidence, and was an expert at dealing with all kinds of people. They were street-smart—they knew which way was up and where and when to hit their marks when it came to people. Though much of what happened to me during the Woodstock summer felt like luck, I believed that I also had the strength to bring things together in a way that worked.

Felix and Jerry produced a large pitcher of ice-cold vodka at the beat-up black-leather-paneled bar off the main room, and quickly prepared me a drink. They asked about my trip, and I told them that it had been fairly hum-drum until I had that run-in with the law in Texas. "Oh, wow, Elliot," groaned Felix, "you must have been scared shitless!" Jerry just shook his head and said, "Texas, man. Yeah, fags like us really have to be careful when driving through places like that. You were fuckin' lucky, Elliot." From the look on his face, I knew that he was serious.

Felix and Jerry were eager for me to start partying with them. To hear them tell it, Hollywood was a hedonistic pleasure palace. There was good California weed everywhere you looked, and the scene was so permissive that finding a hot partner—gay or straight—was as easy as squeezing toothpaste from a tube. At that point however, all I could think of was squeezing a pillow and catching some Zs.

Felix and Jerry helped me carry my bags to one of the huge bedrooms on the second floor. Though tired, I couldn't help but notice that the room was an antiquated delight. It looked like nothing had changed since Marie Dressler's time. Somehow, the old decor made me feel closer to the spirit of old Hollywood. It was like being in a black-and-white movie.

"Get some rest, Elliot. We'll talk more tomorrow," Jerry said. "I guarantee you're gonna love the scene around here. It's just like what we used to talk about back in New York. We can do all those things that we only talked about. We're free out here, man!"

As they were leaving the room, Jerry handed me my own set of house keys and said, *"Mi casa es su casa."* Alone again, it took a moment for reality to sink in. I had finally made it to Hollywood. But I would still be sleeping alone with my duffel bag—just for one more night.

⚘   ⚘   ⚘

It took me a few moments to remember where I was when I woke up the next morning. Then I noticed the high ceiling and recalled that I was pleasantly ensconced in my friends' fixer-upper mansion. The sun was already shining, so I scrambled for my watch. It was a little after eight o'clock in the morning. By my standards, I'd slept late. I didn't want to lose any more time. I needed to get my new life started as quickly as possible. And the first order of business was to get a divorce from my duffel bag, care of a strong steel safety deposit box at the nearest bank.

I tried to descend the stairs quietly. I assumed that Felix and Jerry were asleep somewhere in the mansion. In the daylight, I could now see the house for what it was. It certainly was big, with a distinctive once-upon-a-time glamour tarnished by a decay and neglect. It was obvious that the place needed a lot of work, but I was ready to do what I could.

I got into my car and made my way back down to Hollywood Boulevard, prepared to deposit my money in the first big bank I could find. About three blocks from Hillhurst Avenue, I found my target. Entering the bank, I was introduced to the branch manager, Horace Wilcox, a heavy-set middle-aged man in a blue three-piece suit. Fully aware that I did not look my best, I admitted as much to the banker right away and explained that I wanted the biggest security box they had.

"No problem, Mr. Tiber," Mr. Wilcox said. "That will be thirty-five dollars per year."

I paid for the safety deposit box rental and was then shown to a windowless back room where I could tend to my affairs in private. I emptied my duffel bag into the steel drawer. It was amazing to see all that money fall out of the bag and into the box, some in rubber-banded batches and others freefalling. The heft of the bills was slightly misleading, though. For every halfdozen ten-, twenty-, and fifty-dollar bills, there were hundreds of single-dollar bills. I realized then that Momma had kept the hundreds for her own stash.

It took me two hours to put the money into some type of order. Once I was done, I counted out five hundred in tens and another five hundred in singles. Then I left the vault and made my way back to Mr. Wilcox's desk. Handing him the singles, I said, "I'd like to open a checking account with these five hundred dollars, if that's okay. Do I get a free toaster with my deposit?"

Mr. Wilcox looked at me strangely. Dead silence.

"I guess that's just a New York thing," I said to cover the awkwardness. "Hold the toaster, then. Please give me some temporary checks. Those should work fine."

By the time I left the bank, I had lost my sleeping companion, but I had gained some comfort in knowing that I would finally be able to relax and enjoy my new surroundings. I had money in my pocket, and more cash in the bank. I planned to stay free, even if that freedom was rented.

❀   ❀   ❀

I walked in the front door a little before noon, and found the mansion still quiet. Heading toward the kitchen, which resembled a cavernous movie set, I saw Felix sitting at the counter with a cup of what I thought was coffee. It wasn't—he was drinking what was left of the chilled vodka from the night before.

"Good morning," I said, excited to be a few hours into my first full California day. Felix mumbled a small "Hey."

"Is there a grocery close by?" I asked. "I wanted to pick up some food, and—"

"No, no, no, no!" Felix exclaimed. His entire being seemed to have been plugged into an electrical socket. He hopped up on the counter, grinning and shaking his open hands in front of him like Jerry Lewis after taking a thousand Benzedrine tablets. "No, Elli, no, you don't have to worry about food, man! We've got food. Lots of food! And tonight, I'm going to make you one of the best fucking home-cooked dinners you've ever had in your life!"

Until then, the only home-cooked meals I'd known had been Momma's. And if the army had served her greasy slops to the Viet Cong, they could have ended the Vietnam War in America's favor within five minutes. Anything Felix prepared was bound to be an improvement.

Felix shook his head back and forth slowly. "I'm a great fucking cook, Elli!"

"Sure are, Felix," said Jerry, coming into the kitchen. "Felix is one ultra-groovy gourmand." Just as Felix announced that he was going upstairs to pick out "cooking clothes" for later and ran upstairs, Jerry quickly gestured for me to come over to him by the kitchen doorway.

"Hey, listen," Jerry said, in a conspiratorial whisper, "Felix loves to cook, but he has no idea what the hell he's doing. Don't eat anything he makes. Actually," he chuckled, "you don't have to worry, 'cause he destroys most of it in the oven anyway. I'll order some take-out Chinese ahead of time, as I usually do."

I smiled, and said, "Uh, okay. But is there anything in the fridge that I can eat now? I'm starving! I haven't eaten since yesterday."

"Check this out, man," Jerry said, opening the refrigerator door to reveal a cornucopia of fruits, vegetables, meats, eggs, juices, vodka, and more. "Felix may not be able to cook," Jerry continued, "but he sure does one hell of an impression."

"Just point me toward the bread. I'm sure I can put together a sandwich out of that stockpile," I said.

Once I had downed the lovely veggie-stuffed hero I had created, Jerry and Felix decided to give me a tour of the house. They grasped me playfully by the shoulders and guided me down the main first-floor hallway so I could see what was waiting for me in the Dressler mansion.

"As you will observe, we have seven splendidly appointed rooms here on the main floor," said Felix, really getting into his role as breathless Hollywood mansion tour guide. The hallway had frosted-glass light fixtures running along both walls. Only about half of the lamps worked, though, leaving the hallway dark and dingy.

As we walked, Felix turned toward me and announced each successive room with a sweeping gesture. "This," he said, using his best attempt at a seductive voice, "is where you will find the study . . . the music room . . . the smoking room . . . Here is a room for your public meetings . . . and a room for your most private games." More silly than steamy, his presentation was charming nonetheless.

The rooms were spacious but bare, with some cobwebs in the corner of one room and a broken couch against the wall of another. There was one room that remained locked. Jerry explained that was their office, and that he would show it to me later.

"Next, we have our fully functional and totally exotic South Pacific laundry room on your right," continued Felix, still in full-throttle theatrical mode. Only one of the three washers and one of the three dryers were functional, but I announced my intention to clean my week's worth of clothing that very day. "That's a good idea, El," joked Jerry, showing me the supply of soaps, shampoos, and dry towels at the back of the room.

Felix became very excited as we walked toward a set of twin wooden doors, one of which was missing its handle. "And now, Mr. Tiber, I present to you the magnificent and marvelous Miss Judy Garland Ballroom!" Jerry said, leading the way into a large room about forty feet long and thirty feet wide. It had once been quite impressive, but now there were lots of surface cracks in the ceiling and structural damage along the walls. The wooden floor was still fairly solid, though it dipped slightly in a few spots, and would really need to be relacquered if it were to be beautiful again. Considering the condition Judy Garland had been in when I met her, the name of the ballroom made perfect sense.

"And now," Felix gushed, as we exited the ballroom and moved back down the hallway, "we move onwards and upwards to the deliciously lush second floor of your comfy little mansion. This is where you will find the sleeping quarters in the house, eight amazing feats of stately comfort and architectural delight!"

Jerry led the way back and up the stairs. The second-floor hallway had five crystal chandeliers dangling unevenly from the ceiling, and a gap where a sixth one used to be. Upstairs, the rooms were as spacious as those downstairs, but they had a more intimate feel. Each had large Gothic-style windows that provided sumptuous views of the Hollywood Hills and nearby Griffith Park. The views were even better at night, with all those lights glittering. Several panes of glass were broken, however, and the windows needed to be cleaned inside and out.

All told, the entire place needed major repairs. Jerry said he had identified three major areas that needed work: the roof, the foundation, the interiors. Felix and Jerry had a plan. They would paint the house, fix the cracks, and restore much of the faded glamour or replace it with updated chic. Felix said their hope was to turn the fifty-thousand-dollar investment into a sale of at least two hundred grand *after* taxes. I knew what needed to be done to flip this Hollywood property, but I liked the Golden Age aura that the mansion gave off. Compared to the perpetually wretched El Monaco back in White Lake, this mansion was as opulent as the Taj Mahal.

I could tell Felix was about to announce the end of the house tour when I asked about a door off to the right. "Oh, that's just a single room where I've been staying," Felix said hurriedly, as Jerry led me over. Almost immediately upon entering the room, it felt as if we had walked into the National Museum of Mess. It was as if everything of marginal interest over the past thirty years had been dropped in this room. Everywhere I looked was chaos. There were multicolored bundles of clothing, used towels, tissue boxes, dozens of shoes strewn all over the floor, and the crème de la crème—a male dressmaker's dummy, on which was hung a hot pink taffeta dress. Seeing my horrified reaction, Felix shrugged and said in a mock-serious tone, "Pardon our appearance while we reconstruct." I cracked up. Jerry, taking another look at the room, said to me, "Now you know why he and I stopped living together back in New York!"

Heading back toward the kitchen, Felix asked me what I thought I could do to help them out with the mansion. I was about to give voice to some of my initial ideas when Jerry told Felix that we would all talk about it later, during dinner. That reminded Felix of his earlier promise to produce a killer six-course meal for the three of us. As Felix practically cartwheeled his way back toward the kitchen, Jerry asked me to follow him back to the general office space in one of the larger main-floor rooms. There sat a desk stacked with a variety of papers dealing with different properties all over California.

"This is where we do a lot of what we do," said Jerry, as he lit a joint. He offered me a much-appreciated hit, and I inhaled as deeply as I could. That sweet and even cannabis euphoria hit me fast, like one of those leather-glove slaps to the face that I enjoyed so well. I felt slow and tranquil as Jerry gestured toward a small battalion of telephones across the back of the desk.

"Felix is a master when it comes to these phones, Elliot," he said. "When he's on, he can talk anyone into almost anything."

I was about to ask Jerry about Felix drinking that mug of vodka earlier, but I didn't have to. "Felix has his good days and his bad, you know? When he's up, he can sweet-talk the fucking man in the moon straight out of the night sky. But when he's down . . ."

I told him that I didn't remember Felix being like that back in New York, and Jerry said he really didn't start to see it until they lived together for awhile as a couple. There had been times when Felix got so depressed that it seemed like nothing would shake him out of his funk. "He just goes away inside himself somewhere, and I'm not able to find him at all," Jerry explained. "Since we've been here, it seems to have gotten worse."

"Probably the drinking and the drugs," I suggested.

"Actually," Jerry said with a laugh, "the drugs are the only things that bring him back from the dead. He gets high for awhile, and then he snaps right back in." Jerry paused for a second. "You know what, Elliot? Felix is a good friend. He's an honest person and he loves to party, but he has a demon in him that comes and goes, and there's nothing that he or I can do about it. You'll see him when he's really together, and you'll also see what I see. It isn't easy."

My initial high was wearing off a bit, and I asked Jerry if I could use the phone. I needed to call my parents back in New York and let them know I had made it safely to the West Coast. When my father picked up the line back at El Monaco, I found myself thrilled to hear his voice. My father was pleased that I had gotten to California safely. "A minute, Elli," he said. "Sonia, it's your son!" he yelled out. Distantly, I could hear my mother say, "If he lost the money already, I have nothing to tell him!" There was silence on the phone, and I could imagine my father shaking his head. "She can't come to the phone right now," he said. "She's busy with all the rooms, Elli." I told him that I had heard her, that I had not lost my money yet, and that I understood. We were both covering up the fact that my mother was who she was. At that point, I didn't care. Instead, I told Pop how helpful his maps had been. He said, "It was no trouble, mine son."

I then called my sister Renee. She was thrilled to know that I was finally on my own and in Los Angeles. We talked about Felix and Jerry, and what I was going to do to help fix up the place. I detailed my grand ambition to take Hollywood by storm. "If that's what you want to do, do it," she said, "but do you have enough money to live on?" I had the pleasure of explaining that the Bethel Teichbergs could now afford to be without me, and that I had put away more than enough money to follow my dream. Renee seemed relieved. She said, "Elli, don't be a stranger. Call me when you can. I love you, and I hope you find what you're looking for."

❀   ❀   ❀

Taking a large pad of paper, a few colored pencils, and a yard stick from Jerry's office supplies, I wandered around the house. I took note of what was being done, and what still needed to be done. I also started to draw up floor plans, measuring the dimensions of the rooms, doors, windows, and ceiling heights—everything that would allow me to set the wheels in motion.

I had just about finished doing the first floor when I began to hear festive calypso music playing loudly in the kitchen. Making my way over there, I beheld an unexpected sight. There was Felix, decked out in a long, flowing bright-red evening gown and dancing back and forth in front of a big oven. His head was bobbing, his fingers were snapping, and he was waving his arms above his head in rhythm to the music. Felix shouted along with Harry Belafonte, shaking his ass to the high piping blasts of the band's horn section.

But that wasn't all. It was as if an industrial paint factory had exploded in the kitchen. There were red sauce streaks caked on the wall behind the oven, a blender half-filled with a yellow-orange mix of banana and mango, a bowl of bright purple grapes on the counter next to three leafy heads of iceberg lettuce, and a big metal mixing bowl filled with a puddle of pink cake frosting. I was speechless.

As he spun around dramatically to the music, Felix saw me standing there and exclaimed, "Elliot! I was wondering where you were. Come and dance with me!"

He was wobbling in four-inch-high spike heels. "Tonight, I am Carmen Miranda!" he said, picking up a banana in each hand and shaking them like maracas as he sashayed toward me. "Take me in your arms, lovah!" he teased. Before I could remind him that I wasn't a very good dancer, he grasped me by the hips and started to move me back and forth to the calypso still blasting through four luggage-sized speakers. I found myself laughing as Felix and I danced and spun around. We edged closer to each other, and Felix started to twirl one of his fingers through my hair as the music got a little slower. A few moments later, Felix had his tongue in my mouth. We were both breathless when we stopped.

"Felix," I said, smiling, eyes closed, as he nuzzled my neck, "wait a minute, this is crazy."

"What's crazy, Elliot, is that you haven't been fucked in weeks," Felix said, licking my ear. "Baby, you've had a long trip. You need to relax. Let me help you out, honey." Felix ran his hand across my crotch and dropped to his knees right there in the kitchen. Before I knew it, he had my zipper down and was sucking me off like a pro. I didn't resist. So much had happened to me in the past week, and I *hadn't* had sex in ages. The rhythm was starting to build and I was nearly ready to go off when Felix suddenly pulled me from his mouth and shrieked, "Oh, shit! I forgot about the duck!"

As I stood there in the kitchen, my jeans down around my ankles and my erection unfulfilled, Felix ran screaming toward the oven—only to slip on the hem of his long dress. He got up quickly and opened the oven, which by now was billowing with dark clouds of smoke.

"I ruined it!" Felix cried. "Oh, fuck! I burned the duck!"

"That's all right, Felix," soothed Jerry, coming into the kitchen. "Try making something else instead." He had a look on his face that seemed to say, *I have seen this happen a hundred times.* Me, I was just happy that I had managed to hike my pants back up before Jerry appeared.

Felix took off the Harry Belafonte record and replaced it with the sound-track for the musical *Camelot.* The courtly sounds of the musical's overture resonated in triumph throughout the house as Felix set out to prepare another dinner. I couldn't take the heat of the kitchen any longer, so I accompanied Jerry toward the bar in the study. He handed me a fresh glass of vodka, and then guided me over to the nearby dining room, which featured a stately but somewhat battered table long enough to sit at least twenty people comfortably. What was particularly odd about the table, though, was that it was neatly set for twelve. I turned to Jerry and said, "Are you guys expecting a lot more people over for dinner?"

"No, it's nothing like that. We keep the rooms appointed in this way so that a potential buyer can see what they could do with the mansion," Jerry explained. It sounded like part of a well-rehearsed spiel, and he was only half-convinced of what he was saying. Apparently, he and Felix usually sat at opposite ends of the table. I wondered if they had always had this seating arrangement, or if the time they had spent alone in the mansion had led them to such a distance. For now, Jerry sat next to me, and we started talking seriously about what I could do with the place. I could see now that Jerry had always planned to talk only with me, since Felix would probably interrupt the conversation needlessly. Once I starting outlining my plans, though, it became clear that Felix would have to be a part of the process, too.

I told Jerry that I thought we should build on what was already great about the place. The problems with the roof and the windows would easily be solved with the help of a handyman or two. Inside the mansion, I envisioned a plan in which each room paid homage to a Hollywood classic. The dining room, for example, could be made to resemble the look of *Citizen Kane*. The ballroom could capture the splendor of the genteel Southern ball in *Gone with the Wind*. I gave Jerry lots of other design motifs, but he held up his hand.

"Whoa, Elliot, that all sounds great. But do you know how much it's going to cost to do some of that stuff?" Jerry said.

"Didn't you want me to do a total redesign?" I asked, confused.

"Not a total redesign, El," Jerry gently cautioned. "We only want to fix it up so a buyer can't see any problems with it. It'll be the buyer who decides what he wants to do with the place after it's his. We just have to make it look clean and presentable—fill the cracks, paint the walls and ceilings, that kind of thing. And we figured that since you're a painter, it would be your area of expertise."

That wasn't exactly what a professional interior decorator like me wanted to hear. But I reminded myself that I was their guest. They had said I could stay at the mansion as long as I helped them out. I decided to go along with what Jerry wanted, and asked him if he had any supplies purchased yet for the work. "We've got a lot of paint," he said.

Just about then, Felix half-tripped into the dining room in his dress and made a sad announcement.

"Hey, guys! I'm so sorry, but I dropped all the mashed potatoes to the floor. Anyone want scrambled eggs?" he said.

Jerry gave me a sideways glance, got up from the table, and picked up the telephone: "Don't worry, I'll send for takeout. Chinese okay?"

The doorbell rang just as he went to dial the number. In came a young delivery boy from a nearby Chinese restaurant with a large bag of already ordered food. Jerry gave the young man a tip—they had clearly done this before—and brought the takeout back to the dining room, proclaiming, "Voilà, dinner!" Felix went glumly to the stereo to turn over the record again. I gathered this was an established ritual, and so I told Felix that I was sorry that his dinner hadn't worked out as he had planned.

"Oh, don't worry about it, Elliot. I just wanted to make you feel special, like this was your home," Felix said, his eyes starting to fill with tears.

"Hey, it's okay," I said, and I got up to give him a hug. I understood him. I knew that he was trying his best to be useful and welcoming. I knew also that he'd been having a hard time. For lots of gays, being outwardly gay was not even a choice—it was necessary to conceal your identity. It was fine when you were with your immediate circle of other gay friends. But to the rest of the world, you were someone to be laughed at or scorned, or worse. Just getting through a day without falling apart was often the hardest struggle of all. Jerry came over and we huddled together for a hug. Then Jerry went to get us another round of drinks. He came back with the pitcher of chilled vodka and led the three of us in a toast.

"Here's to our new guest!" Jerry said.

"Here's to the mansion," I added.

"Here's to Camelot!" shouted Felix, as Richard Burton sang those same words on the record. Then he said, "And a big welcome to Hollywood. We're so glad you've come!"

We never did talk about that duck again.

3

City of Angels

Over the next few weeks, I began to figure out how Jerry and Felix and I could best work together to fix up the mansion. If we did things right, we could have nearly all of the work done in four months. I knew that my two mansion-mates were looking to me for inspiration and leadership in an area that was fairly alien to them, and I didn't want to let them down.

During this time, however, I also allowed myself to have a *lot* of fun. After all, I had been dreaming of Hollywood since I was a little boy in Brooklyn. Now, I was really living there. I did everything and anything that I wanted to do. I felt like a big happy kid who never had to go back to work again. I went to the movies in the middle of the day if I liked, and sometimes saw as many as three movies in a row. I spent hours in bookstores on weekday afternoons, and even visited comic book shops in search of some of the great early issues that I used to have when I was kid. I must have dropped hundreds of dollars on rare and hard-to-find comics from the late 1930s and 1940s. Seeing the high prices on these pristine first-edition comic books, I toyed with the idea of calling Momma to tell her how much money she had lost when she threw away my comics. Knowing her, she wouldn't have believed me anyway. Oh well, no matter. I had enough money now for myself, and was totally content during my days—and especially during my nights.

The gay nightclub scene in Hollywood was beyond exciting. In New York, gays and lesbians were mostly relegated to grungy Mafia-run neighborhood bars with flashing lights, loud music, and back rooms. By welcome comparison, the gay bars in Hollywood had a seductive flair and a real feel for show-biz pizzazz. They were decidedly high end, and far more comfortable and inviting than the places I'd frequented back east. I found this change of environment absolutely exhilarating. During my first month in LA, we went out practically every night in search of good music, good drugs, and good bodies. Still, as much fun as it was—and it *was* fun—I never stopped looking both ways before crossing the street after leaving the bars at night. Just like New York, LA had laws that prohibited gay activities. And just as in New York, in LA we also heard about beatings of gay men caught walking on the sidewalk by themselves—acts of violence that never did quite get the attention of the police. Felix, Jerry, and I played it safe; even if we hadn't been friends, it made sense to party as a group. As beautiful gay men in an often ugly straight world, we found strength and comfort together.

We had a nightly routine. Felix would make a call around seven o'clock to one of the two dozen older rich gentlemen whom he had befriended since arriving in Hollywood. Some of these men were openly gay, but just as many were married men. Those men were miserably closeted, and they looked to Felix and Jerry for diversion and release. When one of Felix's sugar daddies drove up to the mansion, Jerry would have them park alongside my Cadillac and invite them into the mansion. A first drink would be served, usually from the tall pitcher of vodka, and then we would get into Jerry's limousine. Most nights, Jerry would drive. His drug of choice was uppers, as they kept him bright and alert. He also liked amyl nitrite "poppers." When broken under your nostrils and snorted, the poppers gave you an amazing rush, best accompanied by orgasm. Later, as he made key contacts in the local drug scene, Jerry also developed a real lust for cocaine.

Sometimes on weeknights, Jerry would make a quick phone call in the office while Felix chatted up our rich middle-aged guest. Then, about fifteen minutes later, a young Chinese man would show up at the front door. He looked a lot like our Chinese food delivery boy. That was because, as it turned out, he was actually the delivery boy's cousin. We called the delivery boy "American-name Sam" and the man "American-name Dave." "American-name Dave" worked as Jerry's personal chauffeur whenever Jerry really wanted to let loose. Talk about your enterprising young man—he was cute, too. "Take us to the promised land, Kato!" Jerry would command, and "American-name

Dave" would drive us and that evening's Daddy Warbucks off to the hot and musky gay club world.

We were regulars at at least a dozen different clubs, going to three to four venues each night, drinking and smoking and sniffing and pilling ourselves to sweet oblivion. Although we loved to ogle the nude male dancers at Goliath's on Melrose Avenue, my personal favorites were Arthur J's on Hollywood Boulevard and Madness Inc. There were hot leather boys there, and all kinds of covert but frenzied sexual activity in the bathrooms. One night, I had sex three separate times with three different men over three hours' time. I even remember seeing Felix slink off to the bathroom with three men at once. Jerry was a little more selective, but he eventually started having an affair with "American-name Dave." Often, they went out to the parked limo to have their own private time; sometimes, they would bring along a third partner whom they both fancied.

At some point during each night, the older man who was underwriting all the partying would introduce Felix and Jerry to other older men. Felix would charm them, and Jerry would talk to them about different properties for sale—or about those other buyers, often from out of state, who were eager to get a piece of the real estate action in Hollywood. Talk always circled back to the Marie Dressler mansion. I was surprised one night, though, when Jerry told an interested party that the mansion had belonged to Clara Bow. On another night, he said it had been the home of Bela Lugosi. And on yet another occasion, he said that the mansion once belonged to Judy Garland. I took Jerry off to the side and asked him, "Hey, I thought you said the mansion belonged to Marie Dressler?"

"What?" said Jerry, over the loud music. When I repeated what I said, he shouted back, "Yeah, uh, right, Dressler. Hey, El, what fucking difference does it make? I'll tell 'em the place belonged to Mickey fuckin' Mouse if it'll get them to buy it!" An hour later, I heard Jerry tell another guy that the house belonged to the Indian actor Sabu after he starred in *The Jungle Book*. Suffice it to say, the Hollywood purist in me was crushed. I really thought I had been living in the Dressler mansion. Now, it was just another big old house in the Hollywood hills, the place where I slept and ate while trying to become a success. Gradually it dawned on me that I hadn't seen Felix and Jerry make a single property sale since I had arrived. And yet there was always a supply of drugs and booze and food around the house. *So much for dreams,* I thought, as I watched Felix lead the old man of the evening into one of the bathrooms at the back of yet another neon-lit homo house—to deliver rendered "services," I suspected.

Once I had gotten in my fair share of partying, I knew I needed to start looking for additional work as a set decorator. I tried to get tips from the men I met at the gay clubs. One man in particular, a makeup artist named Darren, explained to me that I needed to become a member of the motion picture set designers unions if I wanted to be eligible to work. He directed me to an office about eight miles north of the mansion, on West Burbank Boulevard. I got one of my two suits dry-cleaned and even bought myself a new polka-dot pattern magenta-colored tie. A few days later, I drove to the union office, which was on the third floor of a nondescript building. I introduced myself to the receptionist, a pretty young black woman, and explained that I was an artist who wished to apply for membership in their union. She handed me an application to fill out, and explained that it must be accompanied by a nonreturnable processing fee. I paid the fee in cash, and asked the receptionist if I could show my work portfolio to the admissions office director.

It was right before the lunch hour, so she said she would check to see if he had time to see me. A few minutes later, she called out, "Mr. Tiger." Although I was the only one in the waiting room, it took me a while to realize she was referring to me. *Hey, maybe that's how they assign you your stage name,* I thought, as I was buzzed into the office. There I came upon a middle-aged man in a pinstripe suit. Mr. Rose shook my hand and asked to see my portfolio. He seemed all business, which impressed me. For about two minutes, he looked through the photographs of my Fifth Avenue storefront work, model room sets, and extensive mural installations. He looked up at me and said, "This work is quite impressive, Mr. Tiber. I think you could do well as a set decorator. I'm sure your application will be approved. If you are accepted, you will be mailed your union card in a few weeks. Just make sure we have your address, and give me a phone number in case we need to call you."

Wow! It all seemed really easy. With a little luck and my talent for design, I figured I could be working in the movies by Thanksgiving. Naturally, I was impatient to get my first job on a bona fide Hollywood motion picture. Things were looking up.

While waiting for my union card, I turned my full attention to the mansion. I had put together a list of projects required to get the place into shape for sale, operating on as tight a budget as possible. First, we needed to deal with the broken glass in the windows and the French doors. Next, we needed to secure the service of a dependable handyman who could repair and refinish the ball-room floor, and also tend to all the cracks in the ceiling and walls. I even had Felix come with me to a lighting fixture shop so we could find replacement bulbs for the chandeliers throughout the mansion. Jerry interviewed at least a dozen handymen before finally picking a jack-of-all-trades who could not only do roofing and carpentry, but also electrical work and plumbing—and he came with an apprentice son to boot.

Because I expected to be getting movie jobs very soon, I wanted to work fast to repay Jerry and Felix for their generous welcome. I took over the painting, creating a schedule for Felix and myself to cover different spots in the mansion. I would paint for three hours each morning until lunch, and Felix would paint from after lunch until mid-afternoon.

A few weeks into the painting project, I was pleasantly surprised to note that Felix seemed a lot more like the guy I used to know back in Brooklyn. Maybe it was the physical labor, or maybe it was the paint fumes. Whatever it was, he seemed to understand the importance of sticking to the schedule and remained dedicated to his portion of the house painting. Since he hardly ever woke up before eleven in the morning, Felix usually did his work while still wearing a robe—though he would occasionally paint in the nude. For the most part, the discipline seemed to do him good.

When I mentioned this change to Jerry, he didn't seem to make anything of it. In fact, Jerry seemed far more on edge than usual. He had visits at the mansion from people I had never seen before. They would meet with Jerry for about ten minutes in his office and leave as swiftly as they had arrived. I was too busy to really think too much about it, but I did notice that Jerry seemed different. I even heard him fighting with Felix late one night about money. By Thanksgiving, the feeling in the place started to get a little more desperate.

Felix didn't even bother to make a big turkey dinner for the three of us. Instead, we ordered pizza and drank beer.

After dinner, I walked over to Jerry's office and asked how he was doing.

"Fine, fine, I'm just tired, man," he said, sighing wearily and rubbing his eyes. "What about you, El? Did you hear back from that union guy yet?"

"Not yet," I said.

"Yeah, well, don't worry," Jerry said, "I'm sure things will work out." But he didn't sound sure, and I didn't feel sure, either.

"Listen, Jerry," I started, feeling I needed to broach the subject, "we've been having a lot of visitors here at the house. Who are they, anyway? I mean, they don't seem to be coming here to check out the mansion."

"What are you asking me, man?" Jerry said in a wary voice.

"I hate to ask, but I've seen a lot of drugs around here lately," I said, finally letting my worry bubble to the surface. "Jerry, are you selling or what?"

"Elliot," Jerry said, very quietly, "we're all working together here to fix up the place and get it sold. Felix and I have something we're looking to build out here with real estate, just as you're trying to build a career in the movies. Trying to keep this shit going isn't easy," he continued, his face getting tighter, "and I'm only doing what I gotta do to make it happen."

That really didn't tell me much, but I could see I was upsetting him. I told him I was sorry.

"It's all right, Elli," he continued, guiding me out of the office, "but it's better for us both if you don't ask too many questions. You stick to your thing, and I'll stick to mine." He closed and locked the door—not only to the office, but to any further discussion.

I didn't really know what to think. For the first time since I'd come to California, I started to feel a bit vulnerable. I also began to wonder if it was just a matter of time before our place was busted by the narcs. I didn't have much to lose, but I definitely didn't want any new kinds of trouble in my life. So on that Thanksgiving night, before I went to sleep, I gave thanks—thanks that I had put all my Woodstock money into a safe deposit box. At least I had a small measure of control over that area of my life.

As we headed into the final weeks of 1969, we kept piling into Jerry's black stretch limo in search of love—or at least sex. But the sense of adventure and fun we'd had in those first weeks had waned. Jerry would just stand at the bar, drinking endless shots of anything liquid. Felix, once he was drunk, would wander around the clubs, flashing his tremendous white-toothed smile and hitting on the handsomest guys. When that didn't work out, he hit on anyone who would talk to him. I would only have one or two drinks before feeling high enough to try and make out. Nothing varied in our routine except for the locations.

After a few hours one night, we weren't feeling it, so Jerry drove us back home in the limo. We sat in silence, having nothing to say to each other. Even in the company of my friends, I was beginning to feel just as alone as I had been before Woodstock. You could have all the sex in the world and still be lonely. Something was missing. I knew what it was, but I didn't want to think about it. It was a long ride back to the mansion.

❀   ❀   ❀

The week after Thanksgiving, I received a call from Mr. Rose at the union office. He told me I had been accepted, and could join the union by paying the initial membership dues of two thousand dollars. When I said to Mr. Rose that the fee was higher than I had anticipated, he said flatly, "Well, it's up to you. You can try to go with International Artists instead, but you'll have a hell of a time trying to get work right away. With us, you have the comfort of knowing that we're all about what you need. By paying us, you're paying yourself with the best chance you can have to find work."

I realized this was my shot at being able to do the work I had come to do, so I withdrew the cash from my safety deposit box at the bank and gave it directly to Mr. Rose.

"Don't worry, Mr. Tiber," he said, "this is the best investment you can make toward a future in Hollywood." I thought of asking him if they gave away free toasters once you paid the dues, but decided to hold my tongue. It was not the time to be a wise guy, since I really had no choice but to go along with the payment and hope that Mr. Rose was right.

I kept working on the mansion with Jerry and painting the interiors with Felix as I waited to hear back from Mr. Rose about job offers. I waited and waited and waited. After the new year had come and gone, my union card had netted me zilch. I called to speak with Mr. Rose, and also visited the union offices a handful of times. Every time I called or walked through the office door, the pretty black receptionist told me that Mr. Rose was away from the office. Then one day I visited the office and found a different receptionist, who told me that Mr. Rose had been convicted of embezzlement and was now in jail. The receptionist then said that a replacement officer would arrive in a few months, maybe. Another card-carrying union designer I met at Arthur J's explained to me that the whole thing was basically a scam. "They'll never call you about a job. There are just too many designers coming to Hollywood every day," he said. "Having a union card is important to get a job at any of the major studios, but finding work in this business comes from being connected. You have a relative in the business, you work. If you're not connected, you're unemployed. That's Hollywood." So there I was, out of luck and painting interiors while I waited for a call from Cecil B. DeMille—a call that I was now sure would never come even if I was ready for my close-up.

I wasn't the only one who had been naïve about Hollywood. For decades, Los Angeles had been a magnet for would-be stars, writers, directors, and even set designers who dreamed of making it big in the movie business. Good-looking guys and beautiful young women were everywhere. They worked at grocery stores, restaurants, gas stations—wherever they could get a job, waiting for their big break. After all, why not? Wasn't Lana Turner discovered at Schwab's Drugstore?

The problem was that most of these success stories were pure hype—made-up tales that never happened but sounded great in a movie magazine. As I was learning, the hard truth was that Hollywood was open only to a small group of people. Yes, luck might play a role, but having a relative or friend in the business played a much bigger one. And unless you understood the barriers that existed, you could waste a lifetime waiting for that one break. Maybe the first months were exciting, but after the first few years, that sense of desperation started to kick in, and that temporary job as a waitress turned into a career. I had been there for only four months, and I could see that my career as a hot Hollywood set decorator might have to be put on hold, at least for the time being.

It was late January 1970, and all I was doing was working on the house. I'd had to dip into my fifty thousand dollars, and I began to hear my mother's

words echoing in my ears again—"If you go broke, don't come to me." *Yikes!
Time to get a job,* I told myself.

I picked up a copy of the *Los Angeles Times* and started looking for a job
in the field I knew best—interior design. One of the ads was for a position at
Bentley's furniture stores, a chain that was popular in Southern California. I
called the number, and set up an appointment to come in. The huge main
store was smartly laid out, with mostly custom furnishings. As I waited to be
interviewed by the store manager, I saw several other decorators at the
entrance windows staring at my shiny Cadillac, which I had parked in front
of the store. I hadn't even thought of my Caddie as an asset, but then again,
this *was* Hollywood. They all probably assumed I was a wealthy client, not
a job seeker.

Edie Schirmer, the manager, welcomed me to her desk. She was quite tall
and smartly dressed. Her demeanor was impeccable, although her hushed
speaking voice made it difficult to hear her questions until I got used to it.

My background at Sloane's, Lord & Taylor, and B. Altman back in Manhattan brought forth a series of approving nods. "It will be a decided advantage for Bentley's to have a New York interior designer. Our staff here is
almost all Californian, and while they are certainly good, I think you might be
able to bring in some fresh new ideas. Welcome, Mr. Tiber. Oh, and please feel
free to park your car out in front of the store. It will help give us the right
appearance," she said with dignity and restraint.

This branch of Bentley's was in Pasadena. To me, it was all California. I
had had no idea that Pasadena was populated by so many well-to-do little old
ladies. My first couple of clients made it clear that creative *moderne* concepts
would not be of interest. Anything other than time-honored, conventional flo-
rals and French Country furniture would be considered unsuitable, suggesting
the outrageous taste of the nouveau riche.

The other decorators, six women and one gay gentleman, seemed to take
an instant dislike to me. Maybe it was because I was from New York—or
maybe they just didn't like Cadillacs. Each of us had an ornate desk, in the
proper French style, on the main floor. The money was good; I was making
three hundred dollars for each job. But I was miserable. I had dreamed of
designing sets for films, not arranging old ladies' interiors, and there were no
opportunities to do any creative or imaginative designing. The women all

wanted either Chippendale or boring Colonial Williamsburg. I tried to suggest contemporary classics like Knoll or Herman Miller, but those went over like lead balloons. One client actually complained to Ms. Schirmer, saying that I was in desperate need of schooling in the Pasadena standards of taste and propriety. *Please!* After only one month of catering to the hellishly bad taste of those nincompoop customers, I couldn't take it anymore. I resigned.

Felix told me to investigate a great high-end decorating salon run by a woman named Felicia Moore, who specialized in contemporary designs for the very rich. It was a good lead. Felicia was a radiant red-headed creature who ran her roost from a gilt throne covered in zebra and leopard skins. She was known for her flamboyant style, and was no stranger to theatrics. *Eureka, this is just what I need!* I thought. I went down to her main offices, and was able to get an appointment with her on the strength of my New York work experience alone. As she turned the plastic sheets of my portfolio, she seemed as impressed with me as I was with her. I told her that I had left out my recent Pasadena projects on purpose. She understood.

"Mr. Tiber, your Fifth Avenue work is superb. The mere fact that you chose to not include your work at Bentley's is proof that you know how to please a client. I'd be happy to welcome you to join the world of Felicia Moore!" she said, taking my hand and giving it a surprisingly firm shake.

I fairly swooned at Ms. Moore's attention, especially since I hadn't really been taken seriously as an artist since I had left my interior design clients back in Manhattan. When I asked her about my salary and hours, she said, grandly, "But you will be treated as all artists must be treated—divinely! You will be with me, and I will give you free reign to design anything you want. You make your own hours, and you work in your own way. All I ask is that it be original, new, exciting, and very expensive, my darling!" I was in love, and ready to create.

From the moment I first started working for Ms. Moore, I felt I had found a place that would allow me the freedom to work as I had in New York. Ms. Moore employed other designers, but they all seemed to work independently. Which was just as well, since Ms. Moore seemed to adopt me as her new little pet—a fact that did not win me the support of my coworkers. I was too high from Ms. Moore's attention to care, though.

"The showroom needs a touch of magic. Make me something marvelous, Elliot," she said to me at the end of that first week, "something that will show the world that Felicia Moore knows a good idea when she sees it." And that's exactly what I did. That weekend, I drew up plans for a new furniture design. I showed the idea to Jerry and Felix, and they loved it. I came back to Ms. Moore's showroom early Monday morning, and set myself to making my new idea into reality. I took three sectional sofas and paired them with an immense ottoman that we had in our warehouse. I dubbed the configuration "The Pit."

Ms. Moore went absolutely ga-ga for it. It was an instant sensation. I did it up in zebra print, leopard print, and leathers, and selected a wild and inspired assortment of colors, including bright yellow and deep orange. In any other showroom, the sofa assemblage would have gone for five hundred dollars, but at Moore's I established the price for my furniture set at two thousand bucks. Within a week, I noticed that Felicia had moved my Pit design to the center of her showroom and begun holding court there with old and new clients alike. She would ask everyone, "How do you like my new design? Divine, isn't it?"

I was annoyed that she gave me no credit for *my* Pit design, and instead gushed about how brilliant *she* was to have come up with the concept. She would turn over a client to me, and then make it clear that I would simply decide the fabrics, designs, and colors that would go into the client's customized purchase of *her* Pit. Like many others in the business, Felicia was all about Felicia. She was a smart businesswoman who knew exactly how to get ahead. And if the fresh new chic designs of Elliot Tiber were to be co-opted by Felicia Moore as her own, then that was the way it would be.

After working there for two months, Felicia remarked that my Cadillac didn't represent me properly. She felt it was rather pedestrian, below my newly gained position. Only a Mercedes or a Rolls-Royce would be acceptable for one of her designers. In Brooklyn, a Caddie had always been a real status symbol; parked in front of Bentley's in Pasadena, it had been a big deal. At Felicia's, though, it was an embarrassment. *Who knew?* I should have known that I was out of my league with my vulgar Eldorado, which Felicia made me park behind the store, out of sight from her wealthy clientele. Things soon became clearer as Felicia shoved me into her Rolls and took me to Beverly Hills to show me a stunning round contemporary house. I assumed it was for a new client, but I didn't realize that the client was me.

"My darling Elliot," Felicia said in her grand manner of speech, "I want you to buy this house. I cannot afford to have you live in Los Feliz! This is not 1922, and Marie Dressler is long gone! I know Buster Keaton and Douglas Fairbanks slept in your bedroom, maybe even at the same time! But they are dead stars, and dead stars don't buy Felicia Moore. I can get you this lovely cottage for just sixty-five thousand dollars. It may be small by neighborhood standards, but it's situated in a place where you can throw parties, invite the right people, and get us a steady stream of new clients. And besides, Elliot, one day, it will be worth triple the price! It's the right thing to do."

Asking Felix or Jerry for advice about Ms. Moore's demands was useless. Felix said she was a delusional slut, and Jerry added, "What does a straight woman know about the decorating business, anyway?" Jerry then went on to say that the rumor was that Felicia was almost certainly a cokehead—which was pretty rich, coming from Jerry. They were of no help whatsoever.

The fact was, I was terrified to comply with Felicia's request, which seemed more like an order. I didn't want to buy a house, nor was I pleased that she was taking credit for my Pit design. I became even more irate when I saw a full-page advertisement she had placed in the trade magazines, showing her posed mid-lounge in skin-colored tights, promoting her brand-new *The Moore, The Merrier Pit.* My Pit!

The job paid well, but it was going to give me an ulcer. I thought it would be best to express to Felicia how I felt. The door to Felicia' office was open, and I could see her sitting at her desk, looking through some papers.

I walked into the room and said, "Felicia, there's something I need to tell you. Can we talk?"

She looked up and said, "Darling, I don't have time right now. I'm a little busy. Be a dear, and come see me at the end of the day, and then you can tell Felicia all about it. " While her smile never left her lips, it was obvious that she was patronizing me.

The salon closed at eight, and I was in front of her office a few minutes after. As I entered the room, she was still sitting at her desk. She pointed to one of the chairs in front of her desk and said, "Sit down, Elliot." As I was preparing to get into the speech I had rehearsed in my head all day, she grasped control of the moment and spoke first.

"Look, Elliot, I know why you're here. I'm taking credit for the Pit design, so you're angry. Well, frankly, I don't give a rat's ass if you are." Her smile was still fixed, but her theatrical affectations went straight out the window. She continued, "I hired you because of the other places that hired you. You obviously showed them you've got talent, and so far you've shown me that you know what you're doing. But in my store—in my world—you work for me. I pay you an excellent salary, and what you produce is mine to reject or use." No longer smiling, she said, "You think I'm a bitch?"

I wasn't sure if she was looking for an answer, but I quietly volunteered one. "Pretty much."

"Right," she said, "and if I were a man, what would I be called? Shrewd? Tough? Forceful? Because I'm a woman, I have to fight for every damn inch of success I can grab hold of. I know what I am. And if I tell you what you need to do to help us bring in more clients, I expect you to do it. If you don't, you know what your options are. Do I make myself clear?"

I suspected that this was not the first time she'd given this speech. I took a moment to think, so that I could reply intelligently with grace and respect. Unfortunately, nothing clever came to mind. All I could say was, "If I wanted to work for my mother, I would have stayed in Bethel. She also wants me to live in her world. That wasn't going to happen there, and it isn't going to happen here. I quit."

Before she had the chance to respond, I got up off the chair and walked toward the door. Then I turned around and said, "And by the way, I *like* my Cadillac." I left her office, cleared out my desk, and made my departure through the back door to the lot where my waiting Eldorado was parked.

By March, I was feeling depressed again. My life was filled with work in the mansion, bar hopping, unsatisfying sexual encounters, getting stoned, and wasting my hours. I was not having a good time. Clearly, my plan to get a foothold in movies was not working out. I was in a dilemma as to the sort of life I should attempt to create for myself. And then, at the end of the month, Jerry showed me an ad in the *Los Angeles Times* for the release of a big documentary by Warner Bros. Films. The film's title was *Woodstock*.

Of course, the three of us went to see the film on the weekend it opened. Although I had been involved with the festival, I had been too busy to see the musical acts up close. I had tried to describe what had taken place during that weekend to Felix and Jerry, but words never did it justice. I had my few dinky reels of film that I shot around the motel grounds, but there wasn't a projector in the house on which to run them anyway. Now, here was a motion picture from Warner Bros. that seemed to capture those three incredible days perfectly. Still, it was bittersweet for me to see a movie depicting one of the most miraculous events in my life, knowing I had had to spend that whole weekend working like a dog at the El Monaco. When the movie ended, I had tears in my eyes. Whether it was the joy I felt from watching the film or the fact that my Hollywood dream still eluded me, I couldn't say.

April turned into May, and I knew I had to make a move before summer hit. But then, one morning, the phone rang at the mansion. It was my sister Renee, calling to tell me that Pop was ill and might need to go to a hospital. She sounded very anxious. I missed Renee very much, and I was concerned about Pop being sick and stuck at the motel with my mad Russian mother. "Please come home, Elliot," Renee said, and my heart just melted. Fighting back tears, I told her I would drive back to New York the following day.

My time in Los Angeles was over. I had seen enough of the Felix and Jerry show, and had been soured on both the movie business and the oppressive world of LA interior design. Besides, I had practically finished the renovation and design work that I had said I would do at the house. I had earned my keep, done my job, and now it was time to back out of this dead end. *So much for Hollywood,* I thought.

I spent my last day in California gathering up my cash from the safety deposit box at the bank. Though I had lost two thousand dollars to the union, I had earned it back in my short stints at Bentley's and Felicia Moore's. All told, I would leave Hollywood with about the same amount of money I had had when I arrived—this time in easier-to-store large cash denominations, of course. I took one more walk through the finished mansion before packing up the Eldorado. The place was beautiful again. And that's when I knew that it had always been Marie Dressler's mansion, no matter who had really owned it. I would miss the place, and hoped the new owners would appreciate the work that had been put into it.

Jerry and Felix watched me pack the last of my stuff in the trunk of the car, unsure what to say. As I was preparing to say goodbye, Felix suddenly asked me to wait and dashed into the mansion. Jerry and I looked at each other and shrugged at our wacky friend. Felix came back out a minute later, and gave me his copy of *Camelot*. "Remember our times here together, Elli," Felix said, in a voice that sounded both happy and sad. "For the three of us, this has been our Camelot."

"You take good care of yourselves," I said. It was Jerry, and not Felix, who hugged me first. I hugged him back, and then Felix joined the hug. I left my two friends just as I had found them—standing together in the driveway like a pair of broken angels. Except now it was Felix and Jerry who were trying to find their way through the darkness, and not me.

So this was where I found myself, less than a year after attaining my first real freedom, using Pop's maps in reverse and driving cross-country once again, traveling east to White Lake—away from a dream, and back to a nightmare.

4

Oh My Poppa— and the Nine Italian Heroes

"*Oy vey!* You're back. I knew it! You lost all your money!"

That was how Momma welcomed me upon my rueful return to our White Lake room-rental rats' nest—enacting one of the great slow burns in contemporary Jewish-American motherhood. I had pulled the car into the El Monaco's empty parking lot late that Saturday morning, and there she was, perched on the porch outside the El Monaco motel office as if she'd never left her post since the day I'd left. She looked like a smug and kosher bird of prey with room keys in its beak, her face flushed red with agitation and her arms crossed tightly against her chicken soup-stained apron. I noticed my father was not there with Momma to greet me.

"No, I did not lose my money! And where's Pop?" I asked, concerned that things might be worse than Renee had indicated when she called me in Los Angeles.

"He's in the hospital, that's where," she said. "Your father is taking tests. *Expensive* tests! We're supposed to be in Florida. He could take tests there. The tests are cheaper in Florida. Do I need this?" Her voice was full of bitter reproach, but there was also a little something that I had never heard from her before—fear. It was strangely quiet at the El Monaco. It felt as if even the motel grounds were scared for my father. After all, over ten years, there had hardly ever been a time when he hadn't been on the premises. Except to take the occasional vacation to Miami Beach with Momma, Pop had rarely left White Lake.

Just as Momma attempted to hand me some bedspreads to bring to one of the rooms, a car pulled up alongside my Cadillac. It was Sol Mandel and his wife, Luba. They owned a decrepit boarding house on the lake near our place, and they had always been kind and considerate neighbors. Over the years, they had been the only friendly folks besides our milkman, Max Yasgur, with whom I could talk. The Mandels were gentle, literate people who had the patience not only to understand me, but to also be friends to my mother. I was glad to see them. Luba even gave me a short hug, which was far more of a comfort to me than the rough words with which my mother had saluted me upon my arrival. Sol took me aside as Momma bemoaned her work load to Luba, and told me to head over to the hospital as soon as possible.

"Your father is very ill, Elliot," Sol said, "and he has gotten far worse in the past week. I think you need to get over there, okay? We can stay here with Sonia, but you need to see him right away." All of my failed Hollywood life was still packed into my car, but I was out of my head with worry and knew I had to move fast. I thanked the Mandels and ignored whatever my mother was yelling to me as I turned the car around and headed toward the hospital.

I drove the seven miles to the hospital at top speed, wanting only to find my father and see what I could do to help him. Had I known just how sick Pop was when Renee called, I would have hopped on a plane instead of driving. I suspected that Renee had not known how unwell our father was. To listen to my mother, you would have thought that Pop was relaxing at Club Med. Clearly, I needed to call Renee and my other sisters that day from the hospital to let them know what was going on. And I knew I might need to take further action. The local hospital did not have the best reputation. In my head, I was already planning to get Pop the hell out of there and into a better hospital—that day, if possible.

At the hospital, I walked over to the reception desk and asked the clerk where I might find Jack Teichberg. The woman was somewhat cold, and seemed bothered that I had prevented her from finishing her crossword puzzle. She took forever to look up my father's room number. It occurred to me that she was probably yet another stunted local who blamed my family for bringing the Woodstock plague to our narrow-minded little town.

When I got to Pop's room, I saw my father lying awake in his bed. He was crying, and seemed not to know where he was.

"Pop?" I said, holding back my own tears. "It's Eliyahu, Pop."

"Elli?" he said, in a state of confusion. I touched him gently on the shoulder, and again told him that I was there with him. His eyes found mine, and he smiled lovingly at me.

"Mine son, my boy," he said. Suddenly, he grimaced. It was obvious he was in discomfort. He told me he had asked the nurse for something to ease the pain, but the nurse said she would first have to clear it with his doctor. In the meantime, an aspirin was the best she could do for him. He closed his eyes, and his body tensed up as the pain engulfed him. It broke my heart to see him suffer. I asked what I could do to help, and he told me how thirsty he was. He asked if he could have some ginger ale, his favorite drink at the motel. I assured him tenderly that I would check with the nurse about getting him whatever he needed. He nodded slightly and closed his eyes again, letting out a small groan from the back of his throat.

I was furious. I went over to the nurses' station and said that the patient in room 104—Jack Teichberg, my father—was in pain. "Why isn't he being given a painkiller?" I asked. The nurse told me the same thing she had told my father. She had already left a message at the doctor's office.

I said, "This is a hospital, right? Can't you get another doctor to prescribe something? My father is suffering."

"The only doctor who can order drugs for the patient," she continued coldly, "is the patient's personal physician."

I couldn't believe it. "Okay," I said, "could you please bring my father some ginger ale? He's thirsty!" The nurse stiffly looked at his chart. The doctor had not listed ginger ale as an approved beverage for my father, and therefore she could not grant my request. That was not what I wanted to hear. I knew yelling at her wasn't going to help my father. So as diplomatically as I could, I said, "I know you have your rules, but the man in room 104 is in great pain. Call whoever you can to get him something to stop it. Please!" And with that, I went back in to Pop's room.

I felt as helpless as Pop looked. His breathing was labored, and his face was hidden behind a mask of pain. I thought to myself, *This is bullshit*. So I rushed out of the hospital, walked across the street to a small deli, and bought an armful of ginger ale bottles. It took me less than fifteen minutes. I touched Pop's shoulder again so he knew I was there, and uncapped one of the bottles for him. Though far weaker than I had ever seen him, Pop gulped the drink in the bottle down swiftly, as if he had been trapped in the desert for weeks without water. Once he was done, he lay quietly for a minute. He closed his eyes and said nothing. I said, "Are you okay, Pop?" He raised his right hand to signify something, and then let out a good long belch. Then he opened his eyes, smiled, and let out a monumental sigh of relief. It brought tears of joy and pity to my eyes to see how appreciative my father was. His voice was weak, so I had to lean in close to his mouth in order to make out his words.

"Thank you, Elli, thank you. Elli, where? Where's Momma? Why doesn't she come take me home? I'm not feeling so good, son."

He asked for more ginger ale, but could only take a sip before he needed to rest. Within a minute, he was fast asleep. Just then, the head nurse came into the room. Seeing the ginger ale that I had brought for Pop, she made a move to scoop up and take away the drinks. I said to her in a hushed voice, "Nurse, do not lay a finger on that ginger ale. It's for me, while I look after my father during his stay in this hospital." She muttered something about calling security, and walked out of the hospital room in a huff.

Fuck her! I screamed in my head. If she could make a call to security, then I sure as hell could make some calls of my own.

I rushed back down the hall to a telephone booth. First, I called one of my older sisters, Rachelle, and her husband, Sam, who lived fifty-five miles west in a place called Lake Mahopac. I explained Pop's dire situation, and begged them to come and help. I then called Renee, explaining that I was now back in White Lake and that Pop was far sicker than either of us had realized. She said that she was sorry to not be there, and would try to be with us by nightfall.

I returned to my father's room and sat with him for the few hours before Rachelle and her husband arrived. I did not know why Pop continued to sleep. I tracked down a doctor, who confirmed that Pop was not in a coma. He explained that Pop was suffering from chronic colitis that had worsened. The doctor also said that he had scheduled a battery of tests for Pop to take the next day.

I studied my father's pale, thin face. He had always been big and strong from his work in roofing, but now his entire body was frail and weak. He looked so small lying there in that bed. I was wiping the sweat from his forehead with a damp towel when I saw my sister Rachelle's face in the window.

I opened the door and let Rachelle and Sam inside. Rachelle burst into tears when she saw our father.

Sam walked over to me and said, "We brought a private ambulance, Elliot. It's parked right in front of the hospital. Don't worry, we are going to get Dad to the hospital over near us in Mahopac." he said reassuringly. "Here, help me get him into this wheelchair."

Rachelle and I dressed Pop, who was now awake but disoriented, and got him into the wheelchair as Sam stood guard at the door. I walked out of the room, and as soon as I saw the nurse leave her station, I signaled Sam to wheel Pop straight out of the room and out toward the front exit. As we passed the admission area, I turned to Sam and very loudly said, "Dr. Levine, I appreciate you and your nurse coming in person to take my father to your sanitarium. You're sure he needs to be isolated from other people, right? " The receptionist took a cautious step back from the counter.

As promised, the ambulance was at the entrance. Pop was placed on a gurney and wheeled into the back of the vehicle.

"Where is Momma?" Rachelle asked as the door to the ambulance was closed. "Why is she not here to help you?"

"Momma didn't have time to come to the hospital!" I responded sarcastically. "She's been too busy waiting for customers. Forget Momma!" I was far too upset to say anything else, so we went to our separate cars and followed Pop in the ambulance back to Mahopac.

❁   ❁   ❁

The fifty-five mile trip took over an hour. Once we arrived at Mahopac Hospital, the two drivers quickly rushed Pop from the ambulance through the emergency room entrance. My brother-in-law Sam was an optometrist, and he knew several of the doctors at the hospital personally. He explained to me that a room was ready for Pop and a top internist was already waiting to see him. We sat in the waiting room, where we all hoped for and dreaded further word from the doctor about Pop. Finally, after three hours, the doctor emerged and explained that he had put our father into the intensive care unit. His expression was sad.

He said, "I'm afraid it's not only his colitis that's causing the problem. X-rays have revealed a large tumor in his stomach, as well as several smaller tumors in his abdominal region." In addition, the doctor explained, there was swelling around Pop's heart. "Based on your father's age, the advanced stage of the cancer, and what appears to be a weakened heart, surgery is not an option. Nor do we have anything available to reverse his condition. Currently, I have him on a morphine drip to make him comfortable." He finished his report to us by telling us that, at most, Pop had a few weeks to live.

We were devastated. Still stunned from the news, I phoned Momma to tell her what the doctor had said. I suggested that perhaps the Mandels could drive her to Mahopac the next day, and that we could then drive back to the motel together.

Momma said she could not leave the motel. If she left, no one would be there to watch the business.

"Mom, it's May. No one is coming up," I said, incredulous. How could she still be thinking of the motel after receiving this terrible news about Pop? "There won't be any customers there until the Fourth of July weekend." Even as I spoke, I realized that nothing short of a nuclear blast or the chance to chant in Hebrew at my nonexistent son's *bris* would ever make Momma close the motel.

Two weeks went by, and Pop continued to hang on in a drugged state. Renee came from her home in New Jersey, and we both used Rachelle and Sam's home as a pit stop to sleep over and wash up when we weren't in Pop's room. I often arrived earlier and left later at the hospital than the others, so I ended up driving back and forth in my car.

It seemed like Renee never left Pop's side at the hospital during the first week. She emerged at one point and came over to me in the waiting room. Rachelle and Sam had already left for the day, so Renee and I were the only ones there. Her face was pale, and her eyes were flooded with tears. "Elliot, the doctor says that Poppa will be slipping in and out of a coma for the next few days, and then—" She couldn't finish her sentence. This was hard news for us to hear, so we hugged each other to protect ourselves from the pain.

At the beginning of Pop's third week at the hospital, Rachelle and Renee and I were joined by our other sister, Goldie, and her rich husband, David. We tried to offer our sister support, but Goldie hardly spoke and wanted only to spend some time alone with Pop. Rachelle, Sam, Renee, and I had all been taking turns sitting with Pop. Goldie's arrival gave us a little time to rest and take care of other matters. Since we had been unable to convince Momma to come see Pop at the hospital, I pleaded with Goldie to fetch Momma. But Goldie just stared at me icily, without explanation.

I stayed at the hospital with Pop all night that Monday, hoping he might wake up again. Early the next morning, as the sun was starting to rise, I woke from a brief nap. I quietly positioned my chair so I was closer to his bed. I sat by his side and talked to him. I tried to awaken him a bit by enclosing his hands in mine. I had never had an opportunity to really hold my father's hands before, so I cherished the moment. Pop was lying there in front of me, in a hospital bed with all manner of scary-looking equipment and tubes attached to him. The doctor had told us it would be pointless to speak to Pop, since he was now in a permanent coma and could not hear us or make any kind of response. Still, I held his hand and told him everything about myself, as I never had been able to do in the past. I told him that I was gay, that I did not believe in God, and that I could never forgive my mother for all her cruelties throughout the years to him and to me. Then I told him that I hoped he would still be proud to have me as his only son.

As the words came out, I began to choke up. I whispered, "I wish I'd been a better son, Pop. You will always be in my heart. If this is your time, don't be afraid to let go. I'm here." Then his seemingly lifeless hand grasped mine. It was not the vise-like grip I had known growing up, but it was a grip nevertheless—an acknowledgment, perhaps, of having heard me.

A moment later, he took a very deep breath, let it out, and stopped breathing. I knew he was finally at peace. No motel to worry about, no debts to pay, and no Momma barking out orders. I kissed his forehead and wept, my face resting against his chest for the first and last time.

    ❁   ❁   ❁

After signing all the papers the nurse handed me, I drove back to my sister Rachelle's house. I broke the news to Rachelle and Renee, and we all cried. My sisters felt it best if Momma were told in person that Pop had died, and it was my fate to be the one to deliver the news.

I arrived at the motel that afternoon. Momma was sitting outside the office, watching the barren highway for any signs of traffic. Sol was keeping her company, but he took one look at the expression on my face and drove back to his place.

When Momma saw me turn on the "No Vacancy" sign, she screamed at me as if I had gone crazy. She rushed to turn the sign back on, but I restrained her. I ushered her into the bedroom, and told her that Pop had died a few hours before. She began to wail and scream. I stood there, frozen in place. I'd seen her behave in a similar way when she felt she was being cheated by a customer or a salesman. But this was different. Suddenly, she turned to look at me.

"What am I going to do?" she screamed. Then, gazing at her reflection in the wall mirror, she continued wailing. "Who is going to fix the plumbing in bungalow nine? You leave me alone like this, Jack, to clean all the rooms and mow the lawns by myself?"

I started to sweat and tremble, as much from shock as from sorrow. I vividly recalled Momma's once-stunning Marlene Dietrich-like looks from pictures of my parents' wedding, taken when she was only seventeen. As the news of her husband's death began to sink in, I found it unbearable to look at her scrunched-up face. It seemed to me she had no clue whatsoever about how much Pop loved her. She was unable to understand that he was now lost to us forever. And I realized she would never know just how much it had saddened him in his final days that the woman he still loved had not come to see him to say goodbye.

Thoughts raced through my mind as I searched for something to say that could penetrate or even overcome her desperate angst and pain. My whole life, I had been a talker. I had something to say about everything, and I had always used humor to deal with my hurt and pain and loneliness. But now, when I really needed to connect with Momma, I was without words. I knew I should have despised her performance at the news of Pop dying, but it was as if I were paralyzed.

Suddenly, I heard a car pulling up to the front of the motel. It was like a cosmic joke—I put the "No Vacancy" sign on, and *then* we get a customer. I went outside, intending to tell the potential guest that the motel was closed due to a death in the family. But Momma's ears were tuned to the sound of the car. And like a predator smelling its prey, she swiftly exited the bedroom. She wiped the tears from her face, opened the office door, and motioned the man in to register. I stood there staring at her, but she didn't even look in my direction.

I took a bottle of brandy from the bar and put a Judy Garland album on the outdoor sound system. As I walked away from the office and toward the swimming pool, Judy's voice echoed in my ears. I collapsed on a chaise and sat there, drinking the brandy. The evening sun was beginning to set, creating an orange glow over the tall pine trees and illuminating the pool water, changing its blue color to bright orange. I couldn't bear to go to the bar to check on how Momma was doing. I just couldn't talk to her at that moment. So I let myself into my old room, far off from the office. Then I fell asleep.

It was quite dark when I awoke. The lights on the motel building were on. The sign on the highway was lit. There was absolutely no traffic, and in my mind, the utter stillness of the moment seemed like a silent tribute to Pop's passing. The bottle of brandy was half empty, yet strangely, I was not at all drunk. I went into the messy, falling-apart office to shut off the sound system. I could see Momma, sitting in a lawn chair outside the office and watching the highway for a potential customer. I couldn't look at her as I passed by and returned to my room.

❀   ❀   ❀

The sound of a car in our parking lot woke me up the next day. I looked at my watch, and was amazed to see it was already noon. The sheets were soaked with my sweat. I got into the tiny metal shower. As I turned on the water, I thought of the hard work my Pop had endured as he installed those cheap metal showers. I had tried to help him, but I was useless when it came to plumbing or building repairs. I reached for a towel after I finished my shower, but of course, there were none in the room. Momma charged guests an extra dollar for towels, and since I had not forked over the cash, I had no towel. Instead, I used the bed-sheet to dry off before I left the motel room.

Rachelle, Sam, and their two sons were talking to Momma. I went to greet them and we hugged for the first time I could remember. Momma looked the other way, clearly uncomfortable. Rachelle said that she had arranged to have Pop's body transported to the funeral parlor in Monticello. Pop's wish was to be laid to rest in the tiny Jewish cemetery facing the former Woodstock festival site near Yasgur's dairy farm.

Over the course of the day, the rest of our family arrived. My sisters Goldie and Renee had worked together to invite all our aunts, uncles, and cousins. They were strangers to me, and not close enough to know what we had gone through. My mother's younger sister Jenny, never one to miss an opportunity—especially if there were no costs involved—had even made sure to bring bathing suits for her family. She and her husband, Monya, checked themselves and their two teenage kids into one of the deluxe rooms. "Deluxe" at the El Monaco meant the room had electricity and running water. With so many relatives now staying at our motel for Pop's funeral, it almost looked like we were a real business. If she hadn't been so busy playing the role of the grieving widow, perhaps Momma might have looked to charge for the rooms and turn a profit.

Not one of my father's five siblings bothered to show up. My father's large family had never been close. My father had been the oldest child. He had worked diligently alongside his father, a roofer. He had used his earnings to pay for his brothers' and sisters' college tuition. His mother had ruled her entire family with an iron fist. She hadn't asked my Pop to fund the education of his siblings—she had decided for him. In return for his sacrifices, Pop's siblings had looked down on him as a common laborer.

Momma avoided looking into my eyes. Poor Renee, the most sensitive amongst us, cried endlessly. Though I tried to give her support, she was only put at ease when her husband arrived with their daughter the next day. *At least she has someone to love,* I thought, wondering if I would ever be so lucky someday.

It took two hard-to-endure days for Pop's body to be attended to at the funeral parlor in Monticello. Both days, my sisters and I drove from the motel over to where Pop was kept. Since they all had spouses and kids to take, I was left to shuttle Momma back and forth. We never spoke during those rides, and my sisters did me a mercy by coming to the passenger side of the car to help Momma out when we arrived at the funeral parlor parking lot.

On the second day, we brought Pop to a chapel to be eulogized. The eight-mile journey to White Lake proceeded quite slowly. A trip that normally took fifteen minutes now took nearly forty-five. Every once in a while, a handful of Monticello residents stopped to watch our unusually long line of cars driving behind Pop's hearse. *For a man who always had to rush from one job to another his entire life,* I thought, *there's no reason on Earth why Pop can't take his time getting to this particular place.*

The chapel had room for only fifty people, but our group numbered at least a hundred. Despite the tensions that had arisen due to my involvement with Woodstock Ventures, my father had been well regarded by the community. People from White Lake lined the walls of the chapel and listened to the rabbi's canned, fill-in-the-family-member's-name speech. I didn't hear one word the rabbi said. I stood in the back of the chapel, utterly mortified by this mercilessly painful ritual. My sisters sat next to Momma, soothing her.

After the eulogy, our family was led behind Pop's casket to the small cemetery that adjoined the chapel. The rabbi invoked the customary Hebrew prayers on my father's behalf, and my sisters began to cry. I couldn't watch. This ceremony had nothing to do with my father's real life and his spirit. Instead, I looked over at Yasgur's farm, thinking about how my father had never gotten the chance to enjoy any of the money the festival had brought into the business.

Suddenly, my mother let loose a barrage of ear-piercing screams. She had thrown herself onto the coffin, which was still sitting on top of the carriage that had transported it to the gravesite. The rabbi and my brothers-in-law had to pull her off. I thought about how strangely she had reacted to the news of Pop's death when I first told her back at her motel bedroom. Maybe these were her genuine feelings, maybe not. Regardless, I still could not forgive the fact that she never went once to be with her husband as he lay there dying in the hospital.

Once my mother had been subdued, the funeral continued. A few of the neighbors made some touching remarks about how Pop had always been cheerful and helpful to anyone who came to him. Max Yasgur was even there to pay his respects, but he stayed at a distance and only nodded to me when I noticed him. At the end, everyone in attendance looked toward me, expecting me to make some closing remarks. I just shook my head. I couldn't do it—I knew I had said everything I had wanted to say to him on his last day in the hospital. After a pregnant silence, everyone got into their cars and left.

We headed back to the motel, and most of the family settled in at the bar. Less than a year before, this had been the place where Pop and I had served the wonderful Woodstock festival revelers. Now all those groovy people were gone, and so was my father. In their place stood a cadre of anonymous relatives who seemed out of step with the world. They might have been family, but they seemed utterly alien to me, and I was increasingly irritated by their intrusion into our moment of grief.

In short order, Aunt Jenny and her brood came into the bar, all decked out in swimming suits. "It's so hot, Sonia," she said to Momma, "and the pool is full of cool water. You mind if we go swimming? It seems such a shame to let it go to waste. Sonia, you have towels for us?"

"Jenny," I said, about to explode. "Go home. Just get the hell out of here!" Aunt Jenny was insulted. She made a big production, squawking about how she and her family had only come to help support Momma and her children in their time of need. No one really paid attention to Aunt Jenny as she fumed and fussed. Even my mother, who was usually the first to pick up a grenade launcher during a family spat, seemed too weak and distracted to acknowledge her nonsense. My aunt got the message. She rounded up her husband and kids, collected their things, and was out of the motel less than two hours later. As their car drove off, I wanted to shout at the top of my lungs, *Where the hell were you for the last fifteen years? It's not like we didn't have rooms available. When my father's dead, that's when you want to vacation?* Instead, I went off to my room and slept. It had been a sad and exhausting day, as befit the remembrance of an often sad and exhausted man.

When I awoke late the next morning, my head ached, my feet hurt, and my stomach churned with hunger. I slowly put on sneakers and jeans and a T-shirt. With my father gone and buried in the ground, I had to figure out what my next move would be. Having barely survived my previous long-term stay at the El Monaco, I was determined that my time at the motel would be temporary—no longer than the summer. It would take me that long to get over the shock of LA and the loss of Pop. The only thing that scared me was the idea of keeping my money anywhere near Momma. There were safety deposit boxes at the White Lake National Bank, and I still had a fairly good relationship with the branch president, Scott Peterson. After all, I had been the one who brought Woodstock mastermind Mike Lang and his magical bags of cash in through the bank's front door. So I decided to stash my money at the bank, under lock and key, until I could sort out my life.

I headed over to the bar, and was thankful to find some sandwiches and salads in the large stock fridge located there. While looking through the leftovers, I heard the outer screen door to the bar open and turned to see my sister Rachelle standing there.

"We went yesterday afternoon and got a bunch of food down at the deli," Rachelle explained. "Renee knocked on your door so you could come and eat with us, but you must have been asleep."

"Yeah, I guess I must have passed out," I said.

"Nearly all the cousins and everyone left yesterday or first thing this morning," she said.

"The smart ones left without having to spend another night in one of the rooms," I said, only half-joking.

"Yeah, well, I didn't get much sleep anyway," she said, looking back out the screen door as she spoke. Then she turned back to me and said, "So now what, Elliot?"

"Now what *what?*" I said.

"What are you going to do now, Elliot?" she asked.

"I don't really know yet," I said.

"Well, I thought you were a big hoity-toity mogul now out in Hollywood," she teased.

"Oy, don't ask," I said, still unable to fully process how much of a failure the trip out West had been.

"I certainly hope you're not going to tie yourself up to the motel again," she said, and I could hear in her voice that she was deadly serious.

"Listen, I hear you, but right now, I just have to get things worked out," I sighed.

"The only thing you need to work out, Elli, is *you!*" she insisted. I knew she was right. Still, while I knew there was no future for me at the motel, the facts were relatively simple. I had no reason to go back to LA, I had no personal relationships waiting for me in Manhattan, and I still felt I owed something to my father for not being the son that I thought he had wanted. Besides, a few weeks in White Lake would help me clear my head, even if it meant having to spend more time with my mother. I told Rachelle that I planned to stick around, but she was having none of it.

Rachelle pointed her finger at the grounds of the El Monaco, and declared the place to be a miserable dump worth nothing. She told me to walk out of the motel and leave Momma. Even though I wanted to go, it had only been one day since my father's funeral, and it didn't feel fair for me to take off. "I owe it to Pop to see things through with Momma and the motel," I explain.

My older sister shrugged, realizing that her sage advice to me, her doomed baby brother, had gone unheeded yet again. I took some potato salad from the fridge and headed back to my room. I ate my fill, and then decided to take a drive. As I drove past the front office, I saw my mother seated on a beach chair, and told her that I was going to get some soda and cigarettes. She didn't even acknowledge me—she remained eerily focused on the highway and possible customers.

❁　　❁　　❁

One by one, my sisters left the motel the next day. First to go was Renee, who assured me that she would call to let me know if she heard of any available apartments in the city. I loved her for thinking of me, and I told her that I would be in touch. Then Rachelle and Sam and their kids got ready to leave. I thanked Sam for being so helpful to Pop in those last days, and he said that he and Rachelle would drop in soon to see how things were going at the motel. But I could see that Rachelle was still furious with Momma for breaking our father's heart in those last days, and I didn't expect them to be coming back too quickly.

And then Goldie and David were off. As the richest faction of our family drove off the property, Momma came rushing out to say goodbye. Maybe they didn't see her, or maybe they just didn't want to see.

When everyone had gone, only Momma and I remained, together and alone. I certainly hadn't planned to be back in White Lake, but there I was. I was overwhelmed by raw emotions and sad memories of my Pop's death. I didn't know what to do or where to go. As much as I disliked my mother, I knew that my father would have wanted me to be there. I might have been lost, but at least I had a place to stay for a few more weeks. I needed some time to think.

So I told my mother that I would be staying at the motel for the following month. All she said was "Good." Then she walked away. That short exchange might have been the most civil conversation I'd had with Momma in years.

I knew for sure that I was not going to stay in White Lake beyond the summer season. There was no chance in hell that I was going to allow myself to be sucked back fully into Momma's vortex. I had to keep my freedom in sight.

I had been back at the motel for three and a half weeks. Every day, I went around to all the rooms and did the customary bare minimum in preparation for the guests I knew would not show up at the El Monaco. Every day, Momma sat in the driveway on her aluminum beach chair throne, waiting for those guests. Of course, there was no season rush, no horde of tourists salivating for deluxe rooms at the El Monaco. A total of eleven guests checked in during the Fourth of July weekend. That spoke volumes about how busy we were that summer. Truth be told, I didn't expect business to pick up.

Earlier, I had received a call from Renee about some apartments in the Greenwich Village section of New York City. That was enough to inspire my return to Manhattan, and Renee had already offered me her couch in New Jersey in case I needed a place to stay at first. I still planned to drive back to Momma and the motel on weekends for the rest of that summer, but it was a big step for me to be city-bound at that point. I planned to go back into interior design. All I had to do was rebuild my reputation.

On the Sunday after the Fourth of July weekend, I began to pack up my belongings. I went into the motel bar and took some cartons of cigarettes to bring with me on the trip back to New York City. As I left the bar, nine black limousines pulled into the driveway. I figured they had come to White Lake for a funeral and continued my packing. I was feeling strangely at ease, contemplating my imminent departure.

The tall, dark-haired, burly man who had stepped out of the first limo approached me. He was wearing a glossy sharkskin suit—definitely not clothing for a weekend vacation in the Catskills.

"Are you the owner of this resort?" he asked politely, extending a hand. I said I was, and he introduced himself as Gino Morino. Another gentleman came up to us. This man wore shiny dark pants and a black-and-white broadstriped shirt. The shirt was buttoned only halfway, exposing a large, hairy chest and more gold chains than Sammy Davis, Jr. wore. I'd spent some time redecorating a mob-owned bar in Manhattan, and I thought I recognized the men's look. They were wiseguys. "This is my brother, Carmine," Gino said.

"I see a big sign out front that says 'For Sale' with a question mark and the word 'Wha?'"

Five years ago, I had painted a half-dozen signs along each of the motel's driveways in a desperate attempt to unload the El Monaco. I had been especially pleased by the one with the huge question mark in deep red. But the signs were old, and this was the first time they had enticed anyone to ask what they were about.

I said, "Yes, the motel certainly is for sale." Momma leapt out of her chair and darted back into the motel. Gino nodded to his brother, who walked over to the cars and knocked on the windows of each vehicle. The car doors swung open, and out stepped nine families. Pointing to the group, Gino explained that these were his brothers, their wives, and their many, many children. He and his brothers were looking to buy property on which the nine families could settle. Gino asked me questions about the size of the property, the number of buildings, and the yearly taxes. I was ready for him, having committed the answers to memory years before, in case anybody ever responded to my signs.

Just as I was about to take Gino and his family on a formal tour of the property, Momma emerged from the office. She had changed from her pink muumuu into her only fancy dress, put on lipstick, brushed back her straw-like hair, and fixed the strap on one of her high heels. Of course, Gino was very charming to Momma. He graciously took her hand to kiss, and I almost choked trying to stifle the wave of laughter I felt watching Momma's attempt to curtsy in response.

As I walked Gino's family around the grounds, Momma traipsed along, talking to several of the wives. She was so excited that she started talking to them in Yiddish. When one of the Italian women cheerfully answered her back in Yiddish, Momma hopped like a jubilant seal that had been thrown a fresh ball to balance on its nose. I did my best impression of a salesman, celebrating White Lake's fresh country air, its first-class schools, and its suitability as a fine place to raise children. Like Charlton Heston playing Moses, I waved toward the crystalline five-mile lake alongside our property. I even showed them the original twelve-room section of bungalows, still sporting the sign advertising Yenta's Pancake House.

Gino spoke up. "Is this a nice community, Mr. Tiber? How is the resort business? What kind of room rates do you get?" he asked.

"White Lake? Gosh, it's a terrific town to live in," I lied. "There are lots of lovely neighbors, and a great schoolhouse only a few blocks from here. And just last summer, we were sold out every single day. Uh, we charged seven hundred and fifty dollars a night and had to turn people away," I neglected to explain that that had been during the Woodstock festival, or that our regular rate was eight bucks a night.

I didn't feel guilty about avoiding the awful truths—namely, that no tourists ever came around here. After all, sales representatives always exaggerate. Making a sale is the thing that matters, right? Okay, maybe I did feel a little bad. But seeing Momma attempt to sell sodas and candy to the Italian wives and their kids reinforced my need to establish a legitimate transaction of some kind.

"During the festival," I told him, "all the bookkeeping records and room rental cards were washed away in the mud and rain."

"What festival?" he asked.

I saw no point in educating him about Woodstock. I didn't believe that anything would come of this meeting. And then there came the surprise left hook.

As we came around to the swimming pool, Gino said, "I'm not worried about the construction of your place, Mr. Tiber, because one of my brothers is a plumber, another's a roofer, another's a chef, another does cement work, and our wives can clean the rooms and wait tables." I could see a gleam of enthusiasm starting to form in his eyes.

Is this guy actually about to make me an offer for this shithole? I wondered. His gleam met my gleam. "Some things need a bit of work, yes, but there's a solid foundation here for you to all do really well," I said, not daring to hope.

"Yes, my friend, this is a beautiful place. Much nicer than the Bronx neighborhood we live in now," Gino explained. "In fact, this would be perfect for us. There's plenty of space for all of our families. We have nine Italian restaurants in the Bronx. We want to open up a first-class Italian restaurant up here. Does that Italian restaurant down the road do good?"

"Di Leo's?" I said, trying very hard not to cross my arms and do a Cossack dance where I stood. "Well, that place has been there for about thirty-five years. The food is pretty bad, though their heroes are all right. And there is no other Italian restaurant anywhere in White Lake."

An hour had passed since the family had arrived. Gino popped the question. "Well, Mr. Tiber, how much would you want for your entire property?" Wily entrepreneur that I was, I made up a number right there on the spot. "We're asking one hundred and eighty-seven thousand dollars, and not a penny less," I said in as calm a voice as I could muster, considering that I was pulling that outrageous sale price right out of my Jewish tushy.

"We will take it, Mr. Tiber," Gino said. He proceeded to lay everything out in rapid succession. "How soon can you move out? Can we come back next week? Alfonse, get some money from my car. Is it okay if we pay you in cash? I give you fifty thousand now, and then we'll bring the balance around next Sunday? Whaddya say?" Alfonse, quite portly, in shiny black trousers with bright red suspenders and pointy black shoes, amiably retrieved a leather bag from his limo.

It was as if I was on an acid trip. Here was Gino Morino of the Bronx, ready to move his nine Italian families on our property the following week so that they could have their new business up and running by the end of summer. I was so desperate that I would have given him the deed and keys for the cash he had in his car.

I quietly briefed Momma on the offer. I wanted to tape her mouth shut so she couldn't screw up the deal. Her eyes nearly popped out of their sockets when Alfonse brought his bag of cash into the bar. She sat hypnotized as Gino counted out fifty thousand dollars. I then suggested that we make arrangements to have a lawyer draw up a formal agreement for the sale.

Gino shook his head. "We don't need anything in writing. We trust the Jews."

We shook hands, and then the nine Italian brothers from the Bronx gathered up their families, returned to their nine limos, and drove off into the sunset. While my mother salivated over the cash, I was excited to think that my years-long nightmare at the El Monaco Motel was now going to end. Add to that a failsafe escape from Momma Sonia? *Mamma mia!*

❁   ❁   ❁

We had just one week until Gino Morino, the leader of our nine Italian heroes, returned with the balance of the cash. Momma spent the entire first day counting and recounting Gino's down payment—fifty thousand, all there in crisp hundred-dollar bills. She didn't even notice that I hadn't turned on the lights for the main buildings or grounds. I telephoned my sisters to tell them of the miracle of the Italian messiah. None of them believed me. They thought that I was drunk, stoned, or that I had finally cracked up from dealing with Momma. Goldie and David read me the riot act, sure there was no way anyone would pay more than twenty thousand dollars for the land—and then only if the motel buildings were completely leveled. Momma didn't have the time to come to the telephone to confirm since she was counting the *gelt* past midnight.

I thought I'd spend the week relaxing, for the very first time, by the pool. I didn't know that Momma's plans for the week would keep me busy round the clock. Momma said we should have a lawn auction of our personal possessions. I assured her that our personal possessions had no value and a lawn auction wouldn't draw flies.

"No value? We got a fortune of stuff in the barn left over from Brooklyn! You don't know a thing, Elli! I'll call Dora Rifkin, the auction lady from Liberty. Dora is a *kluggeh*. We got a fortune in the barn!" Momma said, as if I were simple.

Fully determined, Momma got on the phone and hired Dora. *Will wonders never cease?* I thought. Dora, the "smart lady," said that Saturday would be the best day to get the biggest crowd. For the first time, Momma was ready to ignore the Jewish rules about not touching money on the sabbath. For ten years, Momma had not handled cash from sundown on Friday until sundown on Saturday. Instead, she had made Pop or me handle the money so she wouldn't have to sin. But now all those religious principles could be over-looked. She figured that God would not begrudge a poor grieving widow the chance to make something for herself, even if it was the sabbath.

Dora put ads in the newspapers, declaring that the famous El Monaco, the former headquarters of the Woodstock festival, would hold a lawn auction the following Saturday. She distributed flyers all over the county, proclaiming that Woodstock icons such as Janis Joplin, Richie Havens, and Blood, Sweat & Tears were somehow connected to the countless items going on sale. Mean-while, I got a couple of town drunks to empty out the barn. We had thirty years of stuff left over from my folks' housewares store in Brooklyn, as well as my father's roofing company materials. The drunks schlepped tons of seemingly worthless junk out onto the lawn. There were broken chairs, rick-ety tables, boxes of rusty nails, rolls of tar paper, cartons of family clothing, broken shovels, old shoes and several orphaned skates from my childhood. There were dozens of paper cartons that had never been opened, and signs advertising the Teichberg Roofing Company and Teichberg's Housewares Store. I couldn't imagine that anyone would want to buy this junk, but Momma was on an adrenaline rush the likes of which I had not seen before. What did I care? Soon enough, I would be free.

Momma hired a local policeman to watch the goods overnight so that local thugs wouldn't steal her blind. Of course, she didn't pay the cop money. Instead, she kept him supplied with endless bottles of beer, which suited him just fine. Looking at the growing pile of rubbish, I couldn't help thinking that I'd have to call the fire department to burn it all up when it didn't sell, lest it scare away our deal with Gino.

On the day before the auction, Dora the *kluggeh* showed up with her assistant to inventory the items. She was there for about five hours before she realized that the normal method would not be practical. Dora decided to wing it, going to each item and pointing it out on the spot. That she was even going to hold the auction at all was a shock to me.

Delirious at the prospect of making so much money, Momma wore her-self out and slept soundly; I passed out from exhaustion. Although we had already deposited many of our worldly possessions on the lawn, there were still a lot of things left in the house. *Well,* I thought, *Gino and his family are entitled to the leftovers, since their purchase price was so inflated.*

I woke up at six in the morning, as usual. Heading for the bar to get breakfast, I was shocked to see my drunken helpers schlepping furniture out of the motel. Momma was showing them where to stack it. I told Momma that the motel furniture had been included in the sale. She said she had never agreed to that and I should mind my own business. She was a businessperson, and I should have known better. After all, she had walked to America from Siberia, running through fifty-foot snowdrifts to escape the Russian soldiers who were hot to rape her—and also pilfer her furniture, apparently.

I didn't have time to make a pot of coffee. Although it was early, there were already over two hundred cars and trucks in the parking lot. Under normal circumstances, we had room for maybe fifty cars at best. So people had parked anywhere they could—along the shoulders of the road, on the lawn, and even in the dirt patches near the swimming pool. Apparently, word had spread as far as Pennsylvania, and everybody wanted to see how the infamous Woodstock headquarters, also known as the El Monaco International Resort, was auctioning off iconic pieces of history!

People had come for the long haul, bringing folding chairs, blankets, picnic baskets, and pickup trucks. Momma had dragged the cash register out to a table on the lawn. Over the register, she posted a big sign: "Cash Only."

The first gem that Dora announced was the golf cart we used to haul the wet laundry outside to dry. That it was rusty, had flat tires, and a dead battery was of no apparent consequence, as Dora exclaimed: "Janis Joplin rode on this antique golf cart! What am I offered?" Active bidding started at five dollars, which I thought was about all it might be worth if you stripped it down for metal parts. We had only paid eighty-five dollars for it in used condition five years earlier. Imagine my surprise when the golf cart wound up being sold for $250!

Assorted rakes, shovels, pool equipment, broken dishes, used paint brushes still stuck to empty paint cans, and piles of sheets and towels also went for very high prices. After all, important people had once *touched* these items. I heard Dora cap the bidding for a keg of rusty nails once looked at by Lucille Ball—in truth, anonymous leftovers from our hardware store—at $150. The original retail price? Thirty-five dollars, maybe. The lady auctioneer hardly had time to describe an item before bidders began waving around reams of cash.

Momma was in heaven. During the lunch break, she led some people into the motel rooms. They soon emerged, dragging lamps and broken TV sets from the very rooms in which the band Santana had slept. An air conditioner that had never worked in real life, but was said to have cooled the brow of folk giant Richie Havens, was snapped up for $300.

"Momma!" I said amidst this sales orgy, "We sold the Morinos our motel! They expect the rooms to be furnished. Just stop this *mishegas* already!"

"You are no businessman," Momma yelled. "You don't know what you're talkin'! Did we give Gino a list of the contents?"

It was eleven o'clock at night by the time Dora announced she was totally exhausted and could go on no longer. She announced that the sale was over. With steely determination, Momma grabbed the microphone, and proclaimed immediately that she would finish the sale. I gave up and went to bed. When I woke up the next morning, there were still a few dozen people and farmers with pickup trucks loading their purchases. When I saw a local hotel owner piling the El Monaco highway signs onto his truck, I tried to stop him.

"Those signs belong to Gino, Momma."

"Twenty-five dollars cash is twenty-five dollars cash. You shut up!" she snapped.

We both slept all day that Sunday. Neither of us had an ounce of energy. At about two in the morning, I heard Momma rattling around in the bar kitchen. She was making her "glez tee" (glass of tea). I waddled over to the fridge and got a Pepsi.

"We took in seventeen thousand two hundred dollars from the auction!" Momma said. "And you said nobody would pay anything for all that junk!"

She was feeling wonderful.

"I know this will be a dumb suggestion," I said, "but I think it only fair that we split that money. You've got to admit, I worked like a slave all week."

"You're young and will make plenty of *gelt* in your life. I am an old woman with a condition and you have the nerve to demand from me what little money I have to live on in mine old age? I'm glad your Poppa isn't here to see this!"

It was useless to argue. *A small price to never have to see her again,* I thought as I headed back to my room to sleep it off.

❀   ❀   ❀

On Monday, the first thing I did was drive over to the bank in White Lake to retrieve my money from the safety deposit box. Once I got back to the civilized world of Manhattan, I could take this money and finally put it into a conventional bank account. Then Momma and I drove the seven miles to our lawyer's office in Monticello. Abe Jacobsen ushered us into his conference room. He was skeptical about the entire setup. He kept telling Momma that the sale of the motel was highly unorthodox—and, without the proper documents in hand or the approval of the township, perhaps even illegal. Abe hadn't even drawn up a contract, since he didn't know the name of the buyer or the terms of the sale.

Gino entered with four of his eight brothers. It looked like they were vying for the "Most Gold Jewelry" award, but they also wore ties, which made it clear to me that they took the meeting seriously. Gino smiled with pleasure as he placed his shopping bag of cash on the conference table. His brother, Alfonse, counted out one hundred and thirty-seven thousand dollars in hundred-dollar bills. He pushed the pile over to Momma. She counted the money again to make sure that it was all there.

Abe pulled Momma and me aside and said in a desperate whisper, "Elliot, Mrs. Teichberg! In my forty years as an attorney, never have I done a property sale this way! I need time to draw up an agreement. One hundred and thirty-seven thousand dollars in cash presented in a large bag? Where did all that money come from?" he pleaded.

"Take a few bills across to the bank and just make sure it ain't counterfeit. That's all you have to know!" Momma sternly ordered him.

Abe looked as if he were afraid to disobey Momma, but he made one last plea. "I don't want to assume the worst, but this deal has been presented and agreed to by nine Italian families from the Bronx. Perhaps this money comes from a less-than-legitimate place?"

"Abe," Momma said, growing impatient, "you don't want to aggravate me in my condition! The bank! Go! Now!"

Ten minutes later, Abe came back from the bank and confirmed that the money was real.

Seeing success on the horizon, Momma took me into the adjoining room. She said, "Eliyahu, you are my only son. You don't want to be a rabbi, that's one thing. But you need to start a family. I want you to get married and have babies. You do this, and I will give you ten thousand dollars for every grand-child, up to two children. After two, you pay for them."

I didn't know whether to laugh or cry. Was she serious? I had to make sure she knew what I was about. So I put my face close to hers and said in a low and murderous voice, "I will not marry a woman because I am gay, Momma. I like men. I will *never* get married. And I will live my life the way I choose. There isn't enough money in the world to make me do what you want. Pop did what you wanted him to do for most of his life, and look where it's got-ten him. I just want to be happy. Let's sign the papers and get this over with. Is that clear enough for you?"

She turned around and went back into the office with the others. I assumed that it *was* clear enough for her. We signed over the property to Gino Morino and company. It was finally done.

We drove back to the motel, where our suitcases were at the ready. Gino asked me for the hotel keys, and I handed him our metal box filled with hun-dreds of them, none of which had room numbers attached. He couldn't have cared less.

Momma told Gino and his brothers that they hadn't just bought a beau-tiful resort—they had also bought ten years' worth of hard work and fine motel management, on which she was sure they could build their own big suc-cess. Fortunately, Sol Mandel soon arrived to take Momma and her bulging laundry bag full of cash to a motel in Monticello before she could realize any more of her deluded fantasies about the El Monaco. And I wasn't at all wor-ried about the cash in her laundry bag, because the person had not been born who could have pried that money from Momma's death grip.

I had to take care of a few last things, but then I got ready to leave myself. Shaking hands with Gino, I wished the Morinos the best of luck.

"So where will you go now, Mr. Tiber?" asked Gino.

I told him I was heading back to Manhattan.

"Well if you're looking to take that Cadillac off your hands," Gino continued, "I would be happy to buy it from you right now in cash."

I was thinking very seriously of dropping to my knees and asking Gino Morino to marry me and whisk me off to a grand castle in Venice. Instead, I agreed to sell him the car. Starting to doubt my own reality a bit, I signed over the pink slip and sold the Caddie to him for exactly what I'd paid for it the summer before—three thousand dollars, dispensed from a wad of cash in Gino's pocket. My amazing Eldorado now had a brand-new daddy.

Gino asked if I needed a lift somewhere, but I thanked him and said I'd make other arrangements. I didn't want to spend any more time with the Morinos, in case they changed their minds about everything. If the Morino clan hadn't seemed so happy as they all unpacked their limos, I might have felt guilty at the price they paid for the place. But it was obvious that money was not much of a problem, split nine ways.

As I walked along the highway on Route 17B, my entire body was trembling. At least I was moving downhill, so I could almost trot without looking like I was leaving the scene of a hit-and-run accident. But that was exactly how I felt—like I was escaping a horrible nightmare. It wasn't until I reached the bottom of the hill, out of sight of the El Monaco, that I finally began to breathe easier.

Bernie Federman, our plumber, was driving by.

"Hey, Elliot, is your car broken? Need a lift to town?" he asked.

"I just sold my car! If you could give me a lift over to Monticello, I would appreciate it. I'm heading back to Manhattan."

Bernie wanted to know who the new owners were so he could do the plumbing for them also. In ten years, if Bernie ever showed up for work sober, it was usually a few days too late. As the only plumber in White Lake, he also charged exorbitant fees. I thoroughly enjoyed explaining that the new owners were nine Italian families with ample skills of their own.

"One brother is a plumber. Another is a chef. Another is a roofer. One brother is a gardener. And Gino, the eldest, is a real chef. He has nine Italian restaurants in the Bronx and will be opening a new restaurant in White Lake. Oh, and he is very politically connected, so he is planning on running for town supervisor. It's my gift to the citizens of White Lake."

"Did you say *nine* Italian brothers?"

"Yep, and they're extended family—all from the Bronx."

"Are you saying you sold to the Mafia?"

"I am not saying anything without my lawyer present."

Bernie smiled and dropped me off at the motel where Momma was staying. Marilyn Fegenbush, a real contender for the Hostess of the Highways award, directed me to either room 54 or 55—she couldn't remember which. Her guest register had disappeared the year before, and she couldn't afford to buy a new one.

Momma was seated on a slanted lumpy bed, as I entered room 54—or 55.

"I want to buy a nice little house in town with my money, Eliyahu. Something not too far from the temple and a kosher butcher."

I called Rosalie Goldenberg, the real estate agent.

"Rosalie? This is Elliot, Sonia Teichberg's son. Is there something my Momma can buy immediately for cash? Preferably furnished, and with linens and dishes, close to the *glatt* kosher butcher and the *shul,* very, very cheap. Something that won't fall down for a few seasons?"

Rosalie was so excited to get a client that she came to the motel within the hour, armed with information on a half-dozen properties she had listed. "I have the perfect place for your Momma. Sonia, maybe you even know the owner, Sadie Slotnik? It has three bedrooms, a modern kitchen, a sizeable bathroom, and even a nice porch. So lovely. You can sit on the porch and see all your neighbors coming and going, so you will know what is going on with everyone. You won't feel alone. Not like in White Lake, where nothing ever happens. Sadie wants twenty-five thousand dollars. It has to be cash because she don't take no checks. It only needs a coat of paint inside and outside. It is a dollhouse."

Momma let her go on and on. I could see the gears turning in her head. It didn't matter what Sadie wanted; my mother would dictate the terms of the agreement.

"Let's go see it," Momma said, maintaining a white-knuckled grip on the laundry bag with the one hundred and thirty-seven thousand dollars in cash.

Rosalie drove us a few blocks away. The little "dollhouse" was a white-shingled dump. It was furnished with what appeared to be the leftovers from one of the bungalows we had just auctioned off. While linoleum was a favored flooring choice throughout our county, exemplifying the refined qualities of

Salvation Army colonial, this house even had linoleum on the ceilings and the outside porch steps. It was a *really* high-class setup. But it did have a porch, and it was only two blocks from the temple and one more block to the kosher butcher. Momma liked the dollhouse. We sat down to talk to Sadie, who was sitting in the kitchen.

"So when do you plan on moving out, *dollink?* I need a place right away."

"I'm ready now. I'll even leave my clothing in the closets, the towels, the new bedspreads, the vacuum cleaner, the mops, soap. Everything. And I've kept strictly kosher. There are four sets of dishes. Meat, dairy, and of course, two sets for Passover. The price is thirty-five thousand. Cash. Not one penny less!"

"To me," Momma said, in her best not-one-penny-more voice, "it's only a fifteen-thousand-dollar house. But I see you need a new set of dentures bad. And there is no garage, no driveway, and your torn linoleum has to be removed. Sadie, *dollink,* the house is leaning to the left and right. But I like you, so I'll buy it for seventeen thousand cash."

Rosalie stood up. She was insulted. She started to tell Momma off, but Sadie put her ancient hand over Rosalie's mouth.

"It's a sale! My daughter Ethel is putting me in a retirement home for old women. Ethel said if I didn't sell this house that she hates, she would burn it down!"

Money changed hands. Sadie signed over the deed and asked Rosalie to drive her to the bus terminal as she took her huge pocketbook and stuffed the cash inside. Momma told Rosalie that after she retrieved her suitcases from the motel, she would be paid her commission. I didn't feel sorry for Rosalie because she was used to the nature of her Borscht Belt clientele. And more importantly, in a few hours, I could get the hell out of there.

Momma showed me a little room upstairs that she said would be my room, and she promised not to rent it out. But she also told me that she was already looking for customers to rent it and the other extra bedroom in case I wasn't around. *Well, she certainly doesn't waste any time setting up shop!* I thought. We went down to the kitchen. Momma found a tea kettle and a package of tea—the cheapest brand in the world. We sat at the rickety linoleum-covered kitchen table, drinking the tea, and I decided to take another stab at convincing Momma to give me my share of the motel sale cash. Foolishly, I thought that she might actually consider the payout, since she was settled in her new dollhouse and I was about to depart to *yenne velt*—another world. I knew it probably would be in vain, but I had to try.

"Since I invested five thousand dollars a year out of my decorating salary for ten years, and I worked every summer without taking a penny, it's only fair that you give me a reasonable percentage of the sale price, or at the very least, that you reimburse me fifty thousand dollars. I won't even charge you interest."

I said this as calmly as I could manage, considering that I wanted to shout.

"Did I ever tell you to invest your money into the motel? Is it my fault that was a stupid thing to do? And besides, didn't you get your money back when you went off to Hollywood? You were never smart about money anyway! If you had any *saychel*,"—brains—"you would have known it was a bad investment!" she replied. Ah, yes, the Sonia Teichberg that I remembered.

Arguing was useless. I picked up my suitcase and scooted out of her house and out of her life. I walked to Broadway, the main street in Monticello, to rent a car. I was downright dizzy from the events of that one whirlwind day. I had gotten rid of the motel, the car, and Momma. On the way, I stopped into a deli and treated myself to a corned beef sandwich on rye, the ultimate Jewish comfort food.

Then I rushed to Hertz, rented a car, and blasted back into the open arms of Manhattan. It had taken the loss of my father, the near-murder of my mother by my own hand, and the miraculous appearance of nine Italian families to bring me back to the place I belonged. But I was again free to do whatever I liked, set loose in a magical city where they let you drink as many bottles of ginger ale as you wanted.

5

My French Connection

"Me Hudson, you Jane?"

That was what Gordon, my muscle-bound companion, said as we turned off Hudson Street and headed to my place on Jane Street in Greenwich Village. It was about two AM on a cold April morning. The street was quiet, or as quiet as a New York street can be at that time.

Gordon had a lion's mane of shoulder-length curly black hair, and a wonderfully tight body underneath his heavy leather jacket. I figured he and I could get into some seriously ferocious naked wrestling before the sun came up the next morning. Ten years earlier, I would have been too nervous to even talk to a guy as attractive as Gordon. However, the time I'd spent trawling the clubs in LA had given me a sense of confidence that I had not known before. What I may have lacked in looks, I more than made up for in attitude—and leather. I was definitely of the "butch" persuasion, and preferred a smack in the face to a mere smack on the lips from my conquests.

A definite erotic charge hung between me and Gordon, but I was already growing bored with this juvenile hunk. Even as we walked, I half-expected this encounter to be just another one-night stand. I already had had several of them in the first eight months or so since I had moved back to the city.

"Hey, you like to get high?" Gordon said.

"Sure. How 'bout two floors high?" I joked, as we reached the steps to my apartment.

Gordon looked up at the second floor and laughed. I could see he was fairly wasted. He had already been drunk and stoned when we first noticed each other earlier that night. We had been partying at Julius, a popular gay bar located a few blocks south of my apartment.

Julius was only one of the many hot spots down in the Village that I had frequented since setting myself up again in the city. Having experienced the glitz and glamour of West Coast gay clubs with Felix and Jerry in Hollywood, I now found the East Coast club scene to be a little more grounded—or maybe the term should have been undergrounded. The city might have had its first Gay Pride Parade a year earlier—the indirect result of the Stonewall Riots—but in 1971, New York was still a very dangerous place to be openly gay. The few posh bars that catered to our homosexual community kept low profiles, while the more overtly gay street bars with their loud music, black lights, and tightly packed clientele were usually located in gritty, crime-ridden neighborhoods.

It had been less than two years since I'd left the city, but in that time, New York had really started to change. Not only had the crime rate begun to soar, but everywhere you looked, there was garbage in the streets and graffiti painted on trucks, walls, and subway cars. There had been a sanitation department strike back in 1968, and there was already talk that another major strike might come from the garbage men by the summer. Walking past heaps of trash sitting out in front of buildings that night, I remember thinking that the city was starting to fall apart. Yes, we had a fine-looking mayor, but with every month, the city services seemed to deteriorate a little more.

As inebriated as Gordon and I may have been—and we were—there was never a moment that we weren't instinctively looking over our shoulders. We always had to be careful, out there on the streets.

"How much further, man?" Gordon groaned. We had only just walked up the stairs toward the entrance door of my building. He was a little wobbly, so I put his arm over my shoulders and helped him navigate the half-dozen stone steps. I leaned him gently against the brick wall to the side of the entrance while I fumbled in my pants pocket for my keys. As I was opening the door, Gordon started pressing the buzzers to all the different apartments in my building.

"Hey, quit it!" I whispered, pulling back on the lapel of his leather jacket. He fell toward me, knocking us both to the ground. Realizing how ridiculous we might look to anyone passing by, I bolted up and tried to help Gordon back to his feet. As I pulled him back up to a standing position, Gordon laughed, then impulsively started to hug and kiss me right there in the doorway.

"Okay, okay. C'mon, let's go inside," I said in a hushed voice, feeling like I was talking more to an excitable puppy than a grown man.

"Sure, man," he slurred. One of the neighbors in my building, undoubtedly awakened by Gordon's mischief, spoke some rather foul language over the intercom. Gordon turned, heaved his body toward the buzzers, and shouted a very loud and playful "Hi!" to whoever was still cursing at him through the speaker. I hitched a finger through the belt loop of his jeans and pulled him through the entrance door. At this point, I wasn't even interested in sleeping with him anymore. I just wanted to get him out of the stairwell and into my place, where I hoped he would cool down and keep quiet. Once I got him into the apartment, though, his focus was on me alone, and we started to grope at each other. The leather of our jackets and pants made soft squeaking noises as we ground against each other in lust. *Well, he's got my attention again,* I thought, as we made our way toward the living room couch.

"Hey, now, wait a minute!" Gordon said, like a breathless adolescent at an amusement park. "Where's your sink?"

"My *what?*" I responded.

"Take me to your sink," Gordon said, somehow making that odd request sound sexy, in a non-plumber kind of way.

I wasn't sure where any of this was going, but I led him over to my small kitchenette. He looked at the sink, said it was perfect, and then asked me to fill it with water.

"Why, you thirsty?" I said.

"No, I wanna show you my big turn-on. It's my game, baby. It's what gets me off."

"Okay," I said warily, as I placed the stopper in the drain and slowly turned on the water faucet. "What's your game?"

Gordon then went on to explain that he liked to get fucked with his hands tied behind his back and his head held under water. He told me it was something he did only with guys he trusted. He had started to do it after he came back from Vietnam a year earlier. I moved to shut off the faucet and bring this night to an end, but he begged me not to stop the running water. He then took off his leather jacket and pants in front of the sink. Gordon had a beautifully rugged body, but I felt that something else was happening here.

In the dim kitchen light, I could make out a long scar line on Gordon's lower back. He started to shake as he stood at the sink, watching the water level rise higher and higher. I was suddenly worried for him, and also a little for myself. I shut off the water and tried to guide him away from the sink and over to the couch. Gordon pushed me away and began to bash his head repeatedly into the hard metal lip of the sink. I stopped him before the fourth head bash, grabbing him by the elbows and telling him to calm down. His forehead had a small gash in it, and blood was starting to fall in droplets across his face, mingling with tears from his eyes.

"Hey, it's only a game, right?" Gordon said. Then he pitched forward and passed out in my arms. He was big, and I struggled to drag him over to the couch and lay him down. I checked to make sure that his breathing was steady, unsure if he had passed out from the pills and booze, or if he had given himself a concussion. I didn't have a first aid kit in the apartment, so the best I could do was to clean his wound with a bunch of paper towels I wet in the water from the full kitchen sink. The gash wasn't deep, and the bleeding stopped after a minute or two. As I tended to him, Gordon stirred slightly and opened his eyes a bit, looking like a newborn baby.

"What's up, Daddy?" he said.

"Listen, are you all right?" I asked.

"Why? What happened?"

Is it possible he doesn't remember any of what just happened? I thought.

Apparently he didn't, so I told him simply that he had fainted and hit his head. He smiled a little, said "Oh" in a quiet voice, and settled back down into the couch. Within a minute, he was asleep.

I, on the other hand, was too freaked out to go to sleep. I went back to the kitchen, where I pulled the stopper out of the sink and watched as the water swirled slowly down the drain. I stood there motionless as the water ebbed away and left me all alone. Just as Gordon would do hours later, when he woke up on my couch and made some small talk about our lack of a night together before quickly fleeing the apartment. Just as my father had done months earlier, destroyed by the deliberate absence of the wife he still loved in his final hours. And just as I suspected everyone I ever knew would eventually do.

❀ ❀ ❀

Now that I was back in Manhattan, it was finally time for me to have my vigilantly watched suitcase of Woodstock earnings surgically removed. So I opened up an account at a nearby bank. I kept enough cash on hand for groceries and a steady supply of dime-bags from the hippies who sold pot in Washington Square Park. For once, I had enough money to do what I wanted—and that was to enjoy my time and paint on canvas.

As an undergraduate at Brooklyn College, I had become friends with one of my art professors, Mark Rothko. His abstract style of painting had profoundly affected the way that I approached my own work. I spent most days in my apartment, working on and reworking my new paintings, using his technique. On the weekends, I set up a little spot near the park off MacDougal Street where I would show and sometimes sell my works. I was living the life of an artist without actually doing the whole starving thing.

I had begun to reconnect with the friends I had made before leaving for the West Coast. Some were previous clients of my design business, Plaza Interiors, and others were people I had become friends with while living in the city. Other than Lou and Erica Shapiro—a wonderful couple for whom I had done some decorating work and struck a lasting friendship—and a handful of others, nearly all of my friends were gay. Many of these friends also knew me only as an interior decorator, and probably wanted to know why I wasn't doing that kind of work anymore. They had not been privy to the highs of my Woodstock summer, nor to the lows of my recent Hollywood excursion. Since I really needed the time and space to regroup on my own, I opted instead for a small handful of friends with whom I could enjoy my time without having to answer too many questions.

On the night before my thirty-sixth birthday, I received a call from my sister Renee, inviting me to have dinner with her family the next night at their place in New Jersey. I had always been underwhelmed by birthdays. In fact, the only birthday party I had had, growing up, was the elaborate bar mitzvah that Momma had thrown for me in front of God, the rabbis, and our assorted relatives. Other than my bar mitzvah, no other birthday had ever been celebrated by anyone else in my family. It was especially sweet that Renee wanted to throw me a birthday party, since she herself had never had one in all those years. I felt sad for Renee. I had the feeling that she was lonely, trapped in her "I'm-really-still-too-young-for-this" marriage, even though she had never said anything. The only two things that really seemed to give her pleasure and meaning were her connection to her daughter, Alyse, and her connection to me.

Earlier, she had been pestering me to get a passport. "You should have one, Elliot," she said, "in case you want to travel to Europe or other faraway places. Take in all the sights, y'know? Maybe it will help you figure out what you want to do next." To me, it sounded more like she was trying to figure out what *she* wanted to do next. But I knew it wouldn't hurt for me to have a passport, in case I had to go to France or Italy to attend a film festival some day. So I got a passport.

"Thanks, Renee, for the birthday invitation," I told her that night on the phone, "but I think I'm just going to stay here and try to finish my newest painting." She didn't push. She seemed to understand my need for isolation. Perhaps she even envied it. She wished me well with my work. I thanked her and promised that the new painting would belong to her when I completed it.

After all, it had been Renee who had initially encouraged me to renew my love for painting. And it had been Renee who helped me secure a new apartment in the city. Once I had gotten back to Manhattan the previous summer, I had booked a room at a downtown hotel, figuring it would take me a few weeks to find a permanent place to live. Two days after my arrival, however, Renee had given me a tip on a two-bedroom apartment in the Village that her friend had told her about. I moved quickly. Having lived and worked in Manhattan before, I knew the routine: pay the building's superintendent a few hundred dollars in "key" money under the table, and the apartment was yours. That very day, I handed over the key money and checked out of the hotel and into my new place. The apartment came fully furnished. It wasn't huge, but it offered comfort and peace. After the decadent chaos of living with Felix and Jerry in LA and the trauma of losing Pop, it was precisely the kind of pad I needed.

My daily lifestyle had been peaceful and productive thus far in the city, but there remained for me a certain sadness and lack of direction. But Renee's call reminded me that it was almost my birthday, and that I should do something fun. So I decided to treat myself to a night out at the West Village clubs. I only lasted about an hour. The scene had grown somewhat tedious for me. There really was no zing in the string of my heart any more—or in the zipper of my leather pants, for that matter. I felt indifferent to the dozens of men around me. Before midnight, I left the bar and started to make my way home through the dark and deserted meatpacking district.

Near Greenwich Avenue, the overhead street lamps illuminated a tall man standing in front of a diner. He was dressed in leather, just as I was. Getting closer, I could see that he had a soft and soulful face, like that of a winged cherub. As I passed him, I could hear footsteps behind me. Quickly looking back in a storefront window, I could see that the man was following me. Not sure if I was about to be harassed by an undercover cop, I walked into the White Tower, an all-night burger joint. Among the gay community, this place was known as the "Last Chance Inn." If you hadn't scored yet, you were relatively sure to find guys here who were hungry for *something* there at the burger joint. If you still couldn't score, you'd make sure to leave before the early morning work crowd came in for their coffee and donuts. For me, at least, the White Tower was a safe haven.

The place was curiously empty that night as I took a seat on a counter stool and ordered a coffee. The man who was following me entered the burger joint as my coffee arrived. Ignoring the other empty stools, he gestured to the one next to mine and asked, "Excuse me, is this seat taken?"

The man spoke with a foreign accent. He sounded more French than anything else. He gave his name, shyly, as André, and explained that he was Belgian, from the French district in Brussels. I was pretty clueless about world geography. In my mind, Belgium was associated with waffles and the Congo— and, of course, their famous export, Brussels sprouts, which I didn't like to eat. I was impressed that he had come from such an exotic place like Africa.

I took a closer look at the man. André had a kind and sensitive face, framed by a strong five o'clock shadow. His black hair was short and neatly combed, but starting to grow a bit longer along the back of his neck. His body looked thin but sturdy in his leather outfit. I noticed that his hands were especially delicate, with long fingers and well-manicured nails. As he spoke, he moved his hands in expressive gestures that suited the pace and tone of his words. He sat with a poise and elegance that seemed weirdly at odds with the outfit he was wearing. Had he been dressed in flowing robes, he might have resembled some kind of nobleman or prince that night. I found him dazzling in a quiet and subtle way—far superior to the usual cut of meat that I usually found hanging around the city.

We talked for hours. Since I never had actual conversations with leather-clad guys that I picked up in clubs, this was a rare treat. The more we spoke, the more I liked this mysterious young man with the almond-shaped eyes and sexy smile. I was smitten. André was literate and bright, and he possessed a terrific sense of humor. What's more, he was clearly talented, telling me about the many creative projects with which he was involved.

In Europe, André was a theater director attached to the Théâtre National of Belgium, and had directed plays in Paris as well. Out of hundreds of other directors who had applied, he had won an international fellowship program that allowed him to study theater and film in the United States. The grant funded a two-year stay, providing him with housing, food, travel, and a stipend of a few thousand dollars for each of the two years.

The only problem had been that the grant required the winner to be fluent in English. Although he knew French, Italian, German, Dutch, and even Latin, André had never learned English. He had brought himself up to fluency, however, in six weeks, using only a book. By the time I met him, he had been in New York for nearly a year and a half, and had staged plays at both the Yale School of Drama and Columbia University. I listened in rapture as he described his most exciting adventures.

In addition to his studies and the directorial assignments at the colleges, André was also working on a motion picture. He told me how an up-and-coming film director named Billy Friedkin was shooting a low-budget movie in New York City with mostly unknown actors. I asked André if that was the same William Friedkin who had directed the movie *The Boys in the Band*.

He said, *"Oui!"*

I said, "Wow!"

Mart Crowley had written the groundbreaking play about gay life in 1968, but I had never gotten to see the original theater production, which had premiered in New York. So I had settled for the movie version, attending a daytime screening of Friedkin's movie in Los Angeles. For a straight guy, I told André, Friedkin had done an amazing job with the material. I then asked André about the new film, trying to sound as casual as I could, all the while thinking, *Gosh, this André guy is a movie star!*

According to André, Friedkin's new picture was called *The French Connection,* and the production had needed a French translator. Enter André, who had been recommended to Friedkin through a mutual contact in the New York theater scene. As André told me, Friedkin was quickly impressed by André's cordial and professional manner, and hired him on the spot to play the role of the French interpreter La Valle in the movie. André had already appeared in a few films shot around Paris and Brussels, so he had acting credits. That night, over coffee, he explained to me that he had only just finished shooting various scenes for the film.

Because of his theater background, I thought about telling André about the original plays that I had written and staged over the past ten years in the El Monaco barn—plays that had all failed abysmally. But I felt shy and unworthy next to this accomplished younger man, so I said nothing. As we continued to nurse our coffees, I told him instead about my paintings, and about my previous career as an interior designer. I avoided mention of White Lake, the El Monaco, or the Woodstock miracle, since I didn't feel comfortable telling him about the worst and best moments in my life up to that point. I also wasn't sure if he would even know what Woodstock was, or why it was called Woodstock when the concert wasn't even *in* Woodstock. After all, André was still fairly new to speaking English. I figured it was enough that we had gotten this far in the conversation.

Night turned to day as we talked and laughed and joked and flirted. André had a sweet and seductively winning smile, and his eyes seemed to twinkle as he spoke to me in his adorable French-accented tones. I told him that it was now the early hours of my thirty-sixth birthday. He didn't believe me at first. I gave him a sarcastic look, and responded, "Do you really think I would make up the fact that it's my thirty-sixth birthday?" He admitted that it was too precise an age for me to make up, but he also said that I did not seem that old to him. I liked that.

Our talk began to give way to longer and more significant pauses. Eventually, we realized that nearly every seat in the White Tower was now filled—the usual morning breakfast crowd had arrived. Since there had not been any discussion of sex, André caught me off guard when he asked if I lived nearby, and if he could come home with me. I became lost in his gentle hazel eyes as he spoke. "Yes, of course," I said, "I can show you one of my paintings."

"Yes, Elliot," André said, "I would like to see it."

We were both very much talking about something else, so I paid our coffee tab and we got up to go. We walked casually back to my place—just two guys sharing the early morning sidewalk. But I was practically breathless with anticipation, and couldn't wait to be alone with him. We hadn't even touched each other's bodies yet, but I felt like we had already touched hearts and minds. That was something that had never happened for me before. So as I opened my apartment door and my life to André that morning, I did so with the hot and uncertain expectation of a virgin.

We spent all of that morning and much of the next day making the most tender and passionate love I had ever experienced. It was astonishing to me how totally compatible and in sync we were with each other. Everything was easy, nothing was forced, and all was permitted. I was in complete heaven, and he seemed as happy with me as I was with him. In fact, everything about him was amazing to me. The heated intimacy between us made it feel as if we were making up for lost time.

Around noon, we found ourselves lying on the bed, looking at each other. The mood gradually turned philosophical, as André reminisced about growing up Catholic in Belgium. I told him about growing up Jewish in Brooklyn. He spoke of his childhood fondness for coffee and baguettes; I sang the praises of egg creams and bagels. He told me that he believed in God, but sometimes wondered if he was really up there. I told him that, as an atheist, I knew for a fact that there was no God. I told him it was better to worship art and music and the movies. He listened to me with the rapt attention of a pupil heeding the words of a wise professor. Momma would have keeled over dead from a stroke if she could have heard me.

Then I had a sudden impulse.

"Hey, would you like to hear a joke of mine?" I asked.

"Yes, why not?" André responded with a grin.

"Okay. Knock, knock."

"Who's there?"

"Godot.'"

André looked at me, not quite knowing what to say.

"You're supposed to say 'Godot who?'!" I said.

"I see. Godot who?" he replied.

No answer.

"Now you repeat it. Godot who?" I said.

He did. *Still* no answer.

Then I delivered the punchline. "'There won't be an answer, because we are waiting for Godot.'"

Silence filled the bedroom. Obviously, Belgium was not known for its "knock, knock" jokes. Then, after a few seconds, he laughed, and I realized that he got what I was doing. He understood the reference. He also recognized that I might be a little different from most people, and that seemed to please him. From the amused but confused expression on his face, though, I knew that there might be a few things the Brooklyn kid in me could still teach this Belgian Congolese. I opened my arms to him, and he snuggled up against me on the bed and kissed my neck. His newly growing beard was like sandpaper against my skin, and I told him that he had better grow it out on the double.

"Do not worry, Elliot," André teased me, "I will grow my beard for you as a birthday gift."

I had just turned thirty-six and was now head over heels for a French jungle prince. *Oui!* He and I were so consumed by each other that we didn't even bother to watch the Academy Awards that night. If we had, we might have seen the *Woodstock* movie win the Oscar for Best Documentary. Not that any of that really mattered to me right then. Let the others from Woodstock have their Oscar. I had won an André!

"No, I am *not* from the jungle," André said to me with a gentle laugh. He and I were browsing a record shop off Christopher Street a few days after our first date. "I am from Belgium."

"Yes, but isn't that in Africa?" I responded, sure that I knew where Belgium was.

"No, Elliot," André continued, with the patience of a saint. "You see, Belgium is in Europe, right above France. You are thinking of the Belgian Congo, which is located in Africa. That is far away, and I have never lived *there*."

"Oh," I said, feigning a quiet arrogance in order to shield my embarrassment at having made the mistake. *Gee,* I thought to myself, *Pop has been gone nearly a year and I still need his maps to know where the hell everything is!*

"This is understandable, though," he said, "and I see how you may have thought it." He and I had been together for only three days, so it would have been easy for him to poke fun at my geographical ignorance, but he was kind enough to take my feelings into consideration. I certainly was not used to any such compassion, and it made me like him that much more.

We had been walking around Greenwich Village after a brief corner-café lunch, during which I told André about my Woodstock summer. Previously, all André had known about Woodstock was that there had been a million grungy hippies taking drugs and sliding around naked in the mud as loud rock music played for three days. Having had a unique view of those three days, I thought I would put it in context and explain what it had meant to me and the kids who were there. I first told him about the crazy role I played in getting the concert to take place in Bethel, and the windfall it had provided my parents and me. He couldn't help but laugh at my good luck.

Then I pointed to the window facing out on the street and said, "André, all you have to do is look at the kids going by. They come to the Village every day from all over the country. They are trying to make a statement through their clothing, ideas, language—and especially their music. One new generation trying to tell another, 'We are not you! We don't want what you want. We just want to be us.' And then Woodstock came along to show the country that a brave new world could actually be brought suddenly to life through peace, love, and music. It was incredible!"

"*Mon ami,* I think I understand," he replied, smiling. "But I still do not like rock 'n roll, or drugs, or hippies."

"Well, they're not going away any time soon," I reasoned. "Better get used to it."

After the fervor of our lunchtime talk, it seemed natural that we would wind up in a nearby record shop to check out some music. In those first few days together, we realized that we shared a love for classical music and opera. There were differences, though. I still enjoyed the hard rock from Woodstock, and André preferred jazz and the ballads of French singers like Edith Piaf and Charles Aznavour. Since I had just turned thirty-six and André was only twenty-seven, it would have made more sense if he liked rock and I liked jazz. Rules are made to be broken, though, and André already seemed so self-assured and on-track with his life, unlike me.

I had picked out an album of orchestral pieces by French composer Maurice Ravel when André discovered an item in the record bin that really excited him. "This is fantastic, Elliot," he said, like a child with a favorite toy, "I had a copy of this record when I was growing up. Do you know the American actor Tony Perkins? These are some songs he sang in French. I have not heard this since I was sixteen!"

Of course, I knew who Perkins was. I even remembered that he had a few minor radio hits in the late fifties, around the time my family set up shop in White Lake. It was a surprise, though, to hear about these French songs, and I told André so. He grinned and said, "Then you must hear these songs, and I will buy this album for you as a birthday gift." I was touched by his thoughtfulness, but I laughed out loud with what happened next. As we made our way to the cash register, André asked me if I had liked Perkins' performance as Norman Bates in the Alfred Hitchcock classic shocker *Psycho*. "You know," he said, "the one where he plays the man all alone in the scary motel with his mother."

"André," I said while laughing, "you have no idea!"

On the walk back to my apartment, I told André about many of my tangled motel-hell traumas—and, of course, about Momma. We were walking anyway, so he was free to run whenever he wished. And if he felt a frantic need to swim back to Belgium, I could direct him a few blocks west to the Hudson River. To my immense relief, however, André seemed to take the story in stride, and even laughed to hear about some of my more frustrating run-ins with Momma. He told me that he had friends with overbearing mothers back home as well. Thankfully for him, though, André had a very warm and loving relationship with his family, especially with his own mother, Fanny. He spoke of an upbringing that seemed the polar opposite of my own. Growing up with a mother and father who loved each other and two sisters who always involved him in their lives, André's childhood sounded like some kind of French-accented paradise.

As we neared a street corner, I pointed up at the top of a brownstone building. I explained to André how I used to work with Pop, laying roof tar on similar buildings throughout Brooklyn on weekends when I was a kid. I told André that my father had died the year before, and was surprised to find that thoughts of my father brought back such strong feelings of loss so quickly. André could probably see the grief in my face. He stopped and said, "I am very sorry, Elliot." He placed his hand gently on my shoulder, and we stood together like that for a few seconds. The moment was totally dashed when a few guys walked into us as they rounded the corner. One of the guys grabbed André by the lapel of his jacket and shouted, "Watch where you're walking, asshole!" Another guy barked, "Fuckin' faggots!" as they strutted off.

I asked André if he was okay, as he looked a little shocked. All I could think to say is, "Here in New York, people have an interesting way of talking to each other." After all, we *had* stopped to talk and he *had* shown me affection by placing a hand on my shoulder.

While we continued walking back to my place, I told André about some of my own experiences as a gay man in the city. I explained that being too much of oneself out in public could bring on all kinds of trouble, either from the straights who hated us, or from the cops who were supposed to protect and serve everyone. André shook his head and said, "Well, Elliot, you do not have to really worry about that in my country. The people are a lot more open about their lives over there, and people are able to be who they are a lot more." *What a wonderful place,* I thought. Any country that let people be simply who they were sounded good to me. I did tell him about that night at the Stonewall when we all fought back against the police. But that was just one night. The real work was ahead of us, to be found on any street corner where a thug might be waiting.

We were about two blocks away from my apartment before André spoke again. "Elliot, let me make you a dinner back at the apartment," he said, as we walked past a grocery store. I was worried he was still upset after we were harassed by the guys earlier, and told him that I would take him out to dinner later that night. Though we were both fairly tall, at six foot one, I had a larger build than André. I told him not to worry about anything while he was with me. He smiled at my chivalry, and then insisted that we stop at the grocery so he could get some things. "Okay, André," I sighed, "but no duck."

"Why?" André asked, "are you a vegetarian?"

"Uh, yeah," I quickly responded. "That's right, André. I'm a vegetarian."

❀ ❀ ❀

Armed with only two bags of fresh produce and basic food staples, along with a big loaf of Italian bread, André turned my little kitchen into his very own performance space. I watched in awe and bewilderment as he pulled out pots and pans from the cupboard. He sliced, diced, and spiced up a delicious combination of tomato, avocado, onion, scallion, and garlic, and mixed them with Romaine lettuce, olives, broken bits of gorgonzola cheese, and walnuts. He also cut thin potato wedges, fried them until they were brown, and doused them with a delicious lemon-butter sauce. I put my new album of Ravel's *Bolero* on the record player, which was not as loud as the sound system that Felix and Jerry used in the Hollywood mansion kitchen, but worked just fine for my needs there in my apartment. As André continued to cook to the rhythms of *Bolero,* I pretended to fiddle with my newest painting. But I was really watching André. He moved gracefully from the left to the right, busying himself with the practiced hand of a true cook. Apart from the occasional cold-cut sandwich, soda, or ice pop, I barely knew or cared about what I had in my kitchen. My relative lack of culinary interest was made clear to André when he opened my refrigerator.

"Elliot," André said, "I thought that you might have eggs here. Where are they?"

"They're in the grocery store, down the block. They keep fresher that way," I responded, feeling a little foolish for not knowing what I had in my fridge. "I can go down and get some now," I added.

"Not necessary, but be aware that there will be no omelets with your salad," he said. Turning back to look in the refrigerator, he saw my gallon container of milk and chocolate syrup bottle alongside a half-dozen small bottles of seltzer water.

"Those ingredients are a permanent fixture in there," I explained. "They are what I need to make egg creams. I make a very good egg cream!"

"But why then do you not have any eggs for your egg creams?" he asked.

"I'm guessing you are not familiar with the Jewish cuisine of eggless egg creams, latkes, *cholent,* delicatessens, and heartburn," I quipped.

"I am afraid I am not."

I could see that he was just about finished with what he was making, so I took two dishes and placed them, along with the usual utensils, at the small oval table alongside my living room couch. Then I took a knife and cut the long Italian bread into a dozen or so pieces. While I had paid for the groceries and we were in my apartment, I wanted to contribute something of my own creation to this meal. So I took two tall glasses and mixed two big egg creams. I asked André if he wanted one. He laughed and said "Sure, yes, but if you don't mind, I would prefer wine."

Thankfully, I had a nearly full bottle left over from the last time Renee came to visit me at the apartment. I took another tall glass and filled it halfway with red wine for André. He thanked me with a long, soft kiss on the lips. I felt a little stupid that I had made him an egg cream, but quickly brightened up when I realized that I now had two egg creams all to myself.

André carefully placed some of the salad on each of our plates. He then brought over the browned potatoes, forked about a dozen slices or so into my plate and his own, and used a large spoon to drizzle a nice amount of the lemon-butter sauce from the pan onto the salad servings. Not knowing what to expect, I picked up some of the salad with my fork and gave it a taste. It was quite simply the greatest salad I had ever had, full of fresh, tangy flavor. When eaten with the browned potatoes, it was absolutely scrumptious. "Wow, André," I said, with my mouth full, "this is great! What do you call this?"

He smiled at me, and said "I call it Salade d'Elliot."

I smiled back at him and said, "If it's for me, why not call it the *Marquis de Salade*?"

"Yes," André responded, getting up to turn over the Ravel record. "That is a very good name for your special salad." The first piece on the other side of that record was Ravel's *Pavane pour une infante défunte*—which, as André told me while we ate and listened, meant "Dance for a Dead Princess" in French. I had never known that. I had just heard it on a classical music radio station years before, and instantly loved its gorgeous and somewhat melancholy melody. Fueled by the beauty of the music and the romance of the moment, I raised my egg cream and proposed a toast.

"Here's to you," I said, looking at André, "and to me, and to all of this here tonight."

"Here is to art," he said, looking at me, "and to madness, and to love always."

As the music continued to play, I got two more pieces of Italian bread from the kitchen counter. Though it was still my habit to eat any food placed in front of me—so long as it wasn't Momma's—I noticed that André was very calm and careful about how he ate. He didn't clean his plate, explaining that his mother always told him that it was best to leave a little food on your plate so that your host does not think that you are still hungry. It wasn't exactly how I was raised, and it seemed like a very European thing to do.

We washed the dishes and settled down on the couch in the living room area. André was tipsy from the wine, having finished off the entire bottle during the meal. He asked me what I was going to call my unfinished painting. Without missing a beat, I said, "Salade d'André!" We both laughed. Then, remembering his gift, André stood up and said that he wanted to play some of the Tony Perkins songs from the French album we bought earlier that day. He went over to the record player and placed the needle down carefully at the groove before the final song on one side of the album.

"There is a song that I very much want you to hear, Elliot," André said, a bit more serious than he had been. The music began with a gentle orchestral introduction. Though not formally trained, Perkins had a very charming singing voice that sounded a little like Mel Tormé's. He sang a pretty ballad in French, and I asked André what the song was about. He looked up at me and said, "The singer is saying that if he is ever to die, he will want to die in the spring, in a quiet room of white curtains, and surrounded by roses."

Oh, André, I absolutely love you. That thought hit me so hard at that moment that I almost spoke the words out loud. I couldn't believe that such a profound and wonderful man had waltzed into my life. I wanted so badly to tell him that I was in love with him. I moved in as the song ended and kissed him gently on his forehead. Then, with his hand in mine, I brought him to my bed, and showed him how I felt instead.

6

A May-September Romance

It was the Thursday before Memorial Day weekend. I hadn't really been in touch with Renee—or anyone else, for that matter—in the six weeks or so since André and I had first met. André, on the other hand, maintained a very busy schedule. He was based uptown, at Columbia University, where he was staging a graduate-student production to be performed in June. The piece was an adaptation of an early work of the celebrated experimental European playwright Eugène Ionesco. Though he was acting as the assistant director on the production, André also served as the stage manager.

While André was in the midst of intense study and show preparation, I tried to focus on my paintings. I had become so smitten with André, though, that he had become my primary preoccupation. I wanted only to be with him—to talk with him, sleep with him, and wake up with him.

When I met André, he was living in a Columbia University dormitory room that he'd been provided as part of his study program. That dorm room was where he had all of his things—clothes, books, a suitcase, and a duffel bag that looked very much like my own. Talking about his rigorous schedule, I asked if he wanted to stay with me at my place instead. We had been practically inseparable since our first night together, so it seemed natural for him to be with me whenever he was not at the college theater.

"Are you sure that you want me to live here with you, Elliot?" André asked in his considerate way. His impeccable European manners were always so refined.

"Yes, yes, of course. *Mi casa es su casa,*" I responded, echoing the phrase that Jerry had said to me the night I had moved into that Hollywood mansion. "Think of my place as your home away from home. I'm here for you, babe." We hugged and kissed. Two days later, André had pretty much moved in with me.

He and I were very strongly attracted to each other, and we made love every free moment. His beard was already heavier than mine, although he'd only started growing it after we hooked up. I joked with him that I was jealous of how quickly he had raised his beard. He reminded me slyly that he was only doing what I had *commanded* him to do.

We already had such a nice and easy rapport that it felt like we had been together for months, not weeks. Still, we had not yet said the words "I love you" to each other. It was as if we were worried that speaking the actual words might somehow break the spell of our romance.

"So when do I get to meet your new boyfriend?" teased Renee on the phone.

"Who told you?" I asked, feigning surprise.

"No one had to. You just sound really happy, Elliot," she said.

"Well, why don't you come and meet him this weekend, Renee?" I continued. I figured she might enjoy a little break from married life in New Jersey. Something seemed terribly wrong with her relationship at home around that time. Whenever I asked about her husband, Freddy, and how things were between them, she said they were going through a rough time. While I didn't know for sure, I suspected that Freddy was abusive to my sister—if not physically, then certainly emotionally. As a result, Renee had become increasingly unhappy and wanted less and less to do with anything that might require leaving her very young daughter, Alyse, at home alone with Freddy.

"You know that it's hard for me to come to the city, Elliot," Renee said, "but maybe you could come to New Jersey and have a holiday barbecue with us on Monday."

"Well, I don't know if that's a good idea, sis," I said. I sensed that Freddy was homophobic and hated me for being gay. I had only been to visit at Renee's house twice since I moved back to the city, once for Thanksgiving and again a few weeks later for Hanukkah. Each time I went, it was obvious that Freddy wanted nothing to do with me. Renee had done all the talking, while Freddy found something to do to avoid being in the same room with me. At dinner, he had hardly said a word, sometimes giving me a stare of unspoken disgust. As an interior decorator, I had encountered the same type of behavior many times before. I felt I knew exactly what the source of their fights might have been. While I adored my four-year-old niece, I never wanted my presence to upset my sister. But I wasn't about to jump through hoops in my life now just because some angry straight guy in New Jersey preferred that I hide my true self because it made him uncomfortable. *Besides,* I thought to myself, *maybe he's the one who has something* he's *trying to hide.*

"Don't be silly, Elliot," Renee responded, "you should definitely come to visit. And please bring André, if you like."

"Renee, I'm not going to bring André somewhere where he and I have to pretend we're both old college chums or confirmed bachelors," I retorted.

"You're my brother, Elliot. You are always welcome at my house," Renee said, as only a loving sister would. "Besides, I have someone here who can convince you to come." And then, in a flash, my niece Alyse was on the phone. "Come see us, Uncle Elliot!" she shouted. "Bring me toys!" *Who can resist such an offer?* I thought, and so I agreed to visit. But I didn't know if André would want to go.

"Well, if he's as sweet a man as you've described, Elliot, I'm sure he will come," said Renee. "Besides, he knows what it's like to have a sister."

"Okay, okay," I responded, wondering if it had been a mistake to tell Renee about André. "Let me talk with him about it and get back to you tomorrow."

"How old is he, anyway?" Renee asked.

"He's, uh, twenty-seven. Actually, he's turning twenty-eight next week. Why do you ask?" I wondered aloud.

"Oh, it's nothing," she said, feigning innocence, "Rachelle will probably ask me about it, so I wanted to know what to say. Do you mind if I tell her, Elliot?"

"I have nothing to hide," I responded. "Go right ahead."

Aside from the brief emotional reunion at Pop's illness and funeral, my older sisters and I had not really stayed in touch. That wasn't a surprise to me, though. As for Momma, all I knew of her was what Renee told me. It sounded as if my mother was healthy and comfortable in her new home. Beyond that, I had no further thoughts or concerns about her.

"Hey, maybe we can have an early birthday cake for André if you guys come," Renee said suddenly. "I still have the cake in the freezer that I made for your birthday last month. Not that I want you to feel guilty about refusing my invitation," she joked.

"Let's put it this way, sis," I responded, "if I hadn't begged off that invitation of yours, then we wouldn't be talking right now about André."

"Yes, I suppose that's true," Renee said, with a melancholy air. "Life is weird, right?"

"If you're lucky, it is," I shot back.

"So," she continued, in a mischievous voice, "you're the older man, huh? How does it feel to be robbing the cradle, Elliot?"

"Goodbye, Renee," I said, pretending to be annoyed. "I'll let you know whether to put out a clean tablecloth on the table for Monday."

For the rest of the afternoon, I kept thinking about that age gap, though. I knew Renee was only having a bit of fun with me, but I did find myself wondering if André thought I was too old for him. There was, after all, a nine-year difference between us—practically a decade. And I knew what the counterculturists said: never trust anyone over thirty!

As I awaited André's return to the apartment that night, I dabbed my brushes against my palette, absentmindedly poking little bits of color onto a brand-new canvas, trying to make something emerge. Sitting alone, I started to feel very anxious. I began to think about all the time that André was spending at work in the college theater. I reflected on all the younger men with whom I imagined he collaborated every day. Clearly, he had much to offer, and I felt sure that I wasn't the only one who might have noticed his charms. My insecurities bubbled to the surface. I had hoped André would be the first to voice his feelings for me; that's why I had resisted telling him how I felt. Then the thought struck me. *What if André doesn't really feel as strongly for me as I do for him? Why can't I just enjoy the relationship and stop making myself crazy?*

The apartment buzzer rang. I hit the button that opened the front door, and stood in my doorway, waiting. Until I saw him come up the stairs, smiling as always, I almost didn't believe André would appear. But he did, and his rush to embrace me dissolved my gnawing feelings of doubt.

❀　　❀　　❀

We went out for a late dinner that night. Our favorite haunt was a little Italian restaurant located near Father Demo Square, off Bleecker and Carmine Streets. The first night we had dined there, I told André about how Gino Morino and his eight brothers turned the El Monaco into a big Italian restaurant up in White Lake. The next time we went back to the restaurant, André suggested that I ask the owner if he was one of Gino's cousins. I carefully explained that if the restaurant owner *were* related to the Morinos and found out who I was, then André and I very well might not make it out of the place alive. Thankfully, he stopped asking me after that and we got back to enjoying the antipasti, the pasta, and the wine. I was careful to emulate André's delicate table manners. I didn't dive into the food as I had been trained to do at Momma's table in Brooklyn. Instead, I watched André as he carefully and slowly chewed his food, just as one ought to in order to truly savor the flavor of enjoyable food. I was learning.

I asked André how his work was going at the theater. Instantly, his face lit up, as he excitedly described minute details of the show. He had a humble way about himself that reminded me of my father. Unlike André, though, my father had never really spoken about his work with tar and roofing—up until the Woodstock festival, he had rarely spoken at all. He had simply done his work, and that was that. I was never that quiet, though, and I had learned a thing or two in my life before André about making a splash and getting noticed. Sometimes I worried that André, like my father, might be too modest to get ahead.

During dinner, André talked about some of the more cutting-edge techniques that he saw being applied in the theater. One of the reasons he had been so excited to come to America had much to do with the New York avant-garde performance style, or "street theater," as he called it. Street theater had not yet come to Brussels, and he appreciated being able to learn about it and use its techniques in his production.

"The idea that excites me most now, Elliot," he said, "is to strip away the wall that stands between the actors on the stage and the people in the audience. I want to create work that is defined as much by the people who sit and watch as by those who stand and perform. That is what I have been learning these past months. The theater must *confront* the audience, and I want to direct productions so that they act as a finger aimed straight at the viewers."

"Are you sure that you don't want it to be the *middle* finger, André?" I countered.

He laughed in spite of himself at my gentle jab, but I quickly encouraged him to keep telling me about his work.

"André, I have been to the theater many times over the years," I began. "But beyond placing the actors on stage and speaking their lines, I don't understand what a director actually does. Tell me more about that."

He smiled at me, bemused at my utter lack of knowledge about his craft. "Well, there are so many things that one must do in this kind of work, Elliot. Are you sure to want to hear about this?"

"Yes," I said, hungry to learn as much as I could about his world. "Tell me everything."

"Well," he began, shifting forward in his chair with the look and sound of an eager co-conspirator, "first of all, everything you do must serve the needs and vision of the script; you must realize the intentions of the playwright. A good director oversees all the elements of the production. That way, there is a free flow of concepts between the different people who make the show happen. You are there from the beginning to help secure the cast of a show—the men and women who will act on the stage as characters in the play. Then there is the issue of wardrobe, or what these actors will wear in the show. The clothes the actors wear go a long way toward establishing their characters, as do the hair and makeup. And from the first moment that all the actors sit and read through a play together, you must keep notes on the ways in which people say their lines, interpret their characters, and relate to each other in their parts. It is important to have continuity from day to day.

"Then there is the design of the set. As a director, you must work with a designer or team of artists to interpret and realize the landscape in which the play takes place. There is also the lighting, which similarly helps set the mood. The director works closely with the lighting director to design the placement and use of the lights. And of course, the director helps determine the selection and use of music, if it is desired. The director and the musical director—the one who leads the musicians or controls the recorded soundtrack—need to understand each other and remain in constant dialogue about how the words and voices of the actors blend, combine, and sometimes work at odds with the music that is heard."

"And I suppose you have to sell the tickets at the box office as well?" I kidded.

"Usually not, but if it is a small show with a low budget, you do whatever is necessary."

He sat back in his chair and took a sip of his wine.

"So, that's it?" I joked. Now I understood why André was so busy and how much work he had to do. I was very impressed by the confidence with which he discussed his responsibilities. All this talk led me to recall my own forays into summer stock.

"One summer at the motel," I told him, "I had thirty-three actors in my barn theater. They were doing Shakespeare's *A Midsummer Night's Dream*. On opening night, we had sold just one ticket. For the second performance, I persuaded the cast to perform in the nude. It was probably for the best that Shakespeare was already dead, since I also changed the show's name to *Sex, Y'all Cum*. We sold two tickets at that next show. *Oy vey!*"

He howled at my story. "How I could have used your expertise up there, André!" I said.

"It is funny, you having all those actors in your barn," he observed, "because I really started more as an actor when I studied in Belgium. I thought I would be an actor because I didn't like the way directing was taught—my professors were like cold scientists, making us take lots of notes during their lectures. There was no passion."

"So when did you learn to direct in theater?" I asked.

"I studied film first," he clarified. "In fact, I wanted to do the film with Friedkin not so I could translate for him or appear in the film, but mostly because I was hoping to learn more about film editing. I still hope that I will be able to learn it. I have to wait and see when I can make that happen."

We were well into our second bottle of wine, André in the lead. Waiting for dessert, I asked André again if there was anything in particular that he wanted to do on the holiday weekend. "No," he said, "just to relax and to be with you." The dessert arrived—spumoni ice cream and cannolis, with two double espressos—and I decided to drop the Teichberg bomb on my unsuspecting Belgian.

"I have something to ask you, André," I continued, careful not to sound too desperate. "My younger sister, Renee, wanted to know if I would come to visit her and her family in New Jersey this Monday for the holiday. We can have a barbecue lunch."

"Barbecue? But I thought you did not eat meat!"

"Yeah, well," I said, remembering my stated aversion to duck at André's first home-cooked meal, "my meat-eating is like a condition. It comes and goes. Anyway, Renee told me to bring a guest if I wanted."

André sat quietly, twirling his dessert fork, and said, "Will I be comfortable there, Elliot?"

I looked at him, saw his vulnerability, and suddenly felt very protective. "No, probably not. André, my sister's husband is an asshole, but my sister is great, and her daughter is adorable. They are a big part of my life, and they really would like to meet you. What if I arranged things so that we'll be able to visit with Renee and Alyse only?"

He paused, looked up, and said, "If it means that much to you, Elliot, then I will go." Seeing how pleased I was that he had agreed, he then smiled and said, "I look forward to meeting your sister and her daughter. You must tell me more about them, though, before we go. You know how much I like to research things."

"Don't worry," I returned, "you've already survived just hearing about my dysfunctional family. Meeting them will be a walk in the park."

I winked at him and flagged down our waiter for the check. I paid for the dinner with yet another tiny chunk of my Woodstock savings—the total of which had probably been depleted by another five thousand dollars or so. For the most part, I hadn't been worrying about money much. I'd drawn on my savings only when my art earnings didn't cover my rent and other basic expenses. But after my dinner with André that night, things started to change.

Money had given me freedom, but without direction, I was drifting aimlessly. Now I'd met a man who knew exactly what he wanted out of life, and it made me think. Here was a man, nearly ten years younger than me, who had placed himself at the center of the modern theater universe, and who would soon be appearing in a major film. And here I was, still dilly-dallying with my paint brushes almost a year after returning to New York, one of the most culturally important cities in the world. My life was in neutral, but

André's was most definitely shifting into overdrive. It tormented me to think that André might consider himself too young and too full of promise to settle down with an older and less focused guy like me. *Dollink, it's time to get a job, do something that will enrich your mind,* I told myself.

Unfortunately, I wasn't sure I could get a job that would bring in a nice income while also satisfying my creative urges. I had worked very hard to build my reputation as a successful New York City interior designer in the previous years, but I had also grown tired of obeying my clients' littlest whims—especially when what they wanted and what I felt was the right choice were often vastly different. After the jobs I had had in LA, I didn't want to put myself back in that same old box again.

We had a relaxing weekend in the city, spending some time out enjoying the sunshine on the Great Lawn in Central Park. André brought a book of French poetry to read. Always looking for a little attention, I had with me the new Irving Wallace book, *The Nympho and Other Maniacs.* I made mischief by reading some of the book's juicier passages about history's most famous whores aloud to André whenever people walked by. Eventually, though, my thoughts returned to my future. I still had a dream—to work in the movies. My disappointments on the West Coast hadn't killed my love of motion pictures, a love that was still a large and enriching part of my emotional life. I went to the movies several times a week, preferring the art-house cinemas. Considering that I had been forcibly deflowered in a movie theater at the tender age of twelve by a shadowy Brooklyn stranger, the cinema still held a special allure for me after all those years.

It occurred to me that there were a lot of unique interior design possibilities in movie theaters themselves. I thought I could perhaps do some design work for one of the theater chains, like Fox or United Artists. I didn't tell André what I was thinking, but I had made up my mind: I would try to get a job designing interiors for one of these chains. If I scored a job, I would surprise André with the news. And if I didn't, I would see how I felt about things then. It was a plan, at least, and I hadn't had one of those in quite a while. I had become the director of my own life again.

❀   ❀   ❀

I called Renee on Saturday morning to tell her that I wanted to bring André, but only if Freddy wasn't going to be around. "Don't worry," she said sarcastically, "he told me that he has to go to work on Monday anyway. I'm not sure how many people need to call their accountants on a national holiday, but I don't ask questions anymore."

"Well, at least we have Quasimodo out of the way," I reasoned. "So now I can bring André without any trouble."

"That's wonderful, Elliot," Renee said. "This is going to be so nice, especially for Alyse."

On Monday, we took a bus from the Port Authority bus terminal to New Jersey. We were picked up at the station by Renee and Alyse, who was especially excited that I was coming to visit with a new friend. André was a perfect gentleman with Renee, who was charmed from the minute he kissed her hand in greeting. She blushed a little at André's courtly manner. Alyse, meanwhile, hopped up and down shouting "Uncle Elliot!" until I picked her up and gave her a big hug. As I put her down, I told her to close her eyes and open her hands. I then placed the soft stuffed animal that I bought her as a gift into her palms. She loved it, and then André started to pretend with Alyse that the animal not only spoke, but spoke French! The stuffed animal said things like "*Parlez-vous français, mademoiselle?*" and "*Comment ça va, ma petite fille?*" in a funny made-up voice that Alyse found hilarious. Renee hugged me and whispered "Charles Boyer, eh?" in my ear.

Always the good cook, André went about helping Renee to prepare lunch, while I made up silly stories to amuse Alyse. Renec asked André about his life back in Belgium, and André shared memories of growing up with his mother and father and his two older sisters in the ancient town of Liège. Renee told André about what it was like growing up as the baby in the Teichberg family back in the Bensonhurst section of Brooklyn. It was clear to me that, as the youngest children in their families, Renee and André easily related to each other. Their conversation danced back and forth like the jets of water from the lawn sprinkler through which Alyse ran back and forth in her little bathing suit for most of the afternoon. Everybody seemed so happy. It had been a long time since I had heard Renee laugh as much as she did that day.

When André excused himself to go to the bathroom, Renee grasped my arm excitedly and whispered, "He is absolutely lovely, Elliot. I'm so happy for you!" To know that my sister shared in my joy meant the world to me. At the same time, though, I was concerned to see how unhappy Renee had become in her marriage. I had always been very protective of my sister, so it killed me to have to sit there and not be able to do anything for her. She told me not to worry. "I'll figure things out, Elliot," she said, looking at Alyse. "It's something that I have to do on my own. Now help me put out the birthday cake I have for André before he gets back." Though I understood what she had meant about having to do things on her own in the marriage, it didn't mean that I had to like it.

As soon as André returned from the house, we shouted "Surprise!" and then sang "Happy Birthday" to him, with Alyse, the smallest of us, singing the loudest. André looked a little embarrassed by the gesture. However, he was very gracious and thankful for the chocolate cake that Renee had gotten for the gathering. She had taken mercy on me, sidestepping any acknowledgment of André's age by placing a single birthday candle in the cake.

We had just finished cutting the cake when Alyse decided that she wanted to redecorate it with marshmallows roasted on the grill. I helped Alyse with the marshmallows, while Renee and André sat and had cake and coffee together. Before too long, it was time for us to get back to the city. Alyse cried a little in the car as Renee drove us back to the bus station, but André soon got her laughing again in the back seat by having the stuffed animal do his French voice. As we drove, Renee asked André and me if we wanted to come back to visit on the Fourth of July. I was about to tell her that we might be able to do it when André said casually, "Well, I will be living in Connecticut at Yale by then, and then I will travel as part of my studies to some other colleges before I return to Belgium in September."

Upon hearing those words, I froze. Renee said, "Oh," and gave me a sad, confused look. I gazed out the window, only speaking to answer Alyse's occasional questions as we continued on our way. My mind was jumbled and my heart felt a flurry of distress.

At the bus station, I gave Alyse one of my big Uncle Elliot hugs, and she gave me a few of her crayon drawings—including one of "Uncle Elliot and his friend." André thanked Renee for her kindness, and kissed her on both cheeks, as so many Europeans do. Renee gave André a quick but affectionate hug, and said that she hoped she might see him again before he left. He said he hoped that would be possible. Then, as he crouched down to bid Alyse *adieu* in his special French-accented stuffed-animal voice, Renee and I hugged.

I could tell she wanted to say more to me, but she only said, "Talk to you soon."

"Yeah," I said haltingly, "I'll call you, sis."

André and I waved goodbye as Renee and Alyse drove away. Making our way to the waiting bus, André said, "Well, your sister and your niece are very lovely, Elliot." I smiled and agreed. I took the window seat, leaving André to his preferred seat on the aisle. He asked me if I was feeling all right, and I said that I was fine except for a small headache. Inside, though, my brain felt like it had burst into flames. I had to keep looking out the window so that I wouldn't cry. Having learned that André would only be in the country for another three months was bad enough. But receiving the news in that sudden, matter-of-fact way—as just one of three other people seated in a car—made my deep feelings for André suddenly seem ridiculous. In all the close moments and profound discussions he and I had shared over the past weeks, why in the world had he not mentioned that he was going to have to leave?

A little while into the bus trip back to Manhattan, I turned from the window to André and said, "I didn't know you had to go back to Belgium in September, André."

"Yes, but you understood that I am only here for the duration of my studies, Elliot," André said, sounding a little surprised. "I must return to Belgium when my studies are through," he said, in a voice that thankfully sounded a bit forlorn. "I will be sad to leave you."

"Quiet," I whispered quickly. After all, we were on a public bus, surrounded by people. Although I had a thousand things I wanted to say, I was keenly aware of where we were. "We can talk about it later." A few seconds passed, and I started to look at Alyse's drawings. There was a blank piece of paper mixed in with the fistful of drawings she had given me. I took a pen from my pocket, and wrote on the paper. I showed it to André:

I'm sorry. I was just upset to learn you have to leave so soon.

Understanding that a quarrel between two gay lovers on a Port Authority bus was not a viable option, André took my pen and joined me in a series of scribbled notes to each other:

I am sorry. Are you sad?

I'm fucking devastated!

Why?

Because I'm going to miss you SO much!

I will miss you, too. But we can still have fun while I am here.

You don't understand, it's more than that. I LOVE YOU.

André looked up at me after reading that last note from me. He smiled and quickly broke the silence, saying, "In Belgium, we say 'Je t'aime.'"

I said, slowly, "I don't understand. You have to write it down."

He grinned and put pen to paper yet again. When he handed it back to me, I then read what he had written:

I love you, too.

I almost sobbed in relief at seeing those wonderful words. I looked up at him, and saw the same measure of guarded adoration in his eyes that I also felt. I quickly drew a heart on the paper, and jotted down our initials inside. Then I signed my name on the page. André looked at the little drawing, swiftly drew in the classic arrow going through the heart, and added his signature alongside my own.

"Our first masterpiece," André said proudly. I smiled and nodded, as I reached out to briefly touch his hand, lying there between us on the seat. I would have liked to hold his hand, but we knew the rules. We had to be wary in public. Although we were in love, we had to express our feelings in ways that would pass largely unnoticed by the straights in the crowd. So on that New Jersey bus bound for Manhattan, two gay men communicated love for each other silently.

Before I fell asleep that night with André in my arms, though, it occurred to me that we still had not said the words.

Over the next week, while André was rehearsing uptown at Columbia, I updated my portfolio with photos of my work in California. I took my suit to the dry cleaner, and called my friends Ron and Fran to ask if they would act as references for me in my new job search. I looked through the *New York Times* classified ads. One day, I spotted an opening in the marketing/advertising department at the Trylon Corporation offices, located at 666 Fifth Avenue—a building that was considered haunted by those who believe numbers actually mean something.

The Trylon Palace theaters had done well ever since the mid-1940s, when weekly movie attendance in the United States was the highest it had ever been. Trylon had also come to acquire various types of non-theater-related commercial properties throughout the country, further filling the corporate coffers. Given my design flair, property management skills (as exhibited at the falling-down El Monaco), and love of the movies, Trylon seemed like a perfect place to work. I hoped that a gig with them might yet lead me down the yellow brick road back to Hollywood.

Instead of sending a standard résumé and cover letter in the mail, I put on my suit and tie—the same suit I'd worn to Pop's funeral—and took a cab uptown to the office. I wasn't really interested in the humdrum marketing position described in the ad. Instead, I decided impulsively to tell the young woman seated at the front desk that I had recently arrived from the West Coast and was eager to do some design work for Trylon's movie house division. Though I had no appointment, the confidence with which I had walked into the office seemed to make an impression on the secretary, who went off to relay my message to the back office. I sat in the waiting room for about a half-hour, and then the young lady told me a member of the marketing team would be there shortly to talk with me about the position.

A few minutes later, I was met by a young man with hair that was slightly longer than mine. "Hi there, I'm David Stein," the young man said, shaking my hand. *This guy looks like he just graduated high school,* I thought to myself. In his office, I explained that I had worked for over a decade as a top Manhattan interior decorator, and had recently returned from a stint in Hollywood, during which time I had restored a number of high-priced mansions to their original splendor.

"Wow, really?" David said. "So did you work on the mansions of any bigtime Hollywood names out there?"

"Have you heard of the legendary actress Marie Dressler?"

"Who? What movies has she been in? " he asked.

"She was in a lot of silent screen movies. Joe Franklin talks about her all the time on his TV show. Well, I restored Ms. Dressler's mansion."

I opened my portfolio and showed him my work. He was impressed by the designs, but he wanted to know why I was interested in Trylon after my stint in Hollywood. As David checked out my work, I noticed that he was wearing a thin silver necklace with a small peace symbol hanging from the chain. I explained that the movie scene out in Los Angeles seemed antiquated and hung up on the old ways of doing things, and that that wasn't my bag. I was interested in new ways of doing things.

He said, "I can dig it," and said that he totally understood where I was coming from. On a whim, I then asked him if he had been to the Woodstock festival.

"No," he lamented. "But I saw the movie and have the album and really wish I could have gone. Were you there?"

"Uh, you got a few minutes?" I asked, grinning.

An hour later, I was hired.

Later that night, I shared the news about my new job with André over dinner at the expensive but wonderful French restaurant, Lutèce. André was happy that I had succeeded in getting a job so quickly.

"It's a really great job, André," I said. "This young guy, David, said that his department has been looking for a person who would work well on projects that involved different departments, including the advertising division and the design department."

"So what will you be doing?" André asked.

"Well, David tells me that they'll create a position for me as the director of creative promotion, and it looks like I will be given the chance to introduce some new design concepts for the Trylon movie theaters all across America. So I'll finally be able to get some of my design work into the movies—even if it's not going to be on the screens."

Still, André wondered why I suddenly wanted a job. "These meals, this money," he said. "I hope that I have not been a burden to you, Elliot. You do not need to spend money on me, you know?"

"I know, André, but that's not what this is about," I said. "I just felt it was time for a change, and you inspired me with all your talk about the theater. Maybe a design job like this can lead to even more important things. You have to start somewhere." At least that was my hope. "Besides, I'll be getting a salary of eighteen thousand dollars a year, plus dental! Hey, it's a solid start."

When I arrived at the office that first Monday morning, my hippie interviewer, David, was nowhere to be found. I learned later that day from Janine—the woman at the front desk—that he had just quit. I should have taken that as a bad omen, but the promise of the new job was still alluring. The buzz would wear off soon enough, though. I would come to detest the relative confinement of working from nine to five each day, and at tasks I didn't enjoy.

As it turned out, the work I was given as the director of creative promotion was not creative at all. The opportunities David had said would materialize never did. Instead, I was made to monitor quality control on already existing fixtures and design components in the various Trylon movie theaters around the country. Most of my day was spent shuffling papers and invoices, and reviewing fluorescent lighting, imitation plastic statuaries, and Renaissance-style paintings that served more as wallpaper than as art. I quickly realized that the job David had made up for me was, well, made up. For all I knew, I might have been David's replacement.

At the end of my second day, I asked to meet with the floor manager for my department—a steely-eyed man named Bob Eudell, who wore a bowtie every day and who moved fast and spoke even faster.

"Yes, Mr. Tiber?" he asked snippily.

"I just wanted to speak with you about my position."

"What about it?"

"Well, it's nothing like what was described to me by my interviewer, David."

"Yeah, well, that David was a real fruitcake. Who knows *what* he was smokin'."

"Right, yes. Well, he told me that as director of creative promotion, I would be free to, uh, *create* designs."

"Well, I don't know what he told you but that is *not* the job."

"I understand, Bob, but—"

"It's Mr. Eudell, Mr. Tiber."

"What's that?"

"The name is *Mr.* Eudell. Only my wife and mother get to call me Bob. Now look, what's the problem?"

"The problem," I responded, growing agitated, "is that I am a creative artist, and I am not getting a chance to create."

"Creative artist, you say? Listen, are you too much of an artist to make a good salary with a good company that makes good dollars hand over fist, season in and season out?"

"I don't mean to sound ungrateful," I said, "but I don't know exactly how I wound up with this job. It's not what was told to me."

"Yeah, well," he said, stopping his rapid-fire talking style for a second before continuing. "You say that you want some creative opportunities, Mr. Tiber?"

"That's right. Even the office hallways, they are so drab." They were a pea-green hue that made more sense for a hospital than for a forward-thinking office. "Since this is a place that designs movie palaces, wouldn't it be nicer to have a vibrant and exciting office to work in?"

"That's really not something our department has any control over, Mr. Tiber. However, we'll take your suggestion—and your interest in other kinds of work—under advisement. I will speak with Mr. Wick about your ideas. Meanwhile, we've got a business to run and movie theaters to refurbish. Unless you have anything else you need to talk with me about, let's get back to work."

It seemed that the company had no real need for a change in the formula. Whatever transformation David Stein had envisioned left when he did. As a result, my fresh start had given me exactly the kind of drone-like office job that I had wanted to avoid. I kept at it, though, since I liked having something to share with André each night, instead of sitting in my apartment waiting for him to return.

Mr. Eudell fancied himself some kind of interoffice Gestapo character, hell-bent on making me miserable. He saw me reading the paper one morning. "No reading the newspaper in the office, Mr. Tiber. Company policy," he said. Another day, I was listening to a small portable radio in my office during the lunch hour. "No radios in the office, Mr. Tiber." I half-expected him to follow me into the restroom and stand next to me, drily intoning, "No pissing in the urinals, Mr. Tiber."

The paperwork was dull and relatively easy to finish—so easy, in fact, that I was usually done with my work by eleven o'clock each day. For the rest of the day, I would draw all kinds of doodles, mostly of André. When people entered my office or started to speak to me from my door, I would place a pile of already paid invoices over my doodles and give them my best "Can't you see I'm busy?" face.

I was slowly going crazy, and I wondered how much longer I could keep at it. Maybe there *was* something wicked about the numbers on the side of that building.

In the third week of June, André invited me to see the play he had been working on at Columbia. The small theater was filled with parents and instructors from the theater department. The production was somewhat abstract and very intellectual. While I was intrigued by the chaotic and multi-colored set design and found the lighting to be very inventive, the dialogue in the play—much of it structured around made-up words—flew over my head. It reminded me of those hilarious double-talk routines that Sid Caesar used to do on *Your Show of Shows*. Everyone else seemed to understand the play's meaning, or so I gathered from the applause at the end of the performance.

Later that night, in bed, André tried to explain the complicated text that the actors had recited. I pretended that I got it, since he had clearly put so much effort and meaning into his work, but I didn't understand it at all. What I *did* understand—and what I suspected André didn't yet—was that most people were really quite simple. As long as they didn't question things too much, most people got whatever they believed they had paid for when they went to see a show. It didn't necessarily matter to most if they didn't understand what they were looking at. What mattered was that they were having an experience. This was how I came to define absurdist theater, as a meaningless concept that people with a combined and vested interest mutu-ally agree has meaning. Bullshit, basically. André was honing his absurdist edge with top college theater professors and directors. I had already inad-vertently mastered the concept of absurdity years before under the tutelage of Sonia and Jack Teichberg.

André had only one week to set himself up at the Yale School of Drama for the next phase of his theatrical work. After his production wrapped at Yale, he was to embark on a quick cross-country trip to various regional the-aters in August, taking a few meetings at the same Hollywood movie studios where I had tried to find a foothold the year before. And then André would be back to New York in early September, with only a few days that we could share together before he had to fly back to Belgium from JFK Airport. I remained positive about his plans, and told André that we would enjoy our remaining time together to the fullest. But it was tough not to dwell on the fact that he would soon leave. I was really going to miss him, and dreaded being there in the city without him. The thought of being stuck in an increas-ingly useless job, surrounded by new paintings and old memories, was terrifying to me. I told Renee my fears during a phone call, and she had an interesting take.

"Why don't you leave New York, and go live with him in Belgium?" she asked. The thought had certainly crossed my mind. However, I still worried that our age difference might be a problem and I didn't want it to seem like I was simply hitching a ride on his rocket of rising talent.

"It's a beautiful thought, Renee, but I'm not going to do something like that if he hasn't even invited me to come," I reasoned. "Besides, the only French words I know are 'oui' and 'bonjour,' so I don't think that's going to get me too far."

"Get a French dictionary, El," she said. "This is your life we're talking about. All I know is that if I had found someone I loved and he was going to move away, I'd pick up and follow him anywhere he was going to go. No question about it." I knew that she was really talking about herself and her disintegrating marriage to Freddy, but I wasn't going to jump on an airplane because my sister thought it would be romantic. Later on that night, though, I continued to think about what she had said. *If I had found someone I loved . . .* I didn't sleep too well that night.

André and I made an arrangement. He would stay at Yale during the week, but take a train back to the city each Friday so we could be together on weekends. On that first weekend after he started work at Yale, I took André over to Christopher Street in Greenwich Village. I wanted him to join with me and march in the second annual Gay Pride Parade. As we prepared to march up Fifth Avenue alongside our gay brothers and sisters, I still felt a little fearful. There was always a chance that some homophobic nutcase could pull out a weapon and hurt one of us. But I knew we had to show our solidarity. And so we marched.

As I did, I held André's hand and finally said what I had wanted to say for many weeks: "I love you, André." He told me he loved me, too. Soon enough, André would have to return home to Belgium. But on that day, we belonged to each other. I chose to be happy in the moment as André had suggested, and tried my best not to think beyond September at that point. Trying, however, is one thing. Doing is another thing completely.

❀   ❀   ❀

After the show at Yale—an abstract interpretation of an Oscar Wilde play—André left in late July for his monthlong trip across the country. We knew by then that we were very much in love with each other. I just had to hear his voice each day, and so I said I would phone him every night. He gave me his trip itinerary and contact information at the different hotels along his route so we could stay in touch. And he left some of his things there at my apartment, including some of his treasured books. I took it as a hopeful sign, and did my best to stay committed to my new job without winding up committed to Bellevue, of course.

Eudell left promptly at five each afternoon in order to get home to his wife in Scarsdale. This meant that I could stay late at my office and make calls to André on the office line, rather than my own at home. I reveled in the freedom; I even listened to my little radio, surfing the AM dial to hear either the popular standards of WOR or the rock songs played by the great disc jockey Cousin Brucie Morrow on WABC. For the most part, I tried to reach André at his hotel room after the end of rehearsals and before dinner. He understood that I was phoning from my office, and that it was usually seven or eight o'clock at night by the time I called. We had very good conversations, and it seemed clear that he missed being with me as much as I missed being with him.

Having seen him work with graduate students at both Columbia and at Yale, it was hard not to worry that André would find new friends and lovers on the road—men who were younger and, I feared, better looking than I was. I felt like he was moving toward better things that had nothing to do with me. I felt bitter, dull, and useless. Worst of all, I was terribly in love with a man who was not even there. Though I realized he had his own plans and dreams, I couldn't help but feel jealous and insecure about the relationship. I wanted to be a bigger person, but I felt so small.

Other than its free access to long-distance phone service, my new job had few perks, and grew increasingly stale and monotonous. I had been hired for my creative talents with interior design, but the reality of the office was far from ideal. Everyone in the office looked sad or dejected or dead, and sometimes all three when it was raining out.

In addition, we were expected to wear drab business suits. My one suit wasn't cutting it, so I bought a few more. Truth be told, all those egg creams and sumptuous restaurant meals had made my old suit a little snug. The new suits fit me a little better, but I hated having to conform to that bourgeois cookie-cutter American-dream bullshit in order to earn a salary. It got so I tried not to look at my reflection in shop windows each day on my way to the office.

The calls sustained me. Just hearing André's voice did much to calm my spirit, and I told him funny stories about how I was stuck wearing a suit and was trying to make some sense and money out of my new job. The more we talked on the phone during those few weeks, the more confident I grew in the telling of my humorous stories. I was in pain without André there, but I drew on that pain to fuel my increasingly absurd and outrageously comical stories. André seemed to enjoy my zaniness, and told me I should consider writing some of my experiences down on paper. We were separated in body, but together in mind and spirit.

One Thursday night, I noticed on a wall calendar at my office that it was only a few days before August 15—the anniversary of the beginning of the Woodstock festival that had changed my world so wonderfully a few years before. Eudell had left the office in the late afternoon that day, and was all set to embark on a one-week summer vacation with his wife and mother in the Poconos. This kept me free of his insane power games for at least a few days. I called André at the appointed hour, just after seven o'clock in the evening. As I listened to Mick Jagger and the Rolling Stones playing "Paint It Black" on my radio, I let the phone ring. It rang and rang, and it kept on ringing. No André. I called back a few more times over the next ten minutes, and it continued to ring. There was no answer. André wasn't there. I called the hotel's front desk and asked if a Mr. Ernotte was at the hotel. They confirmed that André had checked in, but that he had not returned to the hotel yet. *That's all right*, I told myself, *I'll just wait and call back later.* Over the next three hours, I called back three times—and each time, I let the phone ring. I didn't make it back to my apartment until after midnight. I had no idea why André wasn't there at the hotel, and felt upset that he didn't try to call me. As I tried to get to sleep, I kept hearing those words from that song over and over in my head. *Paint it black . . . paint it black . . . paint it black.*

The next day was Friday the thirteenth, and there I was, walking into my office at the 666 building. This mix of bad numbers, combined with the

Rolling Stones song that was still in my head, may well have inspired what I decided to do next. Using the interoffice purchase requisition pad, I ordered a dozen cans of black paint and a pair of big-handled and industrial-sized roller brushes. The materials were delivered to my office after the lunch hour, and I waited until the clock struck five before getting to work.

Starting that Friday night and continuing most of the following day, I took a good look at my office and then proceeded to paint it black. And not just the walls, either. I also painted the ceiling, the file cabinets, the desk, the desk chair, and even the window ledge. By dusk, I had even painted my office door and door knobs. André may have been doing theatrical work of his own out there, but I was now directing my own equally dramatic fade to black—literally. My pain had led me again to paint, but the canvas for my work had grown considerably larger.

When I arrived at work on Monday morning, my newly painted black office was nice and dry. There were hushed whispers from my fellow employees as I made my way down the hallway. There stood my newest artwork—my office, a thing of great and immovable black beauty. I figured everyone on the floor now assumed I was a certified lunatic.

It was a little after ten that morning when I looked up to see our department head, Sidney Wick, walk past my office door. I could hear his shoes click-clack on the floor of the corridor. Then he stopped, turned around, and looked back again at me with his utterly expressionless face. "Good morning, Mr. Wick," I said, in my most cheerful tone. He nodded, and continued walking down the hallway. About twenty minutes later, I was called into Wick's office. Mr. Wick invited me to sit down across from his desk.

"Mr. Tiber," he said, calmly, "I wonder if you have noticed the color of the walls here in our offices."

"Yes, they are all pea green," I answered.

"Indeed," Wick continued, looking up at the ceiling and rocking gently up and down in his swivel chair, "indeed they are. And did you notice the color of *your* office, Mr. Tiber?"

"Yes, Mr. Wick," I said, hurrying to explain myself. "You see, I decided to paint my office black over the weekend. I did it on my own time. I find I do better work if I enjoy the colors of my environment. You know what they say," I joked uneasily, "the best businesses are the ones that stay *in the black.*"

Speaking of colors, Wick was starting to turn red in the face from what I suspected might be a surge of blood pressure. He continued to speak in a steady voice while staring straight at me. "So you're telling me that your office is painted black. Is that true, Mr. Tiber?"

"Yes," I responded.

"You sure?" he asked again.

"Yes, Mr. Wick. I painted it myself."

He paused. Then he got up from his chair and walked to his office door. "I would suggest you have another look, Mr. Tiber." Warily, I followed Wick out into the hallway and looked at my office. And there I saw a trio of janitors who had already set themselves up in my office with a bunch of green paint cans and roller brushes. I looked at Wick, who then waved me coolly back into his office. Once I was back inside, he turned to look at me. He had a strange look on his face, like he was trying very hard to stifle a cough or to stop himself from throwing up.

"You mentioned colors earlier, Mr. Tiber," he said, his cold grey eyes practically pinning me against the wall. "You said something about keeping a company 'in the black.' Well, I can tell you that I have done much to keep this company running in the black for more than twenty years now." His red face was turning a curious mix of pink and purple as he quivered in his beige suit. "You know why these walls are all green, Mr. Tiber? Because it so happens that *I* like that color. Green is the color of money, and that's why we're all here. And if you want to stay here working for us, you will never *ever* do anything like this again. Do we understand each other?"

I nodded, and said that I was sorry for the misunderstanding. Wick told me to get the hell out of his office and back to work. As I opened his office door and was preparing to leave, I suddenly thought back to the time I had spent working for Felicia Moore. I wasn't happy then, and I wasn't happy now. Without consciously knowing what I was about to do, I turned to Wick and said, "You know what else is green, Mr. Wick? A traffic light telling you to go, and that's just what I'm going to do right now. I quit."

Wick was speechless at first, since this was probably the only time anyone had ever spoken to him in that way. Then he had his secretary call for a security guard to escort me from the building. I told him that would not be necessary, and that I was only too delighted to go. He turned back into his office and shut the door. I gave the secretary my office key, wished her well, and made my way toward the elevators. As I walked, I thought I could hear Mr. Wick laughing from inside his office, but I couldn't really be sure.

So that was it. I had self-destructed myself out of a job. In fact, it could be said I had effectively black*walled* myself from the movie biz. But I figured anything beat sitting in an office all day surrounded by green paint, grey suits, and pink- and purple-faced people-eaters like Mr. Wick.

When I returned to the apartment in the early afternoon, I was amazed to find André there already. As it turned out, he had been able to finish his trip two weeks earlier than planned and he wanted to surprise me by returning to the city. I told him the news of my resignation from Trylon. He congratulated me on what he deemed a *bonne décision,* and again suggested that I think about writing down some of my funny observations and humorous stories.

We took full advantage of his final two weeks in New York. It was a time of total adoration. We saw films, took in art exhibits, heard some jazz at the Blue Note, and even went to see a wonderful new musical at the Village Playhouse that a friend of André's had recommended. It was called *Jacquel Brel Is Alive and Well and Living in Paris,* and it was a cabaret-style selection of songs—*chansons,* as André called them in French—all written by famed Belgian songwriter Jacques Brel. The songs had been translated into English by producer Eric Blau and the hit songwriter/performer Mort Shuman. The songs were alternately hilarious and poignant, and the four leads performed the songs with an intensity that reminded me of Judy Garland, whom I had seen in concert years before at Carnegie Hall and the Palace Theater. We were delighted and moved by the performance, during which we held hands. Although I had done everything physically possible with others over the years in the darkness of theaters, I had never actually held the hand of a man I loved in public before.

As a Brooklynite, I felt it was my obligation to take André to Coney Island before he left. I wanted him to have a Nathan's hot dog. I tried to explain that a Nathan's hot dog was not just a frankfurter, but also a slice of New York life. Having spent so much time with me over those few months, I think André was finally starting to get what it was to be a New Yorker. He wasn't from New York, though—he was from Belgium. And though we laughed and loved through the end of August, we both knew André had to leave.

On the day that he was due to fly back home to Belgium, I arranged for a limousine to pick André up from my apartment. Before helping him bring his luggage down to the street, I stopped him in the doorway and gave him the gentlest and most loving kiss of my life. We held each other close. I breathed in his scent, and tried to remember how he felt, every sinew and muscle a living piece of my sense memory as my fingers traced his shoulders and back. My head knew it was right and noble to push him toward his home, but my heart wanted to pull him back into my arms. Instead, I put his luggage into the trunk, shook his hand, and gave him another quick hug. He had given me an address in Liège where I could write to him, and he already had my address.

"Write me some of your crazy stories," André said.

"Send me Belgian chocolate, and keep your beard," I said.

And with that, André was gone. I stood there watching for a long time, even after the limo was no longer in sight.

7

What I Did for Love

"WAAAAAAAAAAAAAH!"

"OHH-NOOOOOOOOOOO!!"

"HELLLLLLLLLLLLLLLP!!"

"EE-EE-EE-EE-EE-EE-EE!!!"

I was at an experimental therapy session on a weeknight in early November, several weeks after André returned home to Belgium. I felt despondent and lost after he left, and had seen a story in the *Village Voice* about Dr. Arthur Janov's radical new primal scream therapy. The idea was that people could purge themselves of adult neuroses by returning themselves mentally and physically to a childlike state. I figured I would try anything to lessen my pain.

The treatment room was completely padded—the floor, ceiling, and even the door were all cushioned. Everywhere I looked, there were men and women crawling around or lying on the matted floor. Some were in the fetal position, sucking their thumbs; others were writhing and screaming underneath blankets. It reminded me of the triage unit we had set up outside the El Monaco at Woodstock for concertgoers who were having bad drug trips. At least then we had been able to chill out the people who were screaming. In this therapy session, people were encouraged to scream as a way of getting better. A terrifying hour passed. I had been lying on the floor like the others, but was not yet able to cry out loud.

"C'mon, man," the young therapy supervisor said to me while we were lying on the ground. "Just let out a good cry. You'll feel so much better."

"Okay," I said, and then let out a short yelp.

"That's right, feel that pain buried deep inside," the therapist whispered, as a woman to my left clocked me in the head with her outstretched arm and shrieked "Mommy!"

"Don't lose the feeling," my supervisor said, jamming a baby rattle into my hand, "go back to when you were a baby. Bring out your birth scream, man. Shake it loose!"

"Ahhh-uh, ahem-AH-AHHHHHHH!"

"Don't be afraid to scream. See your mother, see your father, wrap yourself all up inside that pain and *scream* your way out!"

Jeeez, this guy really wants a production, I thought. I had gone to all kinds of shrinks over the years, but I had only screamed like this after I received my bills for the sessions. Besides, the people freaking out around me only made me remember how much screaming there had been in my Brooklyn childhood home. I started to wonder what Momma and Pop would look like there with that group of screeching people. I pictured my father swiftly seeking retreat in the corner and muttering, "Tar tar tar tar." Then I imagined my Russian Momma hopping around the room, hunched down low like a spider and shrieking "TSAR TSAR TSAR TSAR!" The image of my parents convulsing in a manic state actually made me laugh. Within seconds, I was giggling like a madman.

"Ride the laugh, man, ride it into the tears. Find the way to your sadness. Cry, cry, cry!"

That's it, Jack, I thought, *I want off this ride.* So I screamed and screeched, feeling nothing except the beginnings of a sore throat. Then my screaming turned into an unexpected torrent of laughter that began to shake me out of my doldrums. I actually felt a little better—certainly better than the man directly across from me, lying face down and beating his fists against the floor while bleating out "BAH BAH BAH BAH!" over and over like a confused sheep being violated by a sex-starved farmer.

Just as I was about to get up and make for the door, a bell chimed and everyone sat upright as if on cue.

"Okay, thank you," said the trio of therapists. "Remember where you were on the floor and we'll pick it up from there at the next session. Good night, babies."

As the patients departed in an eerie silence, no one dared to look directly at each other. Right then, I knew instinctively that this particular therapy wasn't for me. It had been entertaining, though, and the laughter did make me feel better. That is, at least until I got back home to my apartment. I missed André terribly. The silence of the apartment was deafening, and everything in the place reminded me of him. Even the hush of the place seemed to hold his presence. By nature, he was so quiet that it felt like he might still be there in the apartment—in the corner chair, perhaps, reading a book and reviewing the many pages of production notes for one of his theater productions.

Ever since Rosh Hashanah, I had been thinking about leaving New York and going to Belgium. Renee had brought it up to me again when she called on the phone from New Jersey. "Why don't you go, Elliot? You love him, he loves you. What else is there for you to do?" What she said made sense, but I still felt that it was high folly for me to consider such a brash move without even talking with André about it. After all, he hadn't invited me to come away with him. I had invited him to live with me, and I figured he would have done the same if he had really wanted me there. Then again, he was different from me. I was a big sloppy dog. If I liked you, I would lick your hands and your face forever and keep running across the room every time you threw me a chew toy to fetch. André was a lithe and majestic cat. It was sometimes hard to read him; he could be as inscrutable as the Sphinx.

And yet, the thought kept coming back to me, humming low in the back of my brain like the soft rattle of an air conditioner. I settled on my couch with an egg cream and a chocolate bar, and switched on the television. I clicked past a channel or two before coming upon *The Tonight Show* with Johnny Carson. The actress Suzanne Pleshette was a guest that night, and it was the usual gabfest. In the midst of all the showbiz chatter, I heard them mention a film she had made a few years earlier—*If It's Tuesday, This Must Be Belgium*. I nearly dropped my egg cream on the floor. It seemed beyond coincidence that I would happen upon that show at that channel at that time, only to hear mention of the place where André now was. And it was Tuesday!

That was *it*—a cosmic sign as intense as the one that had brought me and Woodstock Ventures together was now pulling me closer to my fate again. My course was set. I had to unload my apartment, sell off my paintings, and hop on a plane to Belgium so I could profess my love to André and live happily ever after. I was suddenly thankful that Renee had persuaded me to get that passport months earlier. My baby sister was right—my passport was a guaranteed ticket to the kind of personal joy I had yet to keep in my grasp. Two years earlier, a helicopter had descended from the sky and landed at the El Monaco, granting me the freedom to run away from a cruel and dismal nightmare. Now, a Belgium-bound airplane would fly up into the sky and bring me closer to a precious, romantic dream. Just as it had when I was a young kid in Brooklyn, the magic of Hollywood movies had indirectly given me hope. I was lucky that the freakish falsetto-voiced singer Tiny Tim wasn't on the Carson show playing "Tiptoe Through the Tulips" that night instead.

There is one distinction that separates dreams from reality—planning. The next day, I got up early and went with a legal pad to the corner café for a breakfast of coffee and jelly doughnuts. While waiting for my sweet tooth to be satisfied, I began to write down everything I needed to do for the trip. I had enough sense to realize that I had no real idea about where I was going. I knew nothing about the climate, the culture, the language, the form of currency, and the day-to-day reality of living in Belgium. These were all things I would need to learn about if I was going to do this move properly.

After I finished my breakfast, I headed over to the Strand bookstore. I looked through the travel section. Nestled between a book on the Bahamas and another on Brazil was one all about Belgium. It was considerably slimmer than most of the other books, which suited me just fine. The quicker I could learn about the place, the better.

As presented in the travel guide, Belgian culture seemed to center on eating and drinking. The book spoke repeatedly of the country's excellent beer, delicious chocolate, and the renowned mussels that everyone seemed to eat in the city of Brussels. I was intrigued when I heard that Belgium was famous for its French fries, which were notably fried twice. Far less appealing, of course, was the local custom of drowning the crispy fries in mayonnaise. Not my idea of a tasty meal, but as long as I had André, I figured that the rest of my Belgian adventure would sort itself out.

I had gone through most of the book when the phone rang. It was Renee, checking to see how I was doing. When I told her what I had decided the night before, she thought at first that I was joking.

"No, I'm serious, Renee," I said. "As soon as I settle things with the apartment, I am booking a plane ticket and leaving for Belgium. I even went out and bought a French dictionary earlier today!"

Renee was delighted for me, though I detected some sadness in her voice. "You see," she gently scolded, "I told you it was a good idea to get your passport. Now you can go to Belgium, or anywhere else you want to go."

"Listen, Renee," I said, "I wonder if you can come to the city and have lunch with me. I want to see you about something."

"Well, I suppose I could. I'll have to get Freddy's mother to watch Alyse, though. Isn't it something we can talk about now? What's it about, anyway?"

"You'll see," I said. "Besides, who knows when you're going to see me again?"

"Oh, Elliot, you're going to make me cry!" she said, and I thought I heard the hint of a tear already in her voice. "I'm happy for you, and I know that I've been the one telling you to go, but I'm going to miss you so much. What am I going to do without you? Who am I going to call?"

I felt a twinge of guilt about leaving my sister, but I couldn't help feeling excited about hurtling myself into the unknown. I also hoped that I might be able to make her feel a little better when I saw her in person.

"Just find a day this week to drive in, Renee," I said. "Trust me."

I told my super I was leaving, and began to pack up my things. In the back of my mind, though, I continued to wonder what was going to happen when I showed up in Belgium out of the blue on André's doorstep and André didn't want me there. Far too much in love with him at that moment, and high off the fumes of my impending flight, I shoved those thoughts into my denial drawer—tucked behind the new socks, T-shirts, and boxer shorts that I had bought for my trip.

Renee found a sitter for Alyse and came in for lunch that Thursday.

We went to the corner café and ordered lunch. My sister looked adorable, as usual, but also tired and a bit defeated. Our beverages came—two egg creams, just like those we had enjoyed drinking together when we were kids. Renee raised her glass.

"To my brother, Elliot," she said, "for going after what makes you happy. You deserve it."

As we clinked our glasses together, I motioned for her to put down her drink and come close so I could tell her something.

"Renee, I need you to hold onto a few things for me back here," I said, seriously.

"What is it, El?" she asked, looking a bit worried.

I reached down into the knapsack that I had with me, and showed her my small collection of film cans, along with a folded piece of paper in see-through plastic.

"Did you make an X-rated film, Elliot?" Renee asked. We both burst out laughing.

"No," I said through a giggle, "nothing *that* drastic. It's some footage that I took around the motel during the festival. And this," I said, holding up the folded page held in protective plastic, "is that Chamber of Commerce permit from Bethel that allowed us to stage the festival." I shrugged and said, "Call me sentimental, but I want to hang onto these things. Now that I'm leaving, you're the only one I trust not to throw this stuff away on me."

She told me that she understood completely, and was happy to keep them safe for me.

"And now I have something that is for you and you alone," I said, pulling out a tightly rubber-banded white envelope from the inside pocket of my new jacket.

"What is this, Elliot?" she asked.

"Renee," I said, "in this envelope is five thousand dollars. It's for you, from what I cleared in cash during the Woodstock summer. I want you to have it."

She quickly started to protest, and tried to give the envelope back to me. "No, Elliot, I don't want you to give me your money." She was fighting back tears.

"Renee, listen to me," I continued. "I'm your brother, and I love you. I know there's something going on at home between you and Freddy. I want you to take this money. After lunch, we're going to go together to the bank and get you a safety deposit box. That's where you're going to keep this, okay?"

She tried to interrupt me again, but I didn't give her a chance and kept on talking.

"Listen, it took me a long time to find my freedom. I suffered through a lot of years to get there—years that I'll never get back. I didn't need to go through that crap, and since I finally have enough money, you don't need to either. I'm not telling you how to live your life. But if you find you need to change your life in some way, I want you to know you have this. It is yours. No one can take it from you. You can always make a fresh start, Renee. And if the time should come, this will help you take care of Alyse."

She sighed long and deep, like a giant boulder had been lifted from her shoulders. "You're a good brother, Elliot. Thank you for this. I love you."

"I love you, too," I said. We hugged, and then I told her to tuck that envelope deep into her purse.

"C'mon," I said, "after lunch, we'll go and see a man at the bank about a toaster."

On the way to the bank, Renee asked me how I planned to live in Belgium. I explained that I was going to take a healthy portion of the money I had saved in my bank account and convert it into American Express traveler's checks. As for the remaining cash, I was merely going to cancel my checking account and move the balance into a savings account. The idea was to let it accrue interest until I was ready to use it. It was the only thing that made sense to me at that point. I certainly was not going to get on a plane with a duffel bag of cash slung over my shoulder. That was *not* the way I wanted to make my entrance into Belgium.

After we set up an account for Renee at the bank and locked my film reels and Bethel permit in her new safety deposit box, we walked back to my apartment, two siblings making their way through the city together before a long separation. Renee sighed and said, "New York will not be the same without you, Elliot. I hope Belgium realizes what they're getting."

"I'm more concerned with André than with Belgium at this point," I joked, even though we both knew I was serious.

"So do you want me to tell Goldie and Rachelle that you're leaving?" Renee asked.

"If you wouldn't mind," I responded. "Who knows if they'll even care."

"They care in their own ways, Elliot," she countered, a sister sticking up for sisters. "After all, you are their brother."

"Listen," I said, avoiding the topic, "you and I are going to have to stay in touch. You're my lifeline, my link to what's happening here, back home."

"You mean we'll be pen pals?" said Renee, a grin starting to form.

"Exactly. I'll tell you about Belgium, and you'll tell me about New York. And we'll try to cover all the items in between."

She looked at me quietly for a moment, and then said, "You should call Momma, Elliot. You should let her know."

Anxious as that made me feel, I realized that Renee was right. I could only expect Renee to shoulder so much when it came to our family. I was the only son of a crazy Jewish mother.

We hugged again in front of the apartment on Jane Street, and I told Renee that I would be in touch before I left—especially so that I could say goodbye to Alyse on the phone. Somehow, I knew that things were going to be all right for Renee and me. Even with the distance, we would stay connected through our letters. As she began to walk away, I stopped her and then placed a fifty-dollar bill in her hand. "Use this to pay for the parking garage," I said.

Renee started to cry again, but then laughed. "How come it's always the gay ones who are the nicest?"

"It's only those of us who have the nicest baby sisters," I said, smiling through my tears.

Renee went her way and I went mine. She was heading back to Alyse and an uncertain future with Freddy. I was heading back to an empty apartment and an equally uncertain future with André. But before I could embark on my journey, there was a call I needed to make.

The phone rang for what must have been less than a minute, but felt like five. Just when I thought I had misdialed the number and was about to hang up, someone on the other end of the line picked up. I could hear the all-too-familiar sound of that labored breathing wafting through the phone like plague.

"Hello, Momma?" I said.

"Who's that?" she snapped.

"Momma, it's Elliot. Your son," I answered.

"What, the son who never calls? Never visits? No letters. Not even a *farshtunkene* postcard!" she shot back.

"You didn't get any of my letters?" I lied.

There it was again in my ear—that *voice*. Months before, Renee had given me the phone number for Momma's ugly dollhouse back in the faraway land of Monticello. My mother had never bothered to phone me in the city, though I heard from Renee that Momma called my sisters at least once a week. That was fine with me, since I had nothing to discuss with her. Her opinions were useless at best and harmful at worst, full only of recrimination and neurotic poison. I made the obligatory greetings and asked how she was doing, but it didn't matter.

"So, Mr. Fancypants remembers he has a mother. Listen, if you're calling because you need money, I warned you. You're not getting a penny from me!" This, in Momma language, was equivalent to "I'm fine, and you?"

"Momma, I'm calling to let you know that I'm going out of the country for a while. I don't know exactly how long I'll be gone, but I wanted you to know," I said as calmly as I could.

"What do you mean, you're leaving the country? What did you *do*, Eliyahu? Who's after you?" she said.

"Momma, I didn't do anything bad, and no one is after me. It's just that I met a special person who I want to be with. This person happens to live in Belgium, so I'm going there." I hoped this would be enough of an explanation, but I knew it wasn't.

"Is she Jewish? What does her father do? Is he a rabbi?" She sounded like a broken Borscht-Belt robot. "Don't you know how many Nazis still live in Belgium? You can forget about me coming to the wedding, I'll tell you that!"

And then, as if she finally realized the one clear advantage that could come from the phone call, she said, "Well, at least you're going to give me grandchildren."

"Momma, you already have grandchildren," I reasoned. "Besides, the way it looks in this relationship, I wouldn't hold my breath waiting for babies."

"What, she can't have children? You picked one who can't have no children? What's wrong with her? What's wrong with *you*, you *schmendrick*?"

No, what the hell is wrong with you? I shouted back at her in my mind. "Momma," I said loudly, starting to lose my patience, "I told you before. I like men, not women. His name is André and—"

My mother hung up the phone. I wasn't even conscious of the dial tone as I held the phone to my ear and looked out the apartment window. Even though I had known how the conversation was likely to go, it couldn't have been any more hurtful. Whatever acceptance I might have been looking for was not going to come at that particular moment, if ever at all.

Although I had taken occasional domestic flights from New York to Chicago over the years, I had never flown overseas before. As I called to book a one-way ticket to Belgium through Sabena Airlines, I simply didn't care anymore about what I did or didn't know about where I was going. All I cared about was that I was *going.* I received a first-class ticket on an evening flight out of JFK Airport for the following Monday. I chuckled, remembering how my parents had never spent money on planes—not first class, not business class, not even luggage compartment. For their occasional vacations, my parents had schlepped to and from Miami Beach in their beat-up Cadillac. Its once-superb air conditioner no longer worked, so they had just driven with the windows rolled down. Of course, my mother had always rented the back seats in the car to the neighborhood *yentas,* who also refused to throw away their money on airfare.

On the morning of my flight, I made sure that I had everything I needed. I had my passport, an ample supply of money and traveler's checks, and a card with André's home address and phone number written on it. I considered calling André long distance to tell him that I was coming. The more I thought about it, however, the less I thought this was a good idea. I still remembered how terrible I felt that night when I called André at the hotel and he wasn't there. Well, now it was my turn to surprise him. I looked around the apartment one more time and then I said to myself, *Fuck it! That's it, you're ready to go.*

In the mid-afternoon, Renee and Freddy and Alyse picked me up from the apartment and drove me to JFK Airport. It was a fairly tense ride, what with Freddy at the wheel. Renee tried to make conversation with me, reporting that Goldie and Rachelle had said I was crazy to go to Belgium. Alyse asked me if I was going to see "funny André," and I told her I was. All during the ride, Freddy kept quiet and stared straight ahead as he drove the car.

We pulled up at the airport, and it was time to leave. Freddy came around the back of the car to help me with my two suitcases, wished me well, and shook my hand, in spite of his obvious dislike. Then I bent down to give Alyse a big kiss on the cheek. As I wiped away her tears, she said, "Don't go, Uncle Elliot." I told her that if she would be happy and didn't cry, then I would send her a special gift as soon as I could from Belgium.

Renee smiled at me, slowly shaking her head as tears streamed down her cheeks. She reached out to give me a warm, affectionate hug. To my surprise, I had tears in my eyes too. I whispered, "You're going to be fine, sis."

She whispered back, "You're going to be fine, too."

Renee told me that they had a parting gift for me. I unwrapped the box, and was amused to find a *mezuzah* inside. "For your new home," Renee instructed me. "No self-respecting Brooklyn Jew should be without one." Where we had grown up, all the Jewish homes had a mezuzah—a little case containing a piece of parchment with an important prayer written on it—nailed next to the front door. I found it hilarious that she would give me one, since she knew that I was a confirmed atheist. At the same time, the mezuzah was a reminder of our childhood and culture more than anything else. I was deeply touched.

I told her that since our parents were from Europe, my journey signified a return to the Teichberg origins. And I promised to send a postcard as soon as I got settled. I waved goodbye from the curb as they drove off. Then I turned toward the airport glass doors—my life packed up in suitcases, my heart on my sleeve.

As luck would have it, the evening's flight was not full, and I was the only one seated in first class. For the duration of the seven-hour flight, I was looked after by a handsome young Belgian steward named Matthieu. He asked me why I was traveling to Belgium in the middle of October, and I explained simply, "For love."

He nodded and said, "What's her name?"

"*His* name is André," I replied.

Speaking softly, he said, "Well, good for you. I hope you find what you're looking for."

I gave him a big smile, and thought to myself: *Yeah, me too.*

Over the course of the next hour or so, I learned a little more about Belgium from Matthieu. I was surprised to learn that there were three main languages in Belgium—French, Flemish, and German. Of course, I had studied the Flemish painters in college. But I had had no idea that there was a place called Flanders that was a part of Belgium. Matthieu also explained that Brussels was home to the main headquarters for both the European Union and the North Atlantic Treaty Organization, so everyone felt fairly safe in that area.

Matthieu told me about gay life in Belgium. He explained that Belgians were far more tolerant of homosexuality than people in America. Thinking of how careful André and I had to be when we were together in Manhattan, I told Matthieu, "A pity it can't be like that back in New York. Or in the rest of America, for that matter."

"Will you tell me about André?" Matthieu asked.

High up in the air above the Atlantic Ocean and far away from the intolerances of America, and feeling comfortable after having my complimentary drink, I told him, "My love is a beautiful man named André Ernotte."

He stared at me. "You mean André Ernotte, the director? He is one of the great inventive talents of the Belgian theater. I have seen some of his shows at the Théâtre National. You are not alone in your love of him! Be prepared to join an entire country on that score, Mr. Tiber."

I thanked Matthieu, and pushed the seat back so I could recline fully. I tried my best to fall asleep, but my mind was swimming with thoughts. I found that I was no longer worried about culture shock. Now that I was halfway to my destination, what I *was* worried about was that I might not receive a warm welcome from André.

Almost as soon as I fell asleep, I was awakened by a gentle tap on the shoulder. "We are here, Elliot," Matthieu told me enthusiastically. "Welcome to Belgium." As the plane descended, I looked out of the windows at clouds that looked just like American clouds. I then saw the skyline of an industrial city not unlike the one I had left some hours before. So this was Brussels. Once the plane landed, I was surprised to see a few signs for companies like Citibank and Texaco along the tops of large buildings off in the distance. I knew that I was in a different country, but those English-language signs reared up in front of me as if they were part of the residual ghosting effect you get with images after you squeeze your eyes shut.

I got even more confused when I saw a sign for Zaventem International Airport, not Belgium Airport, as I had expected to see. What the hell was Zaventem? To me, it sounded as exotic as the Land of Oz. Still feeling a little sleepy, I worried for a few seconds that I had gotten on the wrong plane in New York. As I kept walking, though, I started to see other signs with the word "Belgium" written on it. And then I recalled hearing the pilot on the airplane announce that we were landing in Belgium, followed by something that sounded like "Zee Gornisht" Airport—which in Yiddish, of course, meant that I had arrived in the airport of "nothing." I certainly hoped that I would not wind up in the land of nowhere once I wound up on André's doorstep.

Waiting for my luggage to appear on the conveyor belt, I became increasingly anxious. I wanted very much to call André. Once I had my luggage, I headed for the money exchange booth to get Belgian bills and coins. I nearly fell to the floor when my two hundred dollars was converted into a little over nine thousand Belgian francs. Wow!

Rolling in Belgian dough, I made my way to a telephone booth. It was a little after ten in the morning, and I expected he would be awake. I struggled with the phone, which looked different from the ones back home. I was sweaty, both from the exertion of carrying around my suitcases and the anticipation of the call. The phone rang three times. I started to worry that he wasn't at home, that he had given me a false number, that he—

"*Âllo?*" It was André. I knew his voice right away, and I reeled just hearing it again.

"So, where's my Belgian chocolates and waffles?" I asked.

"Who is—*Elliot?* Elliot, is that *you?*"

"Hello, André," I said in a teasing sing-song voice, "yes, it's me."

"Oh my, Elliot, but it is so early in the morning where you are. How are you, *mon ami*? I have meant to write, but I have been so busy." He then asked me if everything was all right.

"I'm fine, André, everything is fine."

"But it must be so early in the morning in New York. What time is it, anyway?"

"It's, uh, about ten in the morning," I said.

There was a pause. "Elliot, where are you?"

"Well," I continued, "I am calling you from a phone booth at the airport. I am *here*, André. I am here in Belgium. I took an overnight flight. Surprised?"

Again, a pause. And then André began to laugh. "Elliot, are you pulling a joke over my eyes?"

"No joke! I am now a Frenchman or a Walloon or a Fleming or a Dutch oven cleaner. I couldn't be without you another second, André. I love you and I just had to see you."

"You came all this way for me, Elliot?" he asked, his voice tinged with a fragile tenderness.

"You bet I did, Mr. Ernotte," I kidded, "that is, if you will have me. Am I welcome to come and see you, André? Do you have time to see me, babe?"

"Of course I do, I want you to come to me right away," he said in a hurried and excited tone. "You have my address, yes?"

"Does the Pope wear a robe?" I shot back. "Of course I have your address. But how far are you from the airport?"

"Not far, not far at all," he said enthusiastically. "Get a taxi, and tell the driver to take you to rue Watteau, number twelve. Come here to me, and I will be waiting for you in front of my building."

He still sounded like he was in shock, so I asked again if he minded that I had come without contacting him.

"Elliot, you have made me so happy. I love you, and I cannot believe that you are really here. Come to me as quickly as possible!"

"I'm on my way, baby," I said.

I got a cab. Fate threw me another piece of luck—my driver spoke English. I asked him to take me to rue Watteau, and we were off. In his best English, the cabbie pointed out landmarks as Belgium rolled past me like some kind of idyllic dream country. I nodded appreciatively and tried to take it all in. I marveled at the centuries-old houses, skyscrapers, busy modern shopping centers, and crowds of people dressed far more conservatively than I was used to seeing back home in the States. The stores had signs written in two different languages. Recalling my travel guide and what Matthieu had said on the plane, I realized that I was looking at French and Flemish words. The trolley cars, long since discarded in Brooklyn, seemed to have rolled right on over to Brussels. They were *everywhere*.

The taxi pulled off the main boulevard and into the Sablon *quartier,* or neighborhood. The driver explained that it was a fine locale of art galleries, antique stores, and fine dining restaurants. Soon enough we turned onto rue Watteau. I instantly spotted André in front of his building, his beautiful face shining as the taxi cab approached. I opened the door before the taxi stopped, and was in André's arms within seconds. As he and I embraced, it felt as if I had been holding my breath under water for almost a month and was only coming up for air now. He hugged me close, and then gave me two Belgian welcoming kisses, one on each cheek. Then, before I had a chance to stop myself, I kissed him passionately on the lips. In New York, I had been conditioned to keep any public displays of affection in check. Here in the streets of Belgium, though, I was hugging and kissing another man in daylight, and no one seemed to care. If they did, they kept it to themselves. I paid the taxi driver, and he waved goodbye with an easygoing smile and a casual puff on his cigar. No scowl, no angry looks, and no derogatory words thrown at me for being demonstrative with a member of my own sex. *Wow, I am in gay man heaven,* I thought.

André grabbed my suitcases and led me up the three flights of stairs to his apartment. Whether in New York or Belgium, it seemed I was destined to live in walk-up apartments. The walls of the stairwells displayed stylish contemporary paintings. Several bronze and stone sculptures of Renaissance cherubs on each landing further enhanced the intimate charms of this quaint seventeenth-century townhouse.

Though it was a lovely location, I was taken aback a bit to see that André—by all accounts an accomplished and relatively famous director in Belgium—lived in a tiny attic studio space and not in a substantial apartment. At the height of my success as an interior designer in Manhattan, I had rented an apartment with eight rooms right down the street from Central Park.

Regardless, I was beyond delighted to see André again. We embraced each other and kissed—so fervently, in fact, that I barely realized we were on the floor, groping each other with the desperation of two people fighting in the desert over the last drops of water in their canteen. Minutes later, panting and utterly spent in our mutual erotic release, I playfully whispered in André's ear, "You see, that's what you get for not sending me chocolate."

After our passionate reunion, André helped me empty out my suitcases. When he opened the armoire to hang up my clothing, though, I was surprised to find that there were no other clothes in the closet. The tiny efficiency kitchen, smaller than the one on the plane, contained only a coffee pot, two ceramic cups, two dishes and glasses, and one pasta pot. He went to get me a cold can of soda from the refrigerator, and I noticed there was nothing else in there. The one shelf in the kitchen had a tin of *gaufres,* a regional variation on those famous Belgian waffles of which I and several other Americans had heard so much over the years. André made us cups of coffee, and we settled in at the miniscule dining table.

We sat together in silence for a few moments. Then André looked at me and asked, "But what are you doing here suddenly like this, Elliot? I was not expecting that I would see you here in Belgium."

"Well," I said, laughing nervously, "there was nothing on TV and I had run out of ideas for paintings." I looked at him seriously. "Why do you think I'm here, dummy? I came for you! I love you. I'm in love with you. I want to be with you. Besides, you never wrote or called! What kind of reaction did you expect from your typical Jewish mother?"

He laughed, but it was clear that he had no clue as to what a "Jewish mother" really meant.

"I do not mind that you are here, Elliot, but did you have a specific goal in mind? Are you here only to see me? And how long did you want to visit here with me?"

I looked him straight in the eye, and said, "André, I'm a free man. Since I left that motel back in 1969, I've come and gone as I please and whenever I please. I'm not here to sight-see, baby. I'm here because I can't think of anything but you, every fucking second of the day. And if you'll have me, I want to be with you, by your side—all the time. I want to live with you."

André hugged me close and told me that he wanted to be with me as well. "This is just a surprise, Elliot. I am so happy you are here, but we need to work these things out together. I have a lot happening right now. Let me tell you about it."

André was very animated as he told me about the play he was rehearsing at the Théâtre National. As he spoke, I silently surveyed the tiny room. The daybed doubled as a sofa. There was only one upholstered chair and a small scatter rug. There wasn't even a chest of drawers. There was no lamp, and the ceiling light was a drab commercial fixture. The studio was very neat; there was no evidence that anyone actually lived there. From our conversations in New York, I knew that André was extremely well-read and had an affinity for contemporary art. And yet there was not one book, painting, or sculpture anywhere in André's apartment. No television, not even a radio. I was confused. The mystery continued when I went to the bathroom. It was smaller than the airplane restroom I had used on the way over to Belgium. There was one unused towel, and nothing in the medicine cabinet. No toothbrush, no aspirin bottle, no shampoo—*nothing*.

"André," I asked, "it looks like no one ever stays in this apartment. Have you been robbed? What's the story? Where the hell is everything?"

André let out a deep sigh and sat down next to me. "Elliot," he said quietly, "I have to tell you something." André explained that although his family loved him, he had never told them that he was attracted to men and not women. While the urban areas of Belgium tended to be more progressive, the more provincial towns were less so. André had chosen never to bring the subject up with his family. He kept the studio apartment for show—he didn't want to have to explain that he lived with another man when his parents or sisters came to visit him.

I was surprised to hear that he was still closeted. André had portrayed life in Belgium as so much freer and more liberal than life in the United States, yet despite my home and my comically dysfunctional family, *I* was the one who was able to be honest about my sexuality to my parents. I was also hurt to hear that André had another boyfriend. The man in question was named Joe, and he was a celebrated and popular Flemish opera director. André explained that his real residence was only two blocks away, in a huge luxury townhouse he shared with Joe. He saw the pain in my expression, so he explained.

"In every city across the States these past two years, Elliot, I met a lot of guys. Many of them told me they loved me and wanted me to live with them. I never took it seriously. You are the only one to have traveled to be with me. No one has ever done that for me before, and I am very touched that you are here. But I *did* have a life here before you, Elliot," he concluded.

"This Joe—uh, is he your lover?" I said, feeling like a lovesick moron.

"Joe was my first lover. I first met him when I left Liège and came up to Brussels to study theater. He is twenty years older than me. Yes, we have lived together as lovers and I have shared his home. But I no longer consider him my lover."

He hadn't told me any of this in New York, he now explained, because he hadn't thought that I would ever take the leap and come to live with him in Belgium. "But now"—his voice broke and trembled a bit—"now it is clear to me that you are the only man for me, Elliot." He hugged me close, but I was wounded and confused, unhappy that he had never told me about Joe.

I pulled away from him. "André," I said, fighting to hold back the tears that were starting to burn in my eyes, "this is, uh, a *lot* to hear, in this way. I mean, uh, it's very sudden. I don't know if, uh . . ." I had to keep staring down toward the floor in order to keep talking. I was jealous of this other lover, but also hurt that there was a piece of his life that he had deliberately kept hidden away from me. *What else might he be hiding?* I thought to myself. Then, with all the strength I could muster, I looked up at him and told him that I would return to New York the next day. "I don't want to go," I said. It was hard to talk with the lump in my throat from my emotions. "But I'm not going to stay here if that's what's going on, André."

"No, no, Elliot," André implored, "you do not understand. After I came home from New York, I realized that my relationship with Joe was nothing like the one I shared with you. I realized that my relationship with Joe had always been based on what was convenient for him alone, never for us together. Elliot, I planned to break up with Joe ever since I arrived back here. I have been trying to find the right moment, the right way to tell Joe that he and I are over."

He smiled, ran a finger through my hair and said, "And then you arrived." I grabbed him again, hard, but with love, and I felt love back in his touch. André said he had some errands to run and would return in a couple of hours. I was so exhausted that after I showered, I plopped onto the day bed and fell into a deep sleep.

It was dark when André returned. He brought in suitcases of his clothes. As I would see when we came down for dinner shortly afterward, he had left boxes of his books, scripts, framed drawings, and other personal things from Joe's place in the entry hallway. Schlepping all that up three flights of stairs was not going to be easy. Fortunately, the apartment owner, an art gallerist named Jean-Claude, and his lover, Hermann, were more than happy to help us set up house together.

❀ ❀ ❀

The weekend came, and André didn't have to be at the theater until Monday. He was so tender with me in those first days in Belgium that the initial shock over his relationship with Joe soon faded away. That weekend, André and I explored winding streets, broad boulevards, and outdoor markets. He helped me find a fun postcard with a picture of the *Manneken Pis* (or the "peeing boy") statue. I sent it to Renee with the following note:

Dear Renee,
I have safely arrived. Please tell Momma that they pee in the pool over here!
Love to you and the mishpacha,
Elliot

Seeing what I wrote, André then took my pen and added *"and André"* alongside my name. What a wonderful way for him to let Renee know that we were together.

As we enjoyed the city, it was a little daunting for me to hear people speaking in French and Flemish. Just as disorienting were the moments when I commented or asked a price and the storeowners replied to me in English. Most Belgians did not speak English, but with the large number of American visitors who came to Brussels for the NATO base, many shopkeepers had learned to communicate. Hearing words I could understand made me feel better.

André described for my benefit the different quartiers, and pointed out architecturally significant buildings that had survived centuries of invasions by the Spanish and the French. In Belgium, many of the most prominent buildings were done in the Art Deco style. In addition, almost every neighborhood had ultramodern corporate skyscrapers housing international businesses. Mixed amongst the contemporary architecture were stately classic Beaux-Arts buildings. Of course, there were also average working-class apartments and smaller two-story homes, the majority of which were painted grey. So much of the city seemed familiar from the dozens of foreign films I had seen over the years. It began to dawn on me, though, that Brussels was not a movie set. It was a real place where people lived and worked. I felt like I had finally found a home.

❀　　❀　　❀

Over the next few weeks, I continued to explore the city. Just a block down the hill from where we lived on rue Watteau was rue Haute. This street was teeming with all sorts of food stores, antique shops, art galleries, and even a large American-type supermarket. I soon came to learn that in decades past, rue Haute had been the city's garment center, not unlike Seventh Avenue in New York City. André explained to me that back in 1944, the Nazis had rounded up the Jews of rue Haute and carted them off to German death camps. A wave of fear and nausea washed over me as I reflected on the atrocities these streets must have witnessed.

André took me to the magnificent Grand Place, a huge square of palatial and highly ornamented buildings. Their decorations were gilded, so that when the sun hit them, the buildings took on a celestial appearance, making it clear why the Grand Place had drawn crowds for hundreds of years.

On Sundays in the Grand Place, you could find flower markets, antique stalls, and assorted retail stands. Some vendors set up booths selling plain and fancy birdcages and an awesome variety of birds, which I assumed were meant to be kept as pets. I was delighted—until it became clear that the birds were being bought to eat at home. *Ugh!*

We dined often at Chez Leon, a famous Belgian restaurant that specialized in a dish called *moules-frites.* The first time André ordered it, I immediately recalled what I had read about it in the travel book back home in New York. Here were two huge bowls of mussels, accompanied by a mound of French-fried potatoes. I had never eaten mussels, and didn't want to try it even after André demonstrated how to extract their flesh from the shells. Then I looked around me. And since the people at the other tables—including several other Americans like me—were all enjoying this Belgian specialty, I shut my eyes and swallowed. What a treat! The mussels were actually luscious, prepared in a vegetable broth with fresh celery, carrots, and tiny potato cubes. My palate continued to grow, despite the local presence of a brand-new Belgium fast food place called Quick, which allowed me to indulge my yen for burgers and fries.

Never the athletic type, I found that dragging groceries, dishes, towels, and other necessities up the three flights to the apartment was a major physical chore. Jean-Claude and Hermann helped me if they were around the building and saw me in need. Of course, I had no idea about Belgian or French or Flemish foodstuffs, as I ventured out grocery shopping over the next few weeks. Initially, I avoided the tiny shops, where products were listed in three different languages and you had to speak French or Flemish to order. I favored the huge supermarket nearby. Recognizable American products were housed in the imported aisles, and I found it hilarious to see everyday items from back home, like cans of baked beans and bottles of ketchup, presented as expensive delicacies. Over time, I got used to shopping as the Belgians did, though it took awhile to build up confidence.

André never had time to cook, and I still only knew how to make pasta, hamburgers, scrambled eggs, and grilled cheese sandwiches. So we often ate out. This gave me the opportunity to enjoy a large variety of superb peasant-style Belgian dishes. André took me to restaurants that were not on the usual tourist routes. These were small, local joints unlike those found in Paris, which I would come to learn about later. It was all a fascinating adventure. I gradually became aware that Americans rarely visited Belgium—even Brussels wasn't much of a tourist destination. Most Americans had their sights on splashier European cities like Paris, Rome, London, and Amsterdam. André was proud of his country, though, and he delighted in pointing out for me the various monuments and famous statues that depicted his country's history and folklore. I don't think I would have had the energy and patience to show someone the sights in New York the same way that André showed me everything in Belgium. He took great pleasure introducing me to his country's rich way of life. He was a world traveler, and remained quite sophisticated in his keen appreciation of just about everything.

André had long rehearsals at the Théâtre National, which he took me to visit soon after my arrival. He showed me around the place, and then introduced me to some of the cast and the artistic director of the production he was working on. A few of his colleagues spoke English, which was quite pleasant for me. My cursory mention of my part in the Woodstock festival, however, brought forth furrowed brows and nonplussed reactions in French. André swiftly pulled me aside and told me not to mention Woodstock to Belgians. He explained that in Europe, it was considered an event attended by drug addicts, sex fiends, and degenerates. Of course, I hadn't known that, but I respected André's advice.

André had bought me a locally produced tourist map of the downtown area around the theater, so I spent the rest of that day conducting a solo walking tour of the unique sites nearby. Predictably, I wound up totally lost and was unable to find my way back to the theater to meet André. He had anticipated this, and had written down the name and address of the theater for me to give a taxi driver when I wanted to find my way back.

During my first days living with André, I glanced through his press albums, two volumes of clippings attesting to his talents and reputation. There were huge newspaper and magazine reviews—some of them front-page articles—

celebrating his accomplishments. I recognized some words, but not enough to understand the reviews. But the accompanying photographs always showed him smiling with various celebrities, so at peace and so content with his career. His amazing success made me question his sanity. I wondered why a guy as accomplished and cultivated as he was would want to be with a guy like me. But I didn't dare ask. It was enough for me to believe that he loved me. That was all I needed to know.

⚙ ⚙ ⚙

I had been in Belgium for about three weeks, and André was getting tired of translating everything from signs in shop windows to items on menus. He told me I absolutely had to start learning French, since it would be impossible to function in Belgium without knowing at least the basic rudiments of its primary language. While André was busy with his rehearsals, I began to attend French classes at the high school near our apartment. The first day was grueling, since I didn't have much experience with foreign language studies. André had a natural bent for languages, but I most assuredly did not.

After my first day in school, André returned and asked me to tell him what I had learned. So I spewed out some sentences from my school notebook. I thought I was saying simple things like: *"My name is Elliot. Where is the hotel? May I have a cup of coffee?"*

"What are you saying, Elliot? Your French, if I can call it that, has some other type of accent. And it is definitely not American," he said, puzzled by my struggle to speak correctly. "What is your teacher's name?"

I looked at my class notes and said, "Monsieur Phan."

"And where is this Monsieur Phan from?" André asked.

"I think he said he was from Vietnam," I replied. With that, André began laughing hysterically. At first I didn't understand, but then it dawned on me. I was learning French spoken with a heavy Vietnamese accent. Once we both stopped laughing, André decided he would teach me French himself as we ate, shopped, and saw films.

It would take me another seven months or so, but eventually I was able to get along pretty decently in French. More important, I was learning slang and expressions that were not in the schoolbooks. I was amazed that I was actually speaking French, albeit with a horrendous American accent. Now when we met with his friends or went to parties, I was able to converse with people to some degree. I was quite pleased that I could now speak well enough to make people laugh. Moreover, while André was at work, I was able to ask directions, make friends on my own, and more importantly, absorb Belgian values and culture. Not totally, though, as it turned out.

One afternoon, I was on rue Haute, shopping for that night's supper. I was going to make *ouiseaux sans têtes*, which is French for "birds without heads," a dish of stuffed meat. I stopped by a pair of butcher shops, one next to another. In one window, hamburger meat was priced at 40 francs for a quarter-kilo. In the other, it cost 75 francs for the quarter-kilo. Naturally, I purchased the 40-franc meat. In addition, it sure looked much leaner than the other, which was almost double the price. I also purchased some *frites* and then headed home to prepare supper.

André returned that night exhausted from his ten-hour rehearsal. He said he was too tired to go out for supper. He was delighted when he saw that I had prepared a hot meal. I served the hot plates of *ouiseaux sans têtes*, fries, and endives—a vegetable I had just learned how to prepare. During dessert, he remarked how delicious dinner was. I proudly told him how I'd managed to grab the half-price bargain for the ground beef by comparison shopping at the two butchers. The one with the sign that said *Boucherie* (which was close enough to the English word "butcher" that I knew what was meant) was much more expensive than the other shop, which was marked *Boucherie Chevaline*. I had no clue what "chevaline" meant, but the beef was half the price and much leaner. Upon hearing my story, André made a strange queasy face and said, "Elliot, honey. You bought horse meat! 'Boucherie Chevaline' means 'horse butcher'!"

I rushed to the bathroom, downed a Bromo-Seltzer, and tried desperately not to hear the voice of that talking horse from the TV show *Mr. Ed* back home. Another lesson learned.

❀   ❀   ❀

"It will soon be Christmas, Elliot," André declared one day, "and so it is time for you to meet my family in Liège."

"Hey, I thought you'd never ask," I said. I had wanted to meet them, but André's theater work had kept him completely occupied. He had almost been able to arrange things so that his family could meet up with us in Brussels when

The French Connection was set to open at the big movie theater. Alas, they were unable to come and see André in his American movie debut. For myself, I had been absolutely floored by how intensely director William Friedkin had captured the gritty feel of the New York City streets. The film made me miss my old home for the first time, and more than I had expected. But the really exciting part had been seeing the scenes in which André appeared.He was only in four scenes, but I couldn't take my eyes off him whenever he appeared. It was sweeter still for me because he was clean-shaven for the film, and so he looked exactly as he had under the street lamp the first time I ever saw him.

André had called his family the next day to tell them that they could see the film in Liège if they wanted, but that they shouldn't expect to see him in a starring role. He sounded a little rueful, and I could see he was upset after he hung up. I suppose he was so used to the adulation of his fellow Belgians that his relatively small part left him feeling unsung and underappreciated. He seemed especially upset by his father, who had apparently asked, "Are you even in the film, André?" I could sense that André probably had as much trouble pleasing his father as I had pleasing my mother. When I jovially reminded him that I didn't appear in the movie at all, he laughed and again was the calm and happy André I knew and loved. Yet I could tell he had been bothered by this missed opportunity. I had done my best to make him feel loved that night.

I was excited to see where André had grown up. Liège was Belgium's second largest city, about sixty miles or so southeast of Brussels. His family still lived in a suburb there—Belgians rarely moved any great distance from where they were born and raised. Belgians universally seemed to suffer from an inferiority complex of one kind or another. In the south, French-speaking Belgians, or "Walloons," felt that they were far less exciting than their Parisian neighbors, who, I'd learn, often pretended they didn't understand the Walloons' "polluted Belgian accent." In the north, Flemish-speaking Belgians felt inferior to the Dutch, who sneered at them for having "corrupted" their language. Who knows, maybe the small population of German-speaking Belgians felt inferior to Germans, too! Moreover, there was a fierce antagonism between the Walloons and the Flemings. The Brussels that I knew was very much a sharply divided city. One half was populated by Walloons, and the other half by Flemings, or the "Dutch Bags," as I heard one drunken American say one night outside a café. The two groups did not seem to mix.

We took the one-hour trip to Liège by rail. Along the way, André gave me a running commentary on the villages and towns floating by the train windows. There were grey old factories and apartment houses in every town and village that we passed. His parents, Fanny and Jules Ernotte, lived near the Meuse river in a town called Jupille, which seemed to be made up of mostly two-story homes and tiny mom-and-pop shops. While there, I detected from the local shopkeepers a kind of resentment toward the large markets and department stores.

Before we arrived in Liège, however, André explained that he was not yet ready to tell his family that he was gay, and that I was his lover. So instead, he asked me if I'd mind being introduced as "a friend and fellow theatrical artist from New York." I agreed to go along with the scheme, and reassured him that I would follow his lead during the trip. However, I also told him that we would become much more than friends once we got back to our apartment—maybe even twice.

André's sister Lilly picked us up in her small Renault at the Liège railroad station. The square outside the station was surrounded by dozens of hotels, bars, and restaurants. Lilly was all smiles as she welcomed André. He introduced us, and I held out my hand. She warmly grasped my hand and kissed me politely on both cheeks. Lilly welcomed me to her country in halting but confident English.

We arrived at André's home. It was a modest establishment that looked exactly the same as every other house in the neighborhood. Though I had never really cared about Hanukkah holiday traditions, I did find the many Christmas decorations that adorned the neighborhood colorful and charming, and I could see that André adored the season.

On the ground floor of André's home was a large shop window with a sign that read:

"Madame Ernotte: *Coiffeuse* (Hair Dresser); Baroness Lilly de Calwaert, prop."

The front room of their home was outfitted as a beauty parlor, in which Fanny and Lilly worked. Fanny Ernotte was one of the most loving women I had ever met. Fanny looked exactly like André, and was as sweet and kind as he was, as well. She was smartly dressed in a floral apron, a conservative skirt, and sensible shoes. And though she was plump in that way that seems to come inevitably to middle-aged women, Fanny's vivacious embrace of life and sunny disposition made her every move seem as lithe and effortless as those of a ballerina. This stood in stark contrast, of course, to my mother, whose lumbering gait resembled that of a losing sumo wrestler.

Fanny was overjoyed to see us. She gave André a huge hug and those double-cheek kisses. And then it was my turn—Hug! Kiss! Kiss! And another hug! I handed her the bouquet of flowers that I had bought for her and the family at the Gare du Midi, the railroad station in Brussels. She loved them, and put them in a cut glass vase.

The Ernotte family home was small but tidy. Everything was simple and functional; the Ernottes' limited income prohibited any luxuries. The house was spotless and homey. It was clear that the family was very proud of André's career—the entry foyer was a mini-gallery of posters and newspaper clippings of André's successful theatrical productions.

André's father, Jules, came out to greet us. He was portly, and wore a shirt and tie and pressed trousers held up by grey suspenders. His hair was neatly combed and his shoes were polished perfectly. I gathered that Jules loved his wine, as he sat there drinking glass after glass. He pointed out that his wines were from Paris, and not Belgium. He also pointed out that he was born in Paris, and had met Fanny there when she was visiting some friends. His evident pride for all things French seemed to indicate to me that André's father was not the type of Belgian gentleman who would allow himself to be labeled a mere Walloon.

Neither Fanny nor Jules spoke fluent English, so poor André had to interpret. I came to learn more French over the years I lived in Belgium, but I was still grasping at straws during this first visit with the Ernottes.

We sat outside in the garden behind the house. There was a tiny brick barbecue pit, a clothesline, and a vegetable garden dug next to flowerbeds. Jules was proud to tell us about the vegetables he carefully tended, while Fanny described the many colorful flowers she grew. Brick walls divided their garden from their neighbors'.

A short time later, Lilly and her husband and daughter came downstairs to join us. They lived upstairs, on the second floor of the house. Then along came André's older sister, Claudette. She was a dozen years older, attractive, and, like André, resembled her mother, with a soft, cherubic smile and playful, bright eyes. Lilly looked more like Jules; her face was decidedly more serious, with smaller eyes that appraised the world warily.

Claudette's husband, Samuel, was very thin, with sharp-boned features and a shock of shiny black hair. He and Claudette were grade school teachers who lived a few blocks away. Their teenage daughter Veronique, slender and nervous, was a part-time college student. Their other daughter, Marie, seemed to be physically and mentally challenged. On the train ride to Liège earlier in the day, André explained that Claudette had given birth to Marie when she was in her forties. The doctors believed that Claudette's age might have been a factor in Marie's disabilities; this knowledge had flooded Claudette with guilt. Marie hardly spoke, but she had an enthusiastic and trusting smile. Everybody in the family was very protective of her, which I found poignant.

Everyone was friendly and welcoming to me at that wonderful Christmas-time Belgian dinner, which had been prepared by Fanny. Fanny's tiny kitchen pantry shelves did not hold a single can of food. She had no freezer, so everything was made from scratch. As we sat down to the meal, Fanny brought out a new bottle of Heinz ketchup from the kitchen and put it in front of me. I had to laugh, realizing that André must have told her I had been putting ketchup on nearly everything I had eaten since I arrived in Belgium. None was needed here, though, since Fanny's cooking was superbly tasty and satisfying.

A warm feeling came over me as I observed André's mother. What a contrast to my own mother, seeing how caring and gracious she was toward her guests. To me, Fanny was what a mother should be. No wonder André was kind and gentle, a true mensch. Fanny's maternal understanding and love made it possible for André to enjoy self-esteem and self-assurance. I had never gotten that kind of support from my mother. I don't think that my father had ever gotten that from her, either. Instead, my father and I had developed our own ways to escape, he with his radio, and me with my movies. Fanny's love for her son seemed to extend to the people her son loved. In the five hours we visited, she made an exceptional effort to get to know me. This was quite an effort, since André had to translate continuously.

We were preparing to leave when Fanny retrieved a lovely wool scarf for André. No question, this was not store-bought. She was an avid knitter, and some months later, she would present me with a huge sweater. The sweater was comfy and warm, and it fit me perfectly. It was also in chocolate—my favorite color, after black—and it had antique wooden buttons.

After dinner, I thanked the family for having me, and found myself on the receiving end of yet another big hug from Fanny. As we piled into Lilly's car to head back to the train station, Fanny whispered something to André through the car window. On the train, I asked him what she had whispered. He said she now felt like she had *two* loving sons to adore. Who would have thought that a nice Jewish boy from Brooklyn would have to come to Belgium to find a mother's love? With such a wonderful, affectionate family, André was a very lucky man, and I told him so as we traveled back to our apartment. What I didn't tell him was that I felt his mother knew we were a gay couple. By the time I received her hand-knitted sweater a few months later when we came to visit again, I knew that André would figure it out for himself. And so he did.

❁   ❁   ❁

After that Christmas dinner, André and I began to go to Liège every few months to spend a day or two with his family. During these visits, André would describe whichever current play he was staging at the Théâtre National. Everyone listened proudly and asked enthusiastic questions—especially Fanny. It was only his father who seemed less than supportive. During these conversations, Jules would refill his wine glass and say nothing as he stared listlessly at the table with a blank expression on his face. If he ever did pipe up, it was usually to put down André's work, or to make it seem as if André's accomplishments were never quite up to par.

André invited everyone in his family to the opening nights of his shows, but his father hardly ever came. Jules seemed largely indifferent to his son's accomplishments. Perhaps he was intimidated or envious of what André had accomplished—after all, this was a man who was determined to be regarded more as a distinguished Frenchman than a run-of-the-mill Walloon peasant. Perhaps he suspected that André was gay and he didn't approve. Whatever it was, the relationship between André and his father was somewhat strained, and only got worse as André's career continued to blossom. I felt angry at Jules for the way he often treated his son, but I knew better than to discuss it openly.

The entire city of Liège knew about André's accomplishments at the Théâtre National, making him a local celebrity. By contrast, I must have seemed rather inadequate. Although I had been instrumental in helping to stage the biggest and most important rock concert in the history of humanity, Woodstock remained a taboo topic. Instead, I was known as the pudgy American lummox who had accidentally served horse for dinner.

As for my family, I wrote some letters to my three sisters about my adventures. Only Renee wrote back. She explained in a letter that Rachelle and Goldie didn't approve of my leaving the country, and thought that I was being selfish by not sticking around to help Momma. Renee remained my tie to home, and as ever, she provided me support, humor, and love.

André saw that my other sisters and mother were not interested in me and my life. We both had our own family ties and dysfunction, but we wound up making our own family. As gay men, we would not have the chance to make a child of our own, so it made sense to bring a dog into our lives. Around my birthday, we were walking together and saw some puppies in the window of a local pet shop. André had been interested in getting a large Belgian Shepherd as a pet. I told him that Adolf Hitler had owned German Shepherds, and so I would not have any shepherd breed on principle alone. Instead, we decided upon an adorable black-haired mutt. It was a sprightly little thing that hopped up and down to get our attention as we looked in the window. I named the dog Toto, as homage to Dorothy's little dog in *The Wizard of Oz*. Who knew that this mischievous little mongrel would nearly send us far beyond the rainbow and practically over the edge?

The trouble with Toto was that lively enthusiasm was his only mode of existence. The dog just didn't stop, hopping around the apartment like some kind of crazed drug addict. He chewed things. We bought some rubber bone toys to appease him, but he soon started to gnaw at the legs of the dining table. Toto also had the unfortunate tendency to mark his territory with urine, especially around the apartment. We took him back to the vet, who explained that our Toto was what he called a "little piddler" and would soon stop once he got to know the place. Two weeks later, however, he was still blasting things with piss like an unruly kid playing with a water gun.

Daily walks made things no better. Each time we walked down to the nearby park, Toto would find a new victim to terrorize. It was challenging enough for me to get on with my neighbors, given the language barrier. But now I found myself in a near-permanent state of embarrassment and apology, as Toto whirled around like a tongue-lolling dervish. "*Pardonnez-moi,*" I said, while Toto alternately barked at an old person, tried to eat a poodle, snapped his jaws at a child who tried to pet him, or looked to mark a nearby tree with either piss or shit or both. Here I was, a foreigner who couldn't speak French, bounding around the town with an untrained and unpleasant black mutt seemingly spawned from the depths of hell.

It was the sixth week of Toto's stay when André suddenly slipped and landed ass-first in a surprise turd package in the middle of the kitchen floor. He shouted every French curse word in existence, looked at me with wild eyes, and said, "That is it, Elliot! Enough! *Enough!* Toto must go!" By that point, I was just thankful André was the one to suggest it. It was unlike him to get so agitated—sort of like watching a mime stop in the middle of a performance to suddenly scream.

The next day, we borrowed a car from one of André's theater colleagues and drove out into the countryside with Toto. Stopping at a farm to ask for directions to Liège, we brought him out on a leash. The farmer's daughter immediately fell in love with Toto, who did for her the same cute dance routine that had first won us over. We explained that the dog had belonged to André's uncle, who had died recently. The girl seemed to love the dog, so her father offered to take the dog off our hands. We readily agreed, and within five minutes Toto was off and running around the farm with the farmer's daughter. Maybe it was just as well—our little apartment was no place for a dog with that kind of energy. Besides, Dorothy's dog Toto had lived on a farm in *The Wizard of Oz*. Perhaps this was fate. Regardless, we were free of the crazy canine and glad of it. "If we ever have another dog," André said, "we get a much calmer one, Elliot. And preferably one that does not shit in our kitchen."

Around that time, mysterious objects addressed to André began to show up in our mailbox inside the building's main entrance. One time, it was a little sculpture; another time, a music box. André explained that these were small gifts that he had given his former lover, Joe, over the years, and Joe was returning them, one by one, without any note. It was some kind of emotional blackmail in a pathetic attempt to get him back. I felt strangely guilty at this heartrending situation, as did André. The idea of an older man who had lost his love reminded me only too keenly of myself. In New York, I had worried about losing André, too.

One morning, I suggested to André that it was time we moved to another neighborhood. I wanted us to have a place for just the two of us, where neither of us had already lived before we became a couple. Considering the situation with Joe, he agreed. Near the Gare du Midi, the main Brussels train station, I noticed a ten-story postwar building that seemed to have all the proper amenities, including an elevator. There was an apartment for rent, a modern one bedroom unit with a real kitchen, a real bathroom, a washer/dryer, and lots of sunlight flooding the tiny balcony on the fifth floor. The rent was fifteen thousand Belgian francs a month, high compared to the six thousand Belgian francs we had split down the middle there on rue Watteau. But André had more work coming for the summer months and I was happy to continue using whatever money I had to help us live. To me, francs stilled looked like board-game money anyway. We gave references, and André provided a written check for security. The apartment was freshly painted and immediately available.

For me, the big attraction was that the apartment had an elevator and balconies overlooking a small grassed square, Place Bara. In addition, it was near the tramline that went past the Théâtre National and the television studios. And, perhaps most important, the apartment building was located near a big Godiva chocolate factory, which meant the air was permanently scented with the smell of chocolate.

All we had to do was take our personal items from the old apartment, since it had never had any real furniture. It was easy to furnish the new place. At the local department store, I picked up a few basic pieces, including a large couch for the living room and a brand-new bed for the bedroom. It would take a few weeks for the larger pieces to be delivered to us. The rest of the furnishings were acquired more slowly, in local shops and galleries.

Within a week, we had moved into our new home. We finally had a place with an elevator—with no "Phantom of the Opera" lurking around the building, waiting to pounce, and no Toto the barking monster mutt circling around a corner of the kitchen, waiting to squat. I had love, balance, and harmony in my life, probably for the first time ever. My world was like a tautly stretched canvas: untouched, untainted, and pure. The only blemish on its surface appeared one day soon after André and I moved in, when I entered our build-ing and heard the muffled sound of a woman yelling no more than a block away. As I was soon to discover, the woman screaming at the top of her lungs was a neighborhood fixture that the people had simply learned to endure. Having survived Momma all those years, this kind of thing didn't faze me one bit—at first.

8

To TV
or Not to TV

"Is Barbra Streisand a Jewish princess? Of *course* I will!"

It took me less than a New York minute to give that answer, when asked by two Belgian intellectuals in the summer of 1972 to give a lecture about Woodstock. André and I were at an opening night party for one of his new shows at the Théâtre National. Despite subtle reminders from André not to publicly discuss what he still felt was the disreputable subject of Woodstock, I was honored by this offer to speak about it from an American perspective. The festival's fame and social relevance had only continued to grow beyond the confines of Bethel, traveling out into the world. Yes, they had even heard about my little backyard gathering there in Belgium!

At that opening-night party, I had been introduced to a short and bookish gentleman named Hal by one of the actors in André's production. As it turned out, Hal was at the party with his partner, a tall woman with long, red hair named Catherine. Through the conversation, which was conducted in broken, nonsensical English sprinkled with a dash of French, they explained that they booked lecturers each year to speak to students who were part of the internationally renowned Fulbright Foundation. That year, one of the top lectures was to be held in the Belgian city of Ghent. When they learned that I was an American and had taught art history at colleges in New York, they were curious about me and asked if I had a topic on which I might want to lecture. André was across the room, talking with two young male dancers from the theater. I was on my own.

"Have you heard of the Woodstock concert?" I asked, a Cheshire cat grin on my face.

"*Oui, oui,* yes, but of course," Hal said, and Catherine added a Parisian nod as she drained her glass of champagne. "Why, were you one of those people who went to the concert?"

"Without me," I said calmly, "there would never have *been* a Woodstock concert as you and the rest of the world now know it." They looked at me quizzically, as if to say, "Well, go on!" So I told them about my Woodstock experience and won them over completely. Without a moment's hesitation, they asked me to give a lecture on Woodstock at the summer Fulbright meeting in Ghent. It was no trouble for me to do it. André would be knee-deep in preparation for the fall season at the Théâtre National, and I had pretty much seen the sights in Brussels and Liège.

"*Magnifique,* Elliot," said Hal. Catherine kissed me on both cheeks and explained that the Fulbright Foundation would pay me an honorarium for the lecture and provide car service to and from the train station in Ghent. I told them, "Of course, please understand that my usual lecture fee is ten million francs, paid in coins." They looked at me, confused at first. "But for you, just ten thousand francs!" Hal and Catherine smiled. Of course, I hadn't really been joking. If I had learned anything from Momma, it was that you never know how much people will pay for something that they want.

It all seemed so remarkable to me. After leaving White Lake, it had seemed as if my pivotal role in making Woodstock happen had only grown smaller as the concert's legend grew larger. By the middle of 1970, as it became clear that my attempts to break into the Hollywood scene had failed, I had watched as the documentary film of *Woodstock* was released to huge acclaim. Adding insult to injury, *Woodstock* won a Best Documentary Oscar on the night of my birthday a year later. Of course, that night wasn't a total loss, because that had been the same night I met André. But now it was increasingly clear to everyone in the world that Woodstock had been an important cultural event. Everyone, that is, except André.

"Why do you want to do this lecture on Woodstock, Elliot?" André asked after the party, when we were back home and getting undressed for bed. "You know that there are many here in Belgium—regular people and artists alike—who regard that entire thing as a depraved gathering of drug addicts and sex-obsessed misfits. Like a kind of immensely vulgar American embarrassment."

I was puzzled at André's dislike for the concert, and told him so.

"You don't see it, André," I said, "but Woodstock has impacted the world. And it continues to change things. It set me free, and I'm proud that I helped make it happen!"

"But, Elliot," André said in a concerned tone, "I am afraid that they will mock you. They do not care if you"—he kissed my neck as we cozied down into our bed—"are made to be the fool. I do not want them to make a clown out of the man I love. They do not know you as I do."

"Don't worry," I said, "nobody can make a clown out of me unless I *want* to be a clown! Besides, once they see that I am an exact double of Robert Redford, they will become obsessed with me and will look to embrace my brilliant insights about the universe—including the millions of all-gay leather jacket galaxies that reside beyond the outer reaches of the Milky Way!" I chuckled, but could see that André was totally serious. "I'm a big boy and I can take care of myself. Besides, I still don't have a work visa. So if I can get some work as a lecturer, then I can contribute to our household, too. I'm tired of you having to do everything for us around here. Trust me, okay?"

André looked up at me quietly, his head resting on the pillow. "Are you sure, Elliot?" he asked.

"Absolutely," I responded. "I've been looking to make some new Belgian francs anyway, so I can splurge and get you some more new shirts! I see you only have five dozen in your closet!"

André had always liked to buy shirts—his interest bordered on obsession. We would be shopping in town on a Sunday afternoon and, without fail, André would spot some shirt in a storefront window. André would say, "I only want to look in here for a minute." About twenty minutes later, we would leave the store with two to five new shirts. And it wasn't just shirts—he did this with sweaters, too. During one especially extravagant shopping spree, I had asked him, "Hey, André, what's with you and all these shirts and sweaters? Are you looking to open your own fashion boutique?"

"Darling," he had said, "you have your *frites* and egg creams and old movies. I have my shirts and sweaters. They are my weakness."

"Well, André, I wouldn't say that it's your only weakness," I had said, brushing my hand along the small of André's back through his new shirt. He had blushed slightly. "We will discuss this later, *mon cheri*."

❁   ❁   ❁

Arriving in Ghent for my lecture, I was dressed in a simple pair of jeans with a blazer jacket over a tie-dyed T-shirt. I was met at the train station by a Belgian student who had been sent by Hal and Catherine to serve as my chauffeur and translator. His name was Philippe, and he looked no older than sixteen. He held a sign in front of him, on which was written "Monsieur Elliot Tiger."

"Monsieur Tiger?" he stammered shyly.

"No," I said, "the name is Tiber with a 'b,' as in bearded beauty!"

He laughed. "So sorry, Mr. Tiber," he said. "Since you are from the rock 'n roll world of Woodstock, I suppose they thought that was really your last name."

"Right," I said back, "lions and Tibers and bears—oh my!"

"What?" Philippe asked.

"Nothing—just a little CIA joke," I said.

"You are with the CIA? *Mon dieu!*" he exclaimed, sounding almost afraid of me. Nearly a foot taller than Philippe, I practically towered over him.

"No, I am not with the CIA, but I know who starches all their shirts. And remember that there is no God—*dieu* is dead!"

Philippe laughed again, betraying his nervousness with a slight increase in his walking speed, so he was two steps or so ahead of me. That way, he could break into a run and get away from me if I decided to rip off his clothes and eat him right there at the train station. But then, as we were driving to the university, he pulled out a small joint and passed it over to me. "A-ha, a *landsman* here in Belgium!" I said with a smile and a wink. I doubt that Philippe understood my use of the Yiddish word for a fellow Jew, but he seemed to realize by now that he could relate to me. *Why not accept the boy's Belgian peace pipe?* I thought as I took a first toke.

Several puffs and twenty minutes later, we arrived at the Ghent University campus. The school's administrative and departmental offices were housed in ornate stone and brick buildings made for the university more than a century before. Equally breathtaking were the evenly spaced trees and carefully manicured landscape gardens—some of the most beautiful topiary design I had ever seen. It looked to me like some fantastic Belgian Land of Oz, with an international crowd of students standing in for the little people of the Lollipop Guild.

I was to give my lecture at a large outdoor amphitheater. Incredibly stoned at this point, I felt like I was floating as I was ushered by Philippe into the backstage area. I had only just gotten comfortable when I was hurried out to the left wing of the stage. And then, waiting behind the stage's side curtain, I was gripped by a nearly paralyzing thought: *What if I have to speak French, or maybe even* Flemish, *to these people?* In my zeal to share my Woodstock miracle, it hadn't occurred to me that I might have a language problem until that very moment.

I tried to calm my mind as I looked out at the stage from the wings. The setup was distressingly sparse. There was a single podium, on which sat a single glass of water, and a single microphone on a stand. I looked around for Philippe, but couldn't find him. My anxiety only grew as my mind registered what was waiting for me beyond the curtains. Then, I heard a French-accented voice shout to the assembled audience, "Elliot the Tiger!" Wandering out onto the stage, I was met with a tentative wave of applause. *Showtime, kids,* I said to myself.

In my very best French, which had not yet developed much beyond trivial chit-chat and the requesting of *Frites, s'il vous plaît,* I attempted to introduce myself. I did so first by explaining that my last name was "Tiber—uh, T, I, B, E, R"—and that I was *not* a tiger. Unfortunately, as I would learn later that day from Philippe, what I really told the audience in French was that I was not a man but a cat. I could see quizzical expressions on the faces in the first few rows. Increasingly nervous, I flashed back to the summer of '69. I tried to tell the audience that I was from the Woodstock festival, had lived at a motel for fourteen years, and had thankfully survived all the drugs and the mud of those three days. In practice, what I said actually sounded something like this in French:

"I am the man from the land of Woodstock. I survived many drugs in my mouth for three days after living for fourteen years in the house of mud."

People started to giggle, and I heard a few isolated coughs from the dark back area of the amphitheater. My words were strung together with lots of "uhs" and "ums" and "ehs," which I think led people to believe that I was still suffering the effects of a bad acid trip. Philippe told me afterward that I had gone on to tell the audience that I had lived totally naked on a farm with Jewish cows and was the man who had permitted more than one million rock concerts to be staged for one hippie. The talk wasn't going the way I had planned it.

As I finished describing my Momma as a "Jewish Cossack Nazi," I heard some muffled giggles from the audience, along with some hushed whispers of concern to my left. The series director began slowly walking toward me.

Utterly bewildered, my Brooklyn-boy moxie kicked in and I blurted out, "Does anyone here speak English, or what?"

"We *all* speak English here, monsieur," said the lecture director.

Silence.

"Oh," I said. Dazed and confused as I was, I had simply forgotten that many Belgians actually spoke English quite well. I looked out at the audience and shrugged meekly. "Oops. So, does anyone want to hear any more about Woodstock?"

The entire audience, including the lecture director, began to laugh. I was finally in my element again. I went on to entertain my audience, bringing that amazing Woodstock moment back to life right there on that stage, all by myself.

At the end of my lecture, my hosts opened the floor for questions. A young woman got up. "Monsieur Tiber, can you tell us what it felt like to be there at Woodstock?"

I looked at the girl, and then I asked everyone in the audience to hold hands with the people on either side of them. I waited for a few moments, listening to people shift around in seats and whisper and giggle. Then I asked again. When they were all holding hands, I smiled. *"That's* how it felt for us at Woodstock." I received a standing ovation. *Not too bad for a hippie savage from Brooklyn named Tiger,* I thought.

After the talk, the lecture director introduced me to a number of young students. Several, as it turned out, were Americans who were living in Brussels because their parents worked at the NATO base. I wasn't sure how the Woodstock vibe would resonate with military kids, but it turned out that they really enjoyed hearing about my wacky life and the freedom that I had gotten out of the Woodstock experience. Perhaps they felt they might also achieve their own unique life experiences above and beyond what had been dictated to them by sheer circumstance. I was proof that they could be anything they wanted to be.

On the drive back to the train station, Philippe seemed far more open and communicative than earlier. He told me that his favorite band was the Doors, and that he planned to visit the grave of the band's lead singer, Jim Morrison, at the Père Lachaise Cemetery in Paris when he had the chance. I told him that I used to play the Doors on my little record player back at the El Monaco, before Woodstock came and saved me. Philippe was a nice young kid and an excellent guide, and I made sure to tell him so. As we said our goodbyes at the station, he even gave me a quick but heartfelt hug and thanked me for bringing such good feelings to everyone.

As a lecturer abroad, I had enjoyed an auspicious beginning.

"They gave you an ovation?" André asked, with a big smile on his face.

"That's right," I said proudly, thrusting out my chest. "I told you that you should trust me, right?"

"Elliot, it was the audience that I did not trust. They can be very cruel and unforgiving to Americans."

"Listen, if I could survive the motel, my mother, and a music festival attended by a million people, I could survive a Belgian audience. Public mockery means nothing to me. Besides," I continued, "I'm far too involved with my own way of life and thinking to care what other people think."

"That is remarkable, Elliot," said André, still unable to believe just how excited people had gotten about Woodstock.

"Who knows," I said, "perhaps I could do some teaching and lectures on art as well." I felt almost high with the sense of possibility about the future. André smiled his serene smile, as he often did when we shared our hopes and plans together.

"What have you written down there, Elliot?" André asked, seeing the scribbling in the notebook that I was taking out of my tote bag.

"Oh, that's something I was playing around with on the way back," I told him. "You know, it occurs to me that there may be more humor to this whole Woodstock thing than I had originally thought."

I explained to André how the persona I had projected from the stage—that of a spaced-out hippie trying desperately to communicate in a foreign language, and making all kinds of mistakes along the way—might actually be a funny character. On the train ride back to Brussels, I had written down a skit in which a character called the Woodstock Hippie tries to do ordinary everyday things, like ordering food in a restaurant, picking up his dry cleaning, asking a Belgian where the bus stop is located, and trying to communicate what might be wrong with his arm during a visit to a doctor's office. André read a page of my skit and started to laugh. He said in an offhand way, "You should write some more of these ideas, Elliot. These are very funny, and this hippie character is a good basis for a sketch."

The next morning, I made myself some tea and toast and sat on the couch watching TV. Although I loved Belgium and the new experiences I was accumulating with André, nothing made me miss home as much as seeing some of the American shows that ran throughout the week on the local Armed Forces television station. Hearing those familiar American voices made me yearn to see Renee and my friends back in Manhattan. I knew I ought to watch Belgian shows to improve my conversational French, but the dialogue went by so quickly that I often just zoned out. There were only really three or four channels to watch, anyway; there seemed to be a near-absolute lack of new and creative programming in Belgium, at least from where I was seated.

Mostly, I liked to watch the reruns of *I Love Lucy* that the Belgian stations aired each day. If I wanted to improve my French, I'd pay attention to the French subtitles that ran on the bottom of the screen. But mostly, I watched to enjoy Lucille Ball's genius for physical comedy. That being said, I couldn't help feeling that her character was a total pain in the ass, especially compared to the character Ricky, played by her real-life husband Desi Arnaz. There were some episodes where I simply couldn't understand why Lucy's husband didn't force her onto a guillotine and lop off her head. Still, I found it endearing that Lucy kept on trying to perform onstage with Ricky. She never gave up on that dream, and I admired her perseverance. After all, it was a trait to which I could totally relate. As I watched Lucy come up with one crazy idea after another, I started to think to myself: *Hey, maybe I've got some crazy ideas of my own that I can play with here.* In a land with a surplus of brown overcoats and waffles, I figured my whackadoo thoughts might be just what was needed to shake things up a bit.

Seated in front of the television the morning after the Woodstock lecture, I thought up another skit idea. Instead of focusing on a specific character like the permanently stoned Woodstock character I had first invented, I allowed my mind to go wherever it liked. I wrote down the first idea that came to me. Drawing from clear memories of my primal scream therapy session back in New York, I depicted a group of sobbing adults in diapers, seated ass-down in several large baby cribs. In my story, a man dressed in a Nazi uniform and sporting a Hitler mustache enters. He begins to scream angrily at all the bawling babies, telling them how they have disappointed him. The man keeps shouting until he moves too close to one of the babies, who reaches up and snatches the fake mustache off his face. Then the adult babies start to squirt their milk bottles at the now clean-shaven Hitler lookalike, who runs out of the room in hysterics as the other babies stand up in their cribs and laugh joyfully. They get up out of the cribs and go dancing out of the room, holding hands and singing the Hallelujah chorus from Handel's *Messiah*—all but one. That one adult baby climbs out of his crib, puts the fake Hitler mustache on his upper lip, and goosesteps his way out of the room, singing the chorus to the Sammy Davis, Jr. hit "I've Gotta Be Me."

The first idea had come to me within minutes. But then I wrote down another idea, then another, and then another. I felt like my pen couldn't keep up with my brainstorming. In addition to the Primal Scream Hitler skit, I wrote a skit about a stoned hippie who marries his own aunt for free room and board; an idea for a staged performance of Tchaikovsky's ballet "Swan Lake," presented by ten actors dressed as swans; a sketch about a muscular rabbi who boxes an out-of-shape atheist in a contest to determine whether God exists; and a skit about a TV repairman who intentionally breaks the sets he is sent to fix so that he can take his customers hostage in their homes, forcing them to listen to him sing arias from German operas after he strips down to his underpants.

I was writing a skit in which a chicken and an egg try to beat each other to the front of a movie ticket line when I heard André fitting his key into the lock on our apartment door. I was still seated on the couch, leaning on the table in front of our TV and writing. More than a dozen pieces of torn-out notebook pages were scattered around me, looking like the flat white moths that used to amass against the screen door back at the El Monaco.

"Elliot, have you been writing all day?" André asked.

"I guess so," I said, surprised. "I hadn't even planned it." I looked outside, and saw that the sun was already starting to set.

André asked me what I had written. "Just funny little skits and sketches," I responded, "I didn't even stop to think about it too much. The ideas were in my head. Read 'em if you like."

He did just that, dropping down into the couch gently and scooping up some of the pages. Looking through the pages, André began to laugh a little. And the more he read, the more he began to laugh. "These are hilarious!" he said, sounding happier and more enthusiastic over the next few minutes than he had been in the past few weeks. "Can you write more of these?"

"I don't see why not."

"What if I asked you to jot down an idea for a sketch right away? Do you think you could do it, Elliot?"

"I'll do better than that. Take me out to dinner at a restaurant that has ketchup, and I'll think up as many sketches as you want," I joked, though I really was hungry and wanted to eat.

"Yes, I am hungry, too," he said, walking toward the bedroom. "Let me put on my new shirt."

As we ate, I came up with all kinds of sketches: a blind pantomime and a deaf ventriloquist; a wife and husband who beat each other up with bagged groceries and fresh fruit; and even a trio of nuns—played by men in drag—who try to make extra spending money as a fifties-era doo-wop group that could only get jobs singing at bar mitzvahs. André liked every new idea I made up, and I felt like I had more energy than I had since the days before the Woodstock show.

Later, we talked about his work at the Théâtre National. André was feeling a little boxed in. I was surprised, since André's reputation in the Belgian arts community had only grown stronger in the time I had been with him. I asked him why he was unhappy with the acclaim and adulation. "Because I am not enjoying myself in the work," he said, in a weary voice. "But that is why I am asking you to make these sketches. I really think you have some talent at making things funny," he continued, "and I was recently offered something that we just might be able to work on together."

"*Excusez-moi?*" I said slowly.

He explained that he had recently been offered the chance to direct a variety show program for television. Belgian producer Jacques Bourton had been one of André's classmates at the Institut National Supérieur des Arts du Spectacle et des Techniques de Diffusion, or INSAS, the Belgian film and theater school. Bourton had been developing top programs for the television division of Radio Télévision Belge, RTB TV, for about two years, and had gotten in touch to see if André wanted to direct a new script he had ready for television.

"This is fantastic news, André," I said, as we finished our after-dinner coffee and began walking back to our apartment.

"No, but you see, there is a problem," André said, "While I may have no experience at television, I know a good script from a bad, and the script Jacques has given me is not very good."

We got back to the apartment, and I asked him to show me the script. It was in French, so it was easier for him to read some of the script to me aloud, instantly translating into English. A few pages into the script, I could tell what he meant. The material was not very exciting and the story had been done to death on other shows. When I told him that I agreed with his assessment, he returned to the subject of my skits.

"That is why your sketches are so exciting to me," said André. "There is something in them that is different—yes, also strange, but in a good way. You create situations that have the potential to be made very amusing. I can see in my mind how to direct the sketches in such a way that they will be hilarious." He turned away from me for a moment, and then said, "I want to do television, but I would have so much more fun working with you on these crazy skits of yours than I would if I were to work on what I have been given. I want to do a TV show based on the sketches that you have been writing."

I was shocked. It was as if Lucy had been told suddenly by Ricky that she could come down and perform in his show at the Tropicana Club. Part of me was elated, but part of me was wary. After all, I had only been writing my sketches to entertain myself. Though André had enjoyed my ideas and encouraged me to create more of them, I didn't really know if my stuff was good, or if André was just looking for a change. Then again, I was still feeling inspired by my earlier outpouring of ideas, and I had seen enough Belgian television to know that there was definitely a shortage of original programming. In the end, it was up to André.

"When do you have to make a decision about this offer?"

"Jacques has arranged a meeting for tomorrow afternoon with Pierre Renoult, the president for comedy and variety shows at RTB," André said, frowning.

"You know I will support you in whatever you do," I reassured him. "If you want me to, I'll come to the meeting with you and help you pitch the idea. After all, I'm the lunatic who wrote these nutty sketches, right?"

"Yes, Elliot," André said. "I want you there with me at this meeting."

I was touched by his faith and trust. I was also slightly anxious about the meeting, because I had absolutely no idea what I was doing. I had enough trouble trying to speak French. How in the hell was I going to talk programming with a TV producer? But in spite of my doubts, I felt sure that I would be able to help André. He had been looking to challenge the status quo—to lob a hand grenade into the Belgian artistic establishment. Me? I was a crazy American, an outsider, and a wild card. I had nothing to lose, and everything to gain.

I was totally calm the morning of the meeting. I was ready. When it came down to it, I had a seemingly endless supply of ideas and an insane view of the universe. In other words, I was *perfect* for television. I only hoped that I could contribute to André's success, not failure.

In contrast, André's nerves were on edge. We sat waiting for a few minutes in RTB's shag-carpeted reception area before Renoult came to greet us. He came bounding toward us, all smiles—until he saw me. My heart froze, and I wondered for an instant if perhaps he had stayed at the El Monaco at one point. Then he raised his arms and shouted "Woodstock Man!" He proceeded to shake my hand vigorously, spilling forth an array of compliments in French.

Unable to catch everything that he was saying, I kept smiling at him while André—who was trying hard to stifle laughter—translated. Apparently, Renoult had attended my lecture in Ghent and immediately recognized me as the hilarious American hippie who had gotten everyone in the audience to laugh so much. I was flattered that he remembered me, but I quickly explained in my still-tentative French that I was there only as André's partner and did not wish to interrupt their business.

After the two of them had discussed the show that André had been given, Renoult asked my opinion of the script. His English was as shaky as my French, so André explained to me that Renoult also wanted to know my thoughts on television comedy up to that point, as he was especially interested in the American perspective.

"I think that the best comedy," I said, speaking English slowly and deliberately, "comes from how people act. It comes from crazy kinds of situations, and how people deal with those situations. The best TV comedy shows are about *people*." Then, fumbling for an example of a successful American TV show he'd know, I blurted out, "Like *I Love Lucy,* uh, Lucy and Ricky!" Unsure if he was following what I was saying, I started to sing the show's theme song right there in his office. Delighted, Renoult sang along. So there we were, a Belgian TV producer and a former American motel pool cleaner, standing in an office, singing "Bah-dah-DUM, buh-dah-DAH, doo-DAW!" Before André could translate what I had said into smooth French, Renoult clapped his hands. "So, you write for *I Love Lucy?*" he asked. *"Très magnifique!"* Thinking I had misheard, I turned to André. "What the hell did he say?"

André, smiling at this madness, looked me straight in the eye and said "He thinks you were a screenwriter for the *I Love Lucy* show." *Oh, shit!* I thought, looking at André apologetically.

Renoult then spoke swiftly in French to André, all the while looking at us like he had just told us where in his backyard he had buried the Hope diamond. André listened and translated. "Monsieur Renoult would like to know if you and I would agree to write an original ninety-minute musical comedy special to air on RTB TV in five weeks." I could see that both André and Renoult were waiting now to see what I—supposedly a scriptwriter for *I Love Lucy*—would say. The only thing I could think to do was to raise my arms over my head and say, "Sure, let's put on a show! Why not?"

Several handshakes later, the contract for the musical-comedy special was finalized. Renoult asked us what we wanted to call the show. André looked at me. Apparently, everyone in Belgium was waiting for me to decide what they should watch on television. Then I thought about how hungry I was, and the title came to me: "How about *Sketch-Up?*" I wanted our show to have an English title that was reminiscent of the popular show *Laugh-In* back home. An English title would make the show easier to promote and distribute throughout the world. And since I figured everyone knew about ketchup in Belgium, I felt that *Sketch-Up* would be approved instantly. It was!

Renoult and André loved the title. In French, they began to discuss production details: crew schedules, rehearsal time, studio booking, and the fact that the show would need to be done live, not taped ahead of time. Basically, all the elements that go into making television—details about which I knew nothing at the time, but would come to learn soon enough. What mattered most that afternoon was that I had accompanied my lover to his meeting with a TV network head, and, despite my naïveté, lack of experience, and inability to speak French, I had wound up the co-creator of a brand new Belgian TV show!

Even with his extensive experience, the show was as much a first for André as it was for me. Andre had worked extensively in theater and film, but never in television. In the cab home from the studios, André entwined his hand with mine, squeezed it affectionately, and told me he felt the show's title had to be changed.

"To what?" I asked.

"How about we call the show *André Loves Elliot?*" he said, smiling at me.

We had a sweet time together in bed after a celebratory dinner. As we held each other and I started to drift off to sleep, André said, "We can start to work on our show tomorrow."

"That's fine, honey," I said, kissing the nape of his neck. "We have five weeks until the show, right? That should be enough time."

Then, as I was about to fall asleep, André said, "No, *mon auteur*. The TV show will be performed live in five weeks. The *script* is due in two days."

❁   ❁   ❁

"Nazis!"

"We have those."

"Jews!"

"We have those, too."

"Nazis and Jews!"

"Done already. Remember the fight scene at the bakery?"

"What about *dancing* Nazis and Jews?"

André started to laugh. We had been working on skit ideas since earlier that morning. André typed into French every idea that came to my mind and rolled out of my mouth. We had been called that day by Renoult, who assured André that my work visa was already approved and would arrive to us by mail at our place within a week. Nothing stood in our way except the completion of the script.

"What about soup?" I said.

"What about it?" responded André.

"I don't know, I just think there's something funny about soup."

"How about an argument between a customer and a maître d' about something being in the soup?"

"Yes," I said. "The customer complains that he ordered the cold potato soup, but he receives the hot potato soup. And the maître d' says, 'Call me back over in another ten minutes.'"

André and I started to act out bits of dialogue together, bouncing ideas off each other and even adopting different voices as we continued to carve out all kinds of characters and zany scenarios. The ideas flowed.

"Chocolate!" I suddenly shouted.

André stared at me for a second before responding, "You want to write about chocolate?"

"No," I said quickly, "I *want* chocolate. I'm starving. Break time!"

As we continued to write down ideas and dialogue, we deliberately left room in the script for on-set improvisation. Including this improvisation, André figured the show would easily fill ninety minutes. To make sure we had plenty of material, though, we decided to write more sketches than we needed. It seemed like the best way to avoid coming up short on the running time.

"If we need a lot, then we'll make a lot," I said, with more swagger than knowledge. I could see that André was concerned about getting an entire show together in only a few weeks. As a theater director, he was well aware of the many things that could and often did go wrong in staging a production. And here we were, working in television, a medium in which André had not yet worked, armed only with a collection of sketches written by a newcomer whose grasp of French was shaky at best.

At first, I was not as worried. For one thing, I was somewhat removed from the practical side of the operations. I was working from a place of total freedom, newly and freshly involved in something that was exciting and fun. While I had never done work in television, I had certainly *watched* a lot of television. Besides, I wasn't even being asked to write for TV, per sé. André was simply encouraging me to dream up weird and crazy images and ideas. I had wanted for so long to get involved with show business. Now with my own TV comedy show to write, with my lover at my side to direct it, I felt absolutely invincible.

By eleven o'clock that night, though, I started to worry. We had dozens of ideas written down, some of which André felt would work and as many that he felt would not. I had been so confident about each idea that I never stopped to think about how they could be realized, or the logistical problems they might pose. What came to me effortlessly was the idea of a sketch—I could see each concept as if it were a picture in a magazine or a frozen image on the TV screen. I was thinking strictly in visual terms, and many of my ideas were more like paintings or even silent films. There was a reason for that.

The sketches would have to be written and performed in French. The only thing I knew how to do with French was to mangle it when I spoke. When André told me that we needed to set down French dialogue, my initial rush started to recede and I realized just how much more still had to be done. We hadn't even taken a break for a proper dinner. We had stayed in the apartment all day and into the night, and we hadn't changed clothes or taken showers. I started to feel tired, but I also felt an urge to beat this monster into submission. I didn't want to lose this crazy opportunity.

"Just tell me what else we need to do, André," I said, standing up and taking several deep breaths to reinvigorate myself. "We can do this." And I kissed him as he sat hunched over at the typewriter.

"All right, Elliot, but I have to find a way to keep myself awake," André said, looking around the apartment.

"Well," I suggested, "you love those fucking shirts. Why not put some of them on?"

"Yes, I want to anyway because it is so late and I always get cold when I am tired," he said through a yawn.

"Not me," I said, whipping off my shirt, "I need to keep myself cold if I want to stay awake." I pulled off my pajama bottoms, so that I was standing there in my boxer shorts and my socks. "C'mon, let's write some French!"

André's response? "Oy!"

Hey, my goy boy is learning to speak Yiddish! I thought as André went to the bedroom to get a shirt. He came back out, a turquoise dress shirt half-buttoned over his white T-shirt. And so we set ourselves to the task, André sitting at the typewriter capturing in French the lines that we were reading out loud together in English. Together, we finalized ten sketches in nearly five hours.

Almost twenty-four hours after we started, there we were: André wearing three of his buttoned shirts, a cardigan, and his russet robe; and me, sitting absolutely naked in the living room.

"We still have more to do," André said, "but we have most of what we need now right here. I cannot believe that we did all that work!"

"I told you there was nothing to worry about," I said, grinning. "Let's keep going."

"Are you serious, Elliot?"

"What," I teased, "are you too tired or something?"

"No, I can keep going. But are you able to keep going?"

"Step aside, you crazy Belgian fairy genius," I said, as I sat down naked in front of the typewriter. "Let's keep at it until we've put every single piece of ourselves into the show."

Thirty-six hours after we started our writing marathon, we were finally done. There were more than twenty separate sketches that reflected our work together as a creative team. We were utterly spent, but also very excited, and I wanted to go out and celebrate. It had been such an explosion of creative thought, and I had never felt more alive and vital than I did at that moment.

André asked me where I wanted to go.

"You know where," I responded. And of course, he did. After we shared a blessedly warm and rejuvenating shower, we dressed up in our black leather outfits and headed out to the nightclub section across town. It had been a few months since we had been to the gay bars, and it was time to have some fun. That night, André and I were both in search of the same thing. We wanted to lose ourselves in that wonderfully wild world of leather that awaited us at the bars. We wanted to see brawny, sweat-streaked male bodies, and to abandon ourselves to the music. These younger men in the club were luscious, rock-hard renegades, always ready to hustle and gyrate out on the dance floor. It gave us a thrill when one or another of these guys touched or grabbed us at the club. We enjoyed watching each other be pawed, and would take home all that pent-up erotic tension and release it beneath the sheets. It was so liberating for me to be able to enjoy being openly gay in a club without worrying about potential harassment the minute I walked back outside.

That night, André and I danced for hours. We were like two giddy lightning bugs, hopped up on shared adrenaline and burning our light so intensely that our beams might have punched holes through that dark Belgian night sky.

A week after being signed to do *Sketch-Up,* André and I arrived at the RTB studios to meet with Renoult again. We were ushered into Renoult's conference room and were surprised to find it filled to capacity with various executives, producers, designers, sound and lighting directors, and even student trainees. Wow! Apparently, our show was a hotly-anticipated project. This sure wasn't some Hollywood television pitch. Not that I had ever given a Hollywood pitch before in my life, but I had heard plenty about them when I lived briefly in Los Angeles.

Of course, I couldn't possibly read the French script to the studio myself. Fortunately, everyone knew André personally or by reputation; many had been students with him at INSAS. Renoult introduced me as their newest American television colleague. "I speak French and Flemish fluently, but not on Wednesdays," I said. There was immediate laughter, which increased as those who understood English translated my words for those who didn't. When I announced the title of the show, it drew applause and lively nods of approval.

The following week was a veritable orgy of frenzied, almost hysterical activity in preparation for the live program. First, the show was cast. Two of the performers were particularly easy to find. Having written what we knew, André and I were shoo-ins for two of the characters we had featured in our script: a bearded Belgian and a big curly-haired American who spoke very little French. André had acted before, of course, and his professionalism allowed him to slip seamlessly between acting and directing on set. As for me, I had been cast in my first costarring role on a television show, and a French-language show at that. I hadn't even needed one of those fabled Hollywood agents to get me the job! I had simply done what so many other performers had done before me: I had written a part that only I could play.

André plucked most of the other actors from his troupe at the Théâtre National. These actors were all fairly well known to Belgian theater audiences, and totally experienced. The one I liked best was the actress and comedienne Suzy Falk. Suzy was rumored to have escaped the Nazis in World War II simply by walking through Germany until she reached Belgium. Suzy's entire family had been gassed at Auschwitz during the war. A strong and indomitable survivor, Suzy had created a career for herself as a performer and had played various supporting and leading roles in theaters throughout Belgium. She was the Belgian version of Carol Burnett, a triple threat: a funny girl, a great singer, and a brilliant dramatic actress. André knew how versatile she was and put Suzy in almost every sketch.

I originally grew close to Suzy because she was fluent in English. If I had a question about what was being said in French during a rehearsal, I could always turn to Suzy, my trusted translator. I told her stories about my crazy family—especially about my mother, who claimed to have escaped Russian Cossacks on foot the same way that Suzy had escaped Nazi storm troopers in Germany. I joked with Suzy that if she hadn't been smart and stopped when she got to Belgium, she might have become a crazy Jewish momma running a ramshackle motel in the Catskills.

In addition to André's friends from the Théâtre National, one of the featured performers on the show was an up-and-coming Parisian singer named Catherine Lara. Everyone knew her name. The moment I met her, it was immediately clear to me that she was a wonderful talent—warm, full of life, and an effortless musical interpreter. She was also very much a French, not Belgian, singer. I was surprised that the studio had not engaged a homegrown talent.

Even the television studios where we were rehearsing *Sketch-Up* were divided into French and Flemish sections. There was a white line painted down the middle of the corridors. Renoult explained that he and his employees were never to cross that line. "That side there," he explained, "is BRT. Flemish TV!" Apparently on principle, French-speaking Belgians did not watch BRT and Flemish-speaking Belgians never looked at RTB. *Bullshit,* I thought. What did I care about the rules? Being me, I walked straight—or gay, rather—down the center of the corridors. Since I was an American and everybody assumed me to be a bit nuts, nobody ever bothered me about it. I had spent most of my life crossing lines, and I wasn't about to change my ways for some silly snit between the Walloons and the Flemings!

As we headed into production, it became clear that there was much work to be done. André confided to me early on at the apartment one night that the absurdist sets, costumes, wigs, and even makeup that we had envisioned might be prohibitively expensive. Still feeling invincible, I told André that I would take care of everything myself or tell people what it was I wanted.

André smiled gently. "Elliot," he said in his careful way, "I want you to listen to me. I know that you are very excited about this show, and that we would not be here if not for you. But you have to remember that *I* am the director of this show. This is a new world for you, and you will see very quickly how little you know about it. What I need you to do is let me be the director in front of all these people. Let *me* run the production. If you have an idea, you come and talk to me about it. If you have a concern, you do not shout out loud about it like you are back at that terrible motel with your parents. For us to make this work, you need to know that I trusted you to write the sketches. Now you must trust me as a director to translate the script for television. You understand me, right?"

A part of me was hurt that he thought he had to explain everything to me that way. So I did what any sensitive and complicated artist would do—I pouted. Though I was offended, I did know what he meant. When it came to the various technical aspects of television, I *was* very much out of my element. However, I also knew that despite his apparent composure, André was nervous as hell about directing television for the first time. I cared about him, and I wanted to make something with him. After I got over my hurt feelings, I told him that I understood and would certainly do anything that he wanted. "Just remember, André," I said, "you may be the director at the studio and on the show. But when we get back here at night, I get to be *your* director."

He smiled at me, and said, "That sounds fine to me. Please understand, I believe I can make this show work. In the meantime, why not start your direction of me here, right now?"

I took his hand, and led him to the bedroom. "Okay, then, Monsieur Ernotte—action!"

We hugged, we kissed, we fucked, and then we slept. *Fade out . . . cut . . . print that take!*

As we rehearsed *Sketch-Up,* I did as André asked and let him call the shots in rehearsal and on set. Often during our rehearsal days, André would talk with me about some element of the art design, or whether or not I felt a costume worked. The crew understood that André and I had written the show together, and they knew that André and I were a couple. Slowly, people began to discuss elements of the show with me. I always deferred to André, but ultimately I started to answer questions from people on the crew because we were running out of time and the show's air date was approaching. I made sure that everyone I spoke to understood that my instructions came from conversations I had had with André. And though it was ultimately André's decision as the director, he had told me that he wanted that particular bit of business or that shade of paint used. I suppose the crew saw André and me as two halves of the same creative mind, and I stayed as respectful of that as I could.

A few days after I started to receive questions, I felt that I had to tell André about it. He gave me a mischievous little grin, and said, "Elliot, they only came to speak with you about those things because as the director I told them that you were in charge of those elements of the production."

Instead of feeling pissed because I had not been informed, I was relieved that he already knew. And later that evening, I realized that André in his quiet yet persuasive way had given me my first job as a production and costume designer. I was touched that André had been thoughtful enough to make my failed Hollywood dream come true—in Belgium.

Working hard to finish up preproduction, André and I were putting in fifteen-hour days. Having already worked out his notes with his assistant director at the Théâtre National, André had the opportunity to take time off from the theater's fall season—time that went instead to *Sketch-Up.* For me, finally getting the chance to work on a real set and be a part of a production made every second of the experience an absolute pleasure.

Since I had been placed in charge of costume design by André, I had free access to RTB's large costume department. I rummaged through the stock but was not content with what I found there. Across the hall was another costume department. Inconveniently, this department was located on the other side of the corridor's white line—on the Flemish BRT side. What did I care about that? Had Suzy Falk escaped Nazi Germany as a child only to now be deprived of good costumes because of a silly strip of white paint? So I marched into that huge room bursting with wonderful costumes, and found lots of wigs and out-fits that suited the zany nature of our show. I went to the studio property man-ager's office to sign the items out for production use. The manager, a scrawny, severe-looking woman, searched her paperwork for *Sketch-Up*. She didn't find our show registered, so she began to question me—in Flemish. Stumped and unable to understand what she was saying, I showed her my ID and my copy of the finalized script.

She noticed the RTB logo on the front page, and again spoke Flemish to me in an alarmed tone. The only two things that I clearly understood were "RTB" and "BRT." Worried that she might object, I shoved my items into my RTB props trolley and ran straight past her, crossing back over the white line and into safe RTB territory. Three BRT security men surrounded me just as I reached the door to the RTB studio stage. They were shouting at me in Flem-ish, and I shouted back in English. The woman who was my assistant and the wardrobe seamstress joined me, shouting at the Flemings in French. An old German janitor who had been mopping the floor at the other end of the hall-way bounded over to us, shrieking, "*Halt!*" He must have been one of the Nazis that my mother had told me were hiding in Belgium.

Hearing the ruckus, André came running from the studio stage with some of the other crew members. The BRT guards explained all over again in slightly broken English that I was not to use any Flemish television resources. André calmly took in the situation and asked the BRT security to come with him as he made a telephone call. Within five minutes, M. Renoult appeared with a studio check book and explained that he would rent the chosen costumes from the BRT studio for use by RTB on *Sketch-Up*. It seemed absolutely insane that this was necessary to borrow a few wigs, dresses, and a false nose. Once money changed hands, though, I was left alone to do what I was there to do—help create a TV comedy show.

Each day we had rehearsals in the morning. As we went through the sketches, the lighting and sound designers worked up their plans. The studio at RTB was the size of a small football field, enabling us to construct various sets at once. As a result, André could direct the entire show so it seemed to flow seamlessly from one environment and background to another. Of course, it would only *appear* to be seamless because everyone worked so diligently and with such enormous enthusiasm for the show. Under André's direction, our little band of merrymakers turned into a tight and well-oiled machine.

We always had lunch together in the studio's enormous cafeteria. The food was superb and inexpensive, as it was subsidized by the government. We sat at huge communal tables assigned to the *Sketch-Up* crew. Just as in the hallway, though, the dining hall had another big white line on the floor, dividing the Flemings from the Walloons. We sat on the RTB side, and on the other side sat the BRT cast and crews. Nobody spoke to anyone on the Flemish side of that stupid white line. One day I couldn't stand it any longer, so I took my chair and placed it astride the line, half of it on one side of the line and half on the other. Everyone stopped to look at me, and the immense room grew deathly quiet. I munched half of my meal leaning to the French side of the line, and the other half leaning to the Flemish. Security from both sides appeared out of the woodwork. André knew enough Flemish to explain that I was an American and did not know that their side of the white line was in fact in another country. He then pleaded with me to rejoin him and the rest of the *Sketch-Up* crew over in French-speaking Belgium. By now, dozens of people were discussing my actions. I got up, took my chair back to the table, and kept eating. I had made my point, though, or at least I hoped I had. Suzy took my hand in hers, and said "Good for you, Elliot." Her little boost of encouragement made me proud.

After lunch, I established beyond all doubt that I was a near-illiterate when it came to French. Aware that my French skills were going to remain a problem for the show, André instructed the crew to make special cue cards for me with my French lines spelled out phonetically. Even with the cue cards, though, it was obvious that we would never finish even one scene properly as I continued to hold forth in my Brooklyn-inflected French. I didn't want to fuck up the show. So I told André at the end of that first week that he should have the technical director flash French subtitles along the bottom of the television screen whenever I spoke French.

1972. On the set of *Sketch-Up*. André's the handsome man in the center, and I'm the guy on the left, watching Suzy Falk do her thing with another actor.

1972. With Suzy Falk, mocking the Jewish wedding that Momma always wished I'd have.

1972. On *Sketch-Up,* it was often the egg before the chicken. From left to right: André, me, and Suzy Falk, in costume from our infamous "Swan Lake" sketch.

1972. Guess who the chicken is.

At first, André did not understand. He worried that the critics would think that our team didn't know how to make a proper television program. I reminded André that *Sketch-Up* was as far removed from a proper television show as anything one could imagine. André spoke with Renoult about the idea, and he loved my suggestion. He even declared both me and André total geniuses. My gut feeling was that viewers would easily get the humor of using French subtitles in a French-language broadcast. As long as André had the team properly prepared so they knew when to superimpose the subtitles when I was speaking, then the live show would work.

If any of us had stopped to think about how difficult it was going to be to perform ninety minutes of crazy skits and music stretched horizontally across the huge studio in a live broadcast, that person would have had to be put in a straitjacket and carried off to a sanitarium. At home, André was his usual self because he was used to the crazy rhythms that invade one's life when preparing a big show. I did notice, however, that he drank a little more wine than normal during our dinners. Drinking seemed to help shut his mind down.

While André looked to steady his mind, he also seemed to be somewhat obsessed about his health. I hadn't noticed it in New York, but in Belgium, it became apparent to me that André was quite the hypochondriac. His mother had told me that André had been quite sickly throughout most of his adolescence, and it seemed to me that in winter he was always either nursing a cold or worrying over a little cough. Amazingly enough, he chain-smoked as many cigarettes as I did—and his were those ultra-strong cigarettes that made me sound like Louis Armstrong the few times I took a drag from one.

André and I were opposites in lots of ways. André tended to watch his weight, whereas I didn't worry about mine, at least at that time. He was careful to take lots of vitamins and deliberately stayed positive. I only liked to take pills that changed the color of the walls, and I enjoyed the feeling of depression, going out of my way to watch sad movies and indulging in fits of sadness, looking out the apartment window when it rained. And yet, the health-nut optimist in our home was the one who always felt ill, and the sugar-addict fatalist was the one who never got sick and always got a clean bill of health from the doctor. Go figure.

As we continued to work out production issues before the broadcast, we quickly realized that we needed a laugh track to prompt viewers at home on how to react. The production setup made it impossible to have a live studio audience, and we didn't have the budget to record a proper laugh track. Instead, I took a cassette recorder with a built-in microphone and held it up to our television at home so I could record the audience from the *I Love Lucy* episodes that played each day. I played the laugh track over the studio speakers during rehearsals so that we would know how long to pause between lines, and eventually, we ended up using my homemade track during the broadcast itself. If anything, our stolen laugh track only emphasized the loonier elements of our seriously strange comical program. We were certainly taking the material to the limit—the show was a virtual kaleidoscope of wacky ideas and silly-looking people.

I was committed to making a show jammed with bonkers material. My corrupt version of "Swan Lake," for example, was inspired by the great American comedian and TV innovator Ernie Kovacs. In the late 1950s, Kovacs staged his own version of the ballet using dancers dressed up in gorilla suits. In our skit— one of the first I'd written the day after my Ghent lecture—I had the actors dress up as big swans. The crew designed a scenery backdrop of a lake, and installed signs in both French and English, mostly so I could understand what they said, but also for the sheer absurdity of it. The signs, so similar to the ones I used to put all over the El Monaco property, said things like "Polluted Water," "Beware of Sharks," "Beware of German Submarines," and "Careful of Hot Dogs." For me, the skit was to be the highlight of the entire program.

In our depraved version of this classic, André was to play the black swan. He would enter the scene dancing, or really shuffling, all in black feathers. He looked magnificent—until you saw his monstrously executed leaps and turns, which made him look like a man who had a scared animal stuck in his tights. After André, our troupe of overweight, graceless swans would follow, making their crass attempts at balletic elegance and beauty. This did not last long: Suzy, dressed as an alligator, would enter and chase the pack of swans with a cooking spoon and huge salt and pepper shakers. Finally, I would arrive on the scene, dressed as a huge fat chicken and sitting in a rowboat. On the night of the show, I would have half a dozen live chickens in the boat with me as I rowed over to André's character. His unwillingness to become part of my "swan stew" meant that my chicken character had to make an omelet for the other swans and the alligator.

There was one problem. "Swan Lake" clearly needed swans who were ballet dancers. Unfortunately, our cast did not include even one trained dancer. So André hired the choreographer of the Royal Ballet of Flanders to teach us the basic steps for the swans. It *seemed* like a good idea.

But then we tried it. One of our actresses was over seventy years old and famous throughout Belgium for playing women of the catastrophically obese variety. This lady must have weighed at least four hundred pounds—standing next to her, I looked like Mahatma Gandhi. We put ballet shoes on her feet and had her wear an enormous tutu that was tailored to fit her girth. She was a swan like no other swan in creation. But there was also no way she could dance or even move. I spoke privately with André during a five-minute break, and we decided that we should have her perched on a high black stool that would not be seen underneath her huge tutu. All that the audience at home would see would be a fat-woman swan with dancing feet, hungrily munching sweeties from out of a ten-pound box of Godiva chocolates.

After a day of rehearsing, our thoroughly *mishegas* ballet ensemble was still unable to master the complicated steps the choreographer struggled to teach us. We swans were bumping into one another, and not one of us managed to dance on our toes. I changed into more comfortable sneakers, but this infuriated the choreographer. When I suggested open-toed high heels, she summoned Renoult to the set to show him how disastrous our "Swan Lake" would be. Clearly, she lacked a sense of humor when it came to ballet. We ran through the routine for Renoult, trying our best but failing to approximate anything resembling ballet. As the writer of the piece, I appealed to Renoult, explaining that this was a *parody* of "Swan Lake." The choreographer was insulted and said ballet was never to be a subject of ridicule.

"Fair enough," Renoult said, "but this is *television*. Not ballet. Besides," he said, laughing, "I think it is very funny. Leave the skit as it is."

And just like that, we were free to pursue the skit as intended. The choreographer insisted that her name be taken off the credits. You can't please 'em all!

❀　　❀　　❀

On so many levels, *Sketch-Up* could very well have been a complete and utter failure. It *did* work, however, and more successfully than any of us had dreamed it might. We cruised through each and every sketch effortlessly. André skillfully kept everything moving forward. He succeeded admirably, working first in front of the camera and then behind it, guiding it to the next set piece.

Even with a few forgotten lines and some mistakes with costumes and sets, the show had an incredible energy to it. Caught in the middle of that chaos, I felt totally free and utterly at home. When I went to Hollywood, my dream had been to become a set designer. Here in Belgium, I was creating sets, selecting costumes, playing parts, and writing scripts. My dream had been fulfilled!

Before I realized it, the large clock on the back studio wall showed that more than an hour had gone by. Catherine Lara had sung a handful of torchy Parisian ballads, and we only had a few scenes left. As I finished one skit and ran to get into a costume for the next, I passed André. He reached out and gave my hand a loving squeeze. It lasted only a second or two, but it was his way of telling me that he loved me and that our crazy quilt of a show was a success. I had never felt so happy.

As the recorded laugh track played out the end of the final skit, we stood in place until we heard Renoult's voice from the control room shout, "*Finis! Wonderful show, everyone!*"

We had a rip-roaring time on the show and after, as well. Renoult treated our entire company to a magnificent dinner party at one of the finest restaurants in Brussels. It was a night of many toasts, lots of laughter, and spontaneous blasts of applause and singing from within our large group. Suzy sat with André and me, and Renoult walked around the gathering with a pleased and increasingly inebriated smile on his face.

André and I didn't get home until three in the morning, but we couldn't sleep. We stayed up the entire night, sitting on our couch and looking at each other, two mad doctors who had unleashed our very own Frankenstein monster onto thousands upon thousands of unsuspecting Belgian homes. We had no idea as to how the newspaper critics in this conservative country would react to this new form of mayhem.

So we were pleasantly surprised when the morning newspapers all declared *Sketch-Up* one of the best television shows of the year. Our show became the front cover story of the top regional television guide, and we got major photo coverage in almost every newspaper and magazine in Belgium.

André and I were interviewed in many publications and on radio talk shows. One critic even wrote in his review about how remarkable it was that an expatriate Jewish-American writer like me would know how to write some of the best French humor on television that year.

Renoult phoned us some weeks later to tell us that our show was to be Belgium's official entry for "Best Comedy Special" at the prestigious Golden Rose festival held each year in Montreux, Switzerland. The Golden Roses were considered to be the Academy Awards of world television programming, so our nomination was an incredible honor. We did not win that year. But a new comedy group on the BBC was awarded the Silver Rose d'Or, the second-place award, for doing a show very similar in nature and tone to our own. I remember wondering just who this Monty Python person was and why his Flying Circus was so funny. Once we had the chance to see a few episodes, though, we realized that Monty Python was not a man but actually six—and that the troupe's anarchic approach to television was so extreme and bizarre that it made total sense to describe it as a circus. We were disappointed not to have won an award ourselves, but having all that acclaim and recognition straight out of the gate did much to raise our spirits and bolster our confidence.

RTB, basking in the glow of a major success, immediately signed us to do a second *Sketch-Up* for the next season, with an option to make a third. We hadn't even imagined that it could become a recurring program. If we had done only one show, I would have been pleased about it for the rest of my life.

Our success and popularity in television did not go unnoticed by the theater world. When the manager of the Théâtre National called André in for a meeting, I got excited, wondering if he wanted us to write a new theater piece. Instead, André was given a peevish lecture about how his work on a freeform TV show like *Sketch-Up* might reflect badly on the Théâtre, which was known to be a more traditional and less radical entertainment venue. We got the feeling that the Théâtre also didn't like our TV show stealing any attention away from André's productions at their theater. Of course, they were happy to take any free publicity that André received from *Sketch-Up*. But it was clear that they wanted him to assure them that his association with their theater would remain a top priority. Since his directorial work was still our main source of income, André grudgingly agreed. However, he confided to me that he was feeling bored and a little burnt out with the theater. If anything, he said, he had enjoyed the experience of working with me on *Sketch-Up* more than any other production he had worked on that year.

I was touched that my little skits had led us to such a wonderful collaboration. In many ways, *Sketch-Up* was a wake-up call for both of us. For André, it freed him from working solely within the confines of conventional theater. It allowed him to use his acting and directing skills in as creative a way as he chose. For me, the show demonstrated that the humor that had gotten me in and out of hot water all my life could be transformed into something real and imaginative. The stories in my head could be written down and enjoyed by others. The floodgates had opened and I was never going to close them again. We felt it was time for something new for the two of us. We just didn't know what it would be . . . yet.

9

Getting Higher, Getting Hired, Getting High Street

As we both took deep hits of hashish in the dim Amsterdam coffee shop, it only took about eighteen seconds for the last eighteen months of our tumultuous lives to lift off our exhausted shoulders. André and I were huddled close together at the table furthest from the front door and furthest from the sound of people passing by on the sidewalk. I had been planning this trip for over a month. It was right around the time of André's birthday and mine, which also stood as the anniversary of when we first met, only three years earlier. Sitting there smoking in that coffee shop, we felt languid and secure, like stringed kites whipping to and fro over a seashore—or at least I did.

I had come to savor the cold-hot blast of serenity that seemed to float off the hashish pipe. I loved how the smoke sank slowly into my lungs, like sweet honey dripping down into a cup of hot chamomile tea. After I held the smoke in as long as I could without coughing, I would let it flow from my mouth slowly, watching it rise calmly out into the air like a translucent cloud. Mixing together the best qualities of alcohol, acid, and pot, this high-grade Dutch hashish was equaled in strength only by the thrill of getting high freely and legally in any Amsterdam spot—the two of us holding hands, no less. Accessible by a three-hour train ride out of Brussels, Amsterdam was like some kind of earthly nirvana for us. In the period after our first *Sketch-Up*, André and I came to regard our trips to Amsterdam as amazingly restorative pilgrimages. In Amsterdam, we could let our hair down, recharge our batteries, free our minds and bodies, and then gear up for re-entry into the trenches of Belgium's comparatively small but stressful entertainment community.

We gradually inhaled ourselves into a cozy haven, sinking into that foreign yet familiar inner zone where people and places and things fall away from thought. I looked into my lover's eyes and saw my own love there, wordlessly reflected back at me. I saw something else in André's face that night as well. I saw a good friend and fellow traveler, bent, bleary, spent, and wearied by a multitude of worries that seemed to have aged him years in only a few months.

"Did it hit you yet, baby?" I asked him. "Are you high?"

He looked at me with his shoulders slumped forward and said, "Everything hits me, Elliot. I do not know if I am high yet. Maybe my head is there, but my heart is heavy." He looked away, seeming almost ashamed of his anguish, but quickly grasped his hands together above my own in what looked like prayer. "I am very, very glad to be away from everything and to be here with you." He smiled, as much for me as for him. He was in pain—I could see it.

I squeezed his hands, told him I loved him, asked him to relax. A few minutes later, I asked him again why he wasn't able to relax.

"Don't know," he said, his voice sluggish but his eyes looking around the bar with a kind of haunted concern. "I think—I mean, that movie really freaked me out."

"Oh, c'mon, André," I said, slightly exasperated. "Are you still spooked by that fucking movie? I told you, that stuff is all made up. You know better than to fall for that crap!"

Perhaps if we hadn't seen *The Exorcist* earlier that day, André wouldn't have been so bothered that night by shadows scooting across the brick walls in the coffee shop. The movie seemed to genuinely terrify him, which was not something I had anticipated. The last thing I had wanted to do was take my overworked Catholic boyfriend to Amsterdam just to scare the shit out of him.

We both had wanted to see the film that William Friedkin had chosen to make after winning the Best Director Oscar for *The French Connection*. If you could read a newspaper on the planet back in early 1974, you could not avoid learning about the incredible sensation that was Friedkin's new film, an adaptation of the best-selling William Peter Blatty novel about a girl possessed by evil. We had read about people getting sick in their seats and fainting at the movie's first showings in America, and watched as the film became an international blockbuster practically without precedent. André's mother had said that she believed the film was an agent of ugliness, and that she hoped we would not go and see it. Renee even wrote me a letter about how she had seen the movie with some friends and how the audience went wild. There was also a personal association—after all, André had appeared in *The French Connection* and had gotten to know Friedkin a bit during the production.

Caught up in the stir surrounding the film, we had ducked into a small Amsterdam movie theater for an afternoon screening. Watching *The Exorcist*, my impulse during much of it had been to laugh. As a Jew and an atheist, I wasn't spiritually invested in the film. It seemed to be ruled by an overwhelming sense of doom and dread that I didn't understand. Because I believed in neither a devil nor a God, the film came across as a story about a mother and her child slowly being driven crazy in a house. Wow, months alone in a house with a woman who had gone bonkers. *Gee, what did that story remind me of?*

André, on the other hand, had sat deathly still during the film. I snuck quick sideways glances at him, and he seemed utterly mesmerized. Certain scenes in the middle of the film really upset him. I reached over to hold his hand a few times, but each time he removed his hand from mine after only a minute or so. The film had a quiet scene right before the big finale, in which it was revealed that the old priest who winds up performing the exorcism on the little girl had actually been writing a new book up in Woodstock. Now that was a scene I liked!

At the coffeehouse after the film, André remained shaken and even a bit sullen, despite several hits of good hashish. I asked him again why the film had bothered him so much, and he paused before telling me. "It just got me thinking about my older sister, Claudette. All the trouble she has suffered trying to raise and take care of her daughter, Marie." He looked down again, trying in vain to stop the tears that were welling up in his eyes. "I remember how hard it was for Claudette. And how she felt maybe God was punishing her for having another child in her forties. I cannot believe that God would punish people so."

I felt bad that the movie had reawakened a family sorrow in him, but I quickly reminded André that there was any number of biological reasons that explained his niece's condition.

After helping him laugh away his fears and convincing him that the devil was not hiding in his hashish smoke, André and I spoke together about the things in the film that we each found most interesting. Talking about the ways in which human behavior was explored so nimbly in the film, André seemed to brighten and even shrug off his earlier fears a bit. "Well, that is something that really does fascinate me, Elliot. The importance of the human face and how film is the best medium through which to represent it."

He continued, "From the stage, you can only bring the audience so close. But I would like very much to make a film that is about people. A story about how much we can learn, or never learn, about each other in this life—with the movie camera as my canvas, rather than the stage. I want to go *further.*"

As stoned as he—*we*—may have been, it was marvelous to hear André sound so passionate about this notion. I told him it was great to think about making a film, especially since he had already mastered all other aspects of production as a director.

He shrugged, though, and looked away from me glumly.

"What is it?" I asked.

"Nothing," he responded unconvincingly. "I just hope that—you know, it is a little sad for me to see how well Friedkin has done with this new film. Remember that I was *in* his previous film. I played a part in making that movie happen. Now it is strange to see how big this new movie is. I guess that is bothering me, too."

He lit a cigarette, and looked me straight in the eye. "I admit it. As a director myself, I feel a bit envious. Who knows if I am ever going to get a chance to direct a film?"

"Don't be so sure," I responded, trying to be supportive. "Life has a funny way of bringing you the very thing that you thought you'd never find. Hell—oops, *pardon*—I mean, heck, I found you, didn't I?"

Before going to Amsterdam, it had been several months since André and I had even been out to see a movie. Ever since we had done the first *Sketch-Up* for

RTB TV, in fact, it seemed that not a spare minute went unused by us. Following the success of our first show and the invitation to make another *Sketch-Up* the following season, André and I began to develop more opportunities to work together. André maintained his position as a director at the Théâtre National. It was a job he valued, even though he wished he could direct pieces that were far more radical in technique and tone than the relatively conservative shows he was then being engaged to stage. I continued to write ideas for skits and routines—several of which were brought directly into the next *Sketch-Up* program—and began again to work on my huge Rothkoesque abstract paintings at the apartment. Through Hal and Catherine, I also made myself available as a lecturer, either for the Fulbright Foundation or at various other colleges and cultural centers throughout Belgium.

I gave my talks primarily in English, with a sprinkling of the few French words that I had picked up. The talks were not only about Woodstock and popular culture, but also on a variety of artistic movements. In particular, I spoke about the Art Deco movement, Surrealism, and the Abstract Expressionist paintings. I had done much work on these topics when going for my Master of Fine Arts degree years before in New York, so I felt I was securely in my element. It was nice to have my own steady source of income, but it had become increasingly clear to me that I was going to have to find other ways to generate enough revenue to keep us in food and rent money—and the shirts that André continued to buy, as was his compulsion.

André's creative frustrations were given an outlet when he was asked to stage la Monnaie's annual production of Wagner's opera *Die Walküre*. The man who owned la Monnaie—technically the Royal Theater of the Mint, and home of Belgium's National Opera—was the brother of the man who managed the Théâtre National. André was told that he was offered the job only because the usual director had taken ill and was unable to mount a production for the 1973 season. Completely new to opera, André took delight in turning the established staging practices upside-down and making the production new again. He told me that he despised how la Monnaie had staged the Wagner opera in years past.

André often told me how disturbed he always had been by what had happened to the Jews during World War II. Even worse, in his opinion, was how so many of his fellow Belgians had turned a blind eye to the atrocities of the

Holocaust during and after the war. To André, the Belgians' continued veneration of Richard Wagner—Hitler's favorite composer, symbol of the Third Reich, and a virulent anti-Semite himself—was disgraceful. With the offer to direct the Wagner opera, André saw a chance both to indict ongoing Belgian anti-Semitism—and to *really* get everyone's attention as a director.

I had no clue what *Die Walküre* was about, so André tried to tell me the story.

"This opera, Elliot, is concerned chiefly with the adventures of a mythical hero-warrior named Siegmund. As the good guy," André continued, "Siegmund is called upon to duel with Hunding. He is the bad guy. During this opera, all of human conflict is presided over by the German war god. His name is Wotan, and—"

"Hold it, his name is Wonton?" I interrupted.

"No, it is *Wotan*. Anyway, he is assisted by a group of stout and large-limbed warrior-goddesses called Valkyries. And these women decide who lives in battle and who dies."

"Why, those sword-wielding bitches!" I said, in mock seriousness. "So then what happens?"

"From there, it gets very complicated. Since it is all sung in German, you will not even know what they are saying anyway. But you can see what happens on the stage. And that is where I will mount my own little revolt against Herr Wagner's material and his fans."

André's first production choice was to hire a separate team of skilled dancers who would use movement to interpret the emotions of the characters sung on the stage by the opera singers. In contrast, the opera singers were to stand as still as possible while they sang. André even planned to costume the singers in huge tent-like white robes that would help disguise any sudden movements they might make as they sang. That way, the audience's attention would also be focused on the deliberate movements of the silent dancers as they acted out the emotions conveyed by the opera singers.

To the opera purists and the performers themselves, André's unorthodox decision to use interpretive dance was already a source of dismay. But then André pushed the production even further. He decided to emphasize Hunding's villainy by always having him appear on stage with a coterie of extras dressed as Nazi soldiers. As a counterbalance, I suggested that he have Siegmund be accompanied by extras dressed in the uniform of the Israeli Defense

Forces. In this way, the conflict between good and evil would be underscored by the opposing armies of extras. Moreover, by transforming *Die Walküre*'s ultra-Aryan hero, Siegmund, into a representative of the Jews, André would also be subtly subverting Wagner's anti-Semitism and forcing his audience to confront their own.

By drawing a clear connection onstage between Wagner and Nazi Germany, André not only made it impossible for the audience to ignore Wagner's anti-Semitism, but also challenged European complacency—the ease with which so many Europeans had chosen to forget World War II and shrug off its aftereffects. He certainly hit his target. Opening night was absolute bedlam, with three separate bomb threats stretching what was already a three-hour-plus production into nearly five hours of raw and bravely reinvented opera. Those who had come to see their Wagner opera sung and performed as it had been each and every year were shocked by the wildness of activity and image there on the stage. As directed by André, the production was incredibly alive and ready to pounce on anyone less than engaged in the very real problems of anti-Semitism that still flowed throughout Europe. He had discovered a gaping hole that resided at the dead center of the culture—and as a result, André got himself noticed as a director.

The good news about that production was that it was reviewed on the front pages of all the Belgian newspapers the very next day. The bad news was that the Théâtre National decided they didn't want that kind of trouble on their own stage and fired André as their director. Still, André's daring artistic choice was a success. The entire five-week run sold out, with so many young people flocking to the production that the opera house had to dust off the little-used balcony section of seats, the top tier. André was absolutely shattered by being fired, though. The high levels of anger and controversy generated by his production of *Die Walküre* left him feeling especially vulnerable as an artist.

Always feeling protective of André, I immediately decided to get him to work with me on developing a new two-character musical play. The working title of the piece was *Attention: Fragile*. The play was about a boy and a girl who progress together through life, from crib to nursing home. Though the show featured a man and a woman on the stage—making their relationship more accessible to a heterosexual audience— the couple was really based on various relationships that André and I had had over the years. As so many artists do, we wrote the show about ourselves. We talked together and wrote out our feelings about when we were adolescents, then teenagers, then struggling into early adulthood, and then where we might be in the final years of life.

As I worked out the details of the story, André began to write French lyrics for the songs in the show. For inspiration, André turned to the Belgian singer-songwriter Jacques Brel, and in particular, his album *Ne Me Quitte Pas,* which in French means "Don't leave me." André listened to the album over and over again, savoring the strong emotion in Brel's lyrical songs of love found and love lost. During the time that we worked together on our new show, the album became one of our favorites. André even helped me with the proper pronunciation of the album's French title, so I didn't sound like a doofus when I mentioned it out loud to our friends and colleagues.

André could sing fairly well, and had a way with words, but he was not a musician and had no experience writing song melodies. So for the music, André reached out to his good friend Claude Lombard, a Belgian singer whom he had met in theater school. Claude had moved to Paris a few years before, and had been singing on a series of popular French television shows. With Claude, the three of us were able to create an exuberant and dynamic score. In rapid order, we got Belgian dancer Monette Loza to do the choreography and were able to interest the popular French actors Anny Duperey and Bernard Giraudeau to play the leads in the show. We were quickly reminded how important a name can be in showbiz. When word got out that Anny Duperey was involved, the show was quickly booked by a theater in Paris. This was great for us, as it helped us gain an artistic foothold outside of Belgium.

As we watched Anny and Bernard perform our show on opening night, it felt as if André and I were watching ourselves up there too—the stage had become our own special mirror. *Attention: Fragile* was swiftly lauded by those critics who had previously taken notice of what André had done with his avant-garde Wagnerian opera. Those in Belgium who had wanted to see what André would do next were surprised and delighted to read about the success of our new show. Though André had crammed nearly every inch of stage with people on *Die Walküre,* he went in the opposite direction on *Attention: Fragile,* heightening the relationship between the two main characters by keeping the production fairly minimal. Two main characters and a few dancers, that was it. When the show finally opened in Belgium some months later, André and I still had no way of knowing that our newest collaboration would continue to be staged throughout the French-speaking regions of Europe for more than three years. We were definitely on a roll, both in our work and our relationship.

A few months later, just after the successful second round of *Sketch-Up,* I suggested to André that we do some live improvisational performances in order to flex our muscles a bit. I wanted to recapture the loose spontaneity with which André and I had shouted out simple ideas and built them into *Sketch-Up* skits. So I suggested that we gather together a small ensemble of six actors, including me and André, who would improvise comical scenes based on a simple word. If someone said "dog," we would build a situation around a dog; if someone said "death," we would have to discover through the live improvisation something that would be funny. I suggested we call it the "Outré Improv Revue."

Unfortunately, we didn't have a French star this time to help us find a place to stage our hastily assembled show. However, we *did* happen upon an empty warehouse in the heart of Brussels, located on a long strip of taverns and dance clubs. The building had been closed down only days before due to a broken water pipe, which had left the place with a pool of stagnant water about three inches deep on the hard concrete floor. Seeing the water, I instantly thought up a gimmick where we would tell people that our improvisational pieces had made people laugh so hard that they had cried buckets—and that if they came wearing their heaviest and highest work boots to see our zany new theater pieces, then they, too, would be a part of the biggest live happening in Belgian theater history.

Admittedly, it was a little scary to have to rig the lighting. One wrong move, one electrocuted performer or audience member, and off André and I would go to prison. Then again, I was used to such precarious circumstances. My parents and I had faced that same fear of electrocution for more than ten years at the El Monaco, where the electrical wiring for light bulbs had been unsafely installed either directly above or very close to our mostly curtainless shower stalls. But this wasn't some ramshackle motel with a theater troupe in the barn, though. With a little bit of my interior-design flair—basically the strategic placement of spotlights around a six-foot-high cement platform that acted as the warehouse's interior loading dock—the "Outré Improv Revue" was housed in what could literally be called a wet dream. Nearly every show we performed those few weeks was sold out, with throngs of young people lining up to get into the new Belgian happening—waffles *not* included.

By the end of that show's brief run, the Théâtre National came back with its tail between their legs, asking André if he would agree to be rehired. He said he would come back, but only on one condition: that they hire *me* to be the dramaturg. I was thrilled that he wanted to involve me, but I quickly pointed out that I had never been a dramaturg before. "If it's like a 'drama queen,' then I think I could do it," I said. I didn't want to mess things up for him.

"No, I do not want you to worry, Elliot," André said. "I want someone there who I can *trust*. I know that you always are there to take care of me, and I need to know I have that from now on. As the dramaturg, your job would be to assist me. So you would be there when I audition actors, there to help me once we head into rehearsals. You would also be expected to research the history of those plays that I direct, and to write up the program notes that will be printed and given to audience members at each show. That is something that you know I already do, Elliot. So all you need to do is follow my directions and listen to everything I say about the work here and at home. By the end of this season, you will know how to be a dramaturg for anyone or any other theater."

So there I was again, throwing myself into the deep end of the pool and trusting fate. As artful as we tried to be, the truth is that André and I were often reacting through sheer instinct to all that was happening over those many months. The great thing was that everything seemed to work, no matter what we tried or what was thrown at us. Yet no matter how exhilarating the work was, it was starting to take a toll on us. No wonder we were both exhausted when we left for our Amsterdam retreat—we needed some rest and relaxation from the lives we were leading!

❁   ❁   ❁

On the second day of our long Amsterdam weekend, still trying to cool off from those months of nonstop creation and performance, André and I had a tasty lunch of onion soup and baguettes near our hotel. We then stopped to buy and scarf down a handful of baked pot cookies from one of the corner reefer bars. Those cookies were even more potent than the ones I had fed to Pop and Momma back at White Lake during the Woodstock summer.

While walking together in the park, deep in our own stoned reveries, I started to think about *The Exorcist* again. One thing that had really stayed with me was the near-constant amount of screaming that took place onscreen. It seemed like the last half of the movie was just a series of blood-curdling shrieks voiced over and over again—I had felt like I was back at the motel with my mother. For fuck's sake, what a ruckus! Other than making me happy that I was gay and that I no longer lived with loud-mouth Momma, all the shouting also reminded me of something that I had first witnessed near our apartment about a year before.

I had been walking in the rue Haute neighborhood near our place, which was located directly across from the Godiva chocolate factory. I was heading toward the market near our apartment building on an early afternoon. As I rounded the corner away from our place, I was stopped in my tracks by the fiercest and most despairing howls of pain I had ever heard. To my complete horror, I watched as a wild-eyed middle-aged woman ran wildly toward a public bus that was sitting at its stop. She proceeded to shout and point her finger accusingly at the passengers entering and exiting the bus. Her shrieks were as much cries of anger as they were cries of sorrow.

I had come to understand a little more French in the months since André and I had presented the first *Sketch-Up,* but the deranged woman was hollering in Bruxellois—a mixture of French and Flemish. Since lots of Flemish is similar to Yiddish, I managed to figure out some of what she was screeching about there in the street. The woman was begging people to stop and help her. She grasped desperately at the arm of one person after another. Each person refused to even look at her as they hurriedly walked away. As she grew more and more frantic, she began to scream through sobs that there was no God. She continued to point accusingly at all those who walked past, saying that no one had done anything to stop it. Then, just as the bus engine revved up and began to drive away, the woman started to yank and rip hysterically at her own hair. She pummeled her fists against the glass door and windows of the rapidly departing bus. Struck by the brutality of it all, I was about to cross the street to see if I could perhaps be of some help to the woman, especially since no one else was doing anything. As I moved to cross the street, though, a gaunt and pale man emerged from the nearest cross street and shouted out to her. She turned to look at him, fell silent as a ghost, and followed him back to a nearby apartment. As quickly as this violent scene had begun, it was over.

Over the following weeks, I had seen the woman and man go through this series of actions on several occasions, and it had been exactly the same way each time. And each time, it ended as quickly as it had started. They disappeared into their apartment building without so much as a murmur. I became curious, and wondered if there might be something I could do to help the woman, who I often saw quietly at her fish wagon in the corner market square. I had even bought some fish from her once, and as if on autopilot, she had simply wrapped the purchase and given me my change. She never spoke a word; she only stared at me vacuously. I felt that I should say something to her, but the situation was too uncomfortable and I retreated to my apartment.

Eventually, I had asked an elderly man I knew at one of the nearby market stalls if he knew the story behind the screaming woman and her mysteriously silent companion. "Those two have been doing that on and off for almost ten years now," he had answered without a trace of sympathy. "Sometimes, they take her away and shut her up for a while. Then she comes back, and starts in again after a few days. Hell, it doesn't matter. Plenty of us have good reasons to scream, but we don't dare. Maybe she knows something we don't." Five months later, the woman and man suddenly left the neighborhood. It was as if the two had never even been there.

Still high and walking together through the park in Amsterdam, I reminded André about that strange, sad woman at the bus stop from months before. He had never seen her himself, since he had always been working at the theater on those days when she would go through her madness. However, he had enough of a picture in his mind from my descriptions. I told André that I had never really stopped thinking about that woman and the quiet man who looked after her. "Did you ever hear what the man would shout to her?" André asked.

"It sounded like he said 'Mimi.' You know, maybe her name was 'Mimi' or something."

"So the woman in the street was . . . a screaming Mimi?" With that, André and I both began to laugh out loud. Perhaps it was from being so stoned or relaxed, but we fell into near-hysterics walking along in the park, thinking about the craziness of that scene. "Well," André said, "all I know is that I can relate now to anyone who feels the need to scream each and every day. I wish that I could shout out like that, just once."

Mimi, her silent caretaker, and their mysterious daily ritual stayed in my mind for the rest of our four-day weekend in Amsterdam, hovering as I drifted off to sleep from the perch of my drug highs. It was with me as we traveled back to Brussels on the train. And it was still with me the day after we returned from our trip, when I found myself fifteen pages into writing my own imagined story about what might have happened to these people. As I thought more and more about Mimi, I wondered to myself, *What in the world happened to this woman? Was she reliving a traumatic moment from her past? And how can anybody manage to stay sane in a life as ruthless and cruel as this one is?* I did not yet know the answers to these questions, but I firmly intended to find out, one way or the other.

❀   ❀   ❀

A week after we returned from our Amsterdam holiday, we received a call from an executive at the RTB TV studios: it had been decided that they would not air a third installment of *Sketch-Up*. Pierre Renoult had not called to tell us the news directly, but he did tell the executive to extend his regret on the cancellation. As a show of support and continuance of the station's apology, the executive told us that a signed letter from Renoult would entitle André and me to use any available office space or editing equipment at the RTB studios. Though we were disappointed that another *Sketch-Up* was not in the cards, the cancellation did take some anticipated pressure off our shoulders. Anyway, the "Outré Improv Revue" shows we had done in that dingy theater represented what we really wanted to do in humor. We thanked Renoult for generously allowing us to continue using RTB office space and editing machines. Soon enough, both would prove to be surprisingly helpful.

That same week after Amsterdam, I also received a letter from Renee. Shortly after that letter, she sent another to us in which she broke the news that she had finally gotten a divorce from Freddy. It turned out he had fallen in love with a woman about thirty years older than he was. The woman was a wealthy widow with no children, so I figured Freddy probably saw her as a chance to back out as a husband and a father and be reborn as just another scumbag gigolo. I quickly wrote back to Renee, conveying my condolences for her pain and also my congratulations on her reclaiming her freedom. I told her that André and I wanted her to come with Alyse and visit us that summer in Belgium, and offered to pay for their plane tickets. I wanted them both to have some fun.

She soon wrote back that she already had enough money saved and was going to come to see us in Belgium for a few weeks in July, when Alyse would be off from school and could come along with her. She had already obtained passports, and was so proud that she would be able to bring her daughter to experience Europe at such a young age. Reading the letter, I was so happy that they were going to come and see us that I began to cry. It was only then that I realized how much I had truly missed them.

In early July, we rented a car and drove to meet Renee and Alyse at the airport. The minute that André parked the car outside the airport terminal, I was out of the car and taking large strides toward the arrival gate. I couldn't wait to see them, and I was especially excited to show Alyse that we lived across the way from the immense Godiva chocolate factory. After standing for what felt like four hours, I finally saw my sister and Alyse walking toward us. Renee was schlepping two suitcases, but she managed a great big smile when she and Alyse saw me and André. All at once, I saw in Alyse my baby sister as I remembered her from childhood—and I also saw in Renee the woman and mother who had just gone through a very rocky period in her life. I ran to my sister and my niece with my arms opened wide, and scooped each of them up in a big bear hug filled to the brim with the kind of love that I no longer felt ashamed to show.

The first few days of Renee and Alyse's visit were spent taking them around to sample typical Belgian restaurants, see the wonderful sights of the city, and generally let Renee and Alyse adjust to the time difference and the mild culture shock. As good hosts, we gave them the use of our king-sized bed while André and I took turns sleeping on the couch or on the rollaway cot. André arranged for Renee and Alyse to have a full personal tour of the Théâtre National, which they found fascinating. They were both very impressed with the lives that André and I were living in Belgium. Alyse even said that she wanted to leave New Jersey and come live with us. I told my sister that if my niece were anything like I had been when I was her age, her desire to live with us probably had something to do with that big chocolate factory down the street.

It took a few days before Renee and I really got the chance to talk about things. As I suspected, she was still in a state of shock from the divorce. She was glad to be free of Freddy, though, and wanted very much to start her life over again. "I figure if you were able to start life over and move to Belgium," she said to me, "then maybe I have a chance to start fresh, too." We avoided it at first, but it was inevitable that Renee would tell me about the other members of my family. My sisters Goldie and Rachelle were living precisely as they had been doing before I left—comfortably set with money, but uncomfortably upset by pretty much anything else.

Then it was time to ask about Momma. I wanted to know if she was happy living at her place in Monticello, and if she was still healthy. "Yep, Momma's doing just fine," Renee said, with a bit of a sigh. "She is the loudest and most ardent supporter of the kosher butcher shop there in town, and she never misses a chance to go to the synagogue. At least that's what she tells me when I call. I don't visit too often, but I call at least once a week."

"And does she ever mention Pop to you? Has she ever gone to his gravesite?" It was a question I had not thought about much, but I knew it was the question that I had to ask.

"I don't even ask her anymore," Renee said, sounding very weary. "She keeps telling me that she is going to leave America and return to Israel." My mother had often said that she wanted to be closer to God by living in Jerusalem. "She also says to me how she always tells the local rabbi that her one and only son is doing important work in Belgium. Oh, and that you're not married." At least she was right on one count. I was still single, but I was learning a lot more about the Jews of Belgium than I ever could have imagined.

By the time of Renee's visit, I had already written and typed up about a hundred pages of a manuscript. Without intending to do so, I had started to write a novel shortly after André and I returned from Amsterdam. The book's working title was *The Woman Who Screamed on Rue Haute,* and it was completely inspired by the woman whom I had come to think of as "Mimi." I was haunted by the idea of what it was that made the woman act with such despair in that same single spot for years. Had she been raped? Had she been robbed, never able to bring the thief to justice? Had she witnessed a death there? I figured that I would never know the truth, so I decided to piece together my own version of what happened through writing.

Some members of the Royal Library of Belgium in Brussels had become familiar with me because of my lectures, and granted me access to their archives for the purpose of research. It was at the library that I learned more about Belgium under Nazi occupation during World War II. I read that in 1943, more than forty thousand Belgian Jews were rounded up by the Nazis and sent to their deaths, along with millions of other European Jews, in the camps and ovens of Auschwitz and Buchenwald.

Around that time, I came across a black-and-white documentary on television. I sat there alone in the apartment, feeling totally frozen, as I watched historical footage of Nazis herding Jews into buses right there in the rue Haute section of the city. It was one thing to read of the horrors that had happened in the city where I now lived, but it was another thing entirely to see, both on film and in photographs, the unstoppable force with which the Nazis had gutted the peace and civility of an entire city.

The many other library documents I found pointed out that in many instances, Jewish husbands, wives, and children were separated and taken away from their Gentile spouses and parents. When I read that, I immediately felt that I knew what had happened to Mimi. As I came to write it in my manuscript, Mimi was a guilt-ridden Catholic woman who lost her Jewish husband and child to the German Nazis during the war. Years later, she returned each day to the spot where she lost her husband and child. What was now a bus stop had been the place where Mimi witnessed the Nazi troopers force her husband into a truck filled with other Jews. It was the spot where, during a scuffle, a soldier had knocked Mimi's young son David down to the cobblestone street, hitting his head hard against a stone. Mimi had been kept at bay by a guard, unable to help her son. Then, her child dying in the street, she had watched as the truck with her husband pulled away. Standing nearby was the local priest, staring silently first at the dead child and then at Mimi. She shrieked at him, "How can you stand there and do nothing? You, a man of God—how can you stand there and not help my baby?"

I had most of it figured out, but I still didn't know who the mysterious man was, or why he showed up each day to quietly lead Mimi away from the commotion. Was he a fellow Belgian? I didn't know what place he would play in my story, but I figured that I might discover his part in the secret story as I continued to write. In addition, I decided that the story needed to be told by a witness to the events—a witness who would also represent me and my curiosity. So I invented the character David Rheinhardt. "David" was the same name I'd given Mimi's dead son; reminded of her boy, Mimi would then be motivated to share her story, providing the basic structure for the book. And the last name "Rheinhardt" was chosen as an homage to my old Brooklyn College professor and friend Ad Reinhardt; with such a name, it was obvious that David should also be an American painter.

Because writers write what they know, the character featured many other details from my own life. Being gay, I could only imagine initially that David was also gay. When I told Renee, though, she suggested instead that I make the character straight. "But why should I do that?" I asked. Her response was clearly influenced by what had happened to her with Freddy. "Why not have him be a straight artist who uses women like objects and is never true to any of them? Then," she continued, with a deep sigh, "when he stops and sees the true suffering of this woman, and also witnesses the loyalty of the mysterious man to her, he is forced to question perhaps the largest mystery of all—himself."

It was a good point. A brilliant one, in fact, and I thanked Renee for the suggestion. Maybe it gave her some feeling of closure to be able to stitch her own terrible memories of Freddy into a larger and more meaningful mosaic. My story suddenly had purpose, direction, and a genuine mystery waiting at the end. Now I just had to finish writing it. That would prove more difficult than I could have imagined, even with all that chutzpah running through my veins. It also took André and me into entirely new creative territory.

❀   ❀   ❀

September 1974

Dear Sis,

It's your sweet and gorgeous brother Eliyahoo here. Well, who didja you think it would be, Yul Brynner on a flying carpet?

I wanted to tell you again how wonderful it was for André and me to have you and Alyse with us here in the Land of Waffles & Chocolate. By the way, I hope that you and Alyse haven't already gobbled through the twenty pounds of Godiva that we bought for you as our special "Au revoir" gift. Did it survive in the luggage, or did it get all gooey? I'd like to know, in case I myself should ever choose to return.

You'll be glad to know that I am now more than halfway finished with the first draft of the novel. At your suggestion, I have made David straight so we can be meaner to him. If we ever get a movie made with this story, they'll all say that Elliot gave up the baseball bat and went back to the catcher's mitt! Just think how proud Momma will be of her gay son's decision to finally marry the Monticello rabbi's old-maid daughter—y'know, the one with the big jugs and that rare collection of edible prayer shawls?

André has helped me figure out the identity of the man who is Mimi's partner in her daily ritual of trauma. The way André sees it, the man is a former Nazi soldier who was on the truck the night they took away Mimi's husband and killed her son back in 1943. He returns after the war to look after Mimi as an attempt at amends. I think it's an amazing solution to the mystery. As a result, I've told him that he and I are now co-authors of the book. He also suggested that we trim down the title a bit. It's now called Rue Haute *(which means "High Street" in English, if you're going to be* that *way about it!).*

Meanwhile, I have a surprise. As of last night, André and I are in the smut business!

That's it for now. Write me back if you want to know more. I'm such a tease, right?

Ta ta! (See you at the movies—well, maybe!)

Love & Hugs,
Elliot

❀ ❀ ❀

After Renee and Alyse had returned to America, I had intended to work only on the novel. I still didn't know if I had anything good, but I was thoroughly involved in what I was creating and I didn't question my motivations for a second. However, money was becoming tight and I wanted to contribute to our household earnings. While the lion's share of my Woodstock nest egg was still safely stowed away in my New York bank, I remembered all those years of being nearly bankrupt, and I was never going to do anything to put me back in that dreadful position.

That's when I thought of Victoria. During the production of the second *Sketch-Up* special, André and I had met a French Canadian movie producer named Victoria Waubert. She and her husband Sebastian were working in rental production offices at the RTB studios, dubbing English dialogue onto a slew of European movies for which they had bought American distribution rights. Her English was far better than my French, so we had no trouble understanding each other. Victoria had a charming and boisterous personality, and as we were working in the same space, I often stopped into her office to see what she was up to. Back then, Victoria and Sebastian had offered me a job writing dialogue for them, knowing that I had a certain amount of authority as the cocreator of *Sketch-Up*. At the time, I had been too busy with *Sketch-Up* and our other projects, so I had politely declined the offer. Now pressed for cash, I reconsidered.

So I called Victoria up and said I would be happy to work as a writer for hire on her dubbed movies. I reminded her of my limitations with French, but she said it wouldn't matter at all. I also told her that I knew next to nothing about dubbing; she said it was something she could easily teach me how to do. What she couldn't teach me, and what she needed from me the most, was the ability to write good and interesting dialogue in English. She also needed readers who spoke clear American English and could put on different types of American accents for the dubbing process. Since she was having trouble getting American actors in Brussels, I'd have to secure their availability for Victoria as well. I knew how to write, but the casting process was really André's area of expertise. So I invited André to join the cash-only project, and asked if he could help us find and audition some experienced American actors. That was when André pulled me aside.

"Elliot," he said in a serious voice, "what do you know about these films that you are being asked to dub?"

"Well, Victoria said it would just be writing English dialogue that can be spoken and dubbed into a variety of European movies that they—"

"Yes, yes, but have you *seen* any of these films?"

I stopped for a moment. "Um, no, I haven't. But it sounds like a good way for us to earn some cash quick and easy. Remember that charcoal mohair shirt you saw?"

Before he agreed to get involved with Victoria and Sebastian, André told me that we would have to schedule a meeting to find out what kind of films we would be working on. I called Victoria, who arranged to meet with us at her office in the early evening.

At least André was kind enough not to call me a naïve boob out loud during the meeting. As he had suspected, the Wauberts were distributors of pornographic movies. The forbidden genre had received a jolt of mainstream attention the year before, when *Deep Throat* was released in theaters. Rumored to be yet another low-budget piece of sleaze earning big bucks for the mob back in New York, the film had sparked a new fascination with the porno film as a potential work of art. Even more important, it revved up the market for the many other "dirty" movies that began to play at seedy movie houses running along the Times Square section of midtown Manhattan. There was suddenly all kinds of cash to be made from skin flicks—and we were being asked to write dialogue for them.

The only serious hitch at the time was that Belgium had strict laws that prohibited the making of pornographic films within the country. The films that the Wauberts were peddling, however, were not hardcore features that showed actual penetration. They were what the industry called "softcore" films, in which nudity was shown but any sex was entirely simulated. Frankly, after seeing some predubbed footage from one of the films that night in Victoria's office, it seemed safer to declare these movies to be strictly "borecore"!

All the scenes were edited to cut the action just when things were starting to really get interesting. I was surprised that anyone would even want to see these movies, since they contained so many abrupt cuts. Victoria then explained that hardcore sex scenes featuring penetration would later be spliced back into the films in Amsterdam and then sent on to the American market. In this way, the strict Belgian codes regarding pornography would not be broken. The beauty of the deal, according to Victoria, was that anything brought into New York through Europe was assumed to be the very dirtiest and most erotic of all the pictures. Once the distributors received their cans of trashy sex pictures from overseas, they were convinced that they had something pretty hot on their hands and never stopped to doubt the relative quality of what they had paid to put in the theaters.

Interestingly, we came to learn from Victoria that there were two theaters in downtown Brussels that showed pornos. They were located only a few streets over from our apartment, in fact. André and I went to one later that night after meeting with Victoria, and we discovered that many of the patrons were gay men. The fact that the films featured straight sex didn't seem to bother them. Every night, there were several men getting it on with each other in the balcony and in the few dark stairwells facing the white movie screen. We also learned that although public exhibition of pornography was illegal in Belgium, the local policemen were being paid regular bribes by the theater owners so that the cops would not shut down the films or arrest anyone in attendance.

For me, the whole situation was a surreal return to my early teen years—all that forced yet enjoyable sexual molestation at the hands of those desperately oversexed guys in the Times Square movie houses. And now I was going to be paid to write the horny English dialogue that would be heard by both the abusers and the abused in those horndog sex theaters back home in the Big Apple. André and I would be well paid for our efforts. In order to maintain our legitimate reputations, we chose pseudonyms for ourselves—"Tondalah Yellowitz" was mine, while André opted for "Prince Shlomo Nedogadach."

Victoria and Sebastian's clever business plan involved purchasing uncompleted movies from Germany, France, Spain, Italy, Thailand, and even Russia. Producers who could not find the funding to finish their projects were perfectly glad to sell their raw footage at bargain-basement rates. Victoria would take the beginning of one unfinished feature from Italy, insert the middle part of an entirely different film from Spain, and then conclude the feature with a small length of footage filmed in Bangkok. In this way, she was able to market, sell, and distribute full feature-length movies regardless of what went on in the beginning, the middle, or the end.

In addition, many of the foreign moviemakers from whom Victoria bought work had no funds to record a soundtrack. The actors could be seen speaking in their native tongues, but they could not be heard at all. Once we had our meeting and Victoria spent a few hours showing us how to loop and sync spoken dialogue so that it would match closely to the action captured on film, I was given my first five films to dub. Since there were no scripts, and since there were very different actors and sets in the shabbily spliced-together segments, it was my job as dialogue writer to somehow try to give the story some sense and basic narrative flow. It was experimental filmmaking, all right, but completely by accident. To me, it was totally hilarious. I loved every absurd second of it.

We established a plan of attack. Victoria would hurriedly splice several unrelated and incomplete movies into a single feature, though later she would show André and me how to do it ourselves, giving us that much more practical experience. Once I had a fully spliced movie, I would watch the mouths of the actors and try to improvise English dialogue that would form the kind of storyline I figured most normal Americans would understand. We were told by Victoria that it really didn't matter what we had the actors say. What was important was that the dialogue be synched as closely as possible to the movement of the onscreen actors' mouths. Not that the "raincoat crowd" would be paying attention to the dialogue anyway, of course.

At first, I really tried to make some sense out of what I was being given. In a movie built around a "sexy Zorro" plot, for example, a tall Spanish actor arrived as Zorro on a white horse in the first third of the film. Then in the middle, this Zorro suddenly became a taller and longer-haired Italian actor who rode around on a brown horse. By the final half hour of the movie, Zorro turned into a bald and much shorter actor from Taiwan sitting atop what looked like a sick donkey! Sexy Spanish Zorro—tall with dark hair—leapt through the window of a hacienda. He was greeted upon arrival by a beautiful damsel with bright red hair and a billowy white gown. But in the very next shot, Sexy *Italian* Zorro ran toward the damsel. The formerly red-haired damsel was now a blond, and her white gown became dark red plaid. I had to be especially inventive when it came time to explain the appearance of the Sexy *Taiwanese* Zorro. Looking at the footage in the screening room, André said it would be impossible to stitch together any dialogue that would make sense to a movie patron.

Here was a moment when my twisted sense of humor came in handy. I simply had one of the damsels say:

"Oy vey, Zorro! What a miracle how you changed from a Spaniard to a Sicilian right in front of my very eyes!"

Then as the Italian Zorro, I exclaimed, "My dear, I believe that blond hair suits you better than the red hair! But remember, I'm not paying those fancy-shmancy beauty parlor bills! What kind of a schmuck do you think I am? Go walk the streets later tonight if you're going to pay that faggot hairdresser's outrageous prices!"

And when Taiwanese Zorro appeared, the suddenly black damsel crisply demanded, "Look here, Kato, you remember to bring me that chow mein takeout like I told ya?"

As I continued to work and rework with André the very emotional and deeply upsetting material that was at the heart of *Rue Haute,* those weekly sex flick dubbing sessions became a very entertaining means of escape for us. And the more dialogue we wrote and dubbed into the films, the more work we got.

On one of the more clumsily edited films, there was a long lesbian seduction scene between two naked women. After taking a look at the footage, we both agreed that we were watching one of the classier unfinished foreign films. We came to this conclusion because when the two women started to get all hot and heavy, a magnificent white horse suddenly stepped in front of the camera—and then stayed there. The horse just stood in place and moved its head up and down and around for about five minutes. For fun, I decided to record myself improvising an entire speech as if the horse was talking direct-ly to the audience. Using an exaggerated Brooklyn gangster accent, I had Vito the Horse complain about his early years as a gelding; his constant need for attention, which almost led to him getting the part as Mr. Ed on American tel-evision; the relative quality of Belgian versus Flemish feedbags; and, of course, his hidden and very hot gay affair with the Lone Ranger's horse, Silver. Upon seeing the finished "Sexy Zorro" movie with our English dialogue alongside the newly added sex stuff, André and I thought the end result was hilarious.

The logic of the three Zorros and two different damsels was skewered enough before they added the more explicit sex scenes. But to my amazement, Victoria got reports that our lesbian and talking horse picture was one of her most popular titles.

Looking over our handiwork one night, I saw that we had a few scenes featuring different actors and actresses, all pounding away like troopers while cheaply recorded funk music and jazz droned on in the background. Since I did care a little about the overall quality of these movies, I asked Victoria later that week if we might also be able to dub in the moans and groans during the silent sex scenes. Touched by my commitment to the work at hand, she agreed.

And that's when the NATO wives came into the picture.

I had given another of my more comical lectures for the Fulbright Foundation a few weeks earlier, on the fifth anniversary of the Woodstock concert. André actually took the day off to come and see my presentation, which made me feel both proud and a little nervous. Hal and Catherine were there as well, and they were the ones who introduced André and me to a small group of American women who were seated together in the front row of the amphitheater. As we soon learned, the women were either mothers of Fulbright scholarship students or wives of military men in high positions at the nearby NATO headquarters. They were thrilled to discover that we were involved in the world of theater and television. I told them that we were actually working on several film projects together, which made the women seem to flutter with excitement. Catherine asked if André and I would be willing to offer the NATO wives a little tour of our offices at RTB TV so they could see how a real movie was made. I hadn't expected this, but I knew an opportunity when I saw one. Before André could reveal my exaggeration, I cut in:

"Why," I heard myself say, "we would love to have these enchanting ladies come and see some real live movie magic! Can you join us tonight?"

The ladies were exhilarated by my gracious offer. André was less amused. When one of the wives asked me what they should wear to the event, I told them to dress as stylishly as possible. Catherine mouthed the word "Merci!" to me as André and I left for the car to take us back home.

In the car, I asked André what he thought of my lecture. He said that, considering it was about Woodstock, he was very impressed by my delivery and my enthusiasm. After a few seconds, he turned back to me. "Elliot, what exactly are you planning to do with those five NATO wives at the editing session tonight?"

"Well, my dear," I said, with a mischievous grin, "let's just say that those ladies' voices could be music to our ears!"

We had told the women to arrive no later than eight o'clock, and to make sure to have the front desk officer call up to us at our special RTB phone. Once we had them with us in the editing suite, I explained to the ladies that André and I were currently working on an edgy and somewhat risqué art film. We had a small group of American actresses who were supposed to have come, I told them, but who had been delayed by a week or more as they finished work on another picture.

"André and I had hoped to show you how the dubbing process is done in the movies," I said, my voice forlorn as André looked down at the floor, "but now it looks like it's not going to happen. I'm so sorry, but—"

I waited a beat, looked at the ladies, and said in wide-eyed wonder, "But of course! Yes, it makes perfect sense. André, what if we were to ask *these* fine ladies here to stand in for the American actresses?"

"No, we cannot do that," André said, starting to catch on to what I had in mind. "It is against the studio rules, because these women are not trained members of the acting profession."

"Oh, what can it possibly matter?" I continued, in feigned indignation. "After all, ladies, you have such lovely voices and I would hate for you to have come all this way for nothing."

André again began to wring his hands, seemingly in the throes of a grand ethical dilemma when one of the women said to me, "Please, Mr. Tiber, we are adult women here, not children. What is it, exactly, that happens in a dubbing session?"

I looked at the women, who eagerly awaited my response.

"Well, it's really quite simple," I continued. "You just need to speak into this microphone over here," I said, gesturing toward the microphone clipped in place atop its metal stand. "You stand here and you say certain words and sentences in English as they are needed in the movie. This picture is a kind of symbolic journey of the self. Nothing is what it seems to be in our story, you see? In fact, people and places and things seem to change shape and form throughout. What we need in order to make sense of the journey for the view-er are those English-speaking voices. If you wish, *you* can provide those English-speaking voices tonight."

The five women looked at each other, giggling and blushing a little as they talked it over. Then they turned and collectively nodded their assent to our request.

"That's fantastic!" I exclaimed, "Just watch, this is going to be so much fun. First, let's do some voice tests so we can get a good level on the volume."

André stifled his laughter as I guided each of the women toward the microphone, and asked them to say their name out loud to me in their most seductive-sounding voice. They all seemed like they had been left to stew in boredom for years by their absentee husbands and overachieving kids. Each of them assumed an elegant but sexy persona as they spoke their names under my slightly exaggerated direction. Suddenly, NATO Wife #1—Carol—became *CAHHH-roll*. NATO Wife #2—Janet—was now *Jah-NETT*, while Wife #3—Barbara—turned into *Bah-buh-RAHH* and Wife #4—Dominique—changed into *Dah-mo-NEEEEEK*. NATO Wife #5—Meg, the outspoken leader of the pack—was still Meg, no matter how hard she tried. In order to help her have a good time as well, I told her to go with another name. And so Meg changed into *Joooo-li-ANNE*—for the evening, at least.

I complimented the women on the sounds of their voices and the look of their fancy dresses.

"Now listen, Carol darling—"

"Call me *CAHHH-roll*, you sexy man," she cooed.

"Oh yes, *CAHHH-roll*," I responded, trying not to laugh. "Now what's happening here in this scene is that you play a naughty French maid who has been caught stealing an expensive jewel from your mistress. To teach you a lesson, she bends you over her knee and begins to spank you long and hard." Her eyes were wide like saucers as I continued to weave the spell. "At first you resist, but then the sound of your voice indicates that you really enjoy it. Just when you think you can't take any more of this sweet pain, the master of the house comes walking into the room."

"I will be the voice of the master," André chimed in.

"Yes, and then I will need you to sound really excited, especially when the other French maids"—I gestured at the other four NATO wives when I said this—"also come into the bedroom and join in the fun."

"Wait a second," said Meg, suddenly shaking free of her *Joooo-li-ANNE* persona. "Mr. Tiber, I thought you said this was an art movie! It doesn't sound like one! What kind of movie is this, anyway? This isn't one of those dirty movies we've been hearing about lately?"

"Have you ever seen director Ingmar Bergman's great film *Persona?*" I asked, putting on a cerebral tone and trying my best not to blow things. "Well, that film dealt with the idea of merging identities. You see, the movies we are working on here are also meant to examine desire and pleasure through the use of many different actors and actresses, uh, playing the same roles. Yes, it's experimental in a way, but I can assure you that whatever lovemaking there may be, all the scenes have a limited *explicissity.*"

"Limited what?" she asked.

I was clutching at straws now with my made-up word, but I continued in the most certain tone I could muster. "Limited explicissity. Indeed, yes, that is what it means to show the passion of lovemaking without showing the actual act, uh, itself. Which I think really separates dirty movies from art films."

I turned to the others and tried to point out to them that our experimental art picture would only truly work if they were able to bring every spark of passion and verve that they could to the dubbing sessions. "However," I said, "if you feel that you can't do this, then André and I would certainly understand. We will have to wait for the American actresses to be finished in another week or so."

"No, we *want* to do this," said *Jah-NETT*. "But what do you want us to *say?*"

"That's just it, my dears," I said, building my case. "You don't have to say any words, really. I want you to take those sultry voices of yours and make the most pleasurable sounds you know how to make here into the microphone. Here, let's start with Carol—I mean, *CAHHH-roll*. You watch the scene shown here," I said, pointing at the playback viewing screen in the center of the editing machine, "and use your voices to help make the scene come alive!"

"And do not worry, ladies," André said as he seated himself among them, "since I will provide my voice to the scene as well, I can assure you that your special work here tonight will remain totally anonymous."

"Yes, that's right," I said, grinning slyly, "this can be our sweet little secret. Now, are we all ready for our close-ups?"

With that, I flicked the light switch on the wall near the locked office door, made my way back to the editing machine, and whispered the one word that all people wait to hear when they are making their first movies: "Action!"

That night, André and I made clandestine diplomatic history. We dubbed the erotic moans and groans of five hot and eager NATO wives into a scene that featured naughty French maids pleasuring each other—not to mention the mistress and master of their house—with limited *explicissity*, of course. They voiced their parts so convincingly that I didn't even bother trying to have them sync up to the mouths of the actors onscreen. We did one recording and let nature take its course. André certainly proved he was a brilliant voiceover artist, sounding as aroused as the ladies did. Afterward, we all needed cigarettes.

Just one dubbing session and the NATO wives were hooked. They signed on to become our in-house vocal artists, helping André and me to dub more than sixty movies—and at a very reasonable rate, too. They formed an odd little club. While waiting for us to set up the equipment and cue the scenes, the ladies would either trade recipes or sit patiently and knit. When we were ready to record their voices, they moved into position and gave it their best effort. I really was learning how to succeed in this thing called showbiz!

Unfortunately, everything came to a sudden halt when Belgian and Flemish policemen arrived at the RTB TV studios one night to arrest Victoria and Sebastian as the producers of illegal porno movies. It was our profound luck not to be there doing a dubbing session that night. Instead, all that the policemen found were a few reels of silent film that Victoria had not yet edited together into a feature. We heard through the grapevine that after their release from jail the next day, Victoria and Sebastian had emptied their apartment and completely disappeared. Later, André heard that they had set up a similar operation in Luxembourg. We considered ourselves lucky to have made some money, gained some editing and dubbing skills, and gotten out unscathed. André and I had a terrific time doing it. It was fast, it provided the cash to keep us in food and rent and shirts, and it allowed me to spend my days writing the novel now called *Rue Haute*.

⚘   ⚘   ⚘

In writing the character of Mimi, I tried to draw upon the Jewish women who had come into my mother's shop when I was younger. Many of them had come from Europe after the war. Even as a child, I could see the pain of the war on their faces. It affected the way that they acted and even how they spoke. I recalled women walking about our store with eyes wide open, often skittish and easily rattled by loud sounds. Some of these women spoke softly and were thin like birds, while others were big and tubby and given to sharp gestures and even sharper voices. I saw Mimi as being somewhere in between those two types of women, and I felt that her traumatic experiences in the story would resonate with those who lived through the war and those who were born right after it.

Except perhaps for the cruelty of the Nazi characters, I was never able to draw upon any of my mother's personal traits for the book. As ever, Momma remained a total mystery to me. All that tenderness, all that pain and heartache and broken life that seemed to bleed out of Mimi like the blood of her murdered son senselessly spread upon the cobblestone street—I never for one moment believed that my mother could ever feel that way about me. When I placed the final typed page of my novel face down on top of my man-uscript, I wept long and hard at the loss of Mimi. It was a loss of not just the character I had created, but of the real woman in Belgium whose life story would remain entirely unknown to me.

Having completed the novel, I went out for a walk and found myself day-dreaming. I kept seeing in my mind the characters as they now existed on the page. I kept thinking about how visual the book really was. In many ways, I had actually seen the story in my mind as if it were a movie. I had loved movies ever since I was a little kid, but the bad taste from my failed trip to Hollywood was still in my mouth. Now I had created something that I felt was begging to be turned into a film. As I walked back to the apartment, I started to think about the experience I had gotten doing *Sketch-Up* for TV. I also thought about those dozens of movies on which I had dubbed dialogue. It seemed so clear to me that *Rue Haute* the book was destined now to become *Rue Haute* the movie.

When André got home that night, I told him that I had finished the novel—and I thought we should try to make a film of it. After reading my final pages, André applauded my work and wholeheartedly agreed that it had the makings of a movie. He reminded me, however, that neither he nor I had any film connections or any experience writing a screenplay. I explained to him that I had already been to American Library in Brussels the week before, where I had been led to a lone shelf that held a few dozen American movie scripts. I devoured the scripts, studying their format and taking many notes. I wasn't about to allow a little detail like my lack of know-how or established track record in the film industry prevent me from writing a screenplay treatment and synopsis of a story concerning such a tortured soul as Mimi. I was determined to make a movie that would shine a light on the Holocaust as it had taken place throughout Belgium. Tired from another day at the theater but warmed by my optimism, André simply wished me luck with it and went off to take a hot bath.

Over the next few weeks, I used our not-yet-published novel as a starting point and began to construct my first screenplay. Using published scripts and books on screenwriting that I'd found at the library as a general guide, I carved my manuscript into a screenplay in under two weeks. I might have missed my chance back in Hollywood, but I was determined to get involved in the movie industry now. Never one to just sit and wait for things to happen, I decided to consult the Brussels phone book in search of Belgian movie producers. I made several phone calls, all of which I began with the same question: "Uh, hello, do you speak English?"

The first dozen *producteurs* didn't speak English. Then, finally, a man named Pierre Druot picked up the phone and answered "Yes." *Bingo!* I introduced myself and explained that my partner was the Belgian director André Ernotte. As fate would have it, Pierre and his business partner, Alain Guillaume, had attended the INSAS College around the same time as André had and already knew him. André had studied theater while Pierre majored in cinema studies and Alain went for an entertainment business degree. I took it as a good sign for the project that my cold calls had brought us directly to these two men.

Meeting with the producers at their office, André picked up with them precisely where they had left off in college. Alain and Pierre both liked the film synopsis we presented. They thought it was a remarkable story with strong movie potential. Pierre told André that if he could adapt the full script from English into French, then he would be able to submit it to the Belgian film ministry and apply for a grant. Furthermore, he explained, the film ministry always had funding for developing Belgian directors. Given his newness to the medium of motion pictures, André stood a good chance of being given the necessary funds for us to make the film. His already extraordinary national reputation in theater and television only increased the likelihood that he would be chosen. There was just one stumbling block. André needed to demonstrate that he had some experience in film before the film ministry provided the funds to back a feature film.

Pierre suggested a way around the problem. The ministry would have no problem in funding a short film. Once the short film was finished, it would have to be shown and judged as worthy by the ministry before they approved a feature-length project for production. André looked at me. I looked at him, and then I said, "Not a problem, Pierre. When do we get started?"

I set myself to writing out an idea that André could then direct. A story had occurred to me when Renee had visited with Alyse. One day, Alyse had been talking nonstop to Renee about anything and everything that seemed to pop into her head. Though she adored her daughter, Renee had clearly begun to get a bit frustrated. I saw my sister as a mother at that moment, and it was strange because her maternal role made her seem older than me, even though she was the younger one.

From that memory, I came up with an idea about a mother and daughter. As an old mother sits quietly knitting, her daughter, who is in her thirties, sits with her mother and complains about all that is going wrong in her life. At the end of the daughter's self-indulgent rant, she looks over at her mother and realizes that she has keeled over dead.

André liked the simplicity of the plot. He felt he could do much by cutting between the two women—one face old, the other face young; one woman speaking, the other woman silent—to suggest the incredible gulf that exists between those who are often considered the closest. André decided the film should be titled *Marée Basse* (French for "low tide"). I was a little confused by the title, and asked him about it.

"So what's the title mean?" I asked.

"The title is symbolic, Elliot," André said, sounding a bit like a snooty professor. "It highlights the mother's need to be safe and unbothered in her old age—just like ships that remain safely anchored in port during low tide. Why? What would you call it?"

"How about *Death by Kvetch* as a title?"

"A little too artsy, Monsieur Tiber," André said.

"Okay, then," I retorted, pretending to be hurt. Actually, I didn't care what the title was. He could have called it *Mary Poppins vs. the Colostomy Bag* if he wanted. I only wanted to get us to a place where we could make a film of *Rue Haute*.

With the small budget provided to us by the ministry, we assembled a tiny crew and hired two actresses, shooting in an apartment owned by one of André's theater associates in Brussels. On *Sketch-Up*, André and I had already begun to hone our abilities to develop the shape and pacing of a story. It was a revelation, however, not to have to work live. This freed us up creatively, as we were able to alter camera placement and shot angle, and to explore storytelling through editing—a process that had not been available to us during our live broadcasts.

Everyone was very professional, and I watched André's sensitive direction with the two actresses. In contrast to his brash and sometimes anarchic style in handling live performances, André chose to give his two actresses a range of subtle directions that were perfectly suited to the movie camera. It was really wonderful to see him working for the first time in a brand-new medium, and using my first screenplay, no less. It was a great moment for us both. At this point in our relationship, we were not only best friends. Through my own trial-by-fire entry into the world of theater and TV and film, we were also now equals. We were making artistic statements that would not have existed in that same way if we hadn't been working together.

After the two-day film shoot, André then set himself to the task of editing the film. He had shot the scenes at various angles and with different types of lighting, giving him more than enough footage to play with. André had always been handsome to me, but he became completely beautiful as he worked in his very intense and focused way on cutting the picture. It took about a week for him to put together a final cut, but the finished film presented two solidly defined characters in a small story that resolves itself in the time allotted and that looked quite good on the screen. Pierre told us that the ministry had enjoyed the short—particularly André's deft direction of the two actors—and were inclined to fund a feature.

Encouraged by the positive experience of making the short, André became fully committed to *Rue Haute*. He worked nearly every night until the early morning hours, feverishly translating my English-language screenplay into French and grabbing only two or three hours of sleep a night. In a couple of weeks, the French-language screenplay was done. Pierre submitted it to the Belgian film ministry. A month later, we got an official letter stating that their standard grant for 35 percent of the film's overall budget would be given to André.

Only 35 percent! We were shocked. Since much of the arts in Belgium were completely underwritten by the government, we had expected the ministry to underwrite the entire production. We asked Pierre what had happened, and he explained that it was rare that any film project got full financing from the government. If we wanted to see the film made, we would have to find investors who would cover the remainder of the budget. He assured us that he would make several inquiries, but said that it might take months or even years to find the money we needed.

It seemed clear to me that Pierre and Alain had been placating André, and had not really expected him to do the short or get to the point where we were. In fact, it seemed that they had not given any thought as to how they were going to raise the rest of the money needed for the film's budget. Their previous films had all been produced on very small budgets, and they had usually managed to put together friends to invest. *Rue Haute* was a project with a much larger budget.

Neither André nor I had any experience in raising funds for a full-fledged feature film, but that wasn't going to stop me. I *knew* that I would find the cash. After all, in a single phone call back in 1969, I had convinced Mike Lang and the rest of the Woodstock team to hold their concert in Bethel—a concert that brought several millions of dollars into an economically depressed area of New York. In comparison, I figured it would be far easier to raise the half a million or so Belgian francs that were needed to meet the budget. It was no longer a question of *if*—it was simply a question of *how*. The rules of the game had been revealed to me, and we were ready to play.

10

Our Magical Black Leather Breakfast Meeting

Before I met André, my life had been bereft of love and tenderness. Now, with several successful collaborations under our belts, our relationship seemed stronger than ever. I was bursting with a greater energy and focus than I'd known at any other period in my life. André, on the other hand, seemed more apprehensive than ever. He had already achieved so much as an artist, but he now seemed hounded by doubts and uncertainty. As we tried to get our movie financed, I thrived on the thrill of the hunt. I knew what it was to have to scratch and claw my way to victory, but André felt it was demeaning to have to beg and hustle for the chance to create.

Maybe it was intrepid ignorance on my part, but I simply refused to accept that anything could prevent us from making a feature-length film. André admired my confidence, although I suspected he also felt it was unearned or a tad naïve. He had far more experience than I had when it came to the performing arts. And yet I had always been the more headstrong and vocal half of our partnership. André was a little more cautious about new enterprises than I was; I preferred to jump off the cliff first and look below later. I was nearly ten years older than André, and I could never shake the feeling that too many years had already passed for me. I wanted to succeed at everything we did at that point, because I was worried time would run out.

It was clear to me that we both needed a break again. In addition to his employment at the Théâtre National, André had also taken on new directorial work at two of Brussels' more experimental repertory companies, the

Théâtre 140 and Théâtre de Poche. I could see he was exhausted, so I suggested another sojourn to Amsterdam. Instead, André wanted to spend a weekend in Paris. I thought it was a splendid idea. After all, the City of Light was the birthplace of French cinema's New Wave. It was there that the great film directors François Truffaut, Jean-Luc Godard, and Alain Resnais had made their groundbreaking films in the late 1950s. Maybe we would catch some of their luck and legacy—maybe something would happen that would help get our movie made. So off to Paris we went.

Being a gay couple in Europe wasn't stigmatized as it was throughout much of America in the 1970s. The relative freedom that I experienced while André and I were in Paris only amplified my confidence. I felt centered and resilient; while André was burnt out, I was pleased that he chose to lean on me for support and inspiration. It made our relationship that much stronger, both personally and professionally.

The bright lights and fast pace of Paris were absolutely electric—exactly what we needed. As we explored the artists' quarter on the Left Bank, we gobbled down the tasty baguettes and chocolate croissants available at every corner café. Though I had seen it in the movies and featured it in my lectures at Hunter College, there was nothing quite like seeing Nôtre-Dame de Paris up close and in person. Though I was not religious, I was enthralled by the sweep and grandeur of this magnificent architectural achievement, by the elegance that suffused every glass window and ritual object in the cathedral.

André was especially touched. He even knelt and prayed before the preserved tunic said to have been worn by the Blessed Virgin Mary. André was a Catholic, and although his faith never seemed to make him happy, it helped satisfy his need to understand something beyond this world. André had told me how back in 1968 he had dropped acid with some college friends right before going to see Stanley Kubrick's epic science-fiction film *2001: A Space Odyssey*. "Like many others," André said, "I felt like I had really seen God toward the end of the movie. But I could never get that spiritual feeling back again. I thought maybe it was the acid that enabled my vision of God. So I took LSD a second time, just to see if I could find God again. It did not work. The next day, I went to a church in Liège and prayed that God might reveal himself to me again. I did not see God directly, but I did feel his presence all around me. From then on, I have believed."

When André finished praying and came back to stand with me, I couldn't resist asking him in a hushed tone, "So, is this where they keep Charles Laughton's hunchback or what?" His face went from solemn to amused, and he had to bite his lower lip to stop from laughing out loud in the cavernous cathedral. Surprise, arousal, entertainment, and laughter—these were the tenets of *my* religion.

Later that day, we were walking in the theater district and passed by a large building that was hosting a production of the Jerry Herman musical *Hello, Dolly!*. I had seen several productions of the show on Broadway, with different actresses in the part of Dolly Gallagher Levi—Carol Channing, Ginger Rogers, and even Pearl Bailey, who had appeared in a wonderful all-black version of the musical. Standing in front of the theater that day in Paris, André and I saw that this production starred someone named Annie Cordy. The name was unfamiliar to me, but André explained that she was a brilliant Belgian comedienne and a megastar throughout the French-speaking world. He further explained that she was a major box office draw wherever she performed. She had done only a few minor dramatic films, but none that I knew.

André felt that I might not understand all the French used throughout the show, and suggested we not waste our time on it. I knew the basic story by heart, and was a little homesick, so I insisted that we get tickets. Annie Cordy was astounding in the part. She was so fantastically funny—her gestures and facial expressions had me and the rest of the theater falling out of our seats from laughter.

After the show, over coffee at a café near our hotel, I mulled over Annie Cordy's remarkable performance. In a flash, it came to me. I said to André, "Hey, let's see if we can get Annie Cordy to play the part of Mimi in *Rue Haute!*"

André shook his head vigorously. "No, no, no, Elliot. She is a major star. We could never even get a chance to meet with her. It would be like trying to pitch a script directly to Marlene Dietrich! It absolutely does not happen, Elliot. There is no way," he insisted.

"Well, why isn't there a way?" I shot back. "She is a Belgian celebrity, you are a revered Belgian director, and I am a pushy Jewish kid with a typewriter from Brooklyn. Sounds like the perfect plan to me. I think we should try to get her for the movie."

André laughed, but I was about to remind him just how far I would go to pursue an idea.

The next morning, I called the theater where we had seen the show, introduced myself as a screenwriter who had recently come from Hollywood, and asked where I might reach Madame Cordy in Paris. Amazingly, the mere mention of Hollywood seduced the box office manager, who gave me the name and number of the hotel where she could be reached. I phoned the hotel myself, and asked the front desk to put me through to Madame Cordy's room. The phone was picked up on the second ring by Cordy's personal assistant, who luckily spoke English.

I knew I had a short moment of time to make my case. I explained that I was an American writer who had worked with André Ernotte on the popular RTB *Sketch-Up* specials, and had returned to work on new projects in Belgium. I said that I had seen Madame Cordy in *Hello, Dolly!* and felt she would be perfect to star in a movie I was developing from my own original novel. The secretary then told me that I was welcome to leave the script synopsis at the front desk of Cordy's hotel.

Then I looked at André and said "See? That wasn't hard," all the time thinking, *Holy shit, it worked!*

It took only a moment to run the script over to Annie Cordy's hotel, which was a few blocks from where André and I were staying. At eight in the morning the following day, the phone in our hotel room rang. André answered. Within seconds, the expression on his face went from sleepy to wide awake to almost hysterical. At first, I thought that something terrible had happened, but André's voice remained very businesslike. He politely finished the phone call and hung up. Then he leapt up onto the bed and fell on me in a crazed hug, nearly squeezing the breath out of me in the process.

"El, that was Annie Cordy!" he said. "She wants us to come to her hotel in an hour to have breakfast with her! Oh my God! I cannot believe it. That was Annie Cordy!"

"Now," I teased, "are you sure her name is big enough to get us the rest of the funds to make our movie?" He kissed me on the lips and shouted "Absolutely. Yes!" in an emphatic and triumphant voice. All I could think was, *Yoicks, I pulled it off!*

We scurried about the hotel room in a mad dash to get ready to meet

Annie. We had only packed a handful of outfits for our long weekend in Paris. As luck would have it, we had already worn almost everything we had brought with us—everything except the leather gear we'd packed on the off chance that we might want to visit one of the city's gay S&M clubs. Unfortunately, there was no time to wash or iron anything else. "What are we going to do?" André asked frantically. "The only clean clothes we have right now are our leathers!"

"Then we have no choice," I said, "we're going to have to wear them."

"Are you crazy, Elliot?" André nearly screamed. "I cannot meet Annie Cordy when I am dressed all in leather!"

"Why not? If anybody asks, we can say that we just finished an invigorating early morning ride on our motorcycles!"

"Be serious, Elliot!" André complained. "What fucking motorcycles?"

"The ones that we'll say have been stolen near the hotel if she asks to see them! Who cares? Come on, move your ass! We've got a meeting with Annie Cordy."

The elegant George V Hotel was the most expensive in Paris—a distinction I tried not to dwell on as we walked toward the front desk. The sheer opulence of the decor surpassed even the magnificence of the Plaza Hotel overlooking Central Park back in New York City. The concierge took one look at us—two bearded leather-clad biker types—and was instantly suspicious. His expression became more respectful, however, when we explained that Annie Cordy was expecting us. We were rapidly whisked off to the hotel breakfast room.

Our reception in the breakfast room was no different from the one we had had at the front desk. The maître d' looked like he was going to blow a whistle and have the hotel security throw us out of the George V immediately. Here again, I told them that Annie Cordy was expecting us, and the maître d' suddenly morphed into the most affable servant.

Starting to sweat from the warmth of all the leather he was wearing, André looked as if he were going to faint dead to the floor from a case of nerves. I wasn't nervous. I knew what we needed from this meeting, and I was fully committed to winning over Annie Cordy.

The now-supplicant maître d' sheepishly led us to Annie's table. She was slender and perky, and in front of her was an elegant basket of croissants and assorted marmalades. She looked at us in our leather and didn't pause for even a second. Instead, she boisterously kissed us on both cheeks; introduced us to her husband, Bruno; and recommended that we order the hotel's signature breakfast dish. Without saying a word about our costumes, Annie accepted us as we were. I was practically in love with her from that moment forward. In fact, I started to wonder if she might be too cheerful and winsome to be able to capture the torment of our character, Mimi. She quickly showed me otherwise.

"Mr. Tiber, Monsieur Ernotte," she said, "I read your synopsis for this film, and I even translated it aloud into French for my husband, Bruno, so he could hear it too. I am rarely offered any dramatic roles of any merit. As you may know from watching me in the show the other night, I am a clown—a funny lady—and a singer. That is my image. As a result," she continued, "this chance to play Mimi, your tragic madwoman, poses for me an exceptional challenge. As Monsieur Ernotte knows, I am still a proud Belgian. I know the streets there, so I remain intimately familiar with the area and can still speak Bruxellois.

"My family," she went on, her face a mask of seriousness, "spent the war years hiding in the Ardennes. So many people I knew endured the horrific suffering that your Mimi has gone through in her life. When I read your synopsis, I told Bruno there is no question. I must play this role!"

André and I were overjoyed to hear how enthusiastic Annie was about the film. Though he was normally restrained and courtly, it was only a matter of time before André revealed himself to be one of Annie's biggest fans, recalling to her in immense detail all the shows that he had seen her do in Brussels and Paris over the years. He became so excited, in fact, that I felt certain he was soon going to ask her for an autographed photo. At one point, I carefully slipped my hand under the table and gave André's knee a quick but firm squeeze. He looked questioningly at me, and I shot him a glance that said *Cool it, kid!*.

Before we could talk more about making the film, though, she quickly went on to explain that her husband was also her manager. Late the night before, he had contacted both the head of the Théâtre National and Pierre Renoult at RTB TV. Annie had done many RTB specials, so of course she knew most of the luminaries in Belgium's performing arts scene. "Mr. Tiber," she said, looking into my eyes, "you told my secretary that you had only just arrived here from Hollywood. And yet Bruno learns from Renoult that you have been based in Belgium for more than three years now. Why didn't you tell me that?"

André looked as if he were going to be sick. I was unsure how to proceed. My bluff had been called. Here sat a seasoned show-business professional who had seen and done it all. It was a critical moment, and I recognized that my response would dictate the fate of our movie. So I decided to tell her the truth. "Miss Cordy—"

"Call me Annie," she said.

"Annie," I continued, the weight of all my hopes and dreams on my shoulders, "I have learned that people only get so many chances to connect with a person of your renown. I was afraid that if I told you who I really was, I wouldn't be able to get you to look at my screenplay. You see, I have spent nearly my entire life as the trapped gay son of two crazy European Jews. When I met André in New York four years ago, I was able to finally find love in this world. The time I have spent in Belgium has allowed me to discover who and what I am as a gay man and an artist. But this story that I—that *we*—have written—it has helped me to discover who I am as a human being. When I saw your performance the other night, I felt like everything I had discovered as I brought Mimi to life on the page was something that you understood and were bringing to life on the stage. I know that we only have some television and a short film to our names, but I truly believe we have a chance here to turn Mimi's story into something beautiful. And if you didn't feel the same way, Annie, my heart tells me you wouldn't have invited us here for breakfast."

She smiled, perhaps touched by the passion with which I was making my pitch. "Tell me, Monsieur Ernotte," Annie said to André, "What was your life like before you met Mr. Tiber?"

"A lot quieter," André laughed softly. "Not nearly as happy or as much fun, though. He is my lover and my friend, but he is very much an artist."

Annie put her hands on mine. "I have only one more question for you, Mr. Tiber."

"Call me Elliot," I said.

"Elliot. We know that you have been given 35 percent of your budget from the Belgian film ministry. How much more have you received, and how much more do you need to get this project underway?"

One sharp Belgian cookie, I thought. "We still need all the rest—sixty-five percent."

"Do you have a production company in place to drum up the rest of the budget and guarantee theatrical exhibition and distribution of your film?"

"Yes, the company is called CinéVog Films," I responded, feeling my pulse rate rise.

Silence hung over our table like heavy smoke from a fire. Annie rested her hands on the table. "If I were to agree to star in your film, gentlemen, do you feel that you would be able to obtain the rest of the production budget?"

"Yes," I said.

"Yes, but of course," André added.

Annie and Bruno exchanged a silent glance. "Gentlemen, you have my full agreement to play the lead role in your film. With that as a standing verbal commitment," she continued, smiling warmly, "let me tell you that I am very excited to do this movie, gentlemen. I also hope we can begin and finish shooting within the next six months. After that, I will be going on tour, and my schedule will be crowded for at least a year."

I rushed to call Pierre and Alain in Brussels. Accustomed to my over-the-top humor, neither Pierre nor Alain initially believed me when I told them that Annie Cordy had agreed to play a tragic character. André got on the phone and assured them both that it was the real thing. Pierre and Alain were amazed, and agreed to grab the next express train to Paris to seal the deal.

Pierre and Alain arrived in Paris by that afternoon. We made quite a group: them in their boring accountant-style suits and attaché cases, and André and me in our leather attire. The four of us met up that night with Annie and Bruno at a chic restaurant on the Champs Elysées for a late supper and to further discuss *Rue Haute*. As we all enjoyed the marvelous meal, Bruno studied the contracts thoroughly. After some negotiation with Pierre and Alain, he handed the documents to Annie to sign.

We caught the milk train returning to Brussels. The whole time, André kept saying "I cannot believe it. I simply cannot believe it." André and I didn't sleep for two whole nights after we got back to Belgium—we were that excited. He phoned his mother, who became nearly hysterical with joy to learn of our good news. No use to phone *my* mother, of course, since Annie Cordy would mean less than nothing to her. If I phoned to tell her I was becoming a rabbi or marrying a nice rich Jewish girl, *that* she would get. No matter, though. My lifelong dream of making a movie was becoming a reality.

✿ ✿ ✿

Now that Annie Cordy was on board, we had no trouble getting the film funded. Pierre and Alain quickly raised the cash, and casting began immediately. I had wanted an American star to play the role of David, the better to interest the American market. I instantly thought of Jon Voight, who had been so poignant in his portrayal of the deluded Texan street hustler Joe Buck in John Schlesinger's 1969 film *Midnight Cowboy.*

By a remarkable coincidence, Voight was actually nearby in Bern, Switzerland, shooting a film with the famous German actor Maximilian Schell. Having learned where the location was through some fellow producers, Pierre and Alain arranged to have our script forwarded on to Voight. We learned that Jon read and spoke French fluently. A short time later, Pierre told us that Jon had telephoned him at his home to tell him how moved he had been by our story and the script. He told Pierre that he would be delighted to play the role of David Rheinhardt.

Of course, we were all beside ourselves with excitement—especially Annie, who relished the idea of working with Voight. I couldn't believe our wonderful fortune. Occasionally, I worried that Voight's blond hair and blue eyes might be a bit too Aryan for a character who was so thoroughly based on my own Jewish roots and personality. The only Jewish men I knew who had blond hair were those who knew how to use high-quality bleach. But I was confident that Voight was a brilliant and versatile actor, and that his star power would help us to sell the picture worldwide.

I phoned Renee long distance to tell her what was happening. She was so pleased for us that she began to cry at the news. I cried, too. Renee assured me that she would share the good news with my sisters Rachelle and Goldie, and I asked her to tell Momma that her son was going to make an important film about the Holocaust in Belgium. I'm sure that Renee did talk to Momma, but I never heard anything from my mother about it.

For the supporting roles, we engaged several actors with whom we had worked so well at RTB TV and the Théâtre National. The grant from the Belgian film ministry required us to use a Flemish actor, so we hired Bert Struys for the role of the former German soldier known simply as "the Man." Bert was a naturally pleasant and affable man, given to laughter and friendly conversation. His character, however, was meant to be dark and silent, so André worked hard with Bert to help sustain his German character's deep sense of isolation and brooding. Although most of André's family did not want to appear, we wrote into the screenplay small walk-on cameos for André's mother and for his three-year-old niece, Isabelle.

We invited our good friend Suzy Falk to appear in the film as la Crémière, a woman who sells cheese and milk in the market square next to Mimi's fish stand. The character of la Crémière was inspired by my old friend Max Yasgur, the dairy farmer who had supplied the land for the Woodstock festival. He was a friendly and wise person, and I tried to convey this serenity in writing the character of la Crémière. It was la Crémière who would tell David that others had tried to help Mimi in the past, trying to get her into an institution; we needed an actress who could portray the weary dignity of such a friend. André and I were very glad to have Suzy on the film. We knew that she would be perfect for the role, and hoped that the film might help her secure more film work as well.

André insisted that I appear in the film as David's friend, a writer and fellow American named Mike Mason. In writing this character, I had once again drawn from my memories, naming this American after the clearheaded and reasonable Woodstock Ventures leader Mike Lang. Just as the real Mike Lang had helped me realize that there was more to the world than the El Monaco, the character, Mike, was written in to help David see beyond his obsession with Mimi. I was still uncertain about my acting, though. I told André I would most likely flub my lines, but he insisted I do it. "If anything," he said, "it will give you something else to add to your professional resumé as we do other projects." Who was I to argue?

With the clock ticking down, André and I had to immerse ourselves in this new world of filmmaking. The first thing we did was to sit down with Pierre and Alain to work out a production schedule, which wound up being six weeks from late June to the middle of August. We also put together a shooting schedule, which told everybody in the cast and crew when we would be shooting what. There were as many exterior scenes as there were interior scenes, so we left open the possibility that we would have to shuffle the schedule a bit in case it rained. Of course, it seemed to rain three hundred days a year in Belgium, so we had to hope for the best while we prepared for the worst.

As with our previous collaborations, André relied on me to help manage the production. At home, he told me, "I need you to make sure that everything is being done by the crew so the movie is something that you and I both want. This is going to be *our* movie in every sense of the word." Technically, I was to serve as art director alongside Philippe Graff, who was also acting as our property master. In practice, however, I often acted as André's deputy director, helping to make critical decisions on and off set, as I had done on *Sketch-Up* and our other projects. I was determined to make my mark on the film. For example, I took the liberty of taping an original Woodstock concert poster on the bedroom wall of the set for David's apartment. André understood that the poster was my own little wink at the world, and kept the poster up.

We assembled a very competent crew to help us make the film. There was the costume designer, Yan Tax; the makeup artist Claudine Thyrion, and her small team of assistants; the cinematographer, Walther van der Ende; the assistant director and editor, Susana Rossberg; the set designer, Louis de Meyere; the key grip, Henri Roesems, whose job was to make sure that we had the necessary equipment in each location and that all technical elements of the shoot had been checked for potential danger or damage prior to shooting; and the unit publicist, Liliane Jaquet, with whom I developed ideas for promotion of our film and its eventual release.

It was important to André that everyone on set felt that their contributions were essential to the film. For the most part, the crew was inspired and dedicated to their craft. There were moments, however, when I could see that the right thing wasn't being done. André and I would discuss these problems at home and decide which of us was best suited to address each issue on set. We made it very clear to everyone involved with the film that we were both the primary creators of the film. I calmly but insistently involved myself in every aspect of the filmmaking process—every aspect except camera placement, which was André's area entirely.

As the story of *Rue Haute* begins, a successful but disillusioned American painter, David Rheinhardt, arrives in Belgium to attend a gallery exhibition of his newest paintings. Soon after his arrival, David first witnesses Mimi's explosion of agony and madness. Unable to understand the reason behind

Mimi's volatile and frightened actions, he begins to obsess over her. As a result, David's next gallery exhibition features a number of paintings, all of which are renditions of Mimi's haunting and anguished face.

Since I had written the character of David to closely mirror my own personality and abilities—particularly my skill as a painter—it seemed only natural that I should create the portraits David was to have made of Mimi for his second exhibition. That meant I had to produce at least two dozen separate canvases, maintaining the same style in all the paintings. In every project I had ever been involved with over the years, I had always put myself into it one thousand percent. With *Rue Haute,* I committed myself *two* thousand percent. I devoted myself to the creation of the many paintings needed for our film. I wanted David's paintings to follow the trajectory of my own artistic development. For his first gallery exhibition, David's paintings would be rendered in the Abstract Expressionist style taught to me by Mark Rothko at Brooklyn College. I created more than a dozen canvases in homage to Rothko's 1961 painting "Orange, Red, Yellow," using large swathes of color brushed across the canvas in long strokes to form basic shapes like rectangles and squares.

For the second exhibition, though, David's style became more realistic, the better to highlight his fascination with Mimi. I wanted David's second exhibition to feature nothing but near-identical portraits of Mimi's face. Working from a photograph of Annie, I worked hard to create precise paintings and line drawings of Mimi. Part of his tortured efforts to understand Mimi, the paintings would ultimately prove to David how little he could ever really know about her. In the script, we emphasized that point even further in a scene in which Mimi appears outside the art gallery at the exhibition opening. As she looks inside at the paintings, David sees her, and the viewers realize that her true identity still eludes him. It took me almost two weeks of feverish painting and drawing to create the artwork for the film. I was fairly spent by the time I finished, but in effect, I was able to turn a part of the film into my very own exhibition. Annie was so taken with one of the portraits I painted that when she offered to buy it from me, I presented it to her as a gift instead.

Most of the action was to be shot near where André and I used to live on rue Haute. The production team had done its research and was able to secure a very sinister dark-green bus that had actually been used by the Nazis to transport Jews from Brussels in 1943. It had been kept in a Paris museum, and getting permission to use it was a major coup for us. I suspected that Annie might have had her husband Bruno call the museum director personally to arrange the use of the bus. Everything seemed to be lining up very well for our film.

We were only a week away from the start of shooting when Voight telephoned Pierre's office, quite distraught. Voight had received word that his wife, Marcheline Bertrand, was at risk for some serious complications in her second pregnancy, so he had done what any responsible husband and father would do—he left Bern in order to fly back to Hollywood and be with his wife. Much to the entire team's disappointment, Jon Voight would not be able to star in our movie.

Pierre was frantic. He made inquiries in Paris for an American actor who was fluent in French. Eager to help, Annie suggested her friend Mort Shuman, the Brooklyn-born American songwriter and concert artist who had first become famous for his partnership with Doc Pomus, writing many hits of the late 1950s and early 1960s, including "A Teenager in Love"; "Save the Last Dance for Me"; "This Magic Moment"; and, perhaps most famously, "Viva Las Vegas," sung by Elvis Presley.

Shuman had outgrown his relationship with Pomus and moved on to new artistic collaborations. With Eric Blau, he had developed and performed in the off-Broadway hit *Jacques Brel Is Alive and Well and Living in Paris,* a musical revue of Jacques Brel's songs. As huge Brel fans, André and I had seen the show in New York in 1971, just before André had returned to Belgium. Having enjoyed Mort's performance back then, André and I thought he might be a good fit for the role of David. I had written David to resemble me, after all, and having Mort in the part made much more sense in terms of how I felt the character should look and act. Yet again, fate seemed to be playing a role in our endeavors.

Through Annie, we set up a meeting. Mort Shuman was a great big bear of a man from the Brighton Beach section of Brooklyn, smart, delightful, alternately kind and tempestuous. His French was impeccable and he was quite famous in Paris, where he had done many concerts and television shows. Mort had a brash personality, but there was also a touch of something enormously sad in him, a deep grief and guilt that he seemed to have buried deep beneath his bluster.

We weren't sure how Mort's energy onstage would translate on film. Mort had never acted in a dialogue-filled feature film before. He was intrigued by the script and he wanted to do more work in movies—his only role at that point had been in the filmed version of his Brel musical, and there his acting duties had taken a back seat to his musical performance. André and I were concerned that he might not be able to capture some of the emotional subtleties required of his character. It was clear that he could bark and bellow, but could he also be sweet and mellow? It would be André's job as director to find out.

Annie Cordy arrived in Brussels with her husband, Bruno. It was heartwarming to see how devoted they were to each other. Annie and Bruno had the kind of relationship that André and I shared. Bruno made sure that Annie had everything she needed to make her as comfortable and content as possible so she could attack her role. As soon as Annie got on set, André began a very intense one-on-one approach to developing and rehearsing the character of Mimi. I understood that this was a part of his directorial style, and I didn't question it. I did feel a bit left out, though. It was very hard to not be plugged into the process of making Mimi real, especially as I had done so much to bring her to life on the page.

André was fully engrossed in the film. I could see from his storyboards that he was going to concentrate on the actors' faces, as he had said he wanted to do when we were getting high in Amsterdam all those months before. He was still getting the hang of a feature film production, though the work he did on *Marée Basse* had given us the basic knowledge we needed to make *Rue Haute*. At first, Pierre helped show him the ropes. Before long, however, André no longer required such handholding and began to chafe at the producer's suggestions.

When André felt he was ready to kick free of Pierre's well-intentioned but ultimately counterproductive recommendations, it was my job to run interference, dragging Pierre's focus away from André and the camera and more to what I was doing on the set. I was there to protect the story I had written, the story that my partner was now trying to create with the camera. I was there to listen each day as André continually made changes or slight variations in his shooting script. Though he had never allowed anyone in his theater, television, and writing circles to see his uncertainties or doubts, he would freely discuss all of it with me when we were alone.

To the outside world, André came across as knowledgeable, confident, strong-minded, and firmly in command of every creative aspect on the film. Behind closed doors, however, he seemed close to a nervous breakdown. André wanted desperately for his first major film job to go well. But the movie wasn't merely a springboard to a career in film; André wanted to make a movie that would genuinely touch people's hearts. As a Belgian born during World War II, he had always felt guilty and angry about the savage inhumanity of the Holocaust, and it had become a mission of his to convey that emotion through our movie. What tormented him was the fear that the film might not lead his audience to feel as strongly about the story and the characters as he did. "In the theater," he said to me, "you can see and hear your audience react, and you can sometimes make changes based on their responses. With a movie, though, your audience can be anyone, anywhere. Once it is done, it cannot be changed. That scares me."

His personal investment in the story was so strong that I think it frightened him. It was this wildly intense sense of purpose that enabled him to function, as well as his escalating use of uppers and downers. "Better living through chemistry" had become the mantra of the counterculture, and while André might not have had a fondness for hippies, he didn't give a second thought now to relying on these pills. To me, at least, it seemed that drugs were widely accepted by the artistic community worldwide.

We were both driven men. And without the drugs and our mutual devotion to each other, there was no way that he and I would have been able to meet the creative challenge that we had set for ourselves. For the three-month duration of the project, there was no time to kick back and relax. This was our chance to make something real and raw and profound about the people who had been wounded by the madness of war.

❖   ❖   ❖

Everyone got along exceptionally well with each other during production. On set, Annie was her normal funny, cheerful self, despite the fact that she was portraying a madwoman. At the end of each day's shoot, she regaled the cast and crew with hilarious stories about her life, as if she were playing to a packed house.

There were some in the cast who were still a little disappointed that Jon Voight had not been able to appear as the lead in the film. The cast didn't

1975. André (standing) and me, writing the screenplay for *Rue Haute*.

1975. On location in Brussels for *Rue Haute*. From right: Annie Cordy, Mort Shuman, me, and André (center, in plaid jacket).

1975. Rehearsing my one speaking scene—dialogue improvised—with Mort Shuman (center). André (left), ever the tough director, is giving me notes on how to improve my performance.

know much about Mort apart from his reputation as a singer/songwriter. Mort was sweet and quite approachable from the first day, though, and soon won over the other actors with his wit and work ethic. He was also extraordinarily deferential to André as a director and properly in awe of Annie's remarkable acting talent.

Like me, he was a tough and self-reliant Jew who had grown up under the thumb of a demanding mother who had survived the brutal pogroms of tsarist Russia. It seemed to me that Mort was the brother I never had. In fact, Mort's background was so similar to my own that I came to feel during the shoot as if I was looking at myself while Mort acted before the camera. It was like stepping outside of my body and watching from a safe distance.

We had a large security team to control the hundreds of locals who showed up everywhere we were shooting. They were kept behind barriers as they watched the famous Annie Cordy do her scenes so as not to slow our schedule down. Annie was the consummate professional in every minute detail of her work. We were on a tight budget, so André tried to limit each scene to three takes or less to cut down on time and expense. Fortunately, we had a group of professionals, so shooting was a breeze and we were nearly always on schedule.

⚙️   ⚙️   ⚙️

As an atheist, I find it funny that one of the most important creative moments in my life involved a scene shot in a place of worship. We were in our second week of shooting, and the crew was setting up cameras inside a Catholic church on a Sunday afternoon. The scene called for Annie, as Mimi, to sneak up to the top of the church pulpit and angrily deny the existence of God to a room full of shocked parishioners. Rather than employ extras in the scene, we had our key grip ask the congregants who were leaving the church's Sunday morning mass if they wanted to appear in a movie with the esteemed star Annie Cordy. By the time we arrived on location, there were over a hundred people sitting in the church pews waiting to see Annie.

I could see Annie talking intensely to André by the church side door into the church. Right before they did the scene, André whispered something into Annie's ear. Then he spoke to the assistant director, who told the parishioners that Madame Cordy would be entering the scene from the left side of the altar directly in front of them. André sat behind the two cameras. One was set to film a medium shot that would show Mimi in relation to the parishioners, and the other camera was to track in closer and closer on Annie as she let loose a torrent of despair against religion and order and society. At long last, André called "Action!" and the parishioners looked ahead toward the altar in anticipation of seeing the great Annie Cordy in person.

But as the actor playing the priest began to go through the rites of Catholic mass, Annie instead started to make her way up the spiral stairs to the pulpit *behind* the parishioners. The parishioners all turned in surprise as they heard Annie deliver her momentous line to the priest: "You just stood there and did nothing to save my little boy! There is no God! None!" Annie's unexpected entrance only enhanced the real shock that the parishioners—and the audience—felt upon hearing the torment of a woman made insane by an unfair world.

The scene was done in a single take, and it was one of the most shocking and heartbreaking performances I had ever seen. When the scene was finished, I made my way over to congratulate Annie on capturing the feeling of the scene precisely as I had imagined it when I wrote it. She looked at me, tears still in her eyes from the power of the scene, and then hugged me tenderly, saying, "I am so sorry, Elliot," as I held her close. Before I could ask her what she meant, she simply walked away and went to rest in her actor's chair outside the church. I was mystified.

Later that night, I asked André what he had whispered to Annie before they shot the scene in the church. He said that he had shared with Annie a secret piece of information, and that he sometimes did that when directing his actors. As a writer of the novel and the script, though, I needed to know what he had said to her. He looked at me calmly and said, "I told her that your mother has never once said she loved you, and that you were molested by your rabbi when you were ten."

I felt my hand form into a fist, as I grabbed him hard by the lapel of his shirt. Blindly, I said, "What the fuck did you say? What did you fuckin' tell her about me?" But as quickly as the rage had welled up inside of me, it left me as I looked at André and saw him smile.

"I did not say that to her at all, Elliot," André said, "but you see now that a good director must know how to get someone to react as he wishes."

I immediately apologized to André, hugging and kissing him. It was then that I realized what a remarkable director André truly was. Over the course of the day, I had seen how he used expert direction to fool a church full of people to look the other way; how he sent a fragile actress into precisely the kind of emotional collapse that he needed for a scene; and how he sent me into a totally unexpected rage by pushing my buttons. I was as touched as I was confused by the process, and ultimately thankful that he taught me to respect the value of a secret.

❀　　❀　　❀

On the Friday afternoon in the third week of the shoot, we received the first weeks' developed footage from RTB's studio film lab. Although Bert and Annie preferred not to see their performances until the film was completed, Mort decided to come with André and me to review the rushes—the preliminary prints of footage taken earlier that day or week. We piled into the editing suite where André and I had recorded our softcore dubs only a few months before, and watched about two hours' worth of footage. "Oh, Christ, I look terrible!" Mort exclaimed when he first saw himself on screen. Then, after a few minutes, he started to watch Annie's performance with a growing wonder. We all did, in fact. Watching on set, we could already tell that the intensity of her performance on the set was strong, but looking at the footage, we felt that the performance had been kicked up another notch. Bert's performance was also solid, but in a quieter way. In the end, we were very happy with what we saw in the rushes.

After watching the dailies, André and I invited Mort out to a late supper. Speaking to me in English and to André in fluent French, Mort captivated us with his wonderful storytelling and infectious laugh. Mort regaled us with all kinds of stories about his experiences in the music business, both in the United States and more recently in France. "They actually bill me as *Mortimer* Shuman on my records and TV appearances, because 'Mort' means 'death' in French," he kidded. "But if I went around as 'Mortimer' when I was growing up back in Brooklyn, the kids would've knocked me on my ass for sure."

I asked him what it had been like to cowrite all those chart-topping pop songs. He took another shot from the whiskey bottle on the table alongside

André's wine, and said "Well, El, it was fucking mind-blowing. But there just isn't any art to the songs coming out of America any more. That's why I left." He frowned, and looked a little sad.

This sadness may well have motivated his prodigious bouts of drinking during the shoot. I didn't know if he was a full-fledged alcoholic at the time, but he certainly exhibited the tendencies of one. When drinking, he could be a sweet guy, then a bully; charming, then abrasive; tender, then cruel. While I wasn't a drinker myself, I understood why he drank. Listening to Mort, I realized yet again how much I had in common with him. What united us most in the conversation was the shared theme of departure in our lives. I began to talk about the factors that had driven me to leave my parents and the motel and the paralyzing force of White Lake. I shared my own hidden reserves of pain—the great loss and sorrow that had characterized my early years in Brooklyn, and the lengths to which I would often go in order to feel a connection to other people, mired as I was in a total absence of affection from my own family.

"We all felt that way, El," Mort said. "And you know, you might have kept at it with your folks if you hadn't made that brave choice to get the hell out of there, as I did. You know how many other nice Jewish boys and girls are sitting right now, crying their eyes out in some apartment building somewhere in the Bronx, Brooklyn, Queens, Staten Island? Prisoners, all of 'em!" He had become incensed by the way so many of the Jews of our generation led guilt-ridden lives. The Holocaust had cast a long shadow over the Jews who had survived it—and their children. "Millions of lives lost!" Mort exclaimed. "How do we escape that kind of incredible burden? We've grown up with that tremendous guilt all around us. It's driven so many of us to succeed, because how could we dare to squelch the gift of life in the face of so much senseless death? But it's a trap, man, and we're finally starting to realize it. I'll tell you one thing: we have to live our own lives, not the ones our parents want us to live."

I took the opportunity to tell Mort about my key role in the Woodstock festival. "So that's why there's a Woodstock poster over the bed!" he laughed. He found my story amazing, and gave me a huge bear hug as I finished sharing my story. "I wish I had known you in '69, man. I would have *loved* to play Woodstock!" he exclaimed.

"Well, I might not have been able to get you on stage, Mort," I said, "but getting you tickets to the show would have been no problem at all!"

We had drinks with our dinner. Well, Mort and André had drinks. The kitchen was apparently out of egg creams, so I had water.

"I really admire," Mort said, after a moment, "how you guys have created this story and are making a movie of it. This isn't some bubblegum Hollywood bullshit. You're doing something important here." He got choked up, trying to hold back the tears that began to fill his eyes. Drunk and exhausted from the day's work, André and I both tried to console him. But he had something to say, and it was clear that the night would not proceed until he had spoken his piece.

"Seeing the way that you two work together," Shuman said, "it's really damn special. That's how Pomus and I were for a long while there in New York." He proceeded to pour his heart out about how tough it had been for him to break away from Doc Pomus and their songwriting partnership. Pomus, whose real name was Jerome Felder, had given Mort confidence when he invited him into the songwriting world housed in Manhattan's famous Brill Building. But as their lives changed, so did their expectations.

Pomus had settled into a reasonably comfortable life with his family out on Long Island. Mort was still a bachelor and wanted to keep playing the field. The differences in their lifestyles, coupled with Mort's growing frustration with much of American pop music, led to a split in the songwriting partnership. "It was becoming another goddamn prison," he said, "and I wanted to be free." Pomus—whose bout with polio early in life had left him unable to walk, except with crutches—had taken Mort's departure very hard. Soon before their split, Mort heard that Pomus had taken a very bad fall in Manhattan while trying to get across the street in his wheelchair. The memory of that accident, and the fact that he had not been there to help his old friend and partner, seemed very real and raw to Mort in that moment, sitting in the café with us. "I'm never going to forget that. Here I am, walking around footloose and fancy free, and my old friend is left confined to a wheelchair for the rest of his life. I went to see him once in the hospital, but there was nothing I could do or say. It was too late. I don't know, I feel sometimes like I was a bad brother, a bad son, to have left him then like I did."

This story struck a nerve in André, who began to speak about how much he cared about his mother, Fanny, and how desperately he wished that he could be closer to his own highly judgmental father. There we were, three drunken prodigal sons in the late Belgian night, hoping that we might some-day wash away the pain in our hearts.

❁   ❁   ❁

During my free moments on the shoot, I roamed the Belgian countryside. In the process, I found a tiny village that I thought was perfect for the part of the story in which David treats Mimi and the Man to a pleasant weekend away from the city. Pierre had been doing his own location scouting, and I felt certain that whatever I suggested would be rejected by him on principle.

So I looked for a way around the problem. I became quite friendly with the Belgian film ministry representative who had been sent to observe the shoot. Since he was fluent in English, I made an appointment to visit him in his office. He had been a fan of our TV shows, and was very pleasant. Without my knowing it, he had even gotten a copy of my original English-language script for the film. Our meeting was allotted a single hour, but we spoke for three instead. When I excitedly described the location I had secured—rent free, no less—he told me that he had been born in that village. *Voilà!* I suddenly had my preferred countryside location.

Though we had avoided bad weather for most of the shoot, we had a day out in the countryside when we actually wanted it to rain—and it wouldn't. We were to shoot a scene in which David walks with Mimi to the country village nearby. Once they arrive at the village and begin to take in the sights, Mimi sees a large truck driving past a group of small children playing with an inflated plastic ball and has another of her manic flashbacks. David helps her to regain her composure, and then buys her a pretty shawl from one of the village shops as a gift. As they walk back to the country house, they get caught in the rain, providing a brief and cleansing moment of pure pleasure. At least that's what we had written.

The crew was prepared to stay in one spot for the afternoon, on the chance that it might start to rain. We had stuck to our shooting schedule very carefully, and didn't want to have to stay at the country location longer than we had planned. And since I had selected the location, I particularly wanted to make sure the shoot was not going to be a failure. With the hours ticking by, we finally decided to *make* the weather cooperate. Our movie rain was provided by the fire truck and two fire engines that I asked our Belgian film ministry rep to get a hold of back in the village. We offered to pay the firemen for their help, but they politely declined. They seemed perfectly pleased just to be a part of our movie make-believe, spraying our Hollywood rain from high atop the fire truck.

We needed only two full takes to produce one of the film's most memorable images—Mimi frolicking like a happy child in the rain with David following protectively behind. After all the days of serious work and intense performance, we needed a little bit of fun to relieve the stress. So after we got the shots we needed, I led the rest of the crew out into the field directly beneath our artificial rainstorm. Everyone was thrilled to have a few minutes of fun playing in the rain.

As soon as they had shut off the water and reeled the fire engine hoses back in, our trio of Belgian firemen asked for autographs from Annie and Mort and Bert. Meanwhile, I asked if I could go up to the very top of the fire truck ladder. Sadly, the firemen said no. "That's okay, Elliot," said Mort, smiling as he showed me an unlit and terrifically wrapped joint, "we can get high on this later instead."

In the evening, we had the crew set up in a country house nearby. We were to film a scene in which Mimi would nostalgically sing a song from her youth. Since they were both talented musicians, Annie had no trouble learning the mournful little melody that Mort had written with André's help earlier that day. Framed by the warm fireplace, Annie and Mort were joined by Bert to create a rare moment that spoke volumes about the beauty that had once existed in Mimi's life, long before the clouds of sorrow and rage had buried her. Annie sang Mort's gentle lullaby in a voice that was kind but broken by the brutalities of life. When André quietly called "Cut" to end the scene, we had all been brought to tears.

And then came the bar scenes. As I had written the screenplay, the two bar scenes were meant to show how David changes after meeting Mimi. In the first bar scene, early on in the film, David is established as a happy drunk, mixing with the locals and seducing a barmaid named Lily. When we see him at the bar later in the film, after his concern for Mimi has driven him to the farthest reaches of obsession, he has become a loutish and broken man. While he was charming with Lily on the first bar visit, he now brusquely barks for beer from her and shies from talk or any explanation for his mean behavior.

We aimed to film the bar scenes at night in a working tavern nearby. We needn't have worried about getting the bar to accommodate our shooting schedule—we learned that Mort had been stopping in for drinks every day since we had arrived in town. He had already won over the bar owner, a man named Victor. When he heard that his bar would be featured in a big Belgian movie, Victor got very excited—almost as excited as Mort was when he learned that Victor had declared all drinks free on the first of the two planned nights we were scheduled to shoot.

The pretty actress Louise Rocco was hired to play Lily, and she and Mort seemed to have good chemistry together. Their chemistry might have been a little *too* good for Victor, who seemed jealous of how much attention Mort was paying to people other than him. It was obvious to André and me that Victor was gay, and just as obvious that Mort was very much enamored of women—something that Victor seemed to have totally missed.

When we told Mort about it during takes, he laughed and made his way over to Victor. Then he gave him a big hug, raised a glass of beer, and began to say in French how marvelous Victor had been to let the movie crew shoot in his bar. He took a big gulp of beer from the glass, wrapped one arm around Victor's shoulders, and shouted "Here's to Victor, the tavern king!" The entire bar exploded in applause, and everyone shouted out Victor's name in celebration. Blushing with pride, Victor bowed to Mort and hugged him. The entire bar now filled with a cacophony of voices and clinking glasses, I turned to André and shouted in his ear, "All hail Mort, the peacemaker!" André grinned and nodded, as he cued the cameraman to start filming in different spots around the bar.

As the night began to wind down, André had our cameramen get footage of the locals—mostly older men who would probably be in Victor's bar most nights anyway, regardless of whether or not a movie was being made. We even had a real-life barfly who came in during shooting with a white dog. She sat down at the bar and never spoke. Instead, she nodded her head up and down every few minutes, making small, silly hand gestures to those sitting nearby. It looked like the woman was more the dog's pet than the other way around.

Luckily, we were able to get some footage of her making her goofy little motions with the white dog sitting next to her on a chair.

Because our crew was so efficient, we got all the scenes we needed for the film in one night. That probably pleased Victor, since it meant he could return to charging people for drinks, and would have Mort back to himself again. With most of the extras wrapped for the day, André called for one last take of Louise and Mort slow-dancing in the center of the bar. Both the movie cameras began to roll. As Louise and Mort ended their dance with a kiss, an attractive but decidedly disheveled woman emerged from the background. She spoke briefly to Louise, and then asked Mort to play another song on the jukebox. As he did, the woman walked forward, singing along with the song. I was confused, thinking an extra was about to ruin a take. Standing next to André, I turned to say something in his ear. He placed his hand on my arm and whispered to me, "Watch." The woman continued singing in a plaintive voice, sounding very much like Edith Piaf. She came to a new verse in the song but then stopped and said, "I forgot the words!"

Everyone laughed and applauded—especially André. Still confused, I waited for the take to end before I spoke. "André, did we discover a new star, or what?"

"No, Elliot. That is Henny Alma, a wonderful Dutch actress. She has only just started to act again, after taking a break for a few years. A friend of mine at the Théâtre National told me about her and I got Pierre and Alain to offer her a part. Mort and Louise were the only other people who knew she would be here tonight. I told them to keep it a secret."

I was surprised, but in a good way. I found the unplanned moment very thrilling. "There's only one problem, babe. We don't have that scene anywhere in the script, or the book."

"Well, we do now," he said. It seemed there might be a few sections of our novel that I would have to revise.

While we were shooting the picture, we had an unexpected guest. The visitor, whom we soon learned was named Henri Louvard, was none other than the head of acquisitions for Rossel, the largest book publisher in Belgium. Rossel also owned the most important daily newspaper in Belgium, *Le Soir,*

so its acquisitions head was a person we certainly wanted to know. Nobody had told us that he had been watching the shoot that day. He said he had been fascinated with what he had observed that morning, and wanted to know if we would be interested in doing a novelization of our film's screenplay. Instead, I explained that we had first written a novel—still unpublished—and then created our screenplay. He was thrilled to learn this, and asked if we would like to have our novel published by Rossel at the same time that the film was to be released.

I pinched myself to make sure I wasn't dreaming, while André played it safe and asked that the editor give us a day or two to think it over. By the end of the week, we had a contract with Rossel to publish our book *Rue Haute* in Belgium. We couldn't have asked for better publicity. Thrilled, I wrote a letter to Renee, telling her to let Momma know that I was going to be a published author.

The toughest scenes of the film were saved for last. To play the younger version of Mimi—the Mimi who appeared in our World War II-era flashbacks—we had hired a Belgian actress named Esther Christinat. Before shooting any of her scenes, André had Esther carefully observe Annie's performance in order to tailor her own to it. We then filmed the short scenes of Mimi's earlier, happier life with her Jewish husband and their son, played by a lovely child actor named Claude Batelle.

Finally, the time came to shoot the moment in 1943 when the Nazis take away Mimi's husband and kill her young son. Esther had to put her heart and soul into her performance—the significance of the entire film rested on the raw tragedy of this one scene. André set up the two cameras to film the takes from two different angles. That way, we would be able to decide in the editing room how best to stitch together the performances.

First we shot the interior scene, in which the Nazis arrest Mimi's husband at their apartment; then we moved outside to the street, where the Nazis load Mimi's husband and other extras onto the World War II-era bus we had secured. Because this sequence was the key to Mimi's madness, André wanted to be sure that it stunned and upset the audience. In deliberate contrast to the slow, steady, ghostly tracking shots used throughout the film, we shot this scene with handheld cameras. André himself hoisted one of them onto his shoulder. The finished footage, shaky and uncertain, did much to convey a mood of agitation and dread. This was highly emotional material, and I was very shaken to see my imagined scene come to life.

André kept pushing the actor-Nazis to move faster and more aggressively. He was also being uncharacteristically tough with Esther, pushing her into ever-escalating levels of hysteria. On each take, Esther had to fight to stop the Nazis from taking her husband away. In her mania to get her husband back, she would lose sight of her own child, who would be knocked to the ground and killed by the Nazis.

After seven grueling takes, Esther was practically in tears, as was young Claude, who was very upset to see Esther in such a state. André decided that they had been through enough and that we were done shooting. He wiped away the boy's tears, picked him up gently, and brought him to his parents. He went back to Esther, held her by the hand, and walked her over to Annie, who had come to set to support Esther. The three of them, all tearful by now, joined in a small group hug. The night's shoot had been painful, but also cathartic. The horror had been committed to film, and now it was over.

Before we went to bed late that night, though, André said to me in the darkness of our bedroom, "Elliot, I do not think that I got the scene right."

"What are you talking about?" I said immediately. "It was great. You were great. Esther and the boy were great. I thought it was done beautifully."

He was still doubtful. "Maybe it will work. There is nothing to be done now, anyway. The shoot is almost over, and we have what we have." I assured him again that he had done a sensational job, but I could tell that he still felt unsure about it.

The very last scene that we shot involved only Mort. On her deathbed, Mimi asks David to go meet the bus for her. She hopes that this bus might finally be the one that brings her husband back to her after all her years of waiting. Mort came to me and André before the first take and said, "I don't know how I'm supposed to play this scene, guys. I just don't know how to go about it doing it. Can you help me?"

André rested a hand on his shoulder, pulled him in a little closer, and said, "Imagine that this bus struck your old friend, Doc Pomus. And those people"—he gestured in the direction of the extras on line at the bus stop—

"imagine that all those people did nothing to help him injured there in the street. As Mimi loses her will to live and dies, your character will become the new screech of madness heard among the streets of the rue Haute section. David succumbs to Mimi's horrors, and comes to feel them himself."

It was exactly what Mort needed to hear. We went for the first take and Mort began to shriek like a banshee. He lumbered toward the bus, cursing alternately in French and in English. He pummeled the glass windows of the bus with his fists as tears streamed from his eyes. Looking to replicate the emotional immediacy he'd captured in the Nazi arrest scene, André again took a handheld camera and went up into the bus with it. There was enough length on the electrical cord for him to get to where Mort was, and he filmed Mort in the throes of his breakdown for a very long two minutes.

At last, André called "Cut!" And that was it. A single take, and the shoot was over. André came out of the bus, passed the camera back to a crew member, and he and I went over and embraced Mort. He seemed dazed and upset, but slowly he came out of the scene and back to us. "Thank you, André," he said, breathing heavily after his intense performance, "thank you. I'm okay, man. I'm okay. I think finally got inside my guilt over Doc. I think I've finally forgiven myself."

These final two scenes had been as emotionally draining for Esther and Mort as the breakdown scene in the church had been for Annie and for me. Everyone there on the set began to clap and congratulate each other on the finishing of the shoot. I looked over at André, who was standing silently by one of the film cameras and looking far off down the street. He had pushed himself as a director even harder than he had pushed the actors, so I hoped that the shoot's end had brought him some inner peace. "That's all, folks!" I said, giving a big sigh of relief.

André winced a bit. "Excuse me a minute, Elliot," he said. He lit a cigarette and walked down the street as the crew began to put away the film equipment. Surrounded by celebrating cast members, André looked like the loneliest man in the world. Maybe he hadn't yet fully come out of the scene yet—maybe he never would. Only time would tell.

We had finished the shoot on time, in early August. A large part of me was very sad to see the production reach its end. The filming of our movie had required a tremendous amount of teamwork. We had come to know and rely upon each other so thoroughly. Actors, technicians, and even gofers—we had all grown very close. In a way, I felt like I had been part of a big, loving family for the first time in my life. I gave warm hugs and lots of thanks to everyone in our production, including Mort and Bert and especially Annie Cordy. Without her faith in the dreams of two leather-clad guys who rode imaginary motorcycles, nothing would ever have happened. We were also indebted to Mort Shuman, who had not only written the song that Annie Cordy sang in the film, but who had also offered to compose the film score, writing the incidental music that would contribute to the film's emotional impact.

Of course, the film was far from done. For André, the end of the shoot only signaled the beginning of a state of angst. He fretted about whether the film would be any good; whether the direction had been too heavy-handed for the delicacy of the story; whether Annie Cordy was going to hate how her performance had been filmed; and whether Mort Shuman might beat the crap out of him for letting him look too inexperienced and vulnerable on screen, especially in the final scene at the bus stop. I assured him that Mort had been pleased with his performance during the breakdown. And since Mort had also asked to write the musical soundtrack for the film, it was highly unlikely that he would beat André up over anything, drunk or sober.

Most of all, André worried that the entire film would not come together the right way in the editing room. I told him that he was a genius—in my opinion, he most certainly was—and I reassured him that I wasn't about to let anything happen that would destroy our dreams or betray our shared fate. I had hope for the future.

"Don't worry about everything so much," I said, as I kissed him softly on the lips.

"If you say so, Elliot, then I will believe," he responded, his eyes red with lack of sleep.

"Hey, you never know," I said. "And if we wind up taking meetings in Hollywood, I know a great mansion where we can stay. I think it belonged once to Marie Dressler."

"Who is Marie Dressler?" André asked.

"An old-time American actress," I responded, "but that's not important. I'd like to play the director tonight, if that's okay with you."

We both smiled. I thought about the past fifteen months. The period had been exhausting, yet it had brought everything that we had hoped for in our lives. And to think we were just getting started.

11

Super Elli!

I ran past several tall skyscrapers, ducking in and out of the clogged midtown traffic. Mere mortals who saw me would not have been blamed for assuming that I was racing to put an end to some villain's bad deeds—a kidnapping, or perhaps a bank robbery already in progress. But they would have been wrong. It was for a very different reason that this fleet-footed concrete warrior was running like some dizzy putz with a pack of lit firecrackers stuck down the back of his pants. In my feverish haste to make the plane to New York from Belgium, I had forgotten to pack an umbrella, and now that I had made it to Manhattan, it was pouring rain.

As I found my way through the rain to the shelter of the nearest phone booth just after stepping directly into a puddle, I pulled open my jacket and flipped up my sweater. Nestled against my chest was a slim attaché case, containing one of two copies of my sacred manuscript—a manuscript of a book already destined to become a bestseller in Belgium. I was wet, I was cold, and I was down to my last eighty cents in dimes. But no matter! I was none other than Super Elli, and my mission on that rainy day in early September 1975 was to entice a book publisher into making an offer for the English-language rights to my book.

I dropped a dime into the coin slot, ready to make my eighth phone call of the day. I dialed the number at the Hearst Publications office on West Fifty-seventh Street. "Time to show 'em what you got, Elliot," I heard myself say out loud as the phone started to ring.

My return to New York City had been planned on a dare. Following the film shoot, I had met with the publishing director at Rossel. I asked him if he had looked into selling our book to an American publisher. The director was polite, but he had said there was not the slightest chance that anyone in New York would be interested. I was amazed at Rossel's cavalier attitude. After all, they were sure to do well with the French-language book, as its sales would be supported and encouraged by the release of our film. As the hype built up in the States, it would travel back across the ocean and help create an international sensation! So I proposed that I fly to New York to seek out a deal on my own. The director found that most amusing. I then suggested that I pay for the trip and hotel myself; if I succeeded in arranging a deal, Rossel could reimburse me. The publishing director smiled and agreed.

Since we were submerged in the postproduction of our movie and I didn't want to leave André for too long, I limited myself to just three days in New York—plenty of time to interest a publisher. When I had discussed the mission with André and our film producers, they had all told me that it was highly unlikely that any real New York book publishers would bite. André thought that my ambition was naïve, and that I was chasing after an unachievable and hopeless fantasy. But why should I let reality discourage me? I was no longer Eliyahu Teichberg or Elliot Tiber or even Woodstock Hippie. I was Super Elli! My successes in the last few years made me feel like I could do anything through sheer will.

The pay phone rang five times before someone picked up. It was a little after three on a Wednesday afternoon and I was ready to climb the outside of the building if this person wasn't prepared to invite me in out of the rain.

"Hello, this is Hearst Publications. How may I help you?"

"Hi," I said, "may I speak with the acquisitions editor in charge of fiction, please?"

"Well—"

The young woman on the phone was only doing her job, telling me the same stuff I had heard from the other publishing offices. They all had the same responses: the editor was out to lunch, had left for dinner, was out of town, was in a meeting, was busy on another line, or did not accept any unsolicited manuscripts as a rule. I knew I had to say something to break down the wall.

"Excuse me, miss, I don't mean to interrupt you, but I have recently arrived from overseas and was told by Mr. Bennett Cerf to speak to your top acquisitions editor about my bestselling book."

"Well, yes, I mean," the young woman stammered. "Can you give me your name again?"

She placed me on hold. I felt around in the front pocket of my pants for my few remaining dimes as I waited, in case I had to plunk more coins into the phone to keep the call going. Finally, another voice—a slightly lower and more sophisticated voice—came on the line. "Yes, this is Miss Powers. What did you wish to discuss?"

I introduced myself as quickly as I could, since I was sure the call would soon run out of time. "Miss Powers, this is Elliot Tiber. I'm an American expatriate writer back here in New York from my home in Belgium, and I would like to speak with you about picking up the American publishing rights on a book that I've just had published in Brussels. The novel has already been made into a feature film, and it is sure to be a big bestseller. Are you available to meet with me? I'm only here in the city for two more days, so it's important that I see you today."

"I could see about clearing some time by this—"

"I'm sorry, but it *must* be today, Miss Powers," I countered.

"Well, this is all very sudden, Mr. Tiber. Where are you staying in the city?"

"I am staying at the Warwick Hotel, but I would like to meet you in person. You see, my Belgian publisher is Rossel and they have suggested that I reach out to your house immediately."

"Where are you now?" she asked, after a pause.

"I'm outside your building, standing in a phone booth. What floor are you on?"

"Uh, okay, it's the seventeenth floor. Come up and tell Joyce at the reception desk that you and I have spoken and that I will be out to meet you."

"Great, I will be up in a few minutes. Thank you." *One door closes, another opens,* I thought, as I hoofed it out of the rain and into the building, ready for yet another adventure.

Wilda Powers turned out to be a vibrant middle-aged woman perhaps only a few years older than I was. The first thing I noticed was that she had wire-rim glasses and wore her auburn hair in a messy bun. She was thin and wore an elegant grey silk dress that looked like it had been designed by the then-popular American fashion designer Halston. Given the low salaries of book editors, however, I guessed the dress was probably a copy. No matter. Miss Powers carried herself with grace, and spoke with a strong voice that showed me how serious she was about her job. Add to this the fact that she had agreed to meet with me after a single call, and I figured that people in book publishing were either the best and kindest people around, or they were completely nuts.

"It's a pleasure to meet you, Mr. Tiber," she said, as we shook hands.

"You as well, Miss Powers," I said, immediately apologetic for the dampness of my jacket from the afternoon rain.

"I would expect a Belgian to always carry an umbrella with him," she said, and I could detect in her voice and in her eyes a glimmer of dry humor—at my expense, of course. She then calmly led me back to her office.

We spoke in her office for about twenty minutes, and she was intrigued by my synopsis of the story. I suspect she was even more taken by my chutzpah and naïveté. Miss Powers said she would read my material and get back to me first thing in the morning.

"Thank you very much for seeing me like this," I said. I again offered her my hand.

"Well, you are certainly the soggiest author that I've met this week," she said, smiling wryly. "Let's hope you're not also wet behind the ears when it comes to writing." I smiled, as she advised me in a mock-motherly tone that it was supposed to rain for the next few days and that I should get myself an umbrella. Back out on the midtown pavement, I followed her advice and bought one from a nearby sidewalk vendor. And as it continued to rain, I kept hoping Miss Powers would see things my way.

֍   ֍   ֍

After the meeting, I went straight back to my hotel room. Too exhausted to go out again, I ordered a large salad through room service and then lay on the bed in my clothes, watching television. I was so distracted with thoughts about my meeting with Wilda Powers that I didn't even call Renee to tell her I was in the city. I hardly slept a wink that night. I told myself that if I didn't succeed I would simply scamper off to the airport and lick my wounds back in Brussels. It turned out that Super Elli did have a secret adversary that could injure him—*rejection*.

The next morning, I woke up early and stared at the hotel phone, planning to call the Hearst offices after nine if I didn't hear from Miss Powers. Time slowed to a sadistic crawl. I took a shower for an hour to keep myself occupied. It was still such a luxury for me to take a shower for longer than five minutes without the water going cold, as had nearly always happened at the El Monaco, in my previous life. Then, at exactly nine o'clock, the phone rang. As I made my way out of the bathroom, I prepared myself for the worst.

"Mr. Tiber," I heard on the line, "this is Wilda Powers. I read your manuscript last night, and I must tell you that I think it is wonderful."

I thought I had to be dreaming, but then I saw my reflection in the mirror. If I were actually dreaming, I wouldn't have seen myself—I would have seen Robert Redford standing there in the mirror instead.

"I love the story," she continued, "and I am in a position to acquire the American publishing rights for your novel. We would like to publish *Rue Haute*—retitled for the English market as *High Street*—through our Avon Paperbacks series. If you will come back to our office around noon today, we will have a contract for you to sign." In contrast to the more formal manner with which she had conducted our first conversation, her voice now sounded excited. It was as if Super Elli had found his Lois Lane, and a book contract to boot!

I practically flew from the hotel up to West Fifty-seventh Street. I feared that something might happen between the time Wilda Powers called and the time I showed up to receive and sign my portion of the contract. My fears were unfounded. Once I got there, it was miraculously easy. I was about to shake her hand for a third time in less than twenty-four hours, but I was so overwhelmed with joy that I gave her a big hug instead. She blushed a bit, but I could see that she felt as delighted as I did. After all, the touch of a super-hero can be powerful!

I treated myself to a lunch of Nathan's hot dogs and an Orange Julius shake before heading back to the Warwick to phone André and let him know what had happened. Because of the time difference, it was eight at night in Belgium. When I called, André had just returned to our apartment to get some sleep after a ten-hour session in the editing studio. I could tell he was still groggy at first, so I had to repeat the incredible news to him a few times before he realized what I was telling him. We both congratulated each other across the time zones, and then André begged for me to come home. I could tell that he was excited by the news, but something in his voice sounded very lonely and agitated. I knew that I needed to get back to him with my love and support. After I hung up, I immediately called Renee. She answered the phone with that tired voice that most parents have when they get a call.

"Hello?" she said.

"Hey, guess what? Your big strong brother is in town," I responded casually.

"Elliot? *Elliot!* What are you doing here? Is everything all right? Is André with you?"

"No," I explained, "he's back in Belgium finishing the edit of our movie. I came here to get us a contract with a New York book publisher for the American rights to the novel—and guess what? I *got* one!"

We both giddily chirped back and forth to each other like two freshly hatched baby chicks. She congratulated me. "This calls for a celebration!"

"I know. Why don't you come into the city? I'm staying at the Warwick. Meet me here around eight o'clock. It'll be so great to see you. So much has happened, it's amazing!"

"I can get the sitter for Alyse, and then I'll come in. You see, I have something to tell you as well, Elli," she said, in a voice suddenly shy yet hopeful. "I met a man. It's only been a few weeks, but he's really nice. Who knows, maybe it'll turn into something, huh?"

"That's great, sis!" I said, genuinely excited for her. "Save the rest for dinner tonight. We can talk more then."

We hung up. I felt victorious, but with no conversation to fill it anymore, I suddenly realized that the hotel room was a very quiet and vacant place. For some reason, the silence made me think of Momma. Maybe it was being back in New York again, or maybe it was the fact that this was exactly the kind of silence that Momma made it her mission to disrupt wherever she went. All I knew was that some rather incredible things were happening to me now. Wasn't it natural that I would want to call my mother and tell her how well everything was going for me?

When she came to visit Belgium two summers before, Renee had given me Momma's new phone number for her place in Monticello. I had written it on a slip of paper that I kept in my wallet, but I had never planned to call. Filled with confidence, I dialed the number and waited to hear Momma's voice on the line. It seemed strange to be so excited to speak with my mother, but I felt that I had accomplished so much and I wanted to let her know about it. I even fantasized that my story about Belgium during World War II would finally make her proud of me.

As the phone continued to ring, though, I became increasingly anxious. On the fourth ring, I heard the click of the line and there it was: my mother's voice, barking "Hello?" into the phone. Brought back to my senses by the sound of her voice—the voice that had always expressed disapproval of me— I hung up. Like a fool, I still needed her love. What I *didn't* need, however, was yet another earful of proof that my mother was never going to get who I was.

I knew where I wanted to go. Downtown, to Greenwich Village. Something told me I needed to get as far away from my isolated hotel room as possible. Besides, I wanted to see what it felt like to walk those city streets as a New Yorker returning home on the wings of triumph. I took the subway down to Christopher Street. I found myself in the throes of a sentimental journey around my former stomping grounds. I had done so much in the past few years in Belgium with André at my side, but it felt as if it had been mere days since I had left New York City.

As I wound my way to my old apartment on Jane Street, I was struck by how much louder and brasher Manhattan had become. The streets, the buildings, and the mounds of garbage were exactly as I remembered them. It was the *people* who had all seemed to change. In place of the acid rock of the late sixties and early seventies, there were now two new kinds of music—disco and punk rock—that were changing the look of the people downtown. The fashion I saw around me that day was equal parts glamour and clamor. One block would bring into view long-haired teenage kids wearing hippie clothes similar to those I'd seen at Woodstock years before—flared bell-bottom pants and platform shoes, for example. The next block brought forth hard-edged city dwellers with short, spiky haircuts; ripped jeans; and steel-tipped combat boots.

Most of all, it was the leather that I saw people wearing that got my attention. As I looked around that afternoon, I also saw gay couples in leather walking down the street holding hands. I had grown accustomed to this kind of out-in-the-open affection in Belgium, but it was not something I had expected to see back home in New York. But gay guys weren't the only people wearing leather—straight men and women also seemed to be hip to our style. I couldn't believe it. The subversive and largely hidden wardrobe embraced by those of us in the gay S&M underground had been adopted by those in the mainstream.

I walked past the record shop off Christopher Street where I had taken André after we first met, and was amazed to see a promotional poster for a heavy metal band called KISS. All four members of the band were wearing make-up and dressed head to toe in tight-fitting black leather outfits and sharp spiked gloves. My dick got hard as I looked at that poster. I would gladly have allowed any member of the group to throw me down and have his way with me right on the sidewalk. Sadly, the record store clerk explained that the guys in the band were pretty fervently straight.

Apparently, conventional notions of homosexual love in straight American society were also being challenged by brave new films from Hollywood. After heading back up to midtown, I had a few hours to kill before I was supposed to meet Renee, so I decided to go see a movie. On a few different theater marquees, I saw the unusual title of a movie, *Dog Day Afternoon,* starring the great Al Pacino. Not knowing what to expect, I bought a ticket. I was excited by the story of a panicked bisexual who decides to rob a bank in order to help his gay lover pay for a sex-change operation. The fact that this daring film was based on a real incident that had taken place a few years earlier in Brooklyn was not lost on me. I took the film as a sign. If everything was changing for the better back home in New York, maybe it was time to move back.

I saw Renee for dinner that night. I was thrilled to hear about how much fun she was having with her new boyfriend, her first since the divorce. Jay was five years older than her and also divorced, and he made her feel renewed and attractive again. Perhaps it would get more serious in time, but for the moment, Renee seemed to be enjoying her life again. At last, she was free. She asked me to consider coming back with André to visit New York, and I told her we would see.

The next day, I flew out of New York faster than a speeding bullet, my Super Elli costume packed in my carry-on bag along with the signed publishing contract. *Avon calling, indeed!* André was waiting for me at our apartment when I returned, and he hugged and kissed me right there in the doorway. When I showed him the contracts, he declared me some kind of mysterious wizard. He wanted to call the publishing director at Rossel at home, but I told him that I wanted the pleasure of telling the guy in person and would visit the Rossel offices first thing on Monday. Suffice it to say, the publishing director was quite astonished when I showed him the Hearst/Avon Paperbacks contract. And the business office was just as annoyed when I presented them with the receipts from my trip.

❦   ❦   ❦

By early 1976—about four and a half months after the wrap on *Rue Haute*—the film was still not finished. We had a lot on our plates. In addition to editing the film, we were simultaneously trying to finalize the French-language version of the novel so that it could be published by Rossel on time, in March. At the same time, André was also directing a new comedy by the Brazilian playwright João Bethencourt called *The Day They Kidnapped the Pope*. It became the smash hit of the 1975 theater season in Belgium, giving us some great publicity for the release of the film.

Still, the show put that much more stress on André, who wanted to make sure the proper amount of time was given to editing the film. I could see that he really cherished the picture, and wanted to make it perfect. As for me, though, I found that I no longer thought too much about the story or the film. I felt that I had followed the story of Mimi and David and the silently guilty German soldier to its logical conclusion. It had been exciting enough for me to see the story through, first written on paper and then acted out by real people on real streets and filmed with real movie cameras. It was only when André started to explain to me how he and the film editor Susana Rossberg needed to select and incorporate the various flashbacks into the overall edit that I realized there was much more work to be done.

Whenever André asked me to come see how the editing was going, I gladly went with him. Compared to our short film *Marée Basse*, *Rue Haute* was a much more complicated picture. In the short, we had had two characters and a single, simple set. The editing on the short had been fairly straightforward, with the cuts dictated primarily by the actions and expressions of the two actors. When it came to *Rue Haute,* however, we had bigger mountains to climb. There were more actors, more scenes, and many different takes to choose from. All these factors needed to be considered in editing the film to best depict our story.

One of the major challenges we faced was figuring out how to signal to the audience that Mimi was experiencing a flashback. During the filming, I noticed that André would often arrange to have one of the movie cameras settle on something in the shot that would trigger Mimi's traumatic memories—a bouquet of white daisies or a small group of young kids playing with a ball. As the final edit began to emerge, I could see clearly how these visual cues helped create connection points between the past and the present. Where I had used words in the book to establish the feverishly disoriented state of Mimi's mind, André had used images of everyday objects and activities. So a bouquet of white daisies in 1975 would trigger a flashback to similar flowers Mimi had received from her husband in 1943, soon before he had been taken away.

The first cut was slightly under two hours long, mostly because André wanted to give the actors enough time to reveal their responses to things being said or done around them in a natural, organic way. Mostly, I loved it, though there were a few scenes I felt could be tightened up to keep the film from feeling too slow-moving. The editor, Susana, agreed with me, and I watched as they went back through and recut some of the scenes I had pointed out.

While we waited to receive Mort's music for the film soundtrack, André began to worry that we might not actually like what he sent us. André was concerned that Mort's pop music background might lead him to create music that was too lightweight for the film we had made. I reminded him that Mort had done amazing work on the English translations of Jacques Brel's songs, and that we had absolutely adored the short song he had written for Annie to sing by the fireplace during the scene at the country house.

We received a tape from Mort just after the New Year. There were two compositions, and a note from Mort about how he envisioned each being used. There was one very melancholy piece written for a single piano in one version and arranged for two acoustic guitars in another version. This music was supposed to signify Mimi's life in the present. The second piece featured a dissonant melody performed by a full electric progressive rock ensemble and was meant to be played during flashbacks to the Nazi arrest. André was pleased with this piece—he felt it heightened the tension of the scene. I didn't agree. I felt that silence was the best accompaniment to the disturbing scene, but I trusted André and wanted to remain supportive for his sake.

All told, we were very satisfied with Mort's musical contributions to the film. I was less pleased with my own work as an actor. Even though I had written the scene in which I appeared, I had repeatedly blown my lines on set, perhaps because I was nervous or overworked. Five takes in, I had had to ask André if I could simply improvise my dialogue with Mort's character, David. We did the take, I said what I felt I would say under the circumstances, and finally the scene was done. Still, I was so embarrassed about my performance that I begged André to remove the scene from the movie. The more I asked him to remove it, though, the more he insisted that the scene must remain. After a while, it became a bit of a joke between us. I would pretend to cry and shout, "But no, Monsieur Ernotte, you must remove me from your film—it will *ruin* me!" André would then tease me, much to Susana's amusement, saying, "Monsieur Tiber, I am sorry. I cannot grant your request. The scene must stay."

Whenever he came home tired or distressed, I would make him laugh by springing my objection about my scene in the movie. It was a bit of silliness between us, but it was enough to get him through a number of tough moments, and to remind him that he was the director, and a good one. His happiness meant so much to me.

And in the end, he managed to play a little joke of his own. On Valentine's Day, I met him at our RTB editing room. Turning away from the flatbed editor, André gave me the final cut of the film as a gift, a big red ribbon wrapped around the metal film cans.

"Hey, is this—? Oh, baby, yes! You finished it!" I said. "This is fantastic! We've given birth to a nine pound bouncing bundle of film! Can we watch it right now?"

"Yes, Elliot," André said, as his smile began to droop, "the film is finished. But I am sorry to say I have some bad news."

"What? You couldn't use Mort's music?"

"No," he said, looking very sad, "no, Elliot. It was necessary, you see, for me to eliminate your scene with Mort from the final cut. I am sorry, Elliot."

"Oh, uh, well, that's okay. I understand." I pretended not to be disappointed, but I was.

We watched the film one reel at a time. It began with a montage of photographs that I had taken around rue Haute. Opening credits had been added to the start of the film, and Mort's piano piece immediately set a sad and intriguing tone. Many of the early scenes in the film had a strange and death-like stillness to them, as if everyone were walking on eggshells. The relationship between Mimi and David developed slowly, showing how beautifully Annie and Mort had worked together under André's direction. At the same time, Bert Stuys' performance as the guilt-stricken former Nazi soldier was haunting in a way that transcended language. Watching him, I felt certain that he could have been effective as a motion picture actor in the silent film era, so expressive were his gestures and movements.

Then, about midway through the film, I was caught completely off guard. My scene with Mort hadn't been cut at all. There I was, standing next to Mort and improvising my lines as David's friend Mike in my own relaxed way. It was so strange to see myself as one of the living, breathing characters in our movie. Since I hadn't expected to be in the final cut, I was free to see my performance as a part of something far bigger than myself. In that moment, I looked at Elliot Tiber and thought, *Well, whaddya know? The kid's got talent.*

I looked over at André and he said, "Happy Valentine's Day, Elliot."

What a wonderful way to celebrate everything we had been through. Our movie was born.

Rossel published *Rue Haute* as planned in March 1976, about a month before the film was set to premiere. A few days after the book came out in Belgium, something fantastic and totally unexpected happened. André's mother called just as we were waking up and told us to buy the morning papers as soon as possible. She told André that *Rue Haute* was reported to be the number one bestselling novel both in the Belgian and the Paris newspaper book sections. We were thrilled. It was so exciting for me to see both our names on that bestsellers list.

I was surprised to see, however, that my name had been listed second to André's—both on the cover and in all the press mentions. My role in the creation of the book seemed to have been casually dismissed. I felt hurt. *Rue Haute* had been my idea from day one. I had cultivated it and brought the book to life—though André had certainly assisted me in that process. When it came down to it, his principal role had been to translate the book into French. He had directed our screenplay; I had written the book. Without my original work, though, there would have been nothing to translate and nothing from which to make a movie.

When I shared my anger and disappointment about the situation, André understood completely. As a good director, he knew that creative projects were collaborative, and that credit must be given where credit was due. He called the Rossel office immediately to get some answers. As it was explained to us, Rossel's marketing department felt that André's name should receive primary billing on the book and in all promotional material because he had better name recognition with the Belgian public. It took a while, but eventually this made sense to me.

André was used to being in the papers, but I was still new to acclaim of any kind. I remained happy to see my name on a published book, regardless of its placement. My work on *Sketch-Up* and *Attention: Fragile,* my lectures, and even the dub jobs André and I had done for the skin flicks had given me a certain level of pride and satisfaction. But there was nothing in the world like being a published author, and a bestselling one at that. Ever since I was a kid in Brooklyn, banging away at a typewriter and dreaming up zany stories to make Renee laugh, I had dreamed of becoming an author. And finally that dream had come true. Each morning, I woke up and had to remind myself that I had entered the rarefied sphere of the successful writers. I felt like I had graduated into the world of the creative arts, and that *Rue Haute*—book and movie—were my diplomas.

While André was initially as excited as I was, as time went on, he seemed to grow more agitated and sorrowful. I couldn't understand why, though I knew that he had been working too much and was plagued by the concern that the film would not connect with audiences. He was swallowing Valium pills a few at a time—he was always either heading up on one substance or coming down from another. More than ever, André seemed to be in dire need of inner peace. He told me that his fantasy was to curl up on the couch with an armful of books to read. Me? I did not want that at all. I wanted to savor every second of this incredible high, a high that far exceeded the intoxicating effects of even the strongest hash cookie. I told him to rely on me to keep things going with the book and the film, and he was only too glad to have me take the reins.

The week before the movie opened, Rossel set up a series of appearances and signings in major department stores and book shops throughout Belgium and in Paris. The first event at a Belgian bookstore was not very well attended, and I suggested to Rossel that future events might feature Annie Cordy and Mort Shuman. It was admittedly a little unorthodox to have stars of the film attend a book signing before the film had even been released, but I figured it was worth a try. Rossel said they would look into it, but we didn't really hold our breath waiting for it to happen. André and I were thus happily surprised when we showed up at the famous Parisian store Le Bon Marché on the Left Bank for a book signing and found Annie Cordy and Mort Shuman waiting there for us.

The publicist at Rossel must have worked extra hard to promote the event, because there were at least three hundred people standing with books in hand on a long line that stretched from the guest table to the back wall of the building. Several color banners announcing the book were displayed throughout the store, and there was another large one in the store's street-level display window. Annie, accompanied as ever by her husband, was in a delightful mood, and Mort was also quite cheery, drinking straight from a bottle of cognac and swaying a bit in his chair. Although André and I were sometimes asked for autographs, most of the attention went to the actors who had played our fictional creations. Books were being sold by the dozens. Just when we thought the event couldn't get any better, Mort began singing the Jacques Brel song "Amsterdam" in a fierce voice, bringing on a spontaneous ovation from the audience. The whole event was beyond magical. I felt as if we had all stepped into the pages of some far happier and more successful entity's book.

The popularity of the book led me to believe that the people of Belgium were ready to revisit the sensitive topic of the Holocaust. At the next few bookstore events, where only André and I were in attendance, there were many on line who wanted to shake our hands and thank us for what we had written. We even met a few older Belgian Jews who had lost relatives during World War II. It was incredibly touching to meet those people. I relied on

André to translate everything that was being said by these survivors, but I learned so much more by looking into their eyes. Sometimes I told them how my mother had lost nearly her entire family at the turn of the century in tsarist Russia. André would translate my words into either French or Flemish, and people would nod knowingly.

As the Belgians and I shared our family stories of wounds and survival, no one found it necessary to cry. These people had been driven far beyond the realm of tears, considering what they and their loved ones had suffered. It was justice enough for many of our readers that we had simply told their story. For perhaps the first time in my life, I felt proud of my Jewish heritage. I now understood far better the incredible struggle that the Jewish people had endured over the centuries and throughout the world. It made me that much more grateful to have the freedom to live as I wished, because I knew just how rare that freedom had been for my ancestors. André could see that my exchanges with these survivors affected me deeply, and he was very attentive to my feelings as we headed back home from each event. "If this is how people are responding to the book," I said, "can you imagine what the response will be once the film is released?"

Looking out the window of our taxi, André said, "We will see."

⚘   ⚘   ⚘

The movie's gala premiere, now heavily anticipated as a result of our strong book sales, was held in one of the largest movie houses in Brussels. It was arranged by Pierre and Alain, who knew all the right people to invite. Members of the Belgian press turned out in force, as did the Belgian and French performers and celebrities who went to these events to see and be seen. Pierre and Alain had invited Jon Voight, but to our disappointment, he had not been able to make it. If he had, maybe we would have had a chance to talk with him about doing another film project together. No such luck. Our guests did include the great French actor and singer-songwriter Charles Aznavour, a friend of Annie's, who had shown his support by providing the preface to our book.

André and I arrived at the premiere in a limousine. We were greeted by what seemed liked hundreds of people, many holding copies of the book and asking for autographs. Soon after, Annie arrived, decked out in sequins and feathers and looking very much like the flamboyant comedienne the public had known up to this point. Because of Annie's involvement, people who had not read our book probably assumed the movie was going to be some kind of musical comedy. Boy, would they be surprised when they saw her in the film as a sickly madwoman! Mort Shuman showed up, a little tipsy, with a well-endowed young Parisian lady on his arm. André's family was there, too. His father was in good form, telling anyone who would listen that the Ernottes were originally from France and not Belgium. Fanny, always supportive of André and me, was wearing her finest gown and a fur coat borrowed from a friend. I felt a little sad that Renee and Alyse couldn't attend, and that so many people I had known back in the States were not present to see what André and I had created together.

There were nearly a dozen photographers and various newscasters covering the premiere for regional television and radio programs. Nearly all of them wanted to speak with Annie or Mort before they went in to watch the film. Very few of the reporters paid attention to us, or to Pierre and Alain. That wasn't a problem, though. We knew that movie stars were vital to getting coverage on a motion picture, especially for first-time filmmakers like us. Because we seemed to be largely invisible, though, I didn't even feel like I was going to a premiere of a movie that I helped create. Only when we got inside and took our seats near the front row did it sink in—it was really happening. I looked at André and said, "Wow." He looked behind us at the rows of people, then turned back to me. "Oy."

We held hands as the lights dimmed. The audience was very quiet as the film began, and remained that way for much of the picture. I began to worry that people didn't like the way that we had written the characters. Then came my short scene with Mort, right after the church scene in which Mimi condemns those in attendance and the priest for believing in the existence of God. Maybe it was the way I said my lines, which sounded very off-the-cuff and casual in comparison to the very specifically written lines of dialogue throughout the rest of the picture. All I know is that some folks in the audience started to laugh, which was proof enough for André and me that people were engaging with the movie. As far as I was concerned, if a theater filled with Belgians in the audience could find favor with a scene featuring lines improvised by an untrained actor from Brooklyn, then the movie was working.

But this comic relief was momentary. By the end of our film, most of the people in the audience were wiping away tears. People seemed genuinely touched by the film. We were still seated when Mort got up and began to clap loudly for us. Within seconds, everyone was on their feet and clapping. Pierre and Alain walked over to us and encouraged us to stand up for the applause. So we headed to the front of the theater and took our bows with Annie and Mort and Bert.

Afterwards, pictures were taken. The burgomaster of rue Haute—a short and mildly inebriated-looking man wearing a traditional Belgian costume for reasons I couldn't fathom— presented Annie with a special crest from the city. Unfortunately, both André and I were elbowed out of the picture during the photo shoot. Fed up with being relegated to the sidelines of our own movie premiere, I realized it was time to take action. *Exit Elliot, enter Super Elli!* I thought.

I stepped forward and shouted Annie's name to the crowd in celebration. As they took up the cheer, I started to lift Annie up onto my shoulders. The burgomaster, though shorter than me by at least a foot, didn't want to be out-done in front of all those cameras. So he quickly got some of his subordinates to help me lift Annie, and then had others from his party put him up on *their* shoulders. With Annie on my shoulders and the burgomaster close behind, I proceeded to lead everybody in the theater out into the street, forming a happy procession in celebration of our little big movie.

I looked over at André, standing with me in the midst of all the people and laughter and revelry that surrounded us. He made his way to me, put his arm around me, and said, "I love you" close in my ear. Everything was perfect that night. It was the culmination of so many things for us; a wonderful moment in our careers and in our lives.

Pierre and Alain worked to ensure that *Rue Haute* was booked in many movie theaters, not only in Brussels but throughout Belgium and France. To capitalize on the popularity of Bert Struys, the Flemish actor who played our Nazi soldier, Pierre and Alain arranged for certain prints of the film to have Dutch subtitles so that they could be played in Flemish-speaking regions in Belgium and the Netherlands.

The gala opening in André's hometown of Liège was a special event to which all the local politicos and snobs had been invited. André received a standing ovation when he appeared. I enjoyed seeing how happy he was with this public recognition and the critical acclaim of his work as a film director. After the hard work he had done to make the film, he certainly deserved his share of celebration.

I started to talk with some of the actors and actresses whom I had gotten to know through my work as dramaturg at the Théâtre National. Whenever I was with André at show afterparties, I kept my eyes and ears open for anything that sounded like an opportunity for a screening of the film. Not long after the film had been released, André and I found ourselves talking with none other than the American theatrical producer Joe Papp, who had come with his wife to see one of André's shows. Papp was a kind yet street-smart guy, and it was a pleasure for me to talk to someone from New York about our film. It turned out that Papp—whose last name had been Papirofsky before he changed it—was also originally from Brooklyn. *Jesus, what is it about Brooklyn anyway?* I thought to myself, listening to Papp tell stories of how he had founded the Shakespeare in the Park performance series in Central Park, and how he had established the Public Theater as a venue for all manner of new theatrical works. "If you ever find that you and André want to come back to New York," Papp said, "be sure to get in touch with me."

As we bid Papp and his wife a good evening, the wheels started to turn in my head. I wondered if André might actually consider a return to New York, to get distribution for our film and to see what else might come up. I had felt something special back on those New York streets after meeting with Wilda Powers. Something was once again calling to me. To us both, perhaps.

In early May, Pierre and Alain told us that *Rue Haute* was being considered for a special screening at the prestigious Cannes Film Festival, but then it was not chosen. At the same time, Pierre and Alain submitted our film to the New Orleans Film Festival. We wound up winning the Grand Prix, the festival's award for best film.

And then the next big miracle in my life took place. We received the incredible news that the Belgian film ministry was poised to select *Rue Haute* as the official Belgian entry to the 1977 Academy Awards in Hollywood. While we understood that it was not a certainty, the fact that our film had even been considered struck me dumb with amazement. I was highly entertained by the idea that the town that hadn't allowed me to decorate a single set might now hand me and André a fucking Oscar! The thought kept my mind reeling way over the rainbow, and I held onto that feeling as I promoted *Rue Haute* in the following months.

Despite our success, this was a frustrating and often disappointing time for us. I saw that Pierre and Alain's other movie projects were becoming higher priorities for them. I arranged a meeting to discuss expanding *Rue Haute*'s reach. Pierre and Alain sidestepped the issue, instead offering to set up Belgian distribution for our earlier short, *Marée Basse*. They also suggested that André direct a new film Pierre had recently written, a star vehicle for a young Belgian actress. I'm sure they thought they were being generous, but I knew André would have no interest in working on somebody else's film. I explained to them both that I had been working over those past few months on two new screenplays, *Plexiglass Suicide* and *Elsie and the Pope*. If André and I were to do another film, we already had our own material.

Gradually, though, it became all too clear. While Pierre and Alain certainly needed to run their business, the fact was that they were not going to lift a finger to help us get *Rue Haute* seen around the world. I got the message. If the film was to be promoted, André and I were going to have to do it ourselves. Right then and there, I decided that I was going to spend every single day doing everything I could to keep breathing life into our newborn celluloid baby. At the top of my list now was to find a way to get our film shown in America.

When I told André about the meeting later that night, he seemed to freeze in place. He sat there for a good five minutes in what looked to be a catatonic state. Then, without saying a word, he got up and stood with his back to me, staring at the wall. The silence of the room made me feel worse and worse, and at last I couldn't take it anymore.

"André," I said, losing patience, "what the hell is wrong with you? I can't remember the last time I've seen you smile or laugh or feel happy about a fucking thing. We've got nothing but good things ahead of us. We've done TV shows and theater and written a book, we've made two movies. When are you going to let yourself enjoy what's happening to us? What's the matter with you, babe?"

He looked at me, eyes welling with tears, and began to weep. I held him in my arms and hugged him as he shook with sobs. "Elliot, Elliot," he murmured, "I am just so exhausted trying to remain *me* in the middle of all of this. I have no freedoms as an artist in this work that I do at the Théâtre National. Every time I try to make something new and different, I am pushed back into a box by what other people want to do. I feel like a fucking fool, Elliot! I am losing myself!"

I was genuinely shocked to learn how unhappy and frustrated he was as an artist. "Only with *Rue Haute,*" he said, beginning to smile, "with your story and the chance to direct a film of my own, I finally felt like I was able to make something that was a true reflection of who I am. Each day in the editing room, as I looked at all the different takes and remembered what I found in each part of the performance, the movie slowly became exactly what I imagined in my mind it could be. And as I worked on each scene and edited my vision of the story together with the music, I realized that it was the first time as a director that I felt free. You and me, working to make this beautiful story come to life in film—*that* is the greatest thing that has ever happened to me as an artist."

Then, as he held his face in his hands, he spoke in a voice of flat despair that sent a chill through me. "You, Elliot," and he looked at me with a face filled with sorrow and envy, "you love freedom, but I am tormented by it. If I stay here in this place, I fear that I will never again get the chance to create something that truly comes from *me,* to see my creative visions come true."

"Then we'll leave. We'll leave, André, and go live in Paris or Amsterdam or Morocco or the fucking Congo jungle. Wherever you want," I said, ready to don my Super Elli cape and save the day. By sheer force of will, my sense of humor, and devotion to freedom, I felt certain that I could keep it all going, no matter what.

"Elliot," he said, "I am tired of staying in this one place."

"Say the word, babe," I responded.

He stood silently, deep in thought with chin in hand. "If we are going to have more chances to make films . . ."

"New York?" I guessed, hoping that he was thinking the same thing that I had had on my mind for weeks.

"Yes," he said, "that is the answer." It was as simple as that—fate on a plate. I was amazed by what I heard, even a little surprised by the suddenness of it. "What, you want to go back to America? But I finally started to learn French, André. Last week, I managed *not* to order horse meat at the market."

He laughed. I could always make him laugh, no matter how bad things were.

"Well, if you really want to go back, we can do that, André. I think it will be great for us both, actually," I said, with a growing enthusiasm that turned into a great feeling of pride and exhilaration.

"But one does not just leave the country," André protested. "We need a plan."

"Why?" I replied. "The only plan I had in my mind when I came here was to find you. All the rest fell into place, and that's exactly what'll happen here."

Knowing that he was naturally more cautious with life decisions than I was, I reminded him about the Woodstock money that I had kept in my New York bank account. "It's what I call my freedom money, honey," I explained. "And if I have to use some of that money to help get us set up in Manhattan, then that's what I'm going to do." I had never really invested my money before. But I had total belief in what André and I were capable of doing, and I had no trouble putting my savings into our partnership.

"I do not know what to say," André said. "Thank you, *mon cheri*. I am very touched that you would do this for me."

"I do this for us," I said, holding him close and kissing his lips and his neck. Then I took him by the hand, and we made passionate love—reawakened, reborn, *ready*. We were going to follow our dreams, and right now those dreams were leading us back to America. It was time for us to head west.

12

Summer of Shove

"But I love so many of them. Which should I bring?"

André must have asked me that question ten times as we packed up his shirts the night before our flight to New York. There was no correct answer to the question, either. If I preferred the silk white dress shirt with black polka dots, he wanted to pack the black dress shirt with *white* polka dots. And if I liked the fuchsia turtleneck, he favored the turquoise one. My big mistake came when I tried a bit of reverse psychology, and told André that I didn't think he should bring his ruffled peach-colored shirt.

"What? You don't like this shirt? You told me you loved how it looked on me."

Great, I thought, *another ten minutes of me trying to talk my way out of a quarrel.*

"Really? Is that the shirt?" I said, feigning a look of puzzlement. "Are you sure, babe? Because I thought," I continued, reaching deep into our half-full bedroom closet, "that it was *this* shirt!" With that, I held up in front of him another ruffled dress shirt, nearly identical to the first except for its color.

"No, you got me that brown shirt last year for my birthday. After I had already showed you that I had this peach-colored one."

"André, you know they have these places called stores in New York. And in these stores, they sell all sorts of things—like shirts!"

"Forget it," said André, suddenly in a huff again. "You clearly do not understand."

"Christ, enough with these shirts already! If you can't figure out which shirts to pack, I'll sell them all to the gypsies while you sleep tonight!"

When I made my big move from New York to Belgium five years earlier, I hadn't worried about leaving anything behind. Besides missing Renee and Alyse, I had been only too glad to kick free of most of the material goods that I had accumulated at the Jane Street apartment. A lot had happened, however, over those five years in Belgium. I found it harder to part with the things that had become part of our lives there. It was even more difficult for André, who had to store most of his personal things and treasured items at his family's home in Liège, where his mother kept a watchful eye over all of it.

This, of course, was a major difference between our families. André could entrust his mother with objects of material or sentimental value. But if I asked Momma to look after anything, it would be dismissed curtly as worthless *mishegas* and she would either sell it, toss it in the garbage, or—better still, to her way of thinking—try to sell it to the garbage man.

André announced to the Théâtre National that he was stepping down as director, with a plan to direct live theater and new film projects in New York. Given the fractious nature of his relationship with the Théâtre, it was more a relief than a disappointment to all parties concerned. I was happy to see that André felt certain of his need to leave. We explained to the owner of our apartment building that we had been offered some projects in America, and arranged to have our old friends Hal and Catherine take over our rental. If our plans in New York went nowhere and we had to return to Belgium, we could easily get the apartment back from them.

Having made our decision to move to New York City, I called Renee long distance from the general office phone at the Théâtre National to let her know. Renee was delighted that we were coming back to America, but I detected a slight melancholy in her voice. Something was wrong. That's when Momma again entered the picture.

"I haven't had the chance to write you about it," Renee said, sounding a bit flustered. "It's all been so sudden. Elliot, Momma's leaving New York and moving to Israel."

It couldn't be. My mother was moving to the Holy Land? I didn't understand it at all.

"She decided that she's going to Israel just like that?" I asked, surprised but also a little amused by the news. "What, did she get caught trying to steal some *glatt* kosher whitefish from the Monticello deli?" At least that got Renee to laugh. "No, Elliot, nothing that drastic," she said, "but Momma has been talking about it to all of us over this past year."

I felt a twinge of guilt as it dawned on me that when I left New York, the burden of looking after Momma had fallen to my sisters, particularly Renee. Then I remembered the many years I had spent at the motel trying to please that bespectacled ding-a-ling who spawned me. That was more than enough to shut off the guilt inside of me but good.

"Wow, so Sonia Teichberg is going to live in a kibbutz, huh? When is she leaving?"

"Well, she hopes to sell the place in Monticello and be on her way before Hanukkah. At least that's what she said. She also tells me that she's going there because she wants to be closer to God now that Pop is gone."

"That's a classic example of 'too little, too late,'" I said sharply. My wounds from my father's final days were still deep.

"I know, I know, she's impossible," Renee said. "She still tells me that I should forgive Freddy and get remarried so that I can be a respectable woman again."

"She's psychotic, obviously!" It made me almost as psychotic to think that she was trying to push my sister back into a terrible situation like that.

"No, she's just Momma. She thinks she's being helpful," Renee reasoned, always the diplomat of the family. "Anyway, I wonder what she'll do when she hears that you're coming back to New York at the same time she's packing up to leave for Israel."

"That's a cinch," I said, biting my tongue. "First, she'll search me for cash and coins. And then she'll try to guilt me into coming to live with her in the Holy Land. Can't you see me, wearing a yarmulke and a prayer shawl and reciting from the Torah as Momma tries to talk our neighbors into finding me a nice Jewish wife who's still got some good birthing years left to her? *Oy gevalt!* No thanks, baby sister."

The topic veered off Momma and back to my return to New York. I explained to Renee that I wanted to find another place in Greenwich Village, and that I was going to work hard to secure better promotion and distribution for our movie while André looked for work as a theater director. I explained to Renee that this was a very general plan. The fate of the movie would dictate our next moves.

Renee was very sweet and offered to let André and me stay at her home in New Jersey when we arrived. It was great to have the love and support of a family member, but I told her that New York was the only place where we believed we could get ourselves to the next level in our careers. She wished us well, said that she loved us, and told me that Alyse would need to see her Belgian uncles as soon as we arrived. I promised that we would see each other before the New Year.

Once we got back to New York, I figured that I could see about gaining access to the Woodstock money. While we were trying to set up shop in New York, I figured my Woodstock funds would help keep us afloat. Interest had been accruing over the years, and I had arranged for my account statements to be sent to Renee's home while I was abroad. I had nothing to hide from her, and it pleased me to know that there was at least one family member I could trust.

Perhaps if we had already had a solid American movie distribution deal in hand before we left, the move to New York might have felt more permanent. As it was, we packed light and gave the rest of our belongings—including at least forty of those damn shirts—to Fanny, who had rented a large car and driven from Liège to see her "two beautiful sons" off.

After we loaded up the trunk and back seat of Fanny's car with our stuff, the three of us shared a quiet moment. Fanny gently cupped my face with her hands, kissed me on both cheeks, and hugged me. As we hugged, she said to me in English, "Now you will watch over and take good care of my dear André. *Oui*, Elliot?" I assured Fanny through my tears that I would never leave his side. We broke our embrace, and she walked back to get something from the car. She returned with a beautiful black wool sweater. "This is so that you will be warm, and so you will not forget your loving Fanny and how she made this for you." Suddenly, I felt sad, thinking of what I was leaving. I had put down solid roots in Belgium, and I had come to know how wonderful it was to be truly loved.

Fanny turned to André, who was very stoic as he prepared to say goodbye. She touched his face, and said, "Your father and your sisters are proud of you, *mon bébé doux.*"

André smiled and said softly, *"Je t'aime, maman,"* telling his mother that he loved her. Their hug was gentle but dignified, and I felt that there was between them a deep reserve of trust and faith that need never be discussed. Their bond as mother and child would not be severed by thousands of miles and an ocean.

I had arranged for a black limousine to drive us to the airport. The limo pulled up just as Fanny was preparing to drive away. She saw the limo behind her in the mirror, looked at us both and smiled proudly. *"Au revoir, mes fils,"* she called as she began to drive away. As she drove off, I shouted my own heartfelt parting words to Fanny in French.

Turning back to André, I saw he had a mildly amused look on his face. "What?" I asked him.

"Nothing," he said, "it is very sweet to hear you speak French—and correctly, too!"

"Yeah," I laughed, "I finally start figuring out what I'm saying, and then we leave."

We pondered the irony in silence for a few moments, took a last look around, and left the land of waffles and chocolate.

We arrived in New York's Kennedy Airport on November 24, 1976, the day before Thanksgiving. The airport was jammed with all kinds of people whizzing past us and coming from every conceivable direction. *New York hasn't changed at all,* I thought to myself. As we waited for our bags, I kept an eye on our film, which I had carried with me on the plane in my duffel bag—the same one that had held all my Woodstock loot when I drove to Hollywood back in 1969.

About six weeks before we left Belgium, André had pointed out that we needed a print of the film with English subtitles in order to market it to non-French-speaking audiences. Knowing that we were basically on our own with the film by that point, I suggested that we move quickly and instead dub the film into English. Subtitles would have been better, but we were pressed for time and we had the knowledge and contacts to do the dubbing work ourselves. We did some of the dialogue ourselves, but for the rest we called upon some actors and actresses from the Théâtre National who spoke English very well. Fortunately, since the character David was American, the dialogue for many of the scenes was already in

English, simplifying our work. We had also needed new opening credits for the dubbed print, which our editor, Susana, had been happy to prepare for us. With this hastily assembled print of *Rue Haute*—now called *High Street* to accommodate English-speaking audiences—I intended to win over the United States.

Once we got our luggage, we had a taxi take us straight to Manhattan. I had asked the driver to take us to the Chelsea Hotel on Twenty-third Street, knowing what a hot spot it had become in recent years for free spirits. As we drove, I told André about how artists such as Bob Dylan, Allen Ginsberg, science-fiction writer Arthur C. Clarke, and even Janis Joplin had called the Chelsea their home over the years. It wasn't a palace by any stretch, but it was shelter from the storm—and I felt it might inspire us to find an apartment that much faster.

We spent Thanksgiving at a small Chinese restaurant nearby. André ordered the Peking duck, and I opted for vegetables in black bean sauce over a heaping bowl of rice. At the end of the meal, the waiter brought fortune cookies. André opened his cookie and found a message that spoke loftily about the path to the future being lined with acts of kindness. I opened my cookie, only to find that there was no message typed out on the paper—it was blank.

"What does yours say?" André asked. I showed him.

"Well," I kidded, "who knows? Maybe this proves that our future is yet to be written by us, not by some anonymous guy working in a fortune cookie factory."

That elicited a smile from André. I hoped I was right.

Within a week of apartment hunting, we were able to find a furnished studio apartment at the London Terrace Gardens. This residential complex filled an entire square block in Chelsea. The apartments had an Old-World charm, and there were huge courtyard gardens where one could relax and read a book. Because the complex was within walking distance of several book publishers, many of the tenants were writers. Even better, the complex was in the heart of Manhattan's gay community, which had gradually moved north from Greenwich Village and was now settled in Chelsea. As a result, many upscale boutiques, restaurants, and clubs had begun to pop up in the area, too. Electricity was included in the rent, as was unlimited use of an

Olympic-sized swimming pool, a true luxury for a 1930s-era city building. Our apartment was perfect.

Once we had moved into our new place, I called Renee and Alyse to come see us in the city for dinner. When they arrived at our apartment, it was just like old times. I grabbed Alyse and gave her a hug, only sort of pretending that she was too big for me to pick up anymore. We ordered in from a local pizzeria and enjoyed the comfort of our new apartment. Glad to put aside thoughts of plays and films and career decisions for a few hours, André seemed to enjoy spending time drawing with Alyse in her coloring books. That gave me the chance to catch up a little with Renee, who had broken things off with Jay, the guy she had been dating a few months earlier.

"So what are your plans?" Renee asked us.

"Well, we conquered Belgium, so we've come back home to take Manhattan—and eventually, the world," I joked, reminding her of the plans I'd made for world domination when we were kids in Brooklyn.

"But seriously, Renee," I continued, "we've got this brand new film, and the English version of the book will be released soon. With a little luck and a lot of phone calls and meetings, we're going to make names for ourselves as artists here in America."

"Maybe you should concentrate on New York first before you go after the farmers and their wives out in Montana," Renee teased.

"The important thing," André said, serious as ever, "is that we continue to grow and express ourselves creatively."

There was a pause in the conversation, and then Renee looked me and said, "She moved, you know."

"What, Momma moved?" I asked, not quite believing my ears. "Are you serious?"

"Yep. She moved into a small condominium in a little town called Netanya outside Tel Aviv, and is getting to know her neighbors there."

Still surprised, I replied, "Well, I'm happy if she's happy. *Shalom!*" And that was all we said about Momma for months.

The holiday season was in full swing, and while I wasn't all that interested in celebrating Hanukkah, I knew how much André loved Christmas. As a show of love, I bought him a small ceramic nativity scene and placed it on the living room table. Then I went back out and bought a Christmas wreath. I thought it looked like a bagel, and I didn't know where to put it in the apartment. Watching TV earlier that day, I had seen an episode of Don Ho's variety shows. Taking inspiration from his fashion choices, I slung the wreath around my neck like I was wearing a Hawaiian lei.

André came home just as it was getting dark outside. As he walked into the apartment, I met him at the door wearing the wreath and did my best hula dance, singing, "Aloha, Monsieur Ernotte, and a merry Christmas too!" I'm sure I looked like a polar bear trying to ice skate. He cracked up, kissed me on the lips, and danced me gently toward our bedroom. Within a few minutes I went from being lei'd to getting laid.

That night, we went out and bought a small Christmas tree with a red stand and several strands of multi-colored Christmas lights. As a show of his support for me, André also bought a menorah to sit next to the tree, which we placed on one of the end tables in our living room. André explained that we had to keep fresh water in the stand so the tree wouldn't dry out before December 25. I told him that he could be the director of watering the tree, while I would be in charge of tree lighting design.

Watching the New Year's ball drop on TV, ringing in 1977, it was as if we'd heard the starting gun in a marathon race. We had had a month to get settled in New York, and now it was time to begin working on our careers. André had yet to set up any new director jobs, but he began to get in touch with some colleagues at Yale and Columbia. His contacts had not forgotten him—if anything, word of his more recent successes in Belgium had increased his cachet. It seemed likely that he would be hired to guest-direct some shows at these universities, and perhaps even invited to teach. Meanwhile, he started to make advances in the off-Broadway community, going to local plays and afterparties and meeting with various producers and directors. We both understood that he needed to move in the right kinds of circles, and I supported him as best I could.

It was hard for André to have gone from national prominence back in Europe to a state of relative anonymity in New York. There were some nights, even some weeks, when he simply didn't want to go to some show and hang around the cast party in hopes of picking up what he disdainfully called "those little theater bread crumbs." He began to drink more than before, and he sometimes fell into dark moods that lasted for hours. He had worked hard for years, he had paid his dues; most of all, he felt that his work spoke for itself. I had to remind him that unfortunately, most of his work spoke in French, not English—and thus might not be well understood here in the States.

In the meantime, my big goal was to secure distribution for *High Street*. Whenever I wasn't trying to drum up a deal, I was busy working on comedy routines and trying to write a serious stage play. Wanting to be with André as much as I could, I thought that a new play might be the right thing for our partnership at the time. If an opportunity to stage new work presented itself, I wanted us to be ready with material. I already had finished my screenplays for *Plexiglass Suicide* and *Elsie and the Pope*—two strongly absurd works more in keeping with *Sketch-Up* than *Rue Haute*.

In *Elsie and the Pope*, an embittered Jewish woman named Elsie Fogelman successfully kidnaps Pope Pius XII at the end of World War II. She forces the Pope to adopt a strictly kosher diet and convinces him to convert to Judaism. They end up falling in love, but the marriage is never consummated because the former Pope is struck and killed by an ice cream truck as he and Elsie cross the street on their way to the local synagogue. Elsie is so distressed that she cuts off all her hair and becomes a Rosicrucian.

In *Plexiglass Suicide,* two gay men believe that they are both invisible to the world after taking acid. They dream up various ways to cleanse modern society of corruption and hate, especially targeting those who are prejudiced against gay people. By the end of the play, the two men realize that they can never change the world around them, though they have changed themselves for the better.

Around this time, we became good friends with one of our neighbors in London Terrace. Frank Fleinowski—his friends called him Flynn—was one of the department heads at the New School University for Social Research. The New School was a university founded in 1919 by progressive thinkers, and had served as a haven during World War II for scholars who had been persecuted in Nazi Europe. When Flynn learned that I had taught at Hunter College, he expressed interest in getting me to teach some courses at the New School. As an established director, André was also of serious interest to the school's theater department. Since I had received no responses to my film inquiries yet, I figured that teaching might be a good move.

Flynn brought André and me to meet his close friend, the Dean of Faculty, Lou Falb. Dean Falb was bright and very friendly, with a prominent nose and a cheerful smile. I had told Flynn about *Rue Haute,* and both he and Dean Falb were interested in seeing the film. Impressed by our book of press clippings and André's impeccable theatrical background, he offered André a job teaching a few courses in theater arts. Falb then turned to me. He had been told by Flynn that I had already taught college-level art and design, but I explained to Falb that I was no longer interested in teaching those subjects. In light of my new success as an author, it seemed reasonable to instead teach creative writing. When Falb asked me what I would call the course, the first thing that came to mind was "Absurd, Twisted Comedy Writing."

Dean Falb loved the concept and thought it would make an excellent class. I was told that the school standards board required that at least twelve students be registered in order for a course to be held. Imagine my surprise when I heard that almost forty students had signed up! In order to accommodate all those students, the school had to add two more sections of the class. Once again, Super Elli had flown in and created another fantastic opportunity. I was now a college professor of humor.

I had no idea that my course would be so successful, or that I would wind up teaching it for the next seventeen years. Both André and I were proud to be affiliated with this prestigious college. Teaching not only helped us with the bills, but it also gave us a little extra authority amongst the New York theater community. Moreover, my classes were held two nights a week, leaving me ample time to pursue theater and film projects. While we waited for the American market to recognize the virtues of our film, we would work hard to nurture our artistic careers.

❁   ❁   ❁

High Street, the American edition of *Rue Haute,* had been published by Avon Paperbacks in spring of 1977, and served as a useful sales tool as I tried to secure distribution for the film. I had initially had some doubts about the American treatment of our book—the cover art made it seem like pulp fiction, worlds apart from the sweet and courageous story we had told. Still, we trust-ed that the folks at Avon knew what they were doing, and I sent a thank-you card to Wilda Powers for believing in us and putting the book into print. I always made sure I had a copy of the book on hand to show to theater owners.

When it came to selling *High Street* in the States, though, Super Elli was more like Stupor Elli. I had no experience at all when it came to arranging for distribution. It wasn't that I was completely clueless about the process, but it was relatively new and unpredictable to me. Still, I was ready to go down any avenue—First or Twelfth—to acquaint people with *High Street*. I read in the local papers that the Chelsea Cinema had a new owner. I knew the theater well, as I had seen many foreign movies there over the years. I called the theater and made my case for the film. To my delight, after seeing the film for himself, the new owner agreed to play the movie for a month. I was ecstatic.

I put in two calls. The first was to André, to tell him the news; the sec-ond was to Annie Cordy in Belgium, inviting her to the American premiere. Unfortunately, Annie was scheduled to do a concert at the Olympia Theatre in Paris, and her new TV series with Charles Aznavour was set to debut shortly afterward. Without her there, the premiere would not be as special as I had hoped.

Unable to get Hearst to chip in for advertising expenses, we had no money to get any kind of attention in the media. We certainly could not afford to hire a publicity firm to set up interviews and other notices. How naïve we were! We didn't know that we were supposed to hold previews of the movie for film critics, or that we needed to buy large display ads in the newspapers. We were counting on a big word-of-mouth response. We figured that with the cinema located in Chelsea, the sophisticated folks who lived in that area and who often went to see foreign films would flock to see our dramatic and important Holocaust-themed movie.

We had both hypnotized ourselves to live from dream to dream. But at one point or another, we all awaken from our dreams, no matter how sweet they are. It would take several months of heartbreaking effort before we learned just how immense the odds were against launching our film in Amer-ica. The true film fans had always had a certain love for French movies. But Belgian films? Not so much.

Besides, the Hollywood movies that were popular at the time seemed intended more for an audience of little kids and pimply-faced teens than for a group of discerning adults. That summer belonged to the worldwide phenomenon known as *Star Wars,* which was to make more money than any film before it. Spending a weekend at Renee's place in New Jersey, André and I decided to take Alyse to see this blockbuster from *American Graffiti* director George Lucas. *Star Wars* was certainly an exciting film, but it seemed to be more interested in robots and spaceships than in the performances of its real-life actors. I remember André saying to me as we left the theater, "I guess this is the kind of thing that Americans want to see now." We understood that by its very nature and theme, *High Street* was never going to be a big mainstream hit. It was then that we realized that we couldn't simply wait for our audience to come to us—it was going to be an uphill battle to attain public recognition.

☸   ☸   ☸

With *Star Wars* fresh in my mind, and only a few more days to build an audience for the premiere, I kicked myself into high gear. I presented myself to more than half a dozen Jewish community centers throughout the city, sharing my feelings about our film's serious exploration of the Holocaust. And like the good son I was, I told them that my mother had seen the film and instantly given it the Jewish Momma Seal of Approval—meaning that it should make everyone feel guilty. That alone helped fill half of the five hundred seats in the theater.

Still pushing, I told my students at the New School about the screenings and also contacted friendly Hunter College colleagues with whom I had reconnected. Renee invited all of our relatives who were still breathing, even the ones who hadn't been in touch since Pop died. In turn, my relatives proceeded to invite anybody conscious enough to understand they were there to see a film and not just consume buckets of popcorn and unwrap hard candies during the movie. André had the wisdom to approach the Belgian Embassy about the film. The name Annie Cordy drew much interest, as we knew it would.

André and I stood on Eighth Avenue and watched as a workman set out the letters for our names and the movie title on the theater marquee. We stood for over an hour, half-expecting passersby to stop in their tracks upon learning that our film was coming to town. A handful of people looked up, but that was only because *we* were looking up. Still, I was so hyped that I coaxed André into going to a diner with me to celebrate with a few chocolate egg creams before he went to a rehearsal. André preferred champagne, but the "Jewish champagne" was always my beverage of choice on significant occasions.

André was caught up in my joyous frenzy, and for once was able to suspend his cynicism. After six years of watching me accomplish the impossible, he believed that I could successfully push *High Street* into the American film market. We didn't have any Hollywood connections, so instead we relied on instinct and hope.

By the day of our premiere, we felt certain that things were going to be great. We greeted our friends and colleagues and my extended family, all waiting on line under the Chelsea Cinema's brightly lit marquee. It was great to have Renee and Alyse there with us. Because Momma was in Israel, we didn't have to worry about getting her a ticket. Frankly, it was a relief not to have her yelling about everything and more once she arrived to the theater.

Soon enough, the movie theater owner arrived, accompanied by a heavily made-up lady in a too-tight dress who looked like she charged an admittance fee. The theater owner seemed a little wobbly, but we pretended not to notice. We had managed to get full attendance at the theater, and there was hardly an empty seat in sight. There was a palpable air of excitement in the auditorium. And then the house lights slowly faded to black. It was showtime.

André and I stood in the rear of the hall. My heart was beating like a jackhammer as the curtains slid open. The houselights dimmed, and the dubbed version of our movie began. The audience applauded when they saw our names in the opening credits, which made us feel both gratified and even more nervous. Things seemed to be going well. After about fifteen minutes, though, the screen suddenly went dark. A few minutes went by and the screen was still blank. I could feel panic starting to set in. I rushed up the stairs to the projection booth. I banged on the door, but the projectionist did not answer. André, normally so calm and composed, practically dragged the theater owner up the stairs by the lapel of his jacket. André was enraged. "What the fuck is happening here?"

"Hey, listen, what can I tell you?" the theater owner said, slurring slightly. "The projector must have broken down or something. Maybe the projectionist in there is high or something. Sorry, guys. Nothing I can do!"

André and I marched back down to the main floor and stood before the movie screen. Trembling from embarrassment, we apologized profusely to the audience and told them that the projector had stopped working. We explained that we would either arrange another screening or make sure that they were given back their money. Renee tried to talk to us a little as the place cleared out, but I told her we would catch up the next day.

We then waited for that moron projectionist to come out of the booth. After two hours had passed with no sign of the guy, I lost my temper. I smashed my shoulder hard against the door, knocking it down. As the door gave way, we saw the projectionist, a gangly kid no older than seventeen or eighteen, passed out on the floor. There was a hypodermic needle near his arm. The owner, who had been standing behind us, pushed his way in to check if the projectionist was breathing. "No problem, man," he said. "It's cool. Let him sleep it off."

"Call a goddamn ambulance now, or I will!" I screamed at him. Once the boy started making moaning sounds, we made a call to the police to report that a person was in need of medical assistance at the theater. This nightmare needed to end.

Resigned to the failure of our film's New York premiere, we retrieved our print from the projectionist's booth and got the hell out of the theater. The following morning, we went to the theater to demand the return of the ticket sales. When we arrived, there was a legal notice taped to the front door of the theater. It was a tax lien. We were shocked to see an unfamiliar name listed as the property owner at the theater. To our horror, we realized that we had been scammed. The guy we had dealt with didn't even own the theater. We sought advice from an attorney, but we had no options, since the guy had disappeared so swiftly.

André was embarrassed and heartbroken. I don't know where I got the courage to move forward, but I did. Mostly, he and I nurtured each other with the certainty that our movie would somehow get the success and recognition it deserved. Trying to drum up interest again, we went from one small independent cinema to another. We didn't know that filmmakers couldn't expect to get a booking just by showing up at a theater with a print of their movie. We discovered later that that was the work of distributors. Still blissfully unaware of how things worked, I wound up trying again with a tiny four-theater complex in the Village called the Quad Cinema, which had a following with local film buffs.

The owner of the theater told us he loved the film and would give it a limited run of four weeks, from mid-June to mid-July. If the movie made money for him, he would extend the run. When it came to talk of regional print advertisements on behalf of our picture, I told the theater owner that I would cover any expenses that might come up. I had the money, and nothing was going to get in our way this time—I would see to that. So when I needed to pay a little more than three thousand dollars to secure some local promotions, I pulled what was needed from my account.

We were pleased to have another shot, but we were wary of being tricked. And we still had no advertising budget, no press agent, and a very limited window of time in which to place a newspaper ad or two. What we had was a compelling and well-made film on a serious topic. We also had the benefit of having been screwed over already. We sure as hell were not going to let anything like what happened to us at that first screening take place again.

I made it my mission to call up each and every person who had come to the disastrous first screening. Since we had not been able to recover any of the money that our guests had paid, I told everyone that we had invited to the first screening that I was personally going to pay for their tickets. Again, I went to the Woodstock coffer.

André was touched, but he was also worried that I was spending so liberally from my reserves. I explained that the money was there to help us. We had worked too long and too hard on the film to not go for the big brass ring. I believed in the film, I believed in André, and I believed in myself.

Renee called to say that she wouldn't be able to make it to the next showing, nor would most of my relatives, who had returned to their homes in Florida. Truth be told, I didn't relish the idea of having my sister and all those relatives there again so soon after the abortive first screening. If something went wrong this time around, I didn't want it to happen in front of family—

their attendance would only increase the likelihood of Momma hearing that her son had flopped in New York.

The first screening at the Quad was a success—meaning that the projector didn't break. In addition to our repeat customers, we seemed to have drawn an art-house crowd, which suited us fine. The film shone on the screen and the audience that night seemed to react to it on a spiritual level, falling under the hypnotic power of Annie's performance. There was a pronounced stillness in the room, but it was borne of attentiveness, not boredom. As the film ended, the audience clapped respectfully and then slowly rose from their seats and left the theater. We thanked the ushers and the house manager, and made our way out to the street.

"Do you think they liked it?" I asked André, as I lit a cigarette.

"I cannot tell," he said, looking serious. "We will know by tomorrow."

Our concerns about the film's reception were shoved aside at daybreak. We received a call from the Quad theater owner, who told us that the film was a major hit with the New York critics. We had even gotten a good review in the *New York Times*. As I hung up the phone, I looked at André and smiled. "Stay here, make coffee, I'm going down to the newsstands!"

I hurried downstairs and made for the corner store, where I bought a copy of each of the local daily newspapers. On the way back to the apartment, I stopped at a bakery to get a dozen bagels and cream cheese—and two delicious chocolate croissants, in memory of the Belgian goodies we had often enjoyed. By the time I came back upstairs, André had the coffee made and poured into two mugs. I spread the magazines and papers on top of our bed, and we got under the covers with our breakfast and started to read. It was appropriate that we were in bed, because the wave of critical acclaim about us and our movie practically put us into a state of mutual orgasm.

I couldn't believe that all our hard work on the picture had finally paid off. The *New York Times* called our film "extraordinary" and highlighted Annie's performance as a "tour de force." A reviewer on CBS Radio declared it "[A] very sensitive movie . . . [and] one of the year's most unusual films." From the hippest paper in town, the *Village Voice*, came the praise that our film was "[A] rich, beautiful experience! Stunning . . . haunting." Although few of the New York papers knew who Annie Cordy was, each gave her exceptionally high marks for her touching performance. *Time* magazine wrote that *High Street* was "extraordinary . . . a movie that wrenches your heart."

It was a great victory for us, and certainly the best moment since we had returned to New York together. We went out for drinks, and then cruised over to the Mineshaft—and then on to the Anvil, followed by the Cockpit—for some serious S&M partying in full leather garb. There was a palpable vibe of "anything goes" in those leather bars, as if all manner of fantasy could be enacted there on the crowded and gloriously sweaty dance floors. These clubs were certainly not for sissies. There were a lot of big and burly guys there who liked their foreplay rough. If you tangoed with the wrong leather daddy at the wrong time, you might very well get knocked right on your ass in an alley outside the club.

For the most part, however, everyone understood that our special pleasures had to have some ground rules—this helped to keep things from getting too wild or violent down in the clubs. Still, gay men and women in New York had to be careful. In fact, we had heard about a series of vicious and still unsolved murders of gay men that had taken place near the gay bars over the past few years. Someone was apparently killing gay men and cutting up their bodies, placing the victim's severed body parts into garbage bags. It was terrifying to think there was someone out there whose sole interest was destroying gay people. As a couple, André and I felt fairly safe at these clubs because we would arrive together and leave together. It was the single gay men who had to be careful. Truth be told, though, the threat of death didn't diminish our taste for adventure. It actually intensified the erotic thrill that so many of us felt as we roamed the clubs.

During the first week of our movie's run, the Quad's 150-seat cinema was usually full. But for the remaining three weeks, it was mostly empty. We didn't know we were supposed to follow up on our success by publishing big ads quoting the rave reviews. We didn't know we could have arranged for TV and radio interviews, or engaged a publicist to set those up for us. Finally, with ticket sales dwindling, our film's four-week run was cut short by two days when a huge power blackout hit the city that July. So there we were again, dead in the water.

André's disappointment in our lack of success increased as the weeks progressed and the summer got hotter. He became even more withdrawn than he had been before, and did everything he could to keep his mind focused on his theater work. The city seemed to be in some kind of mass freefall, with everyone projecting an attitude that hovered somewhere between "Help!" and "Who gives a shit?"

But like some long-suffering character from the Old Testament, I stubbornly refused to give up on our movie. It was time yet again to take stock and move forward. Going through the industry contact list that I had begun to compile back in Belgium, I saw a name that I had not previously considered— Joe Papp. I reminded André how Papp had extended an invitation to come see him if we ever returned to New York. In another of his bleak moods, André was skeptical about going to visit and meet with Papp. André felt that Papp had just been trying to be polite, but I thought he had sounded genuinely interested in doing something with us.

André warned me that Papp was unlikely to remember us. In spite of that, or perhaps because of it, I felt that another seemingly insurmountable challenge had been laid at my feet. *Yet another job for Super Elli!* I thought to myself. I picked up the phone and called Papp's office.

"Mr. Papp, please," I said to the receptionist. "Yes, please tell him that André Ernotte and Elliot Tiber of the National Theater of Belgium are in town and need to speak with him."

After a few minutes, Mr. Papp came to the phone. As I had hoped, he remembered us and gave us an appointment for that same afternoon. For the first time in weeks, André seemed to be happy. We were both excited as we got into our best clothes. Ever since I had first met him, André's favorite colors for clothing were steel grey, khaki that looked like it was steel grey, and any shade of brown that was close to steel grey. When he asked if he should wear the light grey or dark grey dress shirt, I shrugged. "I'm not sure. Why don't you wear the *medium* grey shirt?"

Papp's space, the Public Theater, was housed in the old Astor mansion on Lafayette Street, in the East Village. He had converted the huge building into five theater spaces with a grand, well-designed lobby and a café. He had been clever enough to get ample funding through government and foundation grants and from wealthy investors. Papp's inventive development strategies helped support one of the most eminent theaters in the country.

As we approached the Theater, André was nervous, but I was calm. We walked into the front office and were about to inform the secretary of our appointment, when suddenly there was a buzz from the crowd in the lobby. Joe Papp had emerged from his office and was heading for the exit, arm in arm with actor Farley Granger. Farley was gracious, acknowledging the warm reception he was given by his fans. As they passed by our table, Farley stopped and smiled at André and me. Even with all the celebrities André knew in Belgium and France, he was delighted to see one of his screen idols. Meanwhile, Joe recognized us instantly and welcomed us with hugs.

Papp's interest in our work was sincere. I told him about how important we thought *High Street* was, and that it was in serious contention to become Belgium's entry for Best Foreign Film at the 1977 Academy Awards. He wasn't at all surprised to hear about the difficulty we were having getting the movie picked up for distribution. Joe told us he would set up a screening for himself and a few of his staff members the next day, and asked us to join them. We said we would be glad to come, and left the film cans with him so that the projectionist could set up properly.

The next day, André and I sat at the back of the screening room as the movie unfolded before us for the fiftieth time. We were so nervous. Before I knew it, the lights came up and we were cheered with lively applause from Joe and his staff. Joe was quite enthusiastic about the picture, and thanked André and me for our depiction of humanity. Papp was Jewish, and so our Holocaust film had special significance, moving him greatly.

We had hoped that Papp might have some film industry connections that he could call upon to help us. We sure didn't expect him to personally invest in our movie. In addition to the Public Theater, Papp oversaw six theaters in the city in which he produced plays and musicals. Because he liked the film, he offered to convert one of his playhouses into a cinema to launch *High Street*.

We were astounded by this generous offer, and further blown away some days later when he spent $25,000 to buy a half-page advertisement for *High Street* in the *New York Times*. Christ! That was nearly half of my Woodstock fortune! Sometimes I wondered if Joe Papp was the Messiah come back to the earth. If so, I'd be the first to renounce my atheism and don sandals and robes for Papp the Savior and his ministry of movies and plays.

Joe Papp generously gave us four weeks of screenings. Of course, in a theater with only a hundred seats, our film was never going to show a large profit. What we lacked in profits, though, we made up for in critical and popular acclaim. Learning from our experience at the Quad, André and I beat the bushes a third time to ensure that those hundred seats were always filled. We tried to make every screening a special event, holding a Q&A session after each one. Judging by the spirited applause we received on a daily basis, we did pretty well. Unfortunately, our short-term success failed to result in a legitimate distribution deal. At the end of the four-week run, nothing happened. That was it—kaput.

Despite all our efforts, we were right back where we started: two desperate bearded artists standing on the stoop with our movie packed up in two metal cans. We were down, but we still weren't out.

❀   ❀   ❀

Just when we were ready to heave the film, and ourselves, into the river, fate struck once again. Unbeknownst to us, Sheldon Gunsberg, owner of the Walter Reade theater chain, had come to see our movie at Papp's cinema. We were very surprised when he phoned us to set up a meeting. Mr. Gunsberg, an exceptionally congenial man, said he had a two-week opening at his Baronet Cinema, located in midtown, next door to the elegant Bloomingdale's department store.

Two weeks—that was all the time we could have. He said he hoped that this short engagement might attract movie bookers for a regular run elsewhere. Without any advertising, he warned us that it might very well be difficult to attract attention. I explained to him that we were due a miracle, but there was no need to install a statue of Jesus or the Madonna in the lobby on our account. André pinched me and gave me his *Be serious, Elliot!* look. But I couldn't help myself. "Joan of Arc will be with us. She happened to be my great-great-great aunt, even though she was born a Quaker. I know she will be at the Baronet and shall perform our much-needed miracle."

"So Joan was a *shiksa,* huh?" Sheldon added. André cracked a weak smile, but he did not laugh. While the chase made me feel strong and alive, it made André more and more anxious.

❀   ❀   ❀

Unfortunately, it wasn't long before our dream turned into a humiliating nightmare once again. The film was shown seven times each day. By ten o'clock on the first day, only five people had bought tickets. Perhaps we had gone back to the well a few too many times with our friends and neighbors, because they did not show up either. The handful of Jewish community centers who received our flyers in the week or so before the film's opening seemed to be ignoring us as if we had some transmittable disease.

Who knows? Maybe Momma had made collect calls from Israel to all New York Jews within fifty miles of the Baronet. I could hear her in my mind, shouting: "No one must see this movie! My ungrateful son lives with a secret Belgian Nazi who makes him sleep in a room with swastikas all over the walls! Pray for my Eliyahu in the temple! Ask that the Lord move him to give up on this movie business, and get married to a nice Jewish girl so they can give me nineteen grandchildren! So, do you want to rent a room?"

Dejected, André and I sat in the theater for the final show. In spite of the empty theater, Gunsberg kept the projectionist running the movie. He was a fine mensch, for sure. Gunsberg commiserated with us. He said perhaps it was a film that no one wanted to see at that time. For the next few days, we stayed at home and wallowed in self-pity. This was education at its harshest and least sentimental.

But I was still not defeated. Realizing that I was not going to be able to get the film seen on my own, a few days later, I woke up early and started to call East Coast film distributors in the yellow pages. Several showed interest because of Joe Papp's and Sheldon Gunsberg's endorsements. But the distributors all inevitably asked the same question: "How much do the national and international television rights cost?"

Huh? The first few times, I explained that I was calling about a movie, not a TV show. Finally, one of the people I spoke to explained the problem: "Well, Mr. Tiber, you don't seem to know whether you own the television broadcast rights to your own film. Without ownership of those rights, you haven't a chance in hell of ever making any solid and measurable dollars from your film. Any distributor worth his salt will want to be able to make money on both the theatrical and the TV rights to any movie that they take on. If a movie fizzles on the big screen, you at least stand a chance at some profit selling it off to the little screen. And we certainly aren't in the business of not making money from a distribution deal."

It was as if I, the great and undefeated Super Elli, had been stripped of my magical cape mid-flight and come crashing to the ground. I decided to make a long-distance call to Pierre back in Belgium. He explained to me that André and I could purchase the film's world TV rights—for seventy-five thousand dollars. There was no way that we could pay that sum. André theorized that Pierre and Alain were hurt and jealous that André and I had left Belgium and were trying to move forward with our careers in America. It probably didn't help that Pierre was Flemish and had ambitions of his own to become a film director.

I told André what had happened and explained how I thought I might be able to get those TV rights in hand if I returned to Belgium and had a face-to-face meeting with Pierre and Alain. André looked at me and said sadly, "I think that this is it for our film, Elliot. We have been very good to it, but I think this baby of ours needs to be put to rest."

I was so determined to make things work, to again don the cape and tights of my heroic Super Elli alter ego, that I wasn't sure I heard André right. "Let me make some more phone calls," I said to him, "I'm sure I can get something else to happen here. We can't just give up."

"Well, I can," André said quietly. "We have spent so much time, and you have spent too much of your own money. I think we need to recognize that it is time to stop trying. Elliot, you must learn your limits. Each time you create some brave new opportunity, the more pain and sorrow I have felt when things go wrong. It is not fair to me or to you." He shook his head back and forth slowly, as if waking from a long and nightmare-wracked sleep. "No, Elliot, no. It must stop. This must stop. All of this work to promote the film must stop. This is too much for us. The film is *over*. We must move on, Elliot. It is time to bring the curtain down on this."

Every bone in my body found this kind of defeat impossible to accept. Since I had landed in Belgium seven years before, practically everything I had touched had been a success and had led to bigger and better things. With a Godiva chocolate bar in one hand and a ketchup bottle in the other, I had written an acclaimed TV comedy variety show, delivered a series of well-received Woodstock lectures, written my first best-seller, done the production design for an entire feature film, and talked my way into a book contract with one of the top publishers in America. And now, though I had tried like mad to avoid repeating the failures I had had in Hollywood, I had again fallen flat on my *tuchis*. Worse still, I was making my lover and best friend unhappy. André was in a state of torment—that much was clear to me. "Well, *kemosabe*," I said, using the Lone Ranger's favorite term for his faithful companion, "it looks like there are two kinds of people in this world. There are those who grow and learn from their mistakes, and those who don't."

He nodded. "I do not want this to destroy us, Elliot. We will always have this film, but we may not always have the chance to create new and different stories. Sometimes you need to put your work up on a shelf and be happy that it is even there in the first place."

I wasn't content to see *High Street* wind up on a shelf. It simply wasn't in me to quit. I wanted to set up some more screenings, maybe even rent a car and take the film to be seen in other cities around the country. Perhaps it was foolish, but I really believed *High Street* could find a larger audience—perhaps in the fall, if not in the summer. It would never be *Star Wars,* and I didn't want it to be. But at some level I knew that André was right—the film wasn't going to make a splash, and I needed to accept that.

It was difficult for me to do. I was forty-two years old, and I was running out of time to do all the really great things I wanted to do. I was less and less willing to settle for ordinary life. Giving up was too scary an admission of weakness. Still, I had to admit that I was exhausted and spent, both emotionally and financially, by the months of ceaseless promotion on our little film.

"You're right, babe." The words were hard for me to say. "But I want you to know that I still believe that our film is special and deserves to be seen, and I'll always talk about it and do whatever I can to have it seen by others. And if I live to be eighty, I'll still tell people about the film we made together once upon a time in Belgium."

"If we both make it that long, *mon cheri,* I am sure there will be even bigger and better things to talk about," André said, a soft grin spreading across his face. "One other thing, Elliot," he said, "what is 'key-mo-sah-bee'?"

By the end of 1977, André and I had been thoroughly awakened from our dreams. In more ways than one, *High Street* had left us feeling very low.

I wanted so badly to blame Momma for my troubles, but I couldn't with any semblance of honesty. After all, she and I had practically crossed paths in separate airplanes nearly a year before—I had returned with André to New York just as she was departing with her *mah jongg* and *matzoh*. Perhaps she had intensified the Teichberg Curse as we passed. For the sake of my sanity, I put thoughts of Momma out of my mind, at least for the time being. As for the future, I had learned all too well that you never could tell where the next bend in the road might be.

13

Culture Gaps and Assless Chaps

"Excuse me, do you have a copy of *Mein Kampf?*"

The second I spoke those words to the man at the register in the Strand bookstore, I felt like some vile reprobate.

"I'm sorry, sir. What did you ask for?"

"Um," I stammered, "a copy of *Mein Kampf,* uh, by Adolf Hitler." You could have heard a pin drop.

"Wait here," the bookseller said, in a voice that might have dripped with disdain if it hadn't already been sapped of any discernible emotion. I stood by the counter, feeling the eyes of everyone in the store upon me. It was as if by seeking out the work of that monstrous man, I had somehow helped to conjure him forth in all his villainy. My earlobes burned and my face was flushed from shame. I was a Jew. Why in the world did I want to read that man's book?

I was just about to walk out of the store when the man returned to the register, holding a paperback copy of *Mein Kampf* with a picture of Hitler doing the Nazi salute on the cover. The clerk placed the book in a brown paper bag and rang up the purchase. He read out the total, and I put a twenty-dollar bill down on the counter and took the book. "Keep the change," I blurted out, as I flew out of the Strand and headed home.

I don't know exactly when I had decided to buy and read a copy of Hitler's controversial book. After all, laying out cash in order to read the ravings of the person responsible for the murder of more than six million Jews had not previously been high on my priority list. The decision to read *Mein*

Kampf stemmed from my plan to research the culture of Hitler, Nazism, and the Holocaust more deeply than ever before for the creation of a new play.

A seed had been planted in my mind a few years earlier, in Belgium. During his controversial staging of *Die Walküre,* André had told me that in the late 1960s he had been introduced to Wagner's daughter-in-law, a British expatriate born Winifred Williams. Winifred had married Wagner's son, Siegfried, who was said to be a closeted homosexual. Like so many Germans of her time, Winifred Wagner believed in what Hitler was trying to do. She had even become his friend; he was said to have become enamored of her due to her association with Wagner, his favorite composer. Mrs. Winifred Wagner never disavowed her love for Hitler. He remained a dear friend and cultural hero in her eyes. I found myself perversely intrigued by this woman's ill-advised devotion.

After nearly six years of nonstop hustle and bustle, André and I had settled into a period of relative calm at our London Terrace apartment. The truth was that we were both exhausted. It had been about nine months since we had stopped trying to arrange further screenings of *High Street.* We were still depressed that we hadn't been able to take the movie further than we had, so we spent many evenings sitting at home, trying to relax in front of our television. Having missed out on American television for most of the 1970s, we were ready to kick back and catch up on a lot of great entertainment. When we first learned about new subscription-based cable TV channels like HBO and WHT, which showed commercial-free movies day and night, it was like being turned on to a fantastic new drug. During the week, I'd come home from teaching my humor class at the New School and André would return from whichever play he was working on—whenever he wasn't directing a show abroad, that is—and we would happily retire to our cathode-ray sanctuary.

That spring, we happened to catch a TV miniseries called *Holocaust.* As I watched the miniseries, my thoughts turned more and more to our own film—and how it felt like we had missed our opportunity. My mind also returned to Winifred Wagner, the Nazi-lover. I gradually began to see the makings of what I believed could be a very intriguing story. I suggested to André that that woman's strange and undying loyalty to the cult of Hitler might make for a fascinating play that we could write together. Already consumed with the task of establishing himself more prominently in the New York theater world, André was less than enthusiastic about the idea. "Elliot," he said to me, "if you think that this would be a story worth telling on the stage, then you are going to have to be the one to do it. I cannot take on any more projects now."

I recognized a challenge when I heard it, and decided that very night to begin writing the play on my own. I even had a name for it. "What do you think of *Hitler's Love Songs?*" I asked him. André frowned and told me he thought it was too flippant and insensitive for the subject at hand.

"Not flippant—an attention-getter!" I responded. "Look at what Mel Brooks did with the song 'Springtime for Hitler' in his movie *The Producers*. No one had a problem with that, right?"

"Yes," André countered, "but you must remember that Mel Brooks made a comedy. Do you expect that this play will be a comedy?"

"Yeah, in its own twisted way," I countered. "Don't you?"

"Well, Elliot, that is not for me to decide," he said, cautious as ever. "You need to think about the idea more. Write the play instead of talking about it. You must do some research on the topic first, though. You may be surprised by what you find. And, of course, there is no way that you can use the name of Winifred Wagner in the play. As far as I know, she is still alive. So you will have to make up a name."

"You mean like Brünnhilde Lippenshitz?" I responded in a deadpan voice.

André smiled, laughed a little, and said, "Yes. Right, Elliot. That is exactly what I mean."

Once I got back home from the Strand, I quickly locked the door upon entering our apartment and then slid my copy of *Mein Kampf* out of the package. If I was to write about a real person's obsession, I rationalized, then it would be my job to do some research. I did not tell André that I had bought the book at first, since I didn't want his judgment while I was reading it. Over the next few days, I pored over the Führer's scattered and chaotic plans for the reunification of "the Fatherland." As I read, I didn't know whether to laugh or to scream in response to what that mustache-wearing little putz had to say. Chapter after chapter, page after page, I saw the overwhelming hatred that spewed from Hitler's diseased brain.

From a vantage point that I could only describe as deranged, Hitler described the Jews as relentless vampires and perverse spoilers of humanity. He felt that the Jews polluted and threatened the very foundations of what he called the "Aryan race," a made-up tribe of blond-haired and blue-eyed men and women. No matter that Hitler himself did not have blond hair and blue eyes. He had articulated a belief system that justified all manner of bias, persecution, and violence against the Jews and other "undesirable" people—a belief system that was adopted wholesale by a generation of Europeans.

As I pondered this lunacy, I also began to wonder what it was about the music of Richard Wagner that filled Hitler with such adoration. Heading over to the New York Public Library, I looked at various scholarly books and articles about the use of Wagner's music at Nazi gatherings, at book burnings, and at Nazi youth bonfires. What I found most upsetting, though, was how the Nazis had used Wagner's music at the Dachau concentration camp. Jews who were carted off to Dachau were forced to listen to Wagner's music while being made to work, starve, and die. Having always loved music, and having seen up close how music had helped give birth to the Woodstock miracle in 1969, I felt especially sickened to learn that music had been put to such devious and cruel use by Hitler's henchmen during the Holocaust.

Living with André and having watched him work as a director, I learned a thing or two over the past years. He had often explained to me the importance of an actor's empathy for his or her character, regardless of whether that character was good or bad. Before I could ever hope to get inside that particular mindset, I knew that I needed to listen to Wagner's music. I would have to learn how it would make me feel, before I could to try to write about how it made Winifred Wagner feel.

Around this time, I came into contact with another woman who encouraged me to investigate the Holocaust more thoroughly—albeit in a very different way from Winifred Wagner. About six months after we had last screened *High Street,* I received a call from a woman named Annette Insdorf. As I would learn, Annette had already published an acclaimed book on the films of celebrated French director François Truffaut. She was teaching film criticism at Yale, where André was directing a play at the School of Drama, and had tracked down our number through a colleague.

"I wanted to tell you that I liked very much that film you made with André Ernotte," Annette said. "It has a very fine and fragile feel to it. And I think it captures beautifully the ways in which the Holocaust extended to Belgium. That's something I suspect many still have not fully realized—particularly here in the States. I wonder," she continued, "if you and Mr. Ernotte might be available to speak with me about your film a little more in depth."

I was thrilled by her enthusiasm for *Rue Haute*. She had even referred to our film by its original French title, which told me instantly that she had a deep respect for film. By her flawless pronunciation, I could also tell that she spoke fluent French. *Wow!* I thought—or rather, *Ooh la la!*

"Well, first of all, thank you so much for your kind words about our film. It means more than you can know. Uh, tell me, Ms. Insdorf—"

"Please, call me Annette."

"Yes, okay. Well, Annette, are you looking to write an article about our film?"

"No, I'm working on a book that will examine the Holocaust as depicted by various films from around the world. I'd like to include *Rue Haute* in my survey."

"That's music to my ears, Annette. Just name the date and time, and André and I will be there," I said. I told her I would check André's availability, and she gave me her number so I could call back to confirm.

Wondering why her French sounded so authentic, I asked, "Tell me, Annette. Are you originally from France, or were you the proverbial 'American in Paris'?"

She laughed amusedly. "It's funny you should ask. You see, I was born in Paris, but then my family moved here to New York. What about you?"

I sighed. "I was born in Brooklyn, but then it took me nearly thirty-seven years—and meeting André, of course—to pack up and move to Belgium. We're back in New York, not only for the opportunity to work, but also because I missed the smell of hot pastrami on rye and the taste of those delicious egg creams."

"Well," she laughed, "here's to the ongoing sojourns of two New Yorkers, then."

André and I met Annette the following week at a café, and he found her as charming and fiercely intelligent as I did. After discussing *Rue Haute*, we spoke about many things, including the *Holocaust* miniseries that André and I had seen on TV. André was especially taken with Annette's insights into the films of Truffaut—especially her views on Truffaut's directorial debut, *Les Quatre Cents Coups,* or *The 400 Blows.* I couldn't help telling Annette, much to André's initial embarrassment, the title sounded like it belonged to one of those low-budget skin flicks we used to dub into English back in Belgium. Annette was quite amused as I told her about some of the more ridiculous films we had been asked to dub.

"So, do you have another film planned?" Annette asked.

"Actually, our next project together might be a stage play, not a film," I said. She was intrigued by my story of Winifred Wagner, and wished us well.

We were honored to be interviewed, and I gladly granted her future use in her book of the few movie production stills from *Rue Haute* that we had kept with us after we left Belgium. Being included in Ms. Insdorf's incisive study of Holocaust films would not get us a five-picture deal, but it would go a long way toward validating our creative efforts. It might also give some well-appreciated recognition, respect, and a measure of historical legacy to our little movie. During this difficult period of our lives, meeting Annette was a high point.

My interest in Winifred Wagner revitalized by our meeting with Annette, I attacked the play anew. I had already written and thrown away about a half-dozen drafts of a loosely plotted play. All I could envision was this greatly agitated woman, sitting center stage and waxing rhapsodic about the many virtues of her best friend Adolf. *Who am I going to pair this woman with?* I would think. No matter how I reworked the play, I could never develop it into anything more than a long and increasingly twisted monologue by Winifred. I was stuck for a new way into the material. Something about that old woman ranting alone on the stage kept my writing frozen in place—perhaps Winifred reminded me a little too much of the woman who had brought me into this insane comedy of life.

Meanwhile, André and I found our lives unexpectedly entwined with that of another woman: the great literary and theatrical agent Audrey Wood, whom we had first met a year earlier at one of the *High Street* screenings. She had introduced herself after the film was shown, and told us how taken she was with our work. A unique and highly respected woman in a field that had been dominated by men, Audrey had started as an agent in the 1930s. She first hit it big when she discovered playwright Tennessee Williams at the start of his career. In the late 1940s, she had worked hard to get Williams the deal for the legendary Broadway run of his play *A Streetcar Named Desire*.

As we learned from her later, Audrey had requested a copy of our book from Avon soon after seeing the film. She thought highly of our work, but assumed we had returned to Belgium. Audrey was pleasantly surprised to meet us again at a party given by one of André's fellow theater colleagues. We talked with her for about an hour, and she gave us her card with her address written on it, asking us to meet with her at her home later that week.

Talking with Audrey, it was obvious that she knew the entertainment industry backwards and forwards. Although she still felt that she might be able to get us a hot deal, time was no longer on her side. She had outlived many of her reliable contacts, and thus lost her entry points into the business world. I was happy just to have Ms. Wood's attention and approval, though; I loved hearing her regale us with stories of her past successes. André saw her as a sweet and genuine person looking for a little company, but didn't think anything would come of the friendship.

There seemed to be no end to Audrey's enthusiasm for us. She understood what we were trying to do in our creative collaborations. In many ways, she was a doting den mother to us. We got into the habit of having a meal with her at least once a week at her apartment on the Upper East Side.

Around this time, André and I heard about an intriguing housing opportunity. I had read an article a few days earlier in the *New York Times* about a brand new apartment complex that was set to open in the Times Square area of Manhattan. The complex had over a thousand luxury apartments housed in two towers, each of which had an indoor swimming pool, tennis courts, and rehearsal rooms. In addition, Manhattan Plaza covered all utilities and even provided basic cable TV free of charge. Best yet, the apartments were to be heavily subsidized for low-income New Yorkers—more specifically, for New Yorkers in the performing arts, many of whom worked in the nearby theater district.

The only problem was its location. Manhattan Plaza was in the neighborhood directly north of Chelsea, and a dangerous and seamy place to live at the time. It was a block from the section of midtown infamous for its wealth of porno theaters and grindhouses. Times Square had been rendered in all its sleazy glory by Martin Scorsese in his 1976 film *Taxi Driver*. The sidewalks were piled high with garbage due to ongoing city sanitation department strikes, and hookers and thugs were hanging out right there amidst the trash. Adding to the scene, drugs were sold and consumed on nearly every block in the area, which was within walking distance of the Port Authority bus depot.

Every day from dawn to midnight, thousands of people passed through Port Authority en route to the Broadway theaters. If these starry-eyed tourists were not leapt upon by the hordes of muggers, hustlers, and pickpockets waiting on nearly every street corner, they might have a nice time. For myself, I wasn't afraid of the underworld—hell, I was used to it! Upon reading about Manhattan Plaza, I immediately applied for residence. Through André, we knew many actors and writers who had been approved and had moved in with subsidized rent, so we thought we'd get in easily. A month went by and I had heard nothing from the housing board. Meanwhile, I saw another article reporting that Manhattan Plaza had less than a handful of apartments left for rent, and thousands of applicants were lined up for interviews. I phoned the complex's administrative office a few times a week, but was always met with a cold and indifferent response.

Over lunch with Audrey one afternoon, I tried my best to disguise my frustration, but Audrey could tell something was up.

"What's making my little Elliot so sad today?" she asked.

"It's nothing, Audrey," I lied. "I'm fine."

"No, you're not," she said matter-of-factly. "Come on, darling. What is it? Tell your Aunt Audrey all about it."

"Really, Audrey," André said, "It's nothing that we want to burden you with."

"*Burden* me with? Well, now, this is exciting. Let's hear it, Elliot."

Feeling silly but also genuinely frustrated, I described our difficulty in securing an apartment at Manhattan Plaza. "I've made so many calls, and it's just impossible. Apparently, we have to be approved by some board in order to even be let into the building."

Smiling coyly, Audrey said, "I know someone on that board."

"You do?" I said, starting to feel a small bit of hope for the first time in days. "Who?"

"Me! I'm on the advisory board," she said, laughing. "What? Didn't I tell you?"

Before either of us had a chance to say another word, Audrey already had her hand up for the waiter. "Would you bring me the phone, please?" she asked. André and I sat there in a mild state of shock as Audrey made a brief but assertive phone call. "Yes, well, their names are Mr. Tiber and Mr. Ernotte and they are clients of mine," Audrey said. "That's right, I know them and they should be shown a place as soon as possible. Right, thank you."

Time seemed to have stopped after Audrey hung up the phone. She then looked up at us, smiled and said, "Well, why are you both still here? You'd better get the hell over to Manhattan Plaza. The building manager is waiting there to meet with you."

"Are you serious?" I asked.

"Aren't I?" she said, with a wink and a smile. "Get going, my Broadway babies! Make your Aunt Audrey proud."

Overwhelmed by her incredible gesture, we hugged Audrey. And as we gathered ourselves to leave, I gave the waiter a hundred-dollar bill and told Audrey that the meal was on us.

When we arrived at Manhattan Plaza, we were met by the building manager, Mr. Hengley. He didn't mention hearing from Audrey at all. Instead, he took us by elevator up to the forty-second floor in the Tenth Avenue tower. He said that there were only three apartments left, and that we could select whichever we liked.

The apartment 42-B was a huge, eight hundred square foot space with one bedroom and a huge terrace. It had a view that was simply astounding. Looking north, we could see the George Washington Bridge and the piers alongside the Hudson River; to the west, there was the New Jersey coastline. I fantasized about having Renee and Alyse over so that they could try to locate their house from our terrace.

We discussed rent with Mr. Hengley, who explained that based on our limited teaching salaries, our rent would come to $535.25. This was virtually unheard of for any new building in New York City. At the apartment we had in Chelsea, we had been paying about $400 a month for a studio—and it didn't even *have* a terrace! We were in city-dweller heaven and called Audrey later that evening to thank her.

"That's wonderful news, boys!" she said, "I wanted for you to have a home you can enjoy. I want you comfortable and rested while you are here in the city, especially since I believe that so many great and wonderful things will happen for you both!"

"Not without you, though," I said. "Thank you again, Audrey. We love you for helping us like this!" We would never lose our gratitude for Audrey's help in getting us our new home.

At Manhattan Plaza, we were surrounded by the New York performing arts community. The complex housed more than six thousand actors, writers, musicians, directors, artists, costume and set designers, stage managers, box office workers, lighting technicians, and other people who worked on the Great White Way. It was like living in a magical land of creativity, with constantly overlapping connections.

The best friend André and I made at Manhattan Plaza was the actress Colleen Dewhurst, who was caring and kind in a way that reminded us both of André's mother, Fanny. Given her renown in the theater world—her performance as Josie in Eugene O'Neill's *A Moon for the Misbegotten* had garnered her a Tony in 1974—André and I were a little intimidated when we first met her, sharing an elevator in our building. As we rode up together, I screwed up the courage to introduce myself and André, and to confess what big fans we were of her work. "Why, thank you both so very much!" she said, her beautiful smile telling us that she was far more approachable than we had thought. By the time we got to our floor, she knew our names and had invited us to come and have dinner at her apartment on the forty-third floor.

We shared dinners, either at our place or at hers, whenever we had the time. At our first dinner, she told us she had returned to Manhattan only a few months before, having spent several previous weeks on location in snowy Minnesota for a sweet, sentimental film called *Ice Castles*. "Let me tell you, it was cold out there in the country," she said, knocking back a glass of wine. "But I grew up in Canada, so the cold has never bothered me much."

Although Colleen had primarily done the film for the money, she talked warmly about the work she had done. In the film, Colleen played a former competitive ice-skater who helps train a naturally gifted young girl to a level of success that Colleen's character never had the chance to reach. The part of the young skater was played by a real-life US figure skating champion named Lynn-Holly Johnson, who was totally new to the world of acting. "She had some trouble at the beginning," Colleen said, "but that girl worked her ass off in the part. I helped her through some really tough scenes, and I feel like maybe I taught her something."

Hearing Colleen talk about working with someone new to the game moved André to tell her the story of how he had brought me into his work as a collaborator. Colleen was delighted to hear about how he and I had come to write a top-rated TV show in Belgium, followed by the novel and the making of our film. After André told her about our Belgian adventures, I shared some stories about my crazy early years in Brooklyn as a member of the Teichberg nuthouse. Colleen remarked that my upbringing sounded a lot like that of Woody Allen, with whom she'd worked the year before on his Oscar-winning film *Annie Hall*. I told her that made sense, since Woody had been a classmate of mine at Midwood High School in Brooklyn. "I remember him," I said, "back when he was still Allan Konigsberg and the kids in the schoolyard called him 'Red' because of his hair."

"And what about you, Elliot?" asked Colleen. "What did they call you in the schoolyard?"

"Who, me?" I said. "Actually, I never liked to go out and play in the schoolyard. So the kids used to call me Casper the Ghost."

She let loose one of her priceless laughs, and we all raised our glasses to Casper. In the months to come, Colleen maintained a fairly busy work schedule, cycling from theater to TV to film, and so we saw her every few months or so, when she returned to her place at Manhattan Plaza. But she was wonderfully witty, a delight to spend time with, and an ever-accommodating friend to André and me when we needed encouragement or a warm hug. Out of respect for her friendship, we never asked Colleen to read through or consider appearing in any of our projects. No career move was worth risking our close relationship.

❀   ❀   ❀

We made other friends, too. At one point or another, most of the Manhattan Plaza's residents found their way to the big wall bordering the north side of

the complex. The wall was an ideal spot at which to congregate and meet people. There we would stand around, smoke our cigarettes, get some air, and
take in the big sprawling city all around us. We would hang out and rail about
our latest artistic attempts—the new draft on a play that went nowhere; an
audition for a TV commercial that didn't lead to a part; a meeting over sushi
with a potential film backer that resulted in a bad case of food poisoning; or,
even more distressing, an upsetting phone call from the folks, during which
they said they would pay for you to go to college if you would only come back
home. This was the biggest secret of the Great White Way: more often than
not, the best entertainment on Broadway wasn't in the theaters, it was on the
city streets outside.

We settled into Manhattan Plaza easily enough. Our new apartment was
much bigger than the one we had had at London Terrace, so we took the
opportunity to fill out the space with comfortable modern furniture. We
bought a large L-shaped couch and sofa bed for the living room and two large
mirrors, one for the living room, and one for our bedroom. I structured the
apartment so that all but one of the walls in the living room were filled with
pictures of family and friends, framed programs, and other show mementos
from our time in Belgium. The one bare wall gave me the visual space I needed to start painting again. Against this wall, I set up a huge easel and a dozen
large canvases. I didn't have a particular plan as to what I was going to paint;
I simply put brush to canvas whenever the spirit moved me. Some of my
paintings were landscapes based on color photographs I saw in travel magazines, while others were portraits of people I knew. One time, I started to
paint a portrait of André, but it made him uncomfortable, so I turned the
painting into an abstract composition of sharp diagonal lines intersecting hor-
izontal strips of various colors. When I finished the piece, André asked me
what I called it. I smirked at him and said, "It's called 'Not André.'"

"Touché, Monsieur Tiber," he said, as he went over to the kitchen for a
bottle of wine.

We were so thrilled with our new apartment that we decided to have a little housewarming party. Many of our friends, most from the theater community, came out to see our top-floor paradise and to wish us well. Even my
sisters Goldie and Rachelle came to visit with their families. With our loved
ones in attendance, it was an exciting and pleasurable gathering. We might not

have made it big, but our luxurious digs made it seem like we had. Of course, we saw no need to tell people that our rent was subsidized.

One of the perks of living at Manhattan Plaza was its theater desk, which offered tickets to Broadway and off-Broadway shows for one dollar each. Shows with weak box office sales, or shows that were still in previews—that is, shows that had not officially opened yet—often needed to fill seats in their theaters. Without these subsidized tickets, we could never have afforded to go to as many of the plays and musicals as we did, allowing us to see what other writers, directors, and actors were doing.

André also began to go to Sunday services at the Actors' Chapel—St. Malachy's, a Catholic church a few blocks from our apartment. The services gave him some solace and reminded him of home, so that he did not miss his family so much. Being an atheist, I had no interest in church. I did go with André one morning, though, just to see what it was all about. The mournful dirge of the pipe organ accompanying a ragtag choir of singers made me feel awkward and sad. In addition, the priest annoyed me by telling everybody to get up and then sit back down again. I was used to going through these motions from being dragged to the synagogue as a kid, but I was barely awake, and this continual call for Catholic calisthenics made it impossible for me to take a nap. Perhaps that was the idea, since the priest that morning was about the dullest dude I'd ever heard.

Adding insult to injury, a group of men wearing conservative suits and ties came walking down the aisle with baskets on sticks. When I saw André place a few dollars into one of the baskets, I realized that they were collecting money for the church. *Wow, the Catholics need to raise money to put on their shows, too!* I thought. André seemed a little happier by the end of the service, though. He seemed to draw strength and comfort from the recitations and rituals of the Catholic mass. While I had no plans to come back, I did respect the fact that the church fulfilled a need for André that I was unable to satisfy.

I might not have found religion, but I did start to worship at the altar of physical fitness. Upon my return to New York, I had made a deliberate choice to exercise and eat healthier. As a result, I had lost a great deal of my old chubbiness. I was down from 240 pounds to a relatively trim and well-toned 175 pounds.

I had not struggled with dieting this time, as I had so many other times over the years. I had become highly disciplined, and was on my way to becoming a full-time vegetarian. The cheeseburgers and fries and other rich foods I had formerly enjoyed were gone, replaced by soy products and tofu. I even scaled back on my egg cream consumption, opting for diet sodas most of the time. André and I had begun to get lots of exercise together. When we moved into Manhattan Plaza, we joined the complex's health club, and made it a daily habit to swim laps or participate in their water aerobics classes. My lower weight made me feel more normal than I had ever felt before. I was so much more comfortable with myself, and more confident. Of course, André had never had a weight problem—he had always been trim, with no fat on him at all.

To take advantage of the jobs that were available to him, André started to fly back and forth between New York and Europe—wherever he could get work. He did it without joy or ambition, though. No matter how difficult things had been, André still believed that his future lay in New York. I felt badly for him, and wanted to do something. And so, once again, I donned my imaginary cape and brought Super Elli back to life.

Under Mayor Koch, the city had bought up all the former porno theaters on Forty-second Street, opposite Manhattan Plaza. These buildings were restored and made into what would eventually come to be called Theater Row. Anchoring Theater Row was a large playhouse called Playwrights Horizons. Founded at the Clark Center YMCA in 1971, Playwrights Horizons had moved to Forty-second Street in 1974 and become a sort of mecca for new and experimental theater, the place to go if you wanted to see up-and-coming theater people show off their latest work. It would also prove to be a catalyst in the city's urban renewal movement, helping to recast midtown as a desirable place to be seen. We could see the excitement surrounding the place, and we were very keen to make inroads there.

Armed with André's thick press book, which contained major reviews of his work, I went to the executive offices at the Playwrights Horizons building. I didn't know a soul there. The receptionist told me that I needed to make an appointment, so she handed me a form and I applied for one. I had André's scrapbook open on the receptionist's desk. As I was filling out the form, André Bishop—soon to be the artistic director of Playwrights Horizons and, as I learned, a Yale graduate—came into the office. He stopped at the desk for his messages, and caught sight of the open scrapbook. Evidently he knew enough French to understand the critical acclaim spelled out in André's clippings. He smiled at me and then took a closer look at André's resume. As he ran his finger down the list of various shows André had directed, he stopped at the short list of productions that André had done at Yale and Columbia when he had first been in New York on scholarship.

Intrigued by what he saw, Bishop asked me into his office. Before I sat down, I explained that I was not André, and that I was merely there on his behalf. We went on to speak for over an hour. I filled Bishop in on André's abundant talents as a director, and spoke of his extensive career in European theater. I also explained that we had also moved recently into Manhattan Plaza, and that Audrey Wood was our agent. By the end of the conversation, André B. was very eager to meet André E. Although André E. was overseas wrapping up a play in Paris, he was to return to New York in less than a week—so I made him an appointment with André B.

I was a little concerned that André would be displeased with me for having taken it upon myself to promote him. But André was actually thrilled to hear my news. He was aware of Bishop's excellent reputation, and recognized that an engagement with Playwrights Horizons would be a huge opportunity for him. His meeting with Bishop went well. Bishop said he had recently committed to a new play called *K-2* and cast a gifted young actor named Michael Moriarty to star in it. Would Monsieur Ernotte be interested in directing?

This was the first real break for André in New York. We were both delighted, and went out to dinner to celebrate. Later that night I wanted to make passionate love to André. My newly trimmer figure made me more eager than ever to get physical with André. I was very surprised when André turned me down. Though he was happy that I was healthy, André preferred me as a big and burly bear. My body had changed, and he missed the way I used to look and feel to him when I was heavier.

In fact, he seemed less and less interested in having sex with me at all. More often than not, he would give me a perfunctory hug and a short peck on the lips when he came home from the theater at night. In the past, after we had had a meal, we usually necked on the couch before finding our way over to the bedroom for a romp between the sheets. Now, André would instead pace back and forth in our apartment, often leaving to go get cigarettes around the corner. Sometimes he would be gone for ten minutes; other times, two hours. Occasionally, he wouldn't even have the cigarettes that he told me he had gone out to buy. I didn't ask him where he had been, and he didn't say. Whenever I did ask him where he had been, he would look at me and say, "I was just walking."

We went to the downtown gay leather bars as much as we could whenever André was back from a directing job in Europe. Dressing up in our leather outfits and going dancing helped us to blow off steam. One night at the Anvil, I noticed that one of the men was wearing a full Nazi uniform. Sweat was pouring down his face as he grooved to the music. Suddenly, he stood up straight as a board, shouted "Sieg Heil!," and began goose stepping around the perimeter of the dance floor. Two guys, both of whom looked younger than the costumed Nazi, soon swept him off the dance floor and out of the club. Everybody went back to what they were doing, but I found the image of the man in the Nazi uniform goose stepping to music a strange and fascinating one. Later that night, I began to wonder what it was exactly in the music of Wagner that had seduced Adolf and Winifred and the rest of Nazi Germany so completely.

About a week later, I went out and bought an album of Wagner's most famous pieces. If I was going to get inside Winifred's head for the purposes of the play, then I wanted to see what it felt like to goose step to this notorious composer's music. Standing in our apartment with the windows wide open that balmy but sunny mid-afternoon, I had on a pair of big black boots, but I lacked the traditional Nazi uniform. So I had to improvise, wearing a studded black leather jacket and a pair of assless chaps instead.

I wondered what the Nazis would have thought of me in my black shiny boots and tight leather gear. Perhaps they would have thought me brave. They might even have clapped for me. More likely, they would have pierced my skull with a bullet and dumped my corpse into a mass grave in some far-off concentration camp. As I marched fiercely across our living room in rhythm to Wagner's "Ride of the Valkyries," I found myself moved to shout "Nazi fuckers!" with each booted kick. *Okay,* I thought to myself after I turned off the music, *I think this is something I can write about now.* Suddenly, the phone rang.

"You're not going to believe this, Elliot," said my sister Renee, calling from New Jersey.

"Let me guess—you're pregnant!" I said in mock horror. "But you're not sure who the father is!"

"Bite your tongue!" Renee said. "Having one daughter is about all I can handle! No, no, I just got a call from Israel."

Before I could think of something nasty, I heard myself instead say, "What's wrong? Did something happen to Momma?"

Israel had become an increasingly chaotic place in recent months. There were reports of suicide bomber attacks and other types of violent clashes every week or so. I had been so busy trying to promote our book and film in my first year back in New York that I had hardly ever thought of Momma. But after giving up on *Rue Haute,* I had had more time to keep up with world news, and quickly realized the extent to which Israel was in a constant state of danger. Even with the highly publicized peace accord between Israel and Egypt that had been negotiated over by President Carter in March, Israel was a volatile place to live. It was only natural for me to be concerned about my mother's safety.

"No, she's okay," Renee reassured me.

"So, what did she call you about? Oh, and did she call collect?"

"Yes, but *listen,* Elliot, this is serious," Renee said, sounding more concerned than usual. "Momma tells me that she is getting remarried."

What? I thought, *Sonia Teichberg, again to be a blushing Russian bride?* "Are you kidding, sis?" I asked Renee. "Why in the world would she want to get married again? And, more importantly, who the hell would want to marry her in the first place? What did she say?"

"She didn't say too much, really. In fact, she hung up on me when I told her that I can't go to the wedding. Alyse has school until the beginning of June, and I don't want her to miss any more classes this year. Besides, I can't afford to go."

"I understand, Renee—even if Momma won't, or can't," I told her. I didn't want her feeling bad because of anything that Momma might say or do.

"What about Rachelle and Goldie?" I continued.

Renee explained that she called our two sisters, and that neither was willing to schlep to Israel for a wedding. That left me.

The idea of watching Momma marry a man who wasn't my father was about as exciting to me as the thought of going down on Ethel Merman in a crowded subway car as she sang "Everything's Coming Up Roses" from *Gypsy*. My mother had been so heartless and cruel to Pop for so long that it now seemed unfair for her to remarry—unfair for her to be happy! She had never been happy in all those years with my father, and she had spared no occasion to say so. I looked at my leather-clad reflection in the mirror and fantasized about showing up at Momma's wedding dressed that way. It seemed the perfect wedding gift to give her, considering the life of sorrow to which she had consigned my father.

Later that night, I waited for André to unwind a bit before breaking the big news about Momma's betrothal to a sure-to-be-unhappy Jewish man from somewhere inside the Gaza Strip. André's eyes widened as he stroked his beard. "Are you all right with it?" he asked.

"I honestly don't know," I said. "I can't imagine that she wants to be married again. Hasn't she hurt enough people already?"

I explained that none of my sisters were going to travel to Israel to attend the wedding, and that I certainly wasn't going to step up and do it. Maybe if I hadn't still had those miserable years at the El Monaco stuck in my head like shrapnel, I might have done this *mitzvah* for Momma. But I knew what a visit to Momma would entail, and I wasn't prepared to submit myself to such wanton debasement.

I was so consumed with my own feelings about Momma's wedding in Israel that I forgot to take into consideration someone else's—André's. I was surprised to hear how excited he was to hear about Momma's impending Israeli wedding. "You have to go and do this, Elliot," André said. "Even if you will not go because of your mother, you should do it as a favor to Renee." He reminded me of the letters she had written to me while we were in Belgium, and all the inconveniences that Momma's life had imposed upon my sister. "Besides," he continued, "I want to see the land of Jerusalem. I wish to visit the Holy Sepulchre, to experience for myself the land where Jesus lived. Maybe you and I can also make a visit to the Wailing Wall."

"Me, go to the Wailing Wall?" I said. "What are you, crazy? I'm going to see my mother. Talk about a Wailing Wall—she shouts about everything like she's just escaped from a lunatic asylum!"

"Oh, come on, Elliot," André said. "I know what to expect from your mother by now."

"Yes," I said, "but you don't know my mother like I do. She's totally out of her head. And even with everything that's going on over there, it's still probably more dangerous for you at her house. She'll either hate you because you're not a Jewish girl named Rebecca, or she'll try to sell you dishware. Besides, I don't want to take you away from your work."

"Nonsense," André said with a wave of his hand, "it is only a few weeks until summer starts. I have no show that I need to work on at the moment. So this is the perfect time for a trip. Besides," he continued, with a twinkle in his eye, "do you think I am going to miss the chance to finally meet Elliot's crazy Momma and watch her get married in the land of the rabbis?" I pointed out his new connection with the Playwrights Horizon and André Bishop. "Not to worry, Elliot," he responded, "it will be at least six weeks before I am brought on board as a new director for the fall season. This may be the last time we can go away together for quite a while."

What could I say?

"You know that you're probably going to have to pretend you're a rabbi-in-training from Belgium while we're in her presence," I joked. "You're a *goy*, but at least you have that big and bushy beard going—I mean, *goying*, for you."

We laughed, kissed, and started to talk about our trip to the Holy Land. It seemed ludicrous that I was going to cross an ocean with my lover by my side to watch Momma pretend that she was a seventy-year-old virgin. But I was immensely pleased that he was willing to endure this strange event with me, and that in itself was enough to give me the strength to go through with it. As we held each other and swayed lazily to and fro in the living room, André spotted my Wagnerian leather outfit—the boots, the jacket, and of course, the assless chaps—draped on a chair near the stereo. "What have you been doing here at the apartment while I am at rehearsals, *mon cheri?*" he asked, looking puzzled.

"Well, I don't know," I teased. "You want me to tell you about it, or shall I show you?"

"Why not surprise me?" he said.

We made love that night for the first time in ages, and André quickly fell asleep afterward. I had trouble sleeping, though. Thoughts of my father kept swimming into my mind. I didn't want to betray him by going to Israel, but I felt like I had a responsibility to represent the rest of my family at the wedding. It was only for the sake of other people—Momma and Renee and now André—that I was willing to make the trip. Like it or not, I was now aimed toward the Holy Land like some kind of heat-seeking missile concocted out of a potato knish.

14

An Israeli Wedding and a Manhattan Split

"So where can I buy a pink yarmulke, sis?" I asked Renee the morning after André talked me into making the trip to the Holy Land.

"You mean you're going?" she said, sounding pleased and surprised.

"Yeah, well, you know I always wanted to see where the guilt comes from. Besides, André wants to visit the land where Jesus hung out."

"You've always been so devout, big brother. You better watch out. You just might have a religious experience."

"I had one of those years ago, but I was able to get it removed by a doctor," I quipped.

Renee proceeded to tell me everything she knew about the man who was about to become our stepfather. Our mother had met Boris, a Russian, four months after moving to Israel. She frequently attended a friendship circle where Russian immigrants socialized and helped one another adjust to Israeli culture. The friendship circle offered Hebrew classes, and it was in those classes that Momma and Boris had met. Soon enough, they had hit it off. The whole thing was weirdly romantic. It was strange to think of my mother going soft over someone. She had never exhibited an ounce of sentimentality, at least not in my experience. With Pop, she had always been more like a brutal female dictator.

I felt outraged on my father's behalf. After all, Pop had done everything in his power to please and support and satisfy Momma, who was chronically displeased and dissatisfied anyway. Despite her abusive treatment of him, my father had loved Momma until his dying day. He had thrown himself heart and soul into the sacrificial fires of matrimony for a woman who hadn't even come to visit him on his deathbed. Now, that utterly thankless woman was going to marry another man. I felt as if I was betraying my father by attending this wedding.

I asked Renee how she felt about Momma's remarriage, and she said she was all right with it as long as Boris would be good to our mother. As for myself, I wasn't worried about Momma. She had always taken care of herself just fine, managing to be in total control of herself and anyone else within breathing distance. I told Renee that André and I would bring back a full report about this Boris and how he and Momma treated each other. That seemed to please Renee. Still a bit annoyed that I was going to have to make this trip overseas, I promised my sister that I would ensure that everything was kosher. "I'll even ask Boris if he's been properly circumcised, okay? Better yet, I'll ask Momma." Not that it mattered—I figured it was only a matter of time before Momma castrated Boris anyway.

I wondered if Renee really understood how deeply conflicted I was about the trip. It wasn't just that I felt loyal to my father's memory. I was bothered that even though my mother was about to embark on a new romantic union, she would almost definitely refuse to acknowledge my own. Momma had never been able to take my interest in men seriously. She just ignored it. I was not the married heterosexual rabbi that Momma expected me to be. I was a proud gay man who had a great and loving relationship with another man.

What would happen if I were to bring the man I loved to Momma's wedding? Would she accept who I was? Would she understand that my feelings for André were the same as her feelings for Boris? Or would she find some way to take the relationship that mattered most to me and deliberately screw it up? I had no way of knowing what would happen. I just knew that bringing my life too close to Momma's was always a combustible proposition. But maybe she had changed. Perhaps she had become different in the past few years.

I had underestimated Renee, at least. Sensing my concern, she kindly offered to help by calling Momma and Boris in advance to explain that I would be coming to the wedding with a guest.

"Do you want me to tell Momma that André is your boyfriend?" Renee asked.

"Nope," I said, "I think these things are so much more interesting when she is surprised. Don't you agree? Besides, she should be thankful that I am making the effort to come at all. If you want, tell her I'll be traveling with a friend. And tell her he's half-*goy* and half-Jewish, so no need to ask him if he's kosher when he gets here."

"You never know," Renee responded, "maybe André will win her over."

"Right," I scoffed, "and maybe I'll suddenly have the hots for Marilyn Monroe."

"Just be safe over there, the both of you," said Renee. "And make sure that this is really something that Momma should do—before she walks down the aisle."

To finance the trip, I drew on my steadily dwindling Woodstock stash— only fifteen grand was left from the original fifty thousand. André booked our roundtrip flight and an eight-day stay in a Tel Aviv hotel. He also leafed through a King James Bible in preparation for what he referred to as "the pilgrimage." Knowing that I was going to Israel against my better judgment and by burning through my cash reserves, I sarcastically called this trip "the pillage."

On an early evening in May, André and I boarded an El Al flight out of JFK Airport in New York. For all the concerns about going to Israel at a time of increased terrorist activity, flying on El Al was easily one of the safest experiences that André and I ever had. Perhaps the biggest reason for our sense of security was the intensive preboarding screening process to which El Al subjected passengers before letting them through the gate. They asked André and me totally different questions about our luggage and what we had done in the days leading up to our flight. I was relieved that they didn't ask us which sides of the bed we preferred to sleep on.

André was able to settle in for a very peaceful nap for most of the flight. Of course, the small handful of Valium pills that he took before liftoff might have had something to do with it. I tried to rest, but my sleep was fitful at best. Trying to chill out in my window seat, I kept looking at my reflection in the glass, wondering how I had ended up shackled to yet another round of mirthless Momma *mishegas*. When sleep proved impossible, I read the new bestseller, *Mommie Dearest,* a Hollywood tell-all about Joan Crawford written by her daughter, Christina. Reading a book about someone else's crazy mother somehow made me feel better about mine.

1978. With a *punim* like this, how could the rabbi tribunal refuse Momma's second wedding?

❀   ❀   ❀

"*Shalom,* ladies and gentlemen, and welcome to Israel," the pilot said over the plane's PA system. After we picked up our luggage and I converted my US dollars to Israeli lira, André and I took a taxi to the address provided to me by Renee. The small town of Netanya was about a half-hour drive from Tel Aviv. As we drove, I looked out the window at my surroundings. The first thing I noticed was the comical number of buses everywhere. It seemed as if there were more buses than people. As I watched one bus after another make its stops and then smoothly drive on, I wondered, *Where are all these people going?* With all these Israeli buses driving to and fro, I couldn't help thinking of long-suffering Mimi. I wondered if each bus represented another Mimi, another helpless victim of the Holocaust.

As we headed farther north, away from the airport and closer to Momma, I couldn't stop thinking about sand. *Sand,* I said to myself . . . *hills of sand . . . houses of sand . . . far-off mountains of sand . . . Holy Moses, this entire country is sand!* It puzzled me to think that Momma would willingly live in such a desertlike country. On her summer vacations with Pop, she had barely even set foot on the boardwalk of Miami Beach. What she saw in this place, other than a way to get closer to the Hebrew God, was a total mystery to me.

Momma's condo in Netanya was perched at the top of a hill, on a dusty street lined with green leafy trees. As we approached the building, I had an overwhelming desire to jump out of the taxi and run as fast as I could across the sands of Israel to escape her clutches. Before I could act on this impulse, though, André placed his hand on my knee and said, "There. Elliot, is that *her?*"

As if struck by a strange force of magic, I turned away from André and looked out the taxi window. There she was, all five-foot-one and two hundred pounds of her, standing at the top of the seven stone steps that led from the sandy street right to her doorway. For a shocked moment or two, I stared at this woman who waved at me, her hands held high above a distressingly big smile. *Who in the hell is this?* I wondered to myself. *There's no way that's Momma.* As if in response, the cheery suntanned apparition spoke loudly from the stairs:

"Eliyahu! Is that you, my beautiful *tateleh?* You have come to bring such joy to Momma, mine darling son! Come here, my handsome *boychik!* Your

Momma wants to see you!" Momma began walking toward the taxi. I found myself unexpectedly happy to see her. Suddenly, Momma stopped in her tracks. She had just seen André, and her smiling face quickly changed to the one I remembered—the one in my worst nightmares.

As André came around the side of the taxi, Momma curtly asked, "Who is *this*, Eliyahu? This man here with the big dark beard is your friend? Is he a rabbi? You bring him with you from Belgium, no?" She looked at André with the bitterness of an entire lifetime spent in the shadows of distrust, hatred, and fear. "Who are you?"

I had warned André about Momma several times in the days before our flight, and just a few more times on the airplane. Now it was time to see how well he did with my harshly judgmental mother. Would he declare himself a beautiful gay Belgian prince who had shared all manner of physical delights with her only son for eight years? Would he tell her that he was Pop's illegitimate love child, here to shake Momma down for a hoard of cash that would buy his silence and prevent her good Jewish name from being besmirched in the Holy Land?

Leave it to André, ever the gracious gentleman. Standing by my side, he cheerily explained that he was a good friend of mine who had always wanted to visit Israel in order to be closer to Christ and Moses. He offered his hand in peace and solidarity, but she would not take it—not until she knew for sure. "Wait there a minute," Momma said, squinting her eyes and scratching her chin, "tell me, are you a Jewish man?"

"No, I am not a Jew. I have come, Mrs. Teichberg, to—"

That was it, as far as Momma was concerned. She brought her hand up in front of her face, a guillotine blade waiting to be dropped down on André's neck as he tried to explain his reverence for the land of Jerusalem. Without further discussion, she grabbed my arm and surprised me by giving me a tight yet perfunctory hug. She started to tell me that she could let me stay in the guest room so I had a place to sleep in her house, but I quickly explained that we had booked a hotel back near the airport in Tel Aviv. "So you came, Elli?" she said. Before I had a chance to respond, I saw someone emerge from the house.

"Sonia?" the man said. "Will you not introduce me?"

And with that, Momma made the big introduction: "This, my son, is Boris." Boris was a big man, with hands thick and heavy like twin anvils. As he spoke, however, I began to see that he was intelligent and even handsome. In fact, Boris resembled the British actor Peter Ustinov. He wore a neat suit and a crisp open-collared white shirt. He spoke English well enough and knew a fair amount of Hebrew. Boris shook hands with André warmly, but I could feel Momma's eyes burning through André's head like a red-hot laser beam of dislike and hostility. I was relieved when Boris invited us into the house. Momma walked a few paces ahead of us and never once turned her head to look back at us.

I had not expected to meet a man like Boris. As a Jew, he had survived years of cruel treatment under Russian government in Belarus, only to see his wife and children killed by invading Germans during World War II. After the war ended, Boris had miraculously escaped unharmed and managed to move to Israel. He had many family members in Israel who had also escaped persecution in Russia.

Boris was the exact opposite of my mother in almost every way. He smiled, she scowled; he was generous and kind, my mother was miserly and mean. He had a voice like honey; Momma's voice went into the ear like poison hemlock. Boris was open and expansive about his many Russian relatives, while my mother hardly ever spoke of hers at all. And while Momma's cooking repertoire was limited to leaden bowls of *cholent,* Boris was in fact a very good cook—as we learned when he made a lovely dinner that night.

I was grateful that André didn't have to endure my mother's horrifying dishes. As we ate dinner, Momma told Boris—and only Boris, because she ignored André at every turn—about our lives back in Brooklyn. She prattled on with her recollections, all of which were completely untrue. Momma told Boris that I had begun to read the Torah at the age of three. She also told him that I had spoken often throughout my teenage years about wanting to be a rabbi.

"I remember my only son," she said, "my boy, my darling Eliyahu, wished but to serve God by becoming a rabbi. He would read from the Torah every day when he came home from Hebrew school. He wished only to bring joy to his loving mother. And why shouldn't he, yes? But poor Elli," she continued, with feigned sorrow, "he had too much trouble reading and memorizing his Hebrew. I told him that our god *Elohim* would help him find a way in his life to please his mother."

What in the fuck is going on? I thought to myself, as Momma continued to describe many events in the life of someone who was most certainly not *moi*. I looked in wonder at André, who nodded gently as my mother delivered a near-total hallucination about my childhood in Brooklyn. "My son, what a wonderful athlete he was! He could throw the basketball high up in the air, from Brooklyn to Queens, that's how good he was!"

"Momma," I said, unable to stay silent any longer, "I think you mean football. And yes," I continued, "I think you remember, don't you? How I was the captain of the football team in my senior year of high school?"

She stared at me for an icy second, and then took my lead. "Why, yes, that's right, Elli! It was the football. And such talent you had. Never did the school have such a fantastic player. All the boys looked up to you at the school, while all the girls wanted to be your wife!"

"Ah, yes," I blasted onward, "I was so very popular at that time. But then, of course, there was the accident."

"I'm sorry, the *accident?*" Boris said, genuine concern on his face. "What, there was an accident, Sonia?"

"Well," she said, squinting a little more than usual as she held a smile, "yes, there was an accident. It was out in front of our store, Boris. You see, mine darling son here was carrying a box of expensive dishes from our house a few blocks away to our store. Elli always loved to help his mother with our store. So as he approached our store, he stumbled with the box and fell from the sidewalk out into the street just as a car was driving by and . . ."

"One of the car's tires ran over my hand. It was this hand here, Boris," I said, holding my left hand out in front of me so it dangled loosely at the wrist. "And ever since, my hand has hung just a little limp like this. We tried bandages, hand splints—nothing worked."

"It was a terrible thing for a mother to see," Momma said. "Can you imagine, Boris? A mother's only son being hurt like that and then forced to give up his basketball—"

"That's *football,* Momma," I interjected. "I don't know what I would have done if Momma hadn't found me a strong and capable nurse to give me physical therapy. Each day," I continued, adding to the avalanche of lies, "a young man named Rufus would come to our house and tend to my wounded hand. He applied many soft and sweet-smelling lotions to my skin. Sometimes, he would even give me long sponge baths to make sure I had not lost any skin sensitivity." André hid his laughter by pretending to cough while I kept going further into my story. "Momma and Pop, of course, were always at the family store, so Rufus was never really a distraction to them. I always say, 'Thank *Elohim* that my loving Momma brought home a big, muscular man to ease my pain.'"

Sensing that she was going to lose control of the ludicrous narrative, Momma barked out a quick laugh, sounding a bit like a woodpecker. Then she thrust up her hands and said, "And even then, with his injury, my Elli tells me that he *still* wants to become a rabbi and dedicate his life to serving God! I worried he might not then be strong enough, but who was I to judge? If being a rabbi was what he wanted in life, it was not for me to argue the matter. After all, *something* led him to that decision."

"Oh, yes, Momma," I said, pouring on yet another heap of irony meant only for her—and for André, who clearly knew that something ridiculous was taking place. "I tell you, Boris, that summer as Rufus rubbed me with those lotions and gave me the deep sponge baths, it was hard. *Really* hard," I continued, trying not to laugh. "It was so hard, in fact, that I thought I might just bust . . . from the decision of whether or not to be a rabbi, that is." Momma looked like she might soon require a stiff dose of digitalis to keep her from having a stroke right there on the table.

This tall Teichberg tale was just one of many that Momma and I were to share that night at dinner. She spoke of how much I loved and worried about her, and I spoke of how Momma used to read me bedtime stories when I was a little boy. I even recalled how she loved to sing me little songs after she tucked me into my bed.

"There were so many wonderful songs that you would sing to me, Momma," I said, "I think my *very* favorite must have been . . . what was it again? Was it 'Over the Rainbow'? Or maybe it was 'Mairzy Doats' that you sang? No, no, Momma, I remember what it was—"

The room was absolutely still.

"It was that wonderful song, 'Put on a Happy Face'!" Momma stared at me as if I had just kicked her in the stomach. "You remember, Momma, don't you? Go ahead, sing it for me again. Sing to me, your darling son, here in front of Boris and André!"

"Who?" she said, clearly annoyed.

"*André,* Momma! His name is André!" I shouted back, gesturing toward André.

"Oh, *him,*" she said, with a weak lift of her hands. "André is such a difficult name to remember."

"I don't see why, Momma, since André is also a Russian name," I responded angrily.

The two of us stared at each other, two feral dogs at a standstill. I was about to remind her about the time she said she was abducted by aliens (*goyish* aliens, of course) who flew a UFO over our house in Bensonhurst—when Boris began to sing softly. He was singing a song called "Smile," which had been written by the great silent movie clown Charlie Chaplin for his film *Modern Times.* The song tells us how important it is for us all to smile in the midst of grief and sorrow. As he finished singing the song, Boris began to cry. It was a cry that came from a place of deep loss—loss of family, of friends, of youth. It was clear that Boris had struggled greatly to maintain his belief in the decency of human life, even when that decency seemed to have disappeared almost completely from sight.

André and I were deeply touched. We embraced Boris in empathy and appreciation, as his tears brought forth our own. Momma, on the other hand, remained absolutely unmoved. After a moment's pause, she clapped her hands together crisply and commanded, "Come, Boris—now we clean up!" With that, she got up from her chair and walked into the kitchen. Turned back into her obedient and unquestioning automaton, Boris wordlessly began to clear the table and bring things back into the kitchen. André and I looked at each other.

"What should we do now, Elliot?" André asked.

"Don't do anything," I told him. "The scene is over. This is the intermission."

About ten minutes later, Boris and Momma reemerged from the kitchen. Boris stood up with a glass of thick wine and pronounced in his thick Russian accent, "Elya, I am honored to have you and your friend here with us. As your mother has said, she will become my wife and we will be married in the temple." Though we already knew about the wedding, it was *mazel tov* all around the table at the news. Boris seemed quite eager to assure me that he would be able to support Momma, assuring me that he had a very good pension that had been given to him as part of German reparations after World War II. My gut instinct was to warn him about how bonkers his blushing bride really was. But as he sat with his arm resting lovingly around Momma's shoulders, I thought to myself, *What right do I have to discourage true love?* So instead I turned to Momma and said, "Well, I hope you have a fancy wedding dress!"

On hearing this, she did a forty-yard Olympic dash toward her sewing room. She returned schlepping a huge bolt of dark upholstery fabric, a multi-colored mess of brown, gold, and red. She draped some of it on herself and announced that she was going to sew her own wedding gown. Momma explained that she had gotten the material for next to nothing, which meant that somebody had most likely paid her just to take it off their hands. There was no use telling her that upholstery fabric was much too heavy to be worn as a gown. "Just wait and see how lovely my dress will be for you, *dollink!*" she said to Boris, who looked at my mother adoringly. Then she whisked herself back to the sewing room, shouting behind her, "Boris, drive Elliot back to his hotel! I will be busy making my dress for the rest of the night!"

In the car driving back to Tel Aviv, André seemed quiet. I chalked it up to jet lag. He dealt with the time difference by consuming a slow but steadily escalating stream of alcohol. Then again, perhaps he needed to drink to help protect himself against the slow poison of my mother's passive aggression.

❁   ❁   ❁

The next day, we went to meet Boris's extended family. His relatives all lived in a little house on the beach near Momma's apartment in Netanya. They had set up a long table outside in their backyard garden and covered it with a huge array of salads, Russian snacks, and cookies. There were twenty smiling relatives and twenty bottles of vodka. *Ouch!* André and I were given a warm reception. Everyone was quite lovely, and a few of Boris's relatives even tried to speak a little English or French to us.

We soon learned that the wedding between Momma and Boris was going to have to wait. Apparently, the chief rabbi in Tel Aviv had some concerns about Momma's suitability as a bride, owing to the fact that she had previously been married. As we understood it, a small committee of three Tel Aviv religious judges had to sign some official certificate of approval before the

chief rabbi could perform a wedding ceremony. I, Momma's son, was expected to go answer some questions about her before this certificate could be
obtained. It sounded to me like the same old story—pay up to the powers that
be and your wish will be granted. I told Momma that the rabbi's claim was
total nonsense, and that she and Boris were free to get married without the
judges' approval. I learned very quickly that this was not the way things
worked in Israel. So Momma and I got hold of a *sherut*—a group taxi—and
drove off to see the rabbi and the three judges in Tel Aviv.

I had to keep my staunch atheism in check while talking to the judges.
Momma, who was sincerely worried about the outcome of the meeting, pleaded with me. "Please, Eliyahu, tell these holy men that you keep *shabbos,* that
you are kosher, and that you are married to a nice Jewish girl in Belgium
named Andrea." I didn't give a shit about that, but I didn't want to be the reason that they denied her marriage to Boris.

The rabbi's chambers were severe and exceedingly formal. The judges discussed Momma's religious background, and how and when my father passed
away. They questioned Momma for what seemed like hours, and then they
turned to me. They were pleased that I could speak some Hebrew with them,
but it wasn't quite enough to win them over. They said it was inconceivable
that neither I nor Momma had a copy of Pop's death certificate. This made
them suspicious of us both.

To win these holy men back to my way of thinking, I told them that I was
planning to enroll in rabbinical school back in Belgium. They concurred that
the *goyim* in Belgium needed all the help they could get. And then they asked
me to swear to God that my father was, in fact, dead. I told them, "My father,
Jack Teichberg, died in the early summer of 1970, in a small New York village
called White Lake. He was a devout Jewish man who always wanted the best
for my mother—*always."* This they finally accepted, and then everything was
solved and back on track.

The wedding would be allowed to take place within a few days—the
sooner the better, in my opinion. I had no idea what André thought of any of
this, especially since I had left him with Boris and his family while I went with
Momma to meet with the kosher inquisitors. When we returned to the beach
house and announced that the wedding was back on, everyone cheered.

I couldn't have thought of a less likely place for André and me to be than there in Israel, helping my mother and Boris get married. I told him so when we got a minute to ourselves at the party. His smile was cordial, but he seemed distant.

"What's the matter?" I said to him.

"Nothing," he said, flatly. "I just feel that—" He stopped mid-sentence.

"What, André? What is it?"

"I guess it is just strange for me to see you with your mother like this. As long as I have known you, you have always been strong and free."

"And?"

"And yet," he sighed, "here you are, meeting with rabbis and jumping through all these hoops and trying desperately to win your mother's approval and love."

"Listen," I said in a tense whisper, "I'm doing the best I can in this situation, all right? I'm trying to do the right thing. I don't expect that any of this is going to make things better between my mother and me. You think three days is tough with that woman? Try thirty fucking years!"

"You think you are the only one who has suffered?" André shot back.

"Yeah, okay, so why don't we jet over to Liège after this so I can watch you try to get along with your father?"

I knew the minute the words left my lips that I had wounded him. "Elliot, sometimes you really know how to be an asshole."

"Babe, I'm sorry. I didn't mean to hurt you like that."

"No, I am the one who hurt you. Just forget it. Can we just go back to the hotel, please?"

I tried to get him to look me in the eye, but his eyes were cast downward at the ground. Glancing around the party, I saw Momma watching André and me in the midst of our private argument. I could feel it from across the party—the possibility that she was taking satisfaction in seeing me unhappy.

Since my work on Momma's behalf was done, I saw no need for us to stay. Besides, I needed to get out of her gravitational pull as quickly as I could. So we said a quick goodbye to Boris and Momma, and got a cab to take us to the hotel.

Back at the hotel, I wanted to make love and not continue war. Instead, André told me he had a headache and wanted to get some sleep. He slid into bed and turned away from me, so I stared straight up at the ceiling until I fell asleep. I had strange dreams, including one in which all the roads in Israel turned into immense snakes, rearing up and trying to devour André and me. I woke from the dream, sweating. Everything felt very unreal and far away in that dark Israeli night.

The wedding day came, a Sunday that also happened to be Mother's Day. Arriving at her house, we found Momma in the living room, wearing the wedding dress made from the upholstery fabric she had shown us so boastfully a few days before. "You see, this is a Sonia Teichberg original!"

André and I stood there with our mouths hanging open in amazement. She hadn't just made a dress. She'd also made a matching coat and hat from the upholstery fabric. But she hadn't stopped at the wedding outfit, either. Her sofa and club chairs and walls—even her window drapes—were now covered in that same crazy-quilt material. You could barely see Momma in the midst of all that heavy fabric; she blended right into the furniture. If it weren't for her shrill voice, someone might have mistaken her for a couch and tried to sit on her! Regardless, she was happy that day in her strange outfit, her gold high-heeled shoes, and her newly dyed red hair.

It would have been easy for me to say something sarcastic, but I knew why I was there. I was there to represent my family. So in spite of what was going on in my head, I said "Mom, you have such sparkle and pizzazz! And look, now you are getting married in Israel! Here you know God is close and will bless you and Boris on your wedding day!"

Mom nodded in agreement, smiling, though I could tell that her heavy upholstery dress was starting to tucker her out. Boris arrived at their place at just the right moment. We expected him to be wearing a suit from Momma's upholstery fabric, but he was wearing his own Russian-style suit, too snug and tightly buttoned.

Momma had apparently accumulated a number of new friends since she arrived in Israel, and Boris's extended family helped to fill the wedding hall nearly to capacity. I still did not understand my mother's relationship with Boris, and she made it terribly clear that she did not care to know anything about my relationship with André. And yet I couldn't help feeling a little happy when Boris and Momma broke the wine glass at the conclusion of the wedding ceremony. It took a lot for my mother to break anything that she might be able to sell to somebody else, so clearly this wedding was a big deal to her.

Boris had arranged for the wedding music to be played by a small four-piece klezmer band. When it came time for the newly married couple's first dance, Boris asked the small band to play the Russian song "Ochi chyornye." He announced to everyone at the party, "My family and my friends, this song for our first dance together is dedicated to our wonderful guests, Sonia's son Elliot and his—" Momma cut him off, signaling to the band to start playing and encouraging everyone else to clap and cheer.

After the first dance with Boris, Momma bounded over and introduced me to a rather *zaftig*—make that fat—Russian woman. Clearly, Momma thought this corpulent little *sputnik* and her listless orbit around me might inspire thoughts of marriage. To my relief, this woman only spoke Russian, so I was spared any comprehension of the sweet nothings she whispered huskily into my ear. After another half-hour or so, my unsuccessful would-be bride stood up with the band and began a song. I looked at André and said in his ear, "Well, the fat lady is singing. Let's go." With that, we wished Momma and Boris well and got the hell away from the bizarre matrimonial circus.

It had been an exhausting day. Our flight back to New York was set for the next night, so we had one more day to tour Israel. On that final day, we had planned to visit Jerusalem so that André could pray at the Church of the Holy Sepulchre and see other churches throughout the old city. I didn't have any interest in religious matters, but André had come to stand up with me at my mother's new wedding, and all his efforts to be friendly and make a connection with my mother had been met with rudeness or silence at best. If he wanted to take in more sand and pray in a few more churches, I wasn't about to complain. I *owed* him.

So I was a little shocked when André said that he had visited enough churches and had no interest in seeing anything else in Israel. I asked him why he'd had such an abrupt change of heart. He said, "I just want to go home, Elliot. I want to go home." I wanted to ask him if he meant New York or Belgium when he said "home," but I was suddenly a little scared to hear how he would respond. Instead, we packed our things and caught an earlier flight back to New York.

On the plane, André sat reading a *Time* magazine that he had bought at the airport in Israel. I began to jot down dialogue and general notes that I had for the Winifred Wagner play that I now called *The Music Keeper.* Somehow, seeing Momma at her upholstered Israeli wedding had jumpstarted my thoughts on the still-unfinished play. I had a direction now, even as André seemed adrift.

The trip to Israel had not been as horrible as I had thought it would be. I reported to Renee that Boris was truly a nice man, and that Momma and he actually seemed to get along. Renee was so relieved that Momma was happily remarried that I didn't tell her that I didn't expect that loving feeling to last very long. Considering what I had seen Pop go through, it would be only a matter of time before that instinctive screech of Momma's would direct itself at Boris. Maybe things would be different, but I doubted it.

As it turned out, Boris passed away less than two years after the wedding. Perhaps sharing life with Momma was enough to convince him to enter the afterlife, which the rabbis called *Olam Ha-Ba.* While Pop had been chained to Momma for more than forty years, Boris got the hell out after only two. *Smart man,* I thought.

The first and last time I snorted cocaine was under a hot blur of flashing spotlights at a back table in the ultra-popular Studio 54 nightclub. Back in New York, André and I more than made up for the lack of fun and frolic in Israel. Driven insane by our own pent-up need for physical release, we entered into the summer of 1979 as so many others did: hot, bothered, and ready for action.

It wasn't just the gay New Yorkers who were going wild. The so-called "straight" scene was going through changes as well. The relatively new cultural phenomenon of swinging, or partner-swapping, proved that what had been deemed taboo behavior only a decade before had now been casually accepted into the mainstream. While many gay men had previously confined themselves to the Lower Manhattan leather bars, there were now places where everyone and everything was welcome. Places like Studio 54 and the "no limits" swingers' sex club Plato's Retreat, located in the basement of the

Ansonia Hotel on the Upper West Side, were open to anything short of murder and cannibalism.

The hot glue that brought everybody together in the nightclubs was disco music. At Studio 54, the DJs would play disco long and loud, until nearly everyone wound up on the dance floor. Although disco had arisen out of the gay dance scene, *Saturday Night Fever* had touched off a veritable invasion by straight couples to the disco clubs all over the city. Many of them came into town from the suburbs, the men done up in polyester suits and the women wearing off-the-shoulder satin dresses with fabric flower details along the side.

André and I found ourselves at Studio 54 in early June. We had been lucky enough to gain entrance into the notoriously selective club by mixing in with Andy Warhol's entourage. Once inside, we took in the scene. Even more than the music and crowded dance floor, what really got my attention was the sheer number of recognizable celebrities who were partying at the club. I spotted actors Jack Nicholson and Warren Beatty to my left and Liza Minnelli to my right.

Seated at a table, a blond girl in platform shoes and a pair of tight red leather pants started trying to get me to snort some coke off of her compact mirror. She kept rubbing my shoulder and telling me, "Try it, it makes you see everything *really* clearly!" Both André and I did a line. The girl had told me that I would feel incredible in only a few minutes, but I didn't feel any different. So I did another line, and then another. When I looked up, Jack, Warren, Andy, and Liza were all still there—and the disco music was still playing at maximum volume.

Of course, the *real* high for me was getting in so close to these showbiz giants. Despite our many strikeouts over the past year and a half, I held on to the belief that I might be able to talk one of those personalities into doing a movie with André and me. For most of that night, with those three bright lines of cocaine coursing through my system, I walked up to any celebrities that I saw and tried to chat each one up. The dance music was so loud that I had to shout to be heard. I walked up to Liza Minnelli, said "Hi!" and managed to yell "I once met your mother!" to her. She smiled back at me cheerily before being swept off to the dance floor by some of her friends. *Strike one.*

I then found myself face to face with the legendary Surrealist painter Salvador Dalí, instantly recognizable because of his long waxed mustache. I looked for André to see if he wanted to come with me to talk to the great Spanish artist, but he was nowhere in sight. Never one to hold back, I walked over to Dalí and tried to introduce myself over the loud dance music. I shouted, "Would you consider shaving off your mustache in my movie?" I will never be sure if he heard me. His response was to grow wide-eyed and start shouting something loudly in Spanish that didn't sound like "Sí, señor!" *Strike two.*

I had better luck with the writer Truman Capote. He was even shorter in person than I expected, and was much thinner than he had been in previous years. I could see that he was drunk and probably stoned, but he and I danced together for a song or two. By this point, I had given up looking for André. As the music stopped for a few minutes, I had enough time to ask Capote if he had any interest in doing a film with me and my partner. He waved off my request, staggering slightly as we moved away from the dance floor. He was trying to be cordial, even though I was probably one of thousands who had tried to talk to him about doing some project or another. Rather than shut me down completely, he asked me where I lived in town. "I have a place near the top floor of Manhattan Plaza," I answered, proud that I had such an impressive response.

"You don't *say!*" Truman chirped in that high sing-song voice of his. "My good friend Tennessee Williams just got a new place there a few months ago. Maybe we can all get together at his place sometime—it's less noisy there, anyway."

"Well, yes, maybe we will," I said, trying to be as cool as I could, considering the surroundings and the cocaine in my system. But before I could utter another word, Truman sauntered back to the dance floor. A little while later, I found André standing with a drink in a dark corner near the bathrooms. "Where have you been?" I asked, teasing him about how he had missed the chance to not talk with Liza Minnelli and Salvador Dalí and Truman Capote. I also broke the news that Tennessee Williams—who had been discovered by our agent years before—was now living in Manhattan Plaza, just like us.

"So what? There is nothing remarkable in that, Elliot," he said, sounding annoyed with me. "Even stars need a place to clear their heads." I could see that he was frustrated staying there at the club, so I asked him if he wanted to head back to our apartment.

"No," he said, "I am not ready to go home yet."

His eyes were darting back and forth, and he looked like an animal trapped in a cage. "Okay," I continued, speaking loudly so he could hear me over the dance music. "So where do you wanna go?"

"The Mineshaft, the Ramrod, whichever," he said, "I just want to get out of here. You can stay here if you like, Elliot, but I am leaving!"

"Okay, okay, babe," I said, "come on, let's head downtown!"

I had no problem going with him to the Mineshaft, one of our favorite leather clubs. I was nonetheless a little confused about why André was in such a foul mood. To my way of thinking, hanging out in a club full of celebrities increased our likelihood of getting a new project off the ground by at least a thousand percent. But André looked slightly nauseated by the environment. In fact, he acted like he couldn't get out of there fast enough. We grabbed a taxi and headed back to our place, where we changed out of our more conventional clothing and donned our leather outfits. All the while, I couldn't help but feel that André's mind was somewhere else.

Once in our leather gear, we took another taxi downtown to the Village. We got inside the club, and André made his way over to the bar, where he asked the tattooed bartender to make him a whiskey sour. Never having enjoyed drinking too much, I asked the bartender to give me a beer. We stood together at the bar, looking out at the others on the dance floor and not really talking. As the bartender brought us the round, he told us that there was going to be some exciting stuff happening at the leather clubs in the next few weeks. "Some major movie director is coming to town," the bartender explained, "and he wants to make a movie about us."

"What? Someone's making a Hollywood porno flick about homosexuals?" I asked, curious. André just stood there, looking down at his drink.

"No, man! It's going to be a real movie and it's all going to be shot here in the leather bars. Word on the street is that the director is going to film *everything* that we like down here. Golden showers, fistfucking, circle jerks, whippings, glory holes, you name it. Sky's the limit, baby."

I found it surprising that some Hollywood film director was going to make a feature film about the gay leather subculture. What I heard next seemed like some weird blast of fate.

"So who's the director?" I heard myself ask, to which the bartender responded, "Uh, some guy named Freedberg or something. I think he made *The Exorcist.*"

"William *Friedkin?* William *fuckin'* Friedkin!" I exclaimed, blown away to hear that Friedkin, of all directors, was going to be doing the picture.

"Yeah, that's the dude's name!" the bartender shouted back over the music. "Everyone's excited. Who knows? Maybe one of us will get famous!"

A wave of euphoria that was ninety-nine times stronger than the cocaine came sweeping over me. It felt like the universe was twisting things back around our way. I immediately snapped back into my Super Elli mindset, trying to figure out how André and I might be able to reconnect with Friedkin right there in the clubs. It occurred to me that he might want to call upon me and André to act as advisors on the film, since we knew the leather scene so well. We had always heard about how you needed to know someone in the business to get a picture made, especially in Hollywood. And now, standing at the bar of the Mineshaft, a connection was presenting itself so clearly that it seemed preordained.

As we stood in front of the bar, I could barely keep up with my thoughts. I saw how it would play out: we would come to the bars when we knew they were starting to film; I would do my best to schmooze and get Friedkin's attention there on location; I would then point out to him that his former French interpreter, the great Belgian actor and director, André Ernotte, was my boyfriend; and eventually I would let drop that we were interested in working on his new film.

Had I stopped for a second to think, I would have realized what a schnook I was being. But it wasn't my nature to second-guess. As always, I tended to focus on the dream while ignoring the realities. Nevertheless, it was increasingly clear that André was not pleased to learn that Friedkin would be making his next film there at the sex clubs.

"Are you fucking crazy, Elliot? Are you fucking *nuts?* Do you think for a second that Friedkin is going to give a *shit* that I am prancing around trying to be an extra in one of his movies? If anything, it will be a total embarrassment for him to see what has happened to me since I last worked with him. How can you stand there and suggest that I debase myself and my reputation like that? What kind of a desperate whore do you think I am, anyway?"

With that, André turned and walked out of the bar. I gave the bartender a twenty-dollar bill, and ran after André. Once back out on the street, I asked him what I had done to upset him so much. He wouldn't answer me, but just kept walking until he reached a taxi waiting for a fare.

"André," I said, "Where are you going? Come on, don't be upset. Don't go home. It's still early."

"What makes you think that I want to go home?" he shot back.

"Well where are we going, then?" I asked, getting a little irritated.

"The Ramrod. You do what you like, Elliot, but that is where I am going tonight!"

"Let's go, then," I said, sliding down into the taxi alongside him and asking the taxi driver to take us over to West Street between Christopher and West Tenth. The cab driver, who had probably seen and heard it all in his job, drove us south to the Ramrod. André and I sat still and silent during the ride. The taxi pulled up to the club, and André got out and walked toward the door without so much as a glance at me. I paid the fare and quickly caught up with André, so that we entered the club together.

André headed straight for the dance floor. Within minutes, he was really mixing it up. I followed his lead and began to dance and grind against some of the more gorgeous hard-bodied guys there. Although we were a committed couple, André and I would casually rub against other men in the clubs. It was a bit of fun that had become part of our nightclub routine without ever being discussed. We both used to get an erotic charge out of slapping and grabbing other leather boys around the dance floor.

On this night, however, André took things way further than ever before. Dancing there at the Ramrod, I was shocked to see André kissing several of the men who were dancing with him in the center of the dance floor. While I was certainly no stranger to passion in the leather bars, this was the first time that I had seen André kiss another man on the lips. I couldn't stop looking at André as he kissed the men around him longer and deeper. Eventually I stopped dancing and just stood motionless on the dance floor, watching my lover ravenously give in to all manner of lust with a growing group of men. I felt as if my heart had been stabbed with a sharp icicle that had started to melt, sending cold liquid through my veins.

It was as if I were watching a film running in slow motion. With mounting rage, I saw André close his eyes and teasingly slide his tongue into the hungry, wet mouths of the other men. And I saw him be kissed back by one man, then another, and then another.

I was starting to make my way toward André when I saw a young shirt-less man with a crew cut drop to his knees and start rubbing his hand back and forth against André's crotch. André's cock visibly began to grow harder inside his tight leather pants. My hands squeezed into fists so tight that my finger-nails almost drew blood from my palms. Just as the guy began to pull André's zipper down, I reached André and spun him around so he was facing me. Half-mad with jealousy, I grabbed him by the back of his head and pulled him toward me for a kiss. His eyes closed, André didn't realize it was me. When he opened his eyes and saw it was me that he was kissing, he pulled away, looking agitated. "What?" I mouthed to him, but the loudness of the music and the writhing chaos of the dance floor made it impossible to have a con-versation.

With that, André turned and practically ran out of the bar. I stood there, hurt and confused. What had just happened? As I walked back up to our place at Manhattan Plaza alone, I kept trying to see things from André's per-spective. Try as I might, though, I couldn't help feeling more and more con-fused. Even before our trip to Israel, André had become increasingly distant. Whenever I asked him how things were going, he only mumbled short responses. If I asked what he had been doing while in Paris directing a show, he would get defensive and attack me for being nosy and making him anxious. One time, he said, "Jesus, Elliot, you act as if we were a married couple or something! What is your problem?"

Now, as I walked the Greenwich Village side streets where André and I had first met and lived together, I started to get mad. I felt stupid for having thought that the trip to Israel might bring us closer together. It hadn't done any such thing. André had only grown moodier and more secretive after the trip than he was before. His continued consumption of alcohol and Valium had driven us even further apart.

And now he had thrown himself at those men back at the leather bar. The image of André kissing and being kissed by those men kept playing over and over again in my head, driving me crazy. I closed my eyes, but I could still see him moving to the music, flirting and grinding with those men. I felt sure that the André I'd known and loved had disappeared.

As I walked past Greenwich Avenue, I remembered the first time I saw André—standing there on that corner, silent and beautiful underneath a single street light. Now he had become this temperamental and increasingly bitter person. My thoughts crystallized around the one word that expressed my mind and heart at that crazy moment—"Fuck!"

I proceeded to scream that word with enough force and fury that the people walking toward me on the sidewalk swiftly crossed over to the other side of the street. I began to think of all those other nights over the past few months when André had gone out walking on his own. *What else has he been doing out here?* I thought to myself. *What* else *don't I know?* For the first time, I realized that André might have been cheating on me.

How could he have been so heartless, after everything I had done for him? He would have abandoned so many of his projects if I hadn't been there to push him onward and keep him focused and upbeat. It was I who had persevered to help get *Sketch-Up,* the French-language book deal and then the feature film of *Rue Haute;* the American book deal with Avon Paperbacks; and finally the New York screening runs of *High Street.* Even André's current position at Playwrights Horizons was due to my efforts on his behalf. He needed me, and I had been there for him.

My mind alternated between anger over our artistic struggles and jealousy over André's infidelities. Doubt and anger kept bouncing around in my head: *What happened tonight? Was it something I did? Maybe I'm to blame. Fuck that, it's his fault!*

As I kept on walking uptown, I tried to clear my head. What tortured me was the idea that André had explored other guys sexually without even talking to me about it. To me, his actions demonstrated a casual disregard for my feelings in our relationship. *Shit, maybe all that coke really* is *making me see things clearly,* I thought, recalling what that blond at Studio 54 had told me before I took that first fateful snort.

I returned to Manhattan Plaza around four in the morning—that eerily hushed time of the night when even the cars and taxis seem to have gone to sleep. In the elevator going up to our place, I tried to calm down. I knew that if I continued to think about what had happened at the Ramrod, or the possibility that he was cheating on me, I might rip André's head off his body with my bare hands.

I prepared for a fight, ready to yell and be yelled at the minute I entered our apartment. But when I got to the door, it opened without so much as a squeak. I walked into the apartment and made my way toward the bedroom. It was very quiet in the apartment—so quiet, in fact, that it took me a few moments to realize that I was the only one in the place. André was not there. I was alone in an empty and troubled home.

I couldn't sleep, so I spent the next few hours perched on the edge of the couch, looking out past our terrace to the immense view of the Hudson River. It was a little after seven in the morning when André shuffled through the door. I had planned for us to talk together about our problems, just as the best of friends and lovers should always do. I wanted to be civil, but I was gripped by anger the moment I saw him.

"Where the *fuck* have you been?"

"Out."

"Yeah? Doing what?"

"Just walking."

"Just walking, huh? Did it ever occur to you that I might be *worried?*"

"Hey, I am a grown man. Certainly I can walk down a city street by myself!"

"Not at this time of the morning—and not dressed like that! What if you had been hurt, or attacked by someone? How would I even know where to find you?"

"Jesus! What are you, my mother?"

"Hey, listen, I wouldn't have to talk like this if you weren't being such a goddamn baby!"

"Look who is talking! You did everything except crawl back into the womb when we were in Israel!"

"Oh, you know what? Fuck you! Where the fuck do you get off? That's so unfair! Christ, you know how *fucking* hard that trip was for me. I didn't even want to go until you talked me into it!"

"That is because I thought you might be able to finally share the *truth* with your mother about your life. I thought that since you had achieved your freedom as a man, you would be able to maintain your dignity. Instead, you just sat there and spun all these ridiculous lies. And then when your mother did everything she could to make me feel meaningless, you did nothing to stand up for who you are! You just let her get away with it! You coward!"

"Coward, huh? *I'm* the fucking coward? You're the one who ran away from New York and back to Belgium as soon as you could. The one who hid behind his mother rather than confront his father about who *he was.* The one who said we couldn't get a TV show, who said we couldn't get a movie made, and who thought we'd never get a book deal. And you're the one who went running out of the club last night when you heard that William Friedkin was coming to town with a camera and a Hollywood movie deal. So scared you might have to get down off that precious little pedestal of yours and hustle like the rest of us to get ahead in this motherfucking rat race!"

Everything just stopped. Living together had allowed us both to improve our strengths and cover up our weaknesses. André had brought out the best in me, and I had brought out the best in him. It was only now, hurling unpleasant words back and forth like grenades, that we saw the worst in each other.

Trying my best to defuse the situation, I said, "It's been a long night. Why don't we get some sleep?"

André nodded sadly. "I am so tired, Elliot."

"Me, too, believe me. Let's just go to sleep and try to forget everything we said."

I felt guilty for having attacked André so mercilessly, yet I remained hurt by the thought that he might have been unfaithful. As I looked at André, lying with his back to me, I wished that things could be normal again when we woke up. If I had known what was going to happen next, I would never have let myself go to sleep.

After that night, we buried ourselves in our work. André was busy at the Playwrights Horizons theater. I had the summer off from teaching at the New School, so I continued to work on *The Music Keeper.* Things between us were essentially as they had been before the trip to Israel—not as close and solid as they had been for us only a few months earlier, but certainly a bit more manageable. *Fake it 'til you make it,* I thought. If we could pretend that the fight had never happened, perhaps everything would return to normal.

One night the week after our fight, walking home from dinner, I was busy telling André about the ten-year anniversary of the Woodstock festival, which was going to be commemorated with concerts at Madison Square Garden and out on Long Island. André seemed to have no interest in what I was saying. Back in the apartment, I turned on the TV and André went off to the bedroom. About ten minutes later, he came back to the living room and turned off the TV.

"Elliot, I have to tell you something," he said.

"What is it, babe?" I asked.

"Elliot . . . Elliot, I need, uh, we need—" André stopped. "I need a break from this, from us."

"A break from what? What do you mean?" I asked, dreading his response.

"You know what I mean, Elliot," he said. Of course I did, but I couldn't believe what I was hearing. The more I pushed him to explain, the more desperate I sounded.

"What's wrong? What did I do? What the hell's going on here, André?"

I felt that if I couldn't find out what I had done to lose him, my only choice would be to leap out the window. Way beyond any semblance of pride or restraint, I became frantic. "Why? Why do you want to leave me? Just tell me what the fuck I did wrong. Please, please, please . . . *tell* me!"

"Elliot!" he exclaimed. "I don't want to *fuck* you anymore, okay? How much clearer can I be? I want more! I need to be free. This is not working for me anymore. You are stifling me! We are at a dead end. Nothing is happening. This whole thing is boring. I come home at night, and I cannot stand it. I want to be out there, I want to be with other men, I need to feel alive again. You have already found your freedom—I am still searching. And if I stay and never make this break, I don't know what I am going to do! Elliot, I cannot take it anymore. I am sorry."

As I realized that the man I loved no longer wanted to be with me, the bottom fell out of my world. Before I could stop myself, I began to sob uncontrollably. Nine years spent building a life—sharing laughter and tears and struggles, the very roughest of defeats and the sweetest of successes. And now all of it was suddenly being declared a dead dream.

"Elliot, please don't cry," André said, tears starting to form in his own eyes. I could only look at him and shake my head. *No.*

"Why did you give up on me? Why did you give up on the things we've been trying to do? We've established our own voices together, André, you and me. Why do you want to let that go? Just for some hot young cock? Did you ever think to tell me about your sexual needs? You want to mess around with other men, that's fine, I'm open to it, bring 'em up here. We can do whatever you want, baby. I'll do it, I don't care. I love you. Just don't leave, don't fuckin' leave. *Please don't leave!*"

"Elliot," André said, his face full of tenderness. "You have to understand. I still love you. No one will ever take your place in my heart. I just have certain things that I need to do for *me*."

He went to put his arms around me, but I resisted. I grabbed him by his shoulders, my heart filled with pain, and started to shake him. Eventually, my hands loosened, as my anger trailed off into a deep and lonely despair. We hugged and clung to each other, André gently stroking the back of my head as I howled like some wild dog lying at the feet of his dead master. We stayed that way for a few minutes, and I slowly began to calm down.

As hard as it was for me to hear, the truth was that I understood what André was saying and how he felt. My ten wasted years at the El Monaco had given me great empathy for anyone who felt lost or bitter or afraid about the meaning of their own lives. It seemed absurd for André to move out, but he insisted that he could only go after what he needed if he was away from me. I realized how serious André was when he said he had already removed himself from our joint bank account—we had pooled our earnings ever since we had begun to live together in Belgium. André had also arranged to stay at the apartment of a fellow theater colleague. He didn't bother to share the name, and I didn't ask.

"Can I help you pack at least?"

"I already have packed, Elliot," he said, as he picked up his suitcase from our bedroom closet.

Unable to find any words, I simply watched as André phoned down to the doorman to request a taxi. Then he fished his apartment key out of his front pocket and placed it on the table. We stood in our living room for a few more minutes, not saying very much at all, as it dawned on me that André was really about to leave.

"Listen," he said, "I will give you a call in a few weeks."

I stared at him, unable to speak for probably the first time in my life.

"I will call, just to see how things are going."

"You know the number," I said, feeling low and beaten.

After another pause, André said, "I hope we can remain friends, Elliot."

If I believed in you, God, I'd ask you to stop him from leaving me, I thought as I looked at the man I loved. "You will always be special to me, André." I felt so dizzy from shock that I had to lean against the wall to stop myself from passing out. "Just remember that I'm here for you. If you ever need anything at all, I'm here."

André picked up the suitcase and started to walk toward our apartment door. Then he paused.

"Are you going to be okay, Elliot?" he asked.

"No," I answered, with a sorrow I had never felt before.

My emotions were welling up in me so fast that I was either going to kiss him or kill him if he kept standing there in the doorway. But rather than give in to my despair, I turned to the one thing that had gotten me through hardship time and again—humor.

"Listen, I hope you packed up your favorite shirts, because I'm going to open a small boutique tomorrow and sell all the rest with a big sign that reads 'Worn by André Ernotte'!"

We both laughed, trying not to cry again. "You always know how to make life funny, Elliot."

He smiled. As he turned to go, a thought came to me. I remembered the Jacques Brel album that André and I had listened to so often when we were working on *Attention: Fragile,* back in Belgium, when we were still happy. I remembered that the album's title meant "Don't leave me." And I remembered how André had taught me how to say that title in French.

"*Ne me quitte pas,* André," I said. "*Ne me quitte pas.*"

He hesitated for a moment, and turned back toward me slightly. "No," he said. "No."

"André," I said, not sure what might happen to either of us the minute he left the apartment. "Please promise me something. Be careful out there. Just keep yourself safe. Promise?"

André looked as serene and beautiful as he had been the first time I saw him. He nodded. "*Au revoir, mon ami.*"

15

Stevie Strong
and the Magical Song

My Ten Favorite Movies:

The Wizard of Oz—Dorothy

Meet Me in St. Louis—Trolley Song!

Duck Soup—Freedonia

Animal Crackers—Elephant in pajamas

The Wild One—Brando in that leather jacket—yummy!

All About Eve—Bette Davis, all-time favorite bitch on wheels

King of Hearts (Le Roi de Coeur)—Fun screening this at the
El Monaco "movie theater"

Midnight Cowboy—Joe Buck, Ratso, still remember crying
at the end of this movie

Saló, or the 120 Days of Sodom—Marquis de Sade on film—
talk about a shit-eating grin!

Rue Haute—Wonderful movie, wonderful memories,
a lost cause . . . André

In the days after André left the apartment, I found myself writing down various lists in a notebook. In addition to my favorite movies, I made lists of my least favorite movies—basically, anything with John Wayne—along with lists of literature I still needed to read (including *Moby Dick* and *The Turn of The Screw*); cities I never wanted to visit (such as Raiford, Florida); and my all-time favorite torch songs ("The Man that Got Away" and "Angel Eyes," among others). I was totally depressed, and needed something to occupy my mind. The apartment was so large and quiet without André there, and the near-panoramic view of the city from our windows made me feel even lonelier. I had tried to work on *The Music Keeper,* but found myself frozen in place, unable to move the plot forward.

I wanted to talk to Renee, but she had called a few weeks earlier to tell me that she was taking Alyse on a vacation down to Miami Beach once the school year was done. I hadn't thought to ask where she would be staying. Not being able to tell my baby sister that André had left me made me feel even sadder. I had no course to teach until the fall semester, and nowhere else that I needed to be. So I sat around and moped, left to ponder my great nothing of a life, alone, hour after empty hour. I went through the TV listings with a pen and circled anything that I wanted to see each day, every day, for two weeks in a row. I had turned into my own TV test pattern—it was as if I had placed my life on hold.

Seated on the couch, I clicked from channel to channel. It was summer, so the networks were airing reruns. I couldn't watch sitcoms—the laugh tracks attacked my mind, reminding me of our *Sketch-Up* shenanigans and making me sadder. For the first time ever, I watched soap operas like *Guiding Light* and *Days of Our Lives,* shows my mother had watched every day on the small TV in the office behind the El Monaco front desk. Now, here I was, watching the same exact programs. Oy! Talk about misery. The immense hourglass featured in the opening credits of *Days of Our Lives*—signifying the limited time we all had on earth—was so monumentally depressing that I would probably have laughed at it if I hadn't felt as down as I did.

The only show that gave me any real pleasure was *Welcome Back, Kotter,* but that was because it was set in my old home town of Brooklyn. I watched only one episode of *The Love Boat,* where big-name stars would appear each week and inevitably fall in love as the orchestra swelled romantically on the soundtrack. I hated it as much for its insipid scripts and music as for its capacity to conjure up that botched birthday party I had organized on the Hudson River ferry boat back in 1968. I didn't need any more bad memories.

One morning, about two weeks after the breakup, I got up early and made my way over to the public library. I hadn't been around people, other than the few I'd seen at my local grocery store. I felt lonely, and wanted to interact with someone. I figured that I might meet someone at the library. I had never really thought of the library as potential cruising territory, but I figured it was worth a try. Besides, I felt that it was time to get myself in hand. Now that André was gone, I felt that I needed to make myself into the very best Elliot Tiber that I could be. So I went to the library, eyes open to anyone who looked interesting—or interested—and started to look for some answers.

I leafed through several biographies of great writers, actors, singers, musicians, artists, directors, and began to write down those things that had influenced them. I wanted to see what it was that had made them who they were. Besides, I figured that a few books and a new opera album or two would distract me, help me stop thinking about *him*. As I read, I was not surprised to learn that many of the artists in history that I admired had endured traumatic childhoods and suffered troubled relationships in their adult lives. I drew a small measure of comfort from the knowledge that others had been caught in the same seemingly endless cycle of unhappiness that I now found myself in. It wasn't enough, though, to make me feel any better about myself or my life. And my lingering inner turmoil must have shone through, because no one so much as looked my way there in the library. I felt like a ghost.

It was an impossible situation. I missed André terribly. There was no way around it. Everywhere I went, I found myself wondering where he was, who he was with, and what he was doing. In the two years since we moved back to New York, we had developed favorite spots around the city—restaurants, museums, movie theaters, and especially clubs and bars. I deliberately refrained from visiting the gay leather bars downtown, because I thought I might see him there with someone else, and that was something I didn't think I could handle.

But it was summer, and I ultimately decided that I had a life, too. One Saturday, I was bored of sitting in front of the TV watching reruns, so I went out to see a new movie instead. There was a new comedy playing called *The Main Event*, starring Barbra Streisand and Ryan O'Neal. While waiting for the movie to start, I overheard some men talking about a parade that was being held the next day. Manhattan was always having parades. After eavesdropping a little more, I realized that they were talking about the Gay Pride Parade. I had marched in the second Gay Pride Parade, years ago, but lately I had been so preoccupied, first with my projects and then with the breakup, that I hadn't really given myself the time to think about anything else.

On the way back to my apartment that night, I decided that I would get up early the next day and march in the parade. For one thing, it would be a lot better than watching *Meet the Press*. For another, I felt a certain need to support—and be supported by—the gay community. The recent death of Harvey Milk, the first openly gay man elected to public office, had re-energized the gay rights movement. It felt important to assert ourselves, to fight back against prejudice, and to make the public know that gay people were entitled to a place in society.

I got down to the registration area early and signed up to march, donating some cash to the parade. As I took in the scene, I found some much-needed comfort in being around people like me—people who knew all too well the difficulties that came of being gay. The need for sympathetic friends was as much a part of the gay person's survival guide in the 1970s as it had been in the 1950s, considering the hostility and open opposition we still faced in America. During the parade that day, there were people on the sidewalks shouting insults at us as we marched downtown: "Faggots!" "Back in the closet, queers!" Rather than acknowledge these hateful cries, we ignored them, doing our best to continue merrily on our way. Marching down Fifth Avenue, I surveyed the crowd of happy gays and lesbians. Couples and groups of friends were holding hands and waving pro-gay and pro-lesbian signs as they laughed and moved along the city street. It was a very special moment.

And that's when I saw him—a short-haired, hard-bodied hunk who was the most beautiful young man I had ever laid eyes on.

The man danced jubilantly as the parade moved down Fifth Avenue to Greenwich Village. In spite of the unseasonably cool weather, this luscious Adonis was dressed in a tight hot-pink T-shirt. It stuck to his musclebound arms and chest and six-pack so closely that it looked like it might have been spray-painted directly on his skin. A pair of stonewashed blue denim shorts clung to his finely shaped ass, and I could see from the prominent bulge in the front that he was extremely well endowed. He danced like a pumped-up prizefighter sidling back and forth in his corner of the ring before the bell is rung. Talk about *The Main Event!*

He was very flirtatious in a way that encompassed everyone in general, but no one in particular. As we continued our march downtown, I drank in every sinuous move of his beefcake-y body. I was mesmerized.

I walked closer to him.

"Hi!"

No response. He just kept dancing. I said again, "Hi!" He nodded at me coolly, but kept grooving as we walked. I felt like some ridiculous old fogey from out of town, trying to ask how to get to Grand Central. But I persisted. "So what do they call you back home?"

"Baby," he began, as he continued to gyrate. "Stevie Strong's the name. Stevie Strong! Gonna be a big star, daddy! Who are you?"

"Well," I said, entranced by his lithe moves, "my name is Elliot, and—"

"Elliot? Wow, hey, do you know Elliot Gould? He's famous!"

"I don't know him personally," I hemmed, "but he comes from Brooklyn, like me."

"Wow, you live in Brooklyn? That place is famous!"

"I don't live there anymore. I live here in the city—at Manhattan Plaza."

"Really, you *do?* Hey, Stevie Strong hears that lots of famous people live there. Do you know any of 'em? 'Cause Stevie Strong likes famous people! Stevie Strong's gonna be a star!"

Hmmm, I thought, *this kid only seems to have one thing on his mind.* He also had this odd way of referring to himself only in the third person.

"Yeah," I said, trying to stay near him without getting bumped by his flailing arms. "It just so happens that Tennessee Williams is one of my neighbors."

"Who?" he said, looking confused.

"You know, Tennessee Williams. The playwright. He wrote *A Streetcar Named Desire.*"

Nothing on his face but that slack-jawed, gorgeously dumb look.

"You know," I continued, "that's the play that made a star of Marlon Brando."

"Yeah? Oh, yeah! Marlon Brando. Yeah, Brando. He's . . . famous!"

Something told me that Stevie's favorite cookie was probably Famous Amos.

"I had drinks with Marlon Brando in a club once. He gave me a big manly hug."

Stevie spun around and stood with arms outstretched like John Travolta in *Saturday Night Fever.* "Really? Wow!" A few seconds passed. Then Stevie asked, "Hey, are *you* famous?"

Maybe I could woo this hulking piece of man candy after all. "Yeah," I said, trying not to sound too eager, "I, uh, actually saved the Woodstock concert from being cancelled about ten years ago."

"Woodstock? Yeah, Woodstock! Hey, that's—"

"Famous, I know," I interjected, getting the picture. "I'm also very well known in Belgium."

"Belgium," Stevie responded, thumbing through his evidently thin mental Rolodex. "Is that a famous club?"

I wanted to say, *No, it's a famous jungle in Africa,* but I decided to play fair. "No, it's a country in Europe."

"Oh, wow! Europe. Yeah, that's a famous place. Cool!"

We had reached the Village, the endpoint of the parade, and people were beginning to disperse. Although Stevie's mind was only a little sharper than a bowl of tapioca pudding, his body was on par with Michelangelo's David. Figuring he probably had some shoebox apartment in a sooty brick building off St. Mark's Place, I told him about my great, spacious pad. "Would you like to go have some dinner? Maybe afterward you could come back and see my place?" I said.

"Why don't you come with Stevie Strong and his friends to see the Village People tonight at the Garden?" I was so fixated on Stevie that I had failed to notice the four other guys who were now standing with us on the sidewalk corner. I couldn't believe it—these guys were all gorgeous, too! Standing with these gay young rascals, I suddenly felt a bit self-conscious and *old.* I was about to politely decline the invitation, but then Stevie called out, "Hey, guys! This here is Elliot! He saved Woodstock and the Belgium, and he used to hug Brando in Brooklyn. He's a famous daddy, guys!"

The young men, who were actually quite sweet and friendly, were all *oohs* and *aahs* as they shook my hand. It soon became clear that Stevie Strong was leader of the pack, not only because he was going to be a star, but also because he was very rich. I found out *how* rich when a stretch limousine appeared out of nowhere and Stevie ushered us inside. "Take us to the Plaza so we can get ready to see the show!" The driver steered the limousine back uptown, and away we went.

As we cruised northward toward Columbus Circle, Stevie slammed a cassette into a big boom box that was sitting in the limo. "C'mon, everybody dance! You too, Elliot!" he shouted to me, bouncing happily next to me in the plush leather back seat. Stevie's friends were an interesting bunch. To my left sat a gorgeous young black man with a bodybuilder's physique and a lovely smile. He introduced himself to me gleefully: "I'm Lamont, African prince!" Stevie quickly introduced the other three guys as "my friends from Jersey— Rod, Fast Jimmy, and Ramón!"

"It's not Ramón, it's *Raymond!*" shouted the one in the middle.

"He's just trying to cover the fact that his momma's Puerto Rican!" said Rod.

"At least I know who my momma *is,* bitch!" shot back Ramón/Raymond, which made Fast Jimmy laugh as he looked out the tinted window.

"Quiet down now, you queens!" shouted Lamont. He gently elbowed me in my side and said, "They're jealous that they're not black and beautiful like me!"

"That's what you think, fag!" shouted Rod.

"What, you sayin' I'm wrong?" responded Lamont. "Baby, look at those suntans you boys got on!"

They laughed. Much to my surprise, I found myself joining in. It was just a bit of fun—no real harm to any of it. It made me remember how I had felt when I first came out.

I didn't really know much about the Village People, and this ride uptown was my first introduction to many of their songs. The music was perfect for dancing; like all disco, it was music that simply made you glad to be alive.

"C'mon, we're here!" shouted Stevie, "everybody out!"

Stevie led the way as the six of us walked through the Plaza doors. Actually, I was the only one walking—Stevie and his friends danced to the music on the boom box through the lobby and into the elevator. We drew some stares, but no one bothered us. I got the feeling that Stevie's behavior was tolerated because the staff understood he was rich. I also got the feeling that this kind of forbearance was fairly common in the life of Stevie Strong.

His suite was everything one would expect from the Plaza—a splendidly appointed set of rooms decorated in the Louis XV style. This was the kind of place I had often copied when doing my interior decorating jobs for those wealthy middle-aged Manhattanites in the 1960s. Somehow, this mannered opulence seemed completely out of keeping with the rank and vulgar loudness of Stevie Strong and his posse.

"Stevie Strong is hungry! Let's get some room service. Elliot, what would you like?"

It was late afternoon, and I had only eaten a banana since the march started a few hours earlier. I was hungry, but I felt a little strange having someone pay for my food. "Well, I don't know, Stevie," I said, trying to get a feel for the situation. "I feel funny having you pay for my meal, especially since you're giving me a ticket for the show. Maybe a salad."

Stevie's eyes got big like saucers. "A salad? No fuckin' way, Elliot. Stevie Strong wants all his friends to have a good time tonight. All of us, right?"

As if on cue, Lamont and Rod and Fast Jimmy and Ramón/Raymond shouted, "Right!"

"That's it, then," Stevie continued, "we're only going to have fun tonight! You too, Elliot!"

I moved to thank him with a hug, but he spun in the other direction, toward the large sofa where the hotel menu was placed. Then he picked up the phone, asked for room service, and proceeded to ask for three of everything in the entire menu. "Oh, yeah, and send us your best champagne—bring up a case! And make it quick. Up to Stevie Strong's suite, got it? Thanks!"

He slammed the phone down, rifled through his luggage for a Donna Summer album, picked up a low-seated plush chair and danced his way over to the bathroom. Well, to be more accurate, there were actually *three* bathrooms. I felt like I was hanging out in the court of Caligula—the whole room was positively swimming in decadence. Stevie called out, "Okay, boys, time to take a powder!" As if on cue, they all lined up in Bathroom #1. Stevie produced a large vial of cocaine and asked Fast Jimmy to do the honors. Fast Jimmy got to work. Watching how swiftly he poured out and broke the coke into teensy little lines on Donna Summer's face with a playing card, I could see how Fast Jimmy earned his name. Once he had six lines ready for snorting on the album cover, Stevie said, "Elliot, you go first!"

"No thanks," I said, laughing gently. "I'm fine with my cigarette, a salad, and a little champagne."

"Not a *little* champagne," Stevie shouted, "a LOT of champagne! You sure you don't want, Elliot?" He reached out to me with a hundred-dollar bill rolled tightly into a tube for sniffing.

I smiled and gently shook my head. "No thanks, Stevie."

"Okay, then," he said, and shouted, "more for Stevie Strong then!" He inhaled one line deeply with his left nostril, and another line even more deeply with his right. "Mmm, yeah!" he cooed. The music of the Village People throbbed on the boom box, and Stevie started bobbing his head up and down deliriously as the effects of the coke started to kick in. Once Stevie's mind was properly blown, he passed the bill along to the next in line. "Go ahead, Lamont."

Lamont snorted, followed quickly by Rod and Ramón/Raymond. Fast Jimmy took the final line of blow by licking it right off the album. I noticed he also pocketed the hundred-dollar bill after he was finished, too.

"Now, Elliot," Stevie said, very seriously, "you sit right here in this chair and watch Stevie Strong do his special dance. This is what's going to make Stevie Strong famous. You got the tape, Lamont?"

"Sure do, peach fuzz! You want a 'Say-Hey' now, muthafucka?"

"Yeah!" Stevie said, "punch that shit *up!*"

Lamont laughed all the way over to the boom box. Then he took from his pocket a cassette with "STEVIE!" written across the top in blue felt-tip pen. As Lamont walked back into the bathroom with the boom box, Stevie turned his back to me in a deliberate, slow way. Rod and Ramón/Raymond were jumping up and down behind me on the king-size bed, laughing like hyenas and having a crazy coked-up pillow fight. Stevie took off his pink T-shirt and his shorts and got ready to do his thing. A disco track featuring blaring horns shot from the boom box like a cannonball on the Fourth of July. Stevie looked as if he'd been electrocuted, and suddenly leaped up in the air and turned around to face us, bumping and gyrating to the song. There, tattooed smack-dab in the middle of his rock-hard chest, were the words "STEVIE STRONG" in big stenciled letters.

"You see, Elliot? This is me. I'm Stevie Strong, and I'm gonna be a big fuckin' star! Watch my dance, watch this! I call this the 'Stevie.' C'mon, everybody—do the Stevie!"

I was speechless as Stevie danced maniacally to the music. He was working up a sweat, but he was totally out of sync with the song. Stevie had absolutely no sense of rhythm. He did this shimmy-shimmy move that he must have thought was sexy. In fact, he looked like a mountain man trying desperately to pull his dick out of a wood chipper. I was in agony, biting my bottom lip hard so I didn't bust out laughing. Lamont put his hand on my shoulder, and said, "Look at our boy. Stevie Strong, my man—the Strong is on!"

It was all I could do to make it through the song, but then I clapped and shouted "Bravo!" with the rest of them. Stevie, perspiring and wild-eyed, came over to me and said, "What do you think, Elliot? Do you think this will catch on?"

"Well, I'm no expert," I replied, "but I definitely think you have what it takes." *Yeah,* I thought, *maybe as a failing act on* The Gong Show.

The food arrived with twenty bottles of champagne, and Stevie signed for it, giving the waiter a twenty and a wink. Rod and Stevie got into the Bathroom #3 shower with four bottles and proceeded to pour the champagne over each other, laughing hysterically under the water. Taking a cue from Stevie and Rod, Fast Jimmy and Ramón/Raymond decided to do the same in Bathroom #2.

Witnessing this debauchery, I didn't think I was going to be able to handle the Village People concert. I also didn't think we'd even make it to the concert in time. Besides, it was clear that I wasn't going to make it with Stevie Strong. After only a few hours in his world, all I wanted was a quiet night back in my apartment. It had been an entertaining afternoon, but this was not where I belonged.

I called Lamont from across the room as the other four continued to pour Stevie's money down the drain. "You want to take a shower too, Elliot?" Lamont asked, still smiling but with a look of casual concern.

"No, Lamont," I said, "I already took a shower this morning, and I don't have any—"

"How long since he left you?"

I froze, feeling exposed and awkward. Lamont looked at me with sensitivity, though, and I thought maybe he had gone through a bad breakup, too.

"Almost a month," I said. "How did you know?"

"I just do, that's all," he laughed. I smiled, and he gave me a strong, comforting hug.

"I can't be here. This isn't my—"

"No worries, Elliot. You don't have to explain it to me."

"Thanks, Lamont. What are you going to tell Stevie?"

"No sweat, Elliot. I'll tell him that you decided to head over to the Garden ahead of us. And here," he said, giving me one of the tickets for the show, "take this with you. In case you change your mind."

"That's okay, Lamont," I said, handing the ticket back. "I think I'll sit this one out."

"Well, maybe we'll see you again at the YMCA," Lamont responded, sharing the joke with me.

I shook Lamont's hand, walked out of Stevie Strong's Plaza Hotel lair, and headed back to my apartment at the top of Manhattan Plaza. There was certainly a new kind of energy and excitement for this younger generation of gay men, but it wasn't the kind of energy and excitement I needed for my own journey. While gay Manhattan spent that night jumping and dancing and singing at Madison Square Garden with the Village People, I stayed in my apartment, wondering if André might call. He didn't.

Before I went to sleep that night, I took out my notebook and wrote a simple poem:

I carved on a tree
that "Elliot loves André"
I hope someone sees

July came and went, as I numbly continued to make lists and gaze at my navel. I also wrote poems, some in carefully structured meter and others taken down as quickly as my thoughts came to me. I still had no idea what to do with my play. The various typed and handwritten pages sat there on my desk, waiting to be developed and refined.

Much of the talk in Manhattan Plaza at that time revolved around a call for the New York gay community to stage protests at the leather bars where William Friedkin was shooting his film, now known as *Cruising*. The man leading the charge was *Village Voice* columnist Arthur Bell, who believed that Friedkin's decision to make a film about a murderer targeting gay men was a dangerous one. Bell was concerned that the film might make the public associate all gay men with the leather club underworld. He also worried that it would bring forth new waves of violence and intolerance against gays, undoing the recent work to promote gay rights and acceptance. Hundreds of gay men were moved by Bell's article, and showed up to the shoot locations to protest the film loudly.

I had been at Stonewall—at the very beginning of the gay liberation movement—but I felt conflicted about the protest. As a gay man, I had felt totally comfortable with my experiences at those bars over the past few years. I also didn't understand what the community was getting so upset about. I was a proud leather daddy through and through, so I had no problem at all with a film set in the bars. I saw the leather scene as just one component of a free and diverse gay culture. If anything, I applauded Friedkin for shining a light on a part of the gay world that was not well known.

It was a Friday afternoon in mid-August when I finally received a call from Renee.

"Why don't you and André come to see me and Alyse this weekend?" Renee asked.

"We can't," I said. "What I mean is, uh, André is directing an opera in Brussels right now. And I've been very busy here with my writing." *Two lies in a row, Elliot,* I thought to myself. *Way to go!*

"What," Renee said, "you're too busy to come see your favorite sister and your niece?"

"Be careful, sis. That sounded a whole lot like Momma."

We both laughed it off, and I steered the conversation away from André by asking about Goldie and Rachelle.

"Same as usual, I suppose," she said. "No big changes that I can report. Have you considered calling them yourself?"

"Why should I? When's the last time they called to see how I'm doing?"

"Good point," Renee said.

"By the way," I continued, "you never told me about Disney World. How was it?"

"It was okay, I guess," she said, sounding a little blue. "Alyse had a fun time."

"What about you? Is there anyone new in your life?"

"Nope, It's just me, the single mom with a heart of gold. Hey, that reminds me. Did you hear about Felix?"

"Felix? What, you mean Felix from the neighborhood, Hollywood Felix?"

"Yeah."

The last time I had seen Felix, he'd been in my rearview mirror, standing next to Jerry in the driveway of that crazy old Marie Dressler mansion as I drove off to New York. "Christ, Renee, I haven't thought of him in years. Well, what about Felix, anyway?"

"Apparently, the last phone number they had for you was mine. Jerry called and told me to tell you that Felix died, Elliot," Renee said.

"Died? He *died?*" I was shocked. "What happened? How did he die?"

"I don't know," Renee said. "Some kind of cancer, I think. At least that's what Jerry told me. It must have been a terrible situation. Jerry sounded really broken up about it. He said Felix had been losing a lot of weight. Then he got pneumonia and had to go to the hospital. A week later, Felix was gone."

"That's terrible," I said. I hadn't thought about my old friends out in Hollywood since the day I'd left. The whole thing made me feel even more depressed than I had been before. "Jeez," I muttered, not sure what to say. "I guess we all have to die sooner or later." It didn't sound as cold in my mind as it sounded when I said the words out loud, but Renee seemed to understand and share the shock I felt.

"I much prefer later to sooner when it comes to dying, thank you very much," Renee said. "Are you sure you won't come in to visit for a day or two?"

"I'd really like to, sis, but I can't right now. Let me wait until André comes back, and we'll make plans to get together then. Okay?"

"Okay, then," Renee said, sounding as sad as I felt. "Love you, Elli."

"Love you, too. Talk soon."

I couldn't bring myself to admit to Renee that André had left me. My heart was bruised. Besides, I had always tried to be strong for Renee, and I wanted to keep it that way a little while longer.

I needed to get out of the apartment. Sensing that the summer would be over soon, I thought I would try to enjoy the warm weather while I still could. It was a nice day, so I decided to walk all the way downtown to the Village. I secretly hoped that I might see André down there, but it was clear after I walked around for two hours that I wasn't going to see him anywhere. Saddened, I went back home.

The afternoon shifted slowly to night, as I sat in the apartment and listened to records. One that I hadn't heard in a while was *Lady in Satin,* by the brilliant and tragic singer Billie Holiday. I looked at the album cover as I listened. Posed in profile on the cover, Holiday wore a pearl necklace and grey strapless evening gown. But it was the sadness in her face that really grabbed my attention. She looked as lost and lonely as I felt that night. I then turned the album cover around, and scanned some of the songs listed on the back. It was as if the album represented all of the feelings I was going through after the breakup with André. I felt like fate had led me to listen to that album at that moment.

From song to song, I sat riveted by the beauty and pain that came through in Billie Holiday's voice. Her songs matched my state of mind perfectly, starting with "I'm a Fool to Want You" and ending with the achingly tender "I'll Be Around." I had heard these songs performed by others over the years, including my beloved Judy Garland. But on that night—sitting alone, without André, in our apartment in the sky—the haunting voice of Billie Holiday touched me in a truly unforgettable way. I kept listening to the album, a glass of wine in one hand and my head in the other. A single thought filled my mind: *Come back to me, André, come back.*

A few minutes after I got up to turn the album over for another listen, the doorbell rang. I had no idea who it might be—I wasn't expecting anyone, and Colleen usually called before she came down. I felt a bit tipsy from the wine, and didn't want to let just anyone in.

I walked toward the door, and peered through the peephole. It was André.

I quickly opened the door and looked at him. André stood there exactly as he had on the night he left. I wanted to laugh and cry and scream and kick at him all at the same time. But when he said, "Hello, Elliot" in that beautiful accented voice of his, the rage melted away and I gladly welcomed him into the apartment.

"Hi," I said, wanting badly to hug and kiss him. "So, how are things?"

"Things are—well—" André looked around the apartment. "Things are *things*. How are you?"

"Me? Oh, I'm fine, just fine," I said, trying to make myself sound more confident than I felt.

"I hope you do not mind that I have come to visit," he said, staying near the door.

"No, please, come in," I said.

There we stood, in the living room—*our* living room. It seemed that he was as unsure of what to say as I was.

"Billie Holiday," he observed, as the melancholy sound of "I Get Along Without You Very Well" played on the stereo.

"Yeah, uh, I've been listening to more jazz these days than anything else."

"What, no Wagner?"

"No," I said, smiling a bit at his reference to my still-unfinished play. "That's strictly for work, not for pleasure. I haven't written a new line of dialogue, let alone a page."

"Still stuck on it, then?" he said, looking into my eyes.

"Yeah," I said, trying to figure out how to keep up the conversation. I hesitated for a moment to collect my thoughts and replied lamely, "I'm still stuck on a lot of things, I guess."

We sat carefully next to each other on the sofa bed.

"Elliot," he said, apologetically, "I wanted to see if I might . . . if *you* would be willing to—" He coughed nervously, his voice sounding dry.

"Want some water?" I asked.

"Yes, please."

I went to the kitchen and got him a glass of cold water. I brought it back to him, sat down again—trying to act as nonchalant as I could—and waited for him to take a drink. The album had ended, and there was silence between us.

As he went to place his water glass down on the coffee table, he saw some of the lists that I had left there over the past days.

"What is this, Elliot?" he asked, picking up the pages curiously.

Feeling embarrassed, I blurted out, "Nothing. I've been making lists." I snatched the pages out of his hands and held them to my chest.

"What kind of lists?"

"Oh, I don't know," I said. Then, scanning through the first few pages, I found one that I had written most recently. "Here's one, if you're interested."

André looked down at the page for a moment, then back at me. "These are only the seven days of the week."

"Oh, that," I said, swallowing hard against the lump in my throat. "Um, that was a list of the days in the week when I missed you."

He smiled at me as he traced his fingers over the paper.

"André," I asked, as my heart began to race with anticipation, "why are you here?"

"Well, I—I wanted to know if I might move back in here with you?"

I can't believe it, Billie Holiday, I thought in glee, *he has come back to me!*

"You mean that you want to be with me again," I said.

He waited for a moment before answering. "No. Listen, Elliot, let me tell you about things. I need you to understand what I have been through these past few months, and what I am trying to say to you now, if you will allow me."

He told me he had left so he could move in with an older man. This man, Bill, was a family doctor on the Upper East Side of the city. Bill had left his wife of twenty-six years a year before, when he realized that he was gay. André had met him one night way uptown, at a gay bar called Harry's Back East. This was a more sophisticated venue than the brash leather bars that André and I had frequented on a near-exclusive basis.

"It was on one of those nights when I left the apartment to go out walking. I had heard about Harry's from one of my students. Anyway, he and I—do you mind me telling you about this, Elliot?"

Of course I hated hearing him talk about this other man, but I certainly was not going to tell André how I felt. He was here again with me, so I did my best to compose myself and told him to go on.

"Well, I met this man at Harry's, and he told me about how he had realized after so many years that he had been gay. I found it exciting to have before me a man who was so new to the discovery of his true sexuality. I asked him where he lived, and his place was only a few blocks away. I went with him"—he stopped, took a breath, and continued—"and we had sex that night."

The truth was very hard to take. Perhaps another man would have hauled off and beat the living crap out of André, but I didn't have it in me. I just sighed and blinked my eyes hard to keep them from welling up with tears. Back when we broke up, the thought of André having one-night stands with young guys had made me feel so betrayed and angry. But now, the thought of André forging a serious relationship with another man—and a man older than me—was even more upsetting. When André had originally told me he want-ed to have sex with other men, I had assumed that this desire came from some carnal midlife crisis, a lust for quick trysts with younger men. To learn that he had been with an older man made me realize that he had sought more than physical intimacy. I took it to mean that he wanted new *emotional* intimacy, and that was something I thought that he had only ever wanted to have with me. An affair of the body I could forgive, but an affair of the heart? I didn't know what to say.

"So that is what happened, Elliot. I wanted to move in with Bill to see what kind of lover I could be to someone who needed help discovering who he was in his new life."

"Then why did you tell me you were leaving because you wanted the freedom to have sex with other people?" I asked.

"I did not know if things with Bill would last," he responded. "I figured if I told you I wanted only to have some flings that would be easier for you to hear."

"Naturally," I said, shaking my head.

"What?"

"It's nothing. I was thinking how ironic it is that you're the one to wind up *shtupping* an Upper East Side doctor. In my family, that's on par with winning the jackpot!"

He and I both laughed, helping to defuse some of the tension of the moment.

"Yes, well," André said, "he and I had some nice times, but we were not in love. He and I will remain friends, but I am no longer going to live with him as his lover."

"Frankly," I said, starting to get upset, "that's not something I want to hear about." Things got quiet again. "I still love you, André. That hasn't changed for me, you know?"

"But that is why I am here," André said, excitedly, "that is what you want to know. I still love you, too. I love you, Elliot, more than anyone I have ever known. You are the person I want to live with, and I wish—I hope"—his voice cracked as he tried to hold back what sounded like the start of a sob—"I really hope that we can find some way to live together again."

I got up from the couch and looked out the window toward the lights of the New Jersey shore. As my anger about this other man receded, all I could think was that André had returned to me. This was what I had silently wished for. It was as if by listening to Billie Holiday, I had magically made André appear.

"But there is one condition, *mon amour,*" André said, "I have given this a great deal of thought, and I hope you understand why this is so important to me. I love you, but I must be with other men. And I know that if we were to make love going forward, you would know that I have cheated on you. Over time, you would come to hate me for it, Elliot. This is not what I wish. I do not want to hurt you in this way. And I do not want anything that I do to destroy what we have, and what we've *had,* all these years together."

He took a deep breath. "If I come back, you must agree that we will no longer have a physical relationship with each other. We both can be free to have sexual relationships with others, but we will not bring it up in conversation. We will live together as dear friends, collaborators, and partners in life, but we will never share a bed."

"So what, you figure the floor and the couch could work?" I nervously shot back. I didn't really know what to say without sounding like a stand-up comedian. *You know if one of us gets pregnant,* I joked to myself, *there's going to be a lot of questions to answer!*

"Elliot, I am being serious. Is this something you can agree to?" André asked.

I thought about the many weeks I had sat in the apartment completely alone. And then I knew beyond any doubt that my life was destined to remain entwined with André's. André was my whole world, and I was important enough to him that he had decided to come back. We had everything that a loving couple needed in order to share a life. Well, almost everything—there would be no sex. But then again, there had been no sex for a very long time, since even before we had broken up. I knew he loved me, though, and I held the small hope that he might change his mind. If I could have him back living with me at the apartment, then maybe on some enchanted evening, André and I might again find sexual pleasure together again.

"André," I said, "I'm not going to lie to you. It's difficult for me to not be attracted to you. You've been all I've ever wanted in a lover. But I've missed my partner—my friend—far too much these past weeks for me not to *try* to resist you. So I want you to come home. And I promise that I'm going to try not to get you under the sheets, okay?"

"I feel bad, though, Elliot," André sighed. "I do not want to be unfair to you in this."

"Life's unfair, babe," I said, "but I've been too lonely in this life already. I can't do anything without you by my side. We have to be together, you understand? I love you."

That was it. Tears in our eyes, André and I hugged each other with a devotion and a palpable sense of joy and relief. After a few minutes, we released our embrace. André walked over to the stereo, where I had placed our copy of the soundtrack from Vincente Minnelli's 1951 film *An American in Paris*. "Ah, yes, I always loved listening to this album with you," he said.

"Yeah. Me, too."

"Do you mind if I put on a song?"

"Feel free."

He went over to the stereo, carefully removed the Billie Holiday album from the turntable and placed it back in its jacket. Then he took out the soundtrack, and placed the record player's stylus at the beginning of one of the tracks. It was the beautiful Gershwin song "Our Love Is Here to Stay," as sung by Gene Kelly.

"May I have this dance, Monsieur Tiber?" André asked, moving toward me.

"I would be delighted," I said, letting him lead. We danced together slowly, and it was very romantic. As the song ended, we continued to hold each other. And that was all we did. It was all that we really needed to do.

That night, André slept on the sofa bed. I had told André that he and I could live together in a platonic relationship, but the darkness of the night had a funny way of messing with my best intentions. About an hour or so after we turned off the lights and went to sleep, I got up from my bed and came out to the living room. I saw André laying there quietly on the foldout bed, and I longed for him so badly that my body ached. Standing there, halfway between the kitchen and the living room, I was struck by an almost uncontrollable desire to climb in next to him. But I did not. I could not bear the thought of André leaving my world again. Perhaps there would come a time when we would make love. This was not that time.

The next day, I took a taxi with André to the Upper East Side and helped him pack up whatever clothes and other personal items he had at Bill's apartment. I didn't know what to expect of the guy. I thought I might punch the guy out if I saw any residual affection between him and André.

"Bill," André said, "I would like you to meet my close friend and partner, Elliot."

"Pleasure to meet you, Elliot," said Bill, graciously shaking hands with me. Everyone was pretty awkward, standing there in the entryway to the apartment. Beyond being extremely good-looking—and how!—Bill turned out to be a surprisingly cordial gentleman. It was clear that Bill was very new to being out of the closet, and that he was just looking for friends who would acknowledge and support his now-public identity. I was rather touched. I realized Bill was no threat when he told us that he had met and hoped to have a serious relationship with a man closer to his own age.

"We only met this past week, but I think we might have something together. I'm hoping for the best." *It's tough not to like this guy,* I thought to myself as Bill and I continued to chat. There was no point in staying angry with him. What he had with André could never hold a candle to what I had with André.

"Well, that's all of it," André announced.

We shook hands. "Listen, guys," Bill said, sounding more like an eager fraternity pledge than a medical professional. "Keep me in mind if you ever need help with any medical problems." He took one of his business cards, wrote down his home phone number on the back, and handed the card to me, not André. It was a small gesture that went a long way toward restoring my dignity in the situation.

"Thanks, Bill. That's really nice of you," I said. André wished him luck in his new relationship, and soon we were back in a taxi heading crosstown. Bill wasn't a bad guy. I even told André in the cab that Bill was kind of hot. "That is, if you like that older, stethoscopic type," I said.

After moving André back in and reuniting him with a great many of his shirts, I suggested we take a walk together down to the Village. There, we happened upon a pet store. Standing sweetly in the store's window was a beautiful little Yorkshire terrier. The store owner told us that the dog was about eight months old. She had belonged to an old woman who had died only a few weeks before, and the old woman's son had brought the dog to the pet shop so she might find a new home. André and I fell in love with the dog instantly. She happily licked at our hands and nuzzled her head into our arms as we both took turns holding her. Remembering the last dog we'd had together—that hyperactive and incontinent beast—I said to André, "I think we should name her Toto, don't you?" His look told me I shouldn't press my luck.

We found out that she already had a name, anyway—"Shayna," which is the Yiddish word for "beautiful." The name suited her. We both loved this delightful dog so much that there was no question of us becoming her parents. We wound up bringing her home with us that very night. Before taking her with us, we made certain that she had had all her shots and bought her a small pink collar with little bells attached to it.

It took me about a week of newspaper training Shayna to make sure that she wouldn't go to the bathroom in the apartment. The manager at the pet shop explained that she was already housetrained, but I didn't want to take any chances. She was a very well-behaved dog, though, and had a sweet and tranquil disposition. By the end of her first week with us, Shayna had established a ritual in which she would run and snuggle with Papa André on the foldout bed and then run over to the bedroom and lie for a while with Mama Elliot. She would do this a few times each night, the little bells on her collar jingling merrily as she scooted back and forth to make sure we were safely in bed. Remarkably, it was this sweet dog's love for us both that helped us maintain separate beds without too much angst. Without Shayna, I don't know how we would have made it through this tough time.

16

The Play's the Thing

"You met Gregory Peck? *The* Gregory Peck?"

"Yep," I said to Renee, who had loved Peck ever since she saw him play Atticus Finch in *To Kill a Mockingbird*. "I met the great man himself."

"That's *so* exciting! Where?"

"It was at the opening night of a show."

"Well, what was he like?"

"Tall," I responded.

"Did you get to talk with him?"

"Oh, sure, I told him that he deserved an Oscar for his portrayal of Josef Mengele in *The Boys from Brazil*. Then I threw my arms around him and kissed him for three hours straight!"

"Ha, ha, very funny," she said sarcastically. "But seriously, Elliot, what was he like?"

I didn't have the heart to tell her that I'd only spent about thirty seconds meeting Gregory Peck. Now that André was living with me again at the apartment, we made it a point to go to as many events as possible to get ourselves back into the scene. In a sense, we were acting in front of actors. But the sweet thrill of meeting famous actors and actresses had worn off considerably by this point. It had become an awful grind to keep going to parties. It was a torment to see great stars like Dustin Hoffman, Jeremy Irons, Angela Lansbury, Jason Robards, Alan Alda, Mike Nichols, and Elaine Stritch at these showbiz gatherings—only to exchange an offhand "Hi" with them before they walked away and we slid quickly out of their purview.

You were screwed one way or another. If you didn't have a project to talk to them about, you'd lose the chance to talk. And if you *did* have a project, they would quickly tell you to contact their agent before flying away. Still, I always told Renee about the stars I met wherever André and I went. Renee was farther from the limelight but closer to the joys that sprang from its world, and her excitement helped me survive all my disappointments.

After telling her about Gregory Peck, I finally explained to Renee everything that had happened between me and André that summer. She wasn't entirely convinced the arrangement was a good and healthy one for me, but she couldn't deny that I was happy. And she applauded my new role as a proud white-bearded mother to our dog Shayna.

Meanwhile, I continued my work on *The Music Keeper* and planned lessons for my course at the New School. I had come to love teaching "Absurd, Twisted Humor." My primary job was to help students open their minds so they could create humor in any way that they wanted. This meant that anything could happen, as long as the end result made people laugh. I made it a point to start my class each semester with an assignment that students write a funny short story. I had only one rule: in each story, there had to come a moment in which a character's pants fell down around his or her ankles. By including that absurd suggestion as a pivotal plot point, I helped steer my students into some very weird places.

It was endlessly inspirational for me to teach this course. I wound up with all kinds of students—young college students, middle-aged businessmen, and even older grandmotherly types. I thrived on the zaniness and anarchy that I was able to impart to the students in my class, twice a week, every fall and spring semester. The class gave me a sense of mission and purpose, and it stood as a fixed point amidst the near-total chaos of creation that took place every day in our Manhattan Plaza barracks.

In March 1980, Winifred Wagner—Richard Wagner's daughter-in-law, the very focus of my play—passed away. I had been thinking of using a different name in place of Wagner's, since what I had written was a fictionalized scenario, anyway. Now that she had died, I felt much more comfortable using her real name.

Revitalized by André's return, I had managed to flesh out the plot of the play. Modeled after André, my protagonist, Andrew, is a Jewish graduate student at Columbia University. In the play, Andrew has arranged to meet Winifred Wagner at her home in Germany. He is about to direct Wagner's *Die Walküre* back in New York, and hopes that Winifred will give him her many notes on the history of her father-in-law. He has heard that Winifred also has Adolf Hitler's last manuscripts on how best to continue killing Jews throughout the world with the use of Wagner's music.

Winifred is portrayed as an enormously egocentric woman with one great weak spot: her dedication to the memory of Hitler and the music of Wagner. Sensing that Winifred is lonely, Andrew charms and beguiles the old woman in order to draw out more information. The first act ends with Winifred taking Andrew up to her bedroom.

In the second act, Andrew gets Winifred drunk and persuades her to show him Hitler's notes. She relents and fetches the manuscript—wrapped carefully in linen—from under the red velvet loveseat on which she has been perched during much of the play. Once she hands him the pages, Andrew shoves her back down on the love seat and wipes her lipstick from his mouth in disgust. Winifred is shocked to learn from Andrew that his parents were killed in the Auschwitz concentration camp and that he was raised by cousins in America. He is there in Germany only to avenge the deaths of his fellow Jews, and he tells Winifred that he will present Hitler's final manuscript to the world so that Wagner's music will never be performed again. Driven to madness by Andrew, Winifred has a heart attack and dies in her loveseat. Andrew, having realized his goal, leaves Winifred's house and returns to New York. Poetic justice is served.

After Winifred's death, I reworked the play. I thought back on how the music of Wagner had made me feel as I goose stepped to it—clad in leather— around our apartment. I wanted to imbue the play with the overwhelming rage that had filled me. The more I thought about it, the more I realized the music was actually a third character alongside Andrew and Winifred. I decided then and there to use Wagner's music as a character. The only question was how, and when, that character should appear throughout the play. In order to get it right, I knew that I had to work on it with my Belgian partner.

André was just coming off of a demoralizing production of *Richard III* at

Yale and was ready to attack something new. I asked him if he would start reading through the dialogue I had written for *The Music Keeper*. Since the play now included three characters—Winifred, Andrew, and the music of Wagner—André and I would read the scenes back and forth to each other out loud. Sometimes we switched parts to hear how the dialogue sounded when read by the other. Often, we discovered as we read aloud that some lines worked better if made shorter or longer. We also began to isolate the spots where the music worked best. Though I had written the initial drafts of the play, *The Music Keeper* only came to life once André and I began to work out the dialogue and the music cues between us. Slowly, we found a flow in our work together. It began to feel the same way it had in Belgium. I was pleased to be collaborating with him again, and he also seemed inspired by the work.

By the autumn of 1980, the play had evolved into a tense, icy tête-à-tête between two hugely different individuals. The changes reflected tensions at home. Although André and I were strengthening our relationship as creative partners, we were still figuring out how to maintain a balanced and harmonious home without our former sexual monogamy in place. There were many nights when I wanted him, and sometimes I would flirt with André to see if he was also interested. While he sometimes seemed close to breaking his rule, we never did get physical.

Out of consideration for me, André didn't bring men back to his apartment, but would instead step out to have sex. We arranged things so that we were never at the same club at the same time: if he wanted to go to the Mineshaft, I would go to the Ramrod. But despite all this, I found myself acting like Winifred in the play, trying in vain to hold onto my lover after the initial seduction. Even though I never saw the guys André took up with, the thought of him having sex with other men still filled me with rage, which I tried to purge by getting into rough shoving matches with a wild boy or two on the dance floor. I wanted to get into fights—I liked getting kicked and slapped and punched hard in the stomach. In place of sex with André, I settled for the sweet pain that swept through me as I got knocked and thrashed about by other guys in leather.

No matter how agonizing it was for me to maintain a relationship with André that excluded sex, I saw no other choice. I had become a slave to my unrequited erotic desire. The situation was as addictive to me by then as the cigarettes I continually smoked.

Thus, as I worked on *The Music Keeper,* I wanted the relationship between Winifred and Andrew to represent the tortured codependence I shared with André. But I still had a major problem—the play had no firmly defined beginning or end. As far as I was concerned, there was no answer at all on what I should do at that point, and André was getting busy again with his own projects. So I was stuck again.

It was a cold Monday in early December. Standing outside the Dakota apartment building on West Seventy-second Street, a deranged man had pulled out a handgun and shot four bullets into the back of beloved Beatle John Lennon as he returned home that night with his wife Yoko Ono. Like so many others in the city, André and I heard about the killing on TV and were stunned. By morning, news of Lennon's death had spread throughout the world. The grief and desperation that took hold over the next few days was enormous.

A week later, the press announced that Yoko Ono had asked that a ten-minute vigil of silence be observed in remembrance of Lennon worldwide on the afternoon of Saturday, December 14. André and I took Shayna and got a taxi up to Central Park, so we could stand together with everyone else and pay our respects. We could only get as far as Fifty-ninth Street, as the cab driver told us, "The radio says there are more than two hundred thousand people up there. Unbelievable."

We decided to walk the thirteen blocks to Seventy-second Street. As we made our way up Central Park West, we saw people crying, holding hands, hugging each other, and singing John Lennon songs. Just across the street from the Dakota was an entrance to Central Park. We walked into the park, found a small patch of rock to sit on, and took in the cold wintry scene around us. It was strange for me because the last time I had seen so many people gathered together like this in one place was back at White Lake during what was the birth of Woodstock Nation. And now, only a little more than ten years later, I felt like we were presiding over its death.

When it was announced that the ten minutes of silence was about to begin, everyone retreated into their own private and inner spaces. Even Shayna, wrapped warmly in a wool scarf held close to my chest, was silent as the moment began. It was as if time had stopped and people everywhere around us had been emptied of all life. As we sat and observed the silence, I thought about the awful curse of violence that seemed to have existed since the dawn of humanity. I thought about the terrible cruelties of life that seem always to lurk around the corner, and the ways in which those cruelties never truly seem to disappear from history. I began to think about how broken everything seemed at the start of the new decade. But I also marveled at the triumph of the human spirit in that park—the capacity to stand against the horrors by embracing the glories of love.

When the vigil finished, a recording of Lennon's "Imagine" began to play throughout the park. Some people began to clap, but most dispersed quietly. André and I made our way back down toward Columbus Circle, not saying much. Our cab driver broke the silence. "It's really crazy, y'know," he said, "Lennon wrote a song with the Beatles called 'Happiness Is a Warm Gun,' and he's actually saying the words 'shoot me' during that song 'Come Together.' It's fuckin' weird, y'know? Almost like he knew it was going to happen or something." The spooky sense that something dreadful had happened stayed with us all day and into the night.

That holiday season was uncharacteristically gloomy. Like so many others that year, I bought André the last album finished by John Lennon and Yoko Ono before Lennon died, *Double Fantasy*. When he unwrapped the gift on Christmas morning, he shook his head and laughed. "I bought you the same thing, Elliot!" he said. It was reassuring to realize that we were still close enough to share the same mindset. We kept one copy in its plastic and opened the other to listen to the music. The hopefulness of the album's first song, "(Just Like) Starting Over," felt particularly tragic in view of Lennon's recent death. Still, André and I danced along to the music, two partners trying to find a way into a very dark and uncertain New Year.

❁   ❁   ❁

We finished the play by early January 1981, and we quickly copyrighted the material. André suggested that we might be able to submit the play for separate productions in other countries, if we had a hit on our hands. Though I had dreamt of our play making it to Broadway, and perhaps to Hollywood, André explained that we would be lucky to have run it off-Broadway. He also felt that the material was ideally suited to the stage. He was concerned that on film, our play might come across as a farce. Since I had written *The Music Keeper* as a serious play for serious reasons, I understood and appreciated his protectiveness.

At the end of most weekdays, André would arrive home, often having eaten already, since he and I existed in our own comfortable but decidedly separate orbits. He wanted to cuddle up with Shayna in his arms as we relaxed together on the couch and caught snatches of the world through the TV. Shayna loved the attention.

No matter what was happening, André and I always made time to have dinner together at least once a week. There were a few restaurants close to our place that we liked—mostly Italian restaurants, since we were both vegetarians and enjoyed pasta. During these dinners, we would talk about everything that had happened that week. We would discuss our work, stories in the news, gossip from inside the local theater circles, and any strange encounters we had had with people.

Usually, I did most of the talking and André enjoyed listening and taking it all in. In fact, when *My Dinner with André* came out, starring Wallace Shawn and André Gregory, I joked that the movie was actually about us. "He stole our relationship!" I remember saying. "The only thing he did differently was to make his André the talker instead of the listener. Otherwise, that movie is us!"

Around that time, I got a call from Renee. Sadly, Boris had died from a heart attack. Momma, now the grieving widow, had told Renee that she wanted to return to New York. Renee had Momma stay at her house in New Jersey for a few weeks, until she was able to help my mother find an apartment in Far Rockaway, Queens. It was the perfect community for her—lots of *yentas,* delis, and temples. She would live there for the next ten years.

When I asked Renee if she had talked to Momma about me and André coming to visit, she told me that Momma wanted only for me to come. I could only imagine her screaming and shouting at my sister about it. "Feh! If mine son wants he should come to visit his mother, then why shouldn't he come by himself? I won't have that bearded *goyish* friend of his here in my home! Oy, my son Eliyahu's life is *verfallen!* He won't go to heaven if he lives with that Belgian man!"

"Well, that's it," I told Renee. "If she won't accept André, then I'm not going to visit her. If she cared for me at all, she would accept who I am and

1977. In front of the Baronet Theater in New York, where *High Street* had a brief run.

1982. Receiving a special Humanitarian Award from the Ninety-second Street Y
in recognition of *High Street's* cultural and ethical value. A proud moment.

the way I choose to live my life. And if not, she can go jump in a lake. Better yet, since she'll be in Far Rockaway, she can try the Atlantic Ocean! You can tell her I said that, sis. I mean it!"

❁   ❁   ❁

In early 1982, the Ninety-second Street Y arranged a new screening of *High Street*. They had learned about our film through Annette Insdorf, who had continued to champion it. Following her advice, the event planners for the Y contacted us to do a screening followed by a discussion on depictions of the Holocaust in film and television. It felt wonderful to have someone express interest in the movie after we had given up on it. Annette presided over the panel discussion. The participants included producer Herman Levin and André's friend, the actor Michael Moriarty, who had been featured in the TV miniseries, *Holocaust*, which we'd seen years ago.

To our surprise, at the end of the evening, the Ninety-second Street Y presented us with its Humanitarian Award. Our film had been ahead of its time. A few years after we released *Rue Haute*, French director François Truffaut released his own film about the Holocaust, *The Last Metro*. And in 1982, the peerless Meryl Streep—whom André had directed years earlier in a stage production at Yale School of Drama—gave an incredible performance in the film *Sophie's Choice*. André and I saw the film when it opened, and thought it was brilliant. We couldn't help but see parallels between Streep's performance and Annie Cordy's.

In addition, that Ninety-second Street Y screening also led to my meeting an exceptional woman: Alyce Finell. She showed up in my life at precisely the right time, and soon became one of my best friends. Alyce was a free spirit, and she shared my thirst for new ideas, new opportunities, and new projects. She lived each day with a zestful joy and unending taste for adventure—basically, she was me in a dress. She was as ga-ga over showbiz as I was. It's not too far from the truth to say that if I had been straight, Alyce would have been my soul mate.

We had coffee a few days after the screening. We talked about growing up in New York. Alyce told me about how her grandfather had established the popular A.I. Ross Music Store, and that she had studied to be a professional clarinet player before she fell in love with radio and TV broadcasting while at

Syracuse University. Alyce worked her way up through the industry to become one of the top guest bookers for ABC talk shows. By 1977, she had won an Emmy for a program she created called *Friends of . . .* and went on to become Director of Programming and Supervising Producer for the Hearst/Viacom Lifetime Network. I told her about my art studies, the El Monaco, the Woodstock miracle, and all the amazing things that had happened for me in Belgium with André. Before we realized it, two hours had passed.

"So what is your next project, Elliot?" Alyce asked.

"We have finished a play called *The Music Keeper.* Do you want to hear about it?"

"Of course I do."

I proceeded to tell her the story of the play, and how Winifred Wagner's life had served as inspiration for our fictional construct. "We would love to see it performed here in New York, but there are so many hoops that we would have to jump through that I don't even think we could make it happen. It has been a real frustration, though, because I think it's some of the best work that I have done with André."

"And does André want to direct the play?" she asked.

"He does, though he has a bunch of other commitments, since we have to learn a living. The Goodman Theatre in Chicago wants him to direct a new Tennessee Williams play in April. So he probably won't be back and available to work with me on getting the play staged until the summer."

Alyce sat for a few moments, quietly turning the wheels around in her mind. Then she batted her eyes, and asked me, "What would you say if I could help you to put this play on?"

I batted my eyes back at her. "How about 'Marry me'?"

❀   ❀   ❀

My new buddy Alyce Finell was a very enterprising gal indeed. She helped us secure a month's rental of the South Street Theater, a small performance space on Theater Row. Our show would open in late July and go straight through to the end of August, provided that ticket sales were good. Alyce selected July because it would be after the Tony awards and before the new fall season of shows began to monopolize the public's attention. André was a bit wary and otherwise occupied with his work, but he gave me his blessing to keep working out the details with Alyce. He was also relieved that he would be able to direct our play during the slower part of the season.

Watching Alyce take care of the production process was like taking a master class in speed and efficiency. She was a beautiful woman with impeccable fashion taste, a straight-talking dynamo who knew precisely what to say to ensure that our play would have all that was needed.

Knowing how much this was going to cost, and painfully aware that there was nowhere near as much of my Woodstock money left as there had been even a year before, I told Alyce my concerns about the production expenses. "That's not for you to worry about, Elliot," she said in her lovely, lilting voice. "I will take care of everything."

I was incredibly grateful to have Alyce on our side, but I still felt I needed to contribute something to ensure the proper run of the show. I told Alyce that I insisted on paying for some regional print advertising. Eager to avoid repeating the mistakes we'd made with *High Street,* I wanted to be sure we got plenty of attention for *The Music Keeper.* Alyce helped us hire the publicity firm of the great Broadway press rep Shirley Herz, whose junior staffer, Peter Cromarty, would handle our show. Knowing from bitter experience how important publicity was, I decided to have a chat with Peter to make sure he was up to the task.

We agreed to meet at the water fountain near the entrance to Bryant Park. I told Peter he would know me by my white hair and beard, and by my adorable Yorkie terrier. "I'll also be the one holding up a piece of white oak tag with 'PR NEEDED' written on it in big letters," I joked.

In his crisp single-breasted suit and delicate round tortoiseshell glasses, Peter Cromarty looked more like a young and accomplished yachtsman than a phone-pounding theatrical press agent. It was only when he and I began to talk that I realized how remarkably up to date and appreciative Peter was about the theater world. Peter had studied economics at Columbia University before getting his MFA in theater management. Peter had acted and sang in the Columbia student production of the rarely performed 1920 musical *Fly with Me*—the only show that had been written by Richard Rodgers, Oscar Hammerstein, *and* Lorenz Hart. As it turned out, André and I had actually seen a performance of that very show at Columbia.

We walked together for at least a half-hour, talking about our favorite playwrights, our favorite musicals, and our favorite songwriters. Of course, this led to a talk about Judy.

Judy Garland had been sacred to me ever since I was a kid. As a result, I was especially suspicious of people whose appreciation of her work might be considered superficial. While talking about Judy, I asked Peter, "So, is your favorite Judy song 'Over the Rainbow,' 'Get Happy,' or what?"

"Well, that depends," Peter responded.

"How so?"

"Well, there are different versions of 'Over the Rainbow,'" he said. "You've got the first recording that Judy sang in 1939 for *The Wizard of Oz,* but there's also the version she recorded in 1955 for Capitol Records, after she lost the Oscar for *A Star Is Born*. Finally, there's the poignant version she sang toward the end of the Carnegie Hall concert, so—"

"So," I said, smiling, "which version do you like?"

He looked at me incredulously. "Why, *all* of them, of course!"

Yep, I thought, *this guy is the right publicist for us!*

The fact that Peter had stage experience made us feel that much more secure about his passion and commitment to the theater, and to our play specifically. We were compatible in terms of the work we were going to do to get the show noticed. Considering Peter's stage experience and his great knowledge and love of the theater, I was now certain that he would do wonders for our show. It didn't hurt that he was also properly respectful of André's work, and very enthusiastic about *The Music Keeper* itself. Perhaps this time, we'd manage to get some attention for our work.

Alyce had already spread the word through her theater contacts that we would hold an open audition for a young male actor as one of only two starring roles in a new two-act play. For the part of Winifred Wagner, though, Alyce wanted us to use an actress named Jan Miner. Jan had worked in radio and theater before becoming known as "Madge the Manicurist," the TV commercial character who showed America's homemakers how Palmolive soap not only cleaned dishes, but softened hands. André and I were both uncertain about having the Palmolive lady from TV for our show, so Alyce brought Jan over to our apartment to convince us. We were intrigued to see that Jan was sporting a white-haired wig, and she spoke to us in an incredibly accurate German accent. André and I offered her the role right there on the spot.

Now that we had found our Winifred, we sifted through headshots of lots of handsome actors and were decidedly bored with nearly all of them. Then we found a young Juilliard-trained actor named Dennis Bacigalupi. He was tall, thin, and a little mysterious—exactly how I'd describe André if asked. Since I had based the Andrew character on André, Dennis would be perfect for the part.

Though it had been a few years now since André and I had made love, I tried as often as I could to show him I cared through a loving touch or a hug now and then. As he was getting ready to leave for his flight to Chicago, I wished André well and then pulled him in for a friendly but heartfelt hug. At first he resisted, but then he hugged me back. Shayna was barking a little at André, as if she knew he was leaving and wasn't pleased. I picked up Shayna and stuck her in André's welcoming arms. "Now you wish Daddy a pleasant trip, baby," I said, as Shayna licked his beard.

Alyce agreed to stay at our apartment and look after Shayna so that I could join André in Chicago for the opening of *A House Not Meant to Stand* at the Goodman Theatre. The show looked promising, and André was working with a number of crew members we'd also engage for *The Music Keeper*—Karen Schultz, the set designer, and Rachel Budin, the lighting designer. Being able to forge a working relationship in Chicago meant that things would only go faster once we began work on *The Music Keeper*.

Although we didn't know it at the time, *A House Not Meant to Stand* was to be the last play Tennessee Williams wrote, and André's was one of the final premieres of work that he was able to attend. Both Williams and the Goodman Theatre's artistic director Greg Mosher were very appreciative of André's work on the play. I hadn't seen Tennessee Williams in about three years, but he seemed even more a victim of the booze than he had been earlier. Still, it was an outstanding night for André, one that boded well for our upcoming production.

The next day, André and I caught a flight back to New York and were happily eating dinner together in our apartment by nightfall. I could tell that the success of the play in Chicago had revitalized André. Our only regret was that Audrey Wood, who remained incapacitated from a severe stroke some months before and was cared for now by family in Connecticut, could not be there at the show. She had discovered Tennessee at the start of her career, and come upon André and me near the end. We would have loved for her to have seen André make good at the Goodman that night, not to mention the unveiling of *The Music Keeper* in July.

With the Williams play done, we entered rehearsals for *The Music Keeper*. The first thing André did was to have Jan and Dennis both come to our apartment to listen to some Wagner. As we listened, André encouraged us to talk about our nicest and earliest memories involving music. I talked about my love for Judy Garland and Barbra Streisand, while André remembered growing up listening to jazz and romantic ballads in Belgium. Jan declared herself a fan of all kinds of music, and Dennis talked about rock music.

Afterward, André arranged for Dennis to come back to our apartment the next day, but alone, without Jan. I could tell that André found Dennis attractive, so I thought he might not want me there. But no—he wanted me to read some of the more upsetting passages from *Mein Kampf,* and the Marquis de Sade's *One Hundred Days of Sodom,* while Dennis listened to Wagner. The idea was to get Dennis into the right mindset to play Andrew.

"Do you understand Andrew's motivation?" André asked afterward.

"Absolutely, he's fighting for his life against this music."

"Not just *his* life," I chimed in. "Remember that Andrew is standing up and taking action for the six million Jews killed by the Nazis. Do you feel up to it?"

"Yes, I can do this," he said, smiling but serious.

I looked at André, and he said, "This was a good rehearsal. Come back here in two days, Dennis. Then you and Jan and Elliot and I will start to rehearse the lines of the play."

After working with Jan and Dennis to establish the adversarial relationship between Winifred and Andrew, André dove into the dialogue. André was very particular about the way Jan and Dennis read their lines; there had to be a certain cadence to their readings or the play wouldn't work. By making Jan and Dennis adhere to specific rhythms, it became far easier for André to weave the Wagner excerpts into the dialogue. He would have Jan and Dennis speak their lines very slowly, and then he would work through the same scene with each actor speaking at an accelerated pace. Once André heard several different line readings, he decided which he liked best. Within two weeks, Jan and Dennis had their roles down pat—and Alyce informed us that we now were able to move into the rented South Street Theater, where we would bring the play to life.

In terms of logistics, *The Music Keeper* was a fairly simple production. All the action took place in the living room of Winifred Wagner's opulent home, designed by Karen Schultz to feature a slightly curved staircase leading to Winifred's unseen bedroom. Susan Tsu created two lovely dresses for Jan and a dark suit for Dennis that evoked the clean severity of a Nazi uniform. Rachel Budin's lighting design remained calm and subdued for most of the show, bathing the stage in a faintly warm autumnal orange color. Only toward the end of the show did the lighting become harsh and brighter, changing gradually to underscore Winifred's death by heart attack at play's end.

I was very pleased with Jan and Dennis's performances. They looked and sounded exactly the way I had imagined when I first began to write the play. Even the tech rehearsals were a snap. The only area of concern was the music. Somehow, the music clips were never quite loud enough for André's taste. He wanted the Wagner music to serve as sonic explosions, punctuating the soft and often passive flow of dialogue between Winifred and Andrew. Used this way, the Wagner would approximate the near-hysterical tirades that Hitler delivered to the German people.

"Louder!" he would shout from the director's desk in the front row. "That music has to be much louder!"

Our music supervisor, Mildred, pointed out that if the music was too loud, the house sound system would distort it.

"Good, let the music be distorted," he said, with a deadly serious look in his eye. "Let it hurt the audience, just as it hurt all those people in Europe!"

I understood Mildred's concern, and tried to point out that the music might intrude on Jan and Dennis's performances up on the stage.

"That is what I want to do here, Elliot," he said. "Let the music be so loud that it desensitizes the audience—just as it desensitized Winifred, Germany, all of Europe to the madness playing out around them."

André wanted it that way, so that's what was done.

❀   ❀   ❀

I think what surprised me the most about opening night on *The Music Keeper* was how quickly it flew by. Alyce Finell handled everything with the assistance of Peter Cromarty, who had gotten a number of national and regional theater reviewers to attend. The press list included the estimable *New York Times* theater critic Dick Shepard. Peter reminded us that the fate of nearly every show in town was almost always decided by the next morning's review from the *Times*.

The house lights went down, the stage lights came up, and our play began. Andrew approaches Winifred, who is sleeping on the divan, center stage. Slowly, he raises a revolver and points it at Winifred, creating a powerful tension. The audience is frozen with anticipation, waiting for the gun to go off. The opening was certainly an attention-getter, and did much to sustain the audience's involvement with the two characters as the play progressed. Meanwhile, those loud blasts of Wagner music worked on two levels: they shocked our audience, and also ensured that anybody who might have been nodding off in their seats during the show was quickly awakened. I spent the intermission with André backstage, not wanting to pollute the air of seriousness in our piece by shaking hands and kissing asses out in the lobby.

When the play ended, I noticed that the audience seemed to be divided between those who felt they understood the play's message and those who were left scratching their heads. All told, it was a fast and exciting night of theater. Now it was out of our hands; it was up to the critics to decide whether the play had succeeded.

As it turned out, my great expectations for *The Music Keeper* were never realized. Shepard's review in the *New York Times* was largely positive. He described our play as "an altogether interesting stage piece that, for whatever it lacks to fit the terms of standard drama, holds the attention and gives you much to think about." This was the only good review we received for the play, unfortunately. All the other reviews were very unkind. The *Christian Science Monitor* called it "more thesis than theatrical," and *New York* magazine said it suffered from an excess of "crudeness, dishonesty, pretension, and mindlessness."

The Music Keeper closed after three weeks. Our little team was utterly crushed, though I think that Jan and Dennis were relieved to escape the high levels of agitation that they had to reach during each night's performance. Alyce had been very disappointed that her production hadn't made more of an impact, but I assured her that we would always appreciate her willingness to take a chance on our material. Our friendship remained strong and we only grew closer over the next few years. I could see that André remained a little wary of Alyce, perhaps because our intimacy did not include him. He remained gracious with Alyce, though, and felt that we were very lucky to have made her acquaintance.

With *The Music Keeper* finished, I kept waiting to be clobbered over the head by depression. After all, I had just watched three years of hard work evaporate from the stage in a mere three weeks. Coupled with the realization that my hard-earned Woodstock money had blown away in the harsh winds of Theater Row, I should have been leaping from the Brooklyn Bridge. Instead, I felt a strange sense of calm. I felt confident—even happy. The play had not succeeded as we had hoped, but the play had been performed. It had been real. It had *existed*. It was our first show in New York, and an accomplishment of which I would remain proud.

Still, it had not been as well received as I had hoped. André, worried that I might be upset, kept to himself for several days after the show closed. I was the one who broke the silence one night while we were watching TV.

"Hey, are you okay?" I asked.

"Yes, but I thought maybe you wanted to talk about losing the play. I know that you spent all that money of yours."

"What the hell," I said, sighing myself into a smile. "I'm surprised that it's lasted as long as it has. I've actually been pretty frugal!"

"Maybe I can look again to do some work in Europe again to help with expenses?"

"No," I said, "your home is here with Shayna and me. Don't worry. We'll get by. I'll be back teaching in a few weeks, and I thought I might start painting again. I've sold some good portraits in my day. And who knows—maybe I can get my interior decorating going again."

While we were talking, a commercial came on. It was the Oscar-winning actor John Houseman, extolling the virtues of the investment house Smith Barney. At the end of the commercial, Houseman talked about how crucial it was to earn one's money. Taking it as a sign, I turned to André. "From now on, fella, we're back to earning whatever money we need in order to keep doing what we're doing."

"And what," André asked, "are we doing, Elliot?"

"We're trying, André. We keep trying, babe. What else can we do?"

17

The Gay Plague

"Hey, did you hear about Paul?"

I looked up casually from my classroom desk at the New School that spring semester of 1983 and overheard two of my students talking to each other as they filed out of the room.

"Paul? What about him?" one said.

"Well, I hear he's got that new gay disease people are talking about. You know, that thing they're calling the 'gay cancer.'"

"Holy shit. Really? Wonder how he got it!"

"How do you think, dickhead? From being a faggot, that's how."

"So that's why he's been missing classes. Hey, do you think only fags can get it?"

"I hope so. I sure as fuck don't want to catch it from some homo queer. C'mon, let's get out of here."

I learned two things in that moment. First, there were still a lot of people who hated others for being gay. And second, the stories I had increasingly heard about a terrible illness that was killing gay men had now reached my classroom.

It was exceptionally hot in New York City that summer. Things got so uncomfortable by late June that when Stanley Grier invited us to spend weekends at his beach house way out east, on Fire Island, we were happy to accept. We had met Stanley through Alyce Finell at a Soho gallery opening. He was a successful and very wealthy advertising executive who had various accounts in the fashion industry, both in the United States and in Europe. In addition to the Fire Island beach house, he also had a splendid duplex apartment on the Upper West Side and a palatial mansion on Long Island, in Oyster Bay. Just like Bill the doctor, Stanley had been married to a woman for more than fifteen years before coming out of the closet; they had four children.

At first, I had a hard time believing that Stanley was actually gay. There was something about him that seemed a bit broader and rougher and louder than necessary—in short, he seemed straight. He was lovely and handsome, though, with a strong and muscular build and long strands of salt and pepper hair combed back tightly from his forehead. He was maybe a year or two older than I was, but his thick, lustrous hair seemed to mock my own speedily receding hairline. While both André and I remained committed to full beards, Stanley was clean shaven and maintained an effortless tan.

After a series of theatrical letdowns, André and I both welcomed the change of scenery. Alyce promised to house-sit and look after Shayna for us—she liked staying at our place anyway. Over a series of weekends throughout July and August, we would take the Long Island Rail Road train out to Bay Shore and then walk about a mile or grab a taxi over to the ferry that would get us over to Stanley's place. Fire Island reminded me of the time I'd spent by the seashore when I was younger. I even fantasized that Fire Island might live up to its name and rekindle the erotic heat that had burned so intensely between us for nearly a decade.

Whenever we arrived at his beach house on Friday afternoon or Saturday morning, we would find Stanley surrounded by a group of young gay men, all of whom seemed as interested in his wealth as they were in his attention. Alcohol was plentiful—ice-cold beers in the fridge and various bottles of hard liquor behind a wet bar that opened out on to a deck facing the Atlantic Ocean. Stanley also kept two refrigerators stocked with steaks that his guests could cook on the three large barbecue grills set up along the deck. A vegetarian like André and me, Stanley had lots of salads and delicious fruit-and-veggie platters. Whenever he ran out of anything at the house, Stanley would simply give a few hundred bucks to somebody to head over to the grocery store and bring more back. Since there was so much free stuff at his place, no one ever ran off with the cash—they would always come back, because Stanley's place was where so many wanted to be.

Stanley's offerings weren't limited to food and booze. In the living room, you could always find a few cigar boxes filled with joints; a sugar bowl on a long, mirrored table, filled with cocaine; and a stash of amphetamines and amyl nitrite that he would give to any guests who wanted to head up to one of the seven bedrooms on the top floor of the beach house. That was probably the greatest attraction of Stanley's place for his weekend guests—at Stanley's, they could do anything they wanted with anyone they wanted. This caused the young men to refer to the Grier house mischievously as the "Fuck Hut."

On our first weekend visit, Stanley told us that Alyce had advised him to pick our brains about the worlds of film, TV, and theater. It was clear that Stanley loved showbiz and had cash to burn. We were grateful Alyce had steered us toward someone who not only had a great beach house, but also might be able to help support our theatrical ambitions. Mostly, Stanley wanted to learn more about becoming a theater producer.

"So what does it take to become a theater producer, anyway?" he asked.

"You want the truth?" I said. "It takes money. That's about it. Just cough up a large enough hairball to finance a production, and you'll quickly become known as a top cat."

"Really?" he asked, looking wary. "I thought you needed to study production—like, in college."

"There is an art to it, Stanley," André piped in. "For example, there are people—"

"Like Alyce," I added in quickly.

"Yes," André said, looking at me a little coldly, "yes, like Alyce. There are those who are born to it and who have a legitimate idea of what makes a good show. These are people who possess a large and bountiful interior life, and who have an appreciation for the creative process. The best producers are the ones who, in addition to having money or the ability to raise it, are driven by the need to tell stories."

"Stories, huh?" Stanley said. "I've got a story or two I could tell you. That's for sure."

"Do tell," I responded.

"Not tonight," he said. "Not yet. Keep coming around to see me here this summer. You have an open invitation. Let's see where things go."

Over the next few weekends, we started to find out a little more about Stanley Grier. Slowly, we came to realize that not everything was as it seemed.

Despite all the revelry, I never once saw Stanley indulge in any sex or affection during those few times that we visited him at the beach house. Then again, I never played around with guys when I was at the house, either. Still, there had been something in the way Stanley presided over the goings-on at the "Fuck Hut" that seemed powered more by rage than anything else.

Sometimes it seemed like everything he did was rushed and aggressive. His movements—even gestures as simple as turning his head—often had a sort of impatience. He didn't simply place an ashtray down on a table; he would let it fall with a clunk from a good six inches or so above the table. When he put down a glass, he slammed it down. He would blast disco music through the huge stereo speakers he had rigged throughout his house, smiling as he invited everyone to dance and have fun. But while everyone else was rubbing up close to each other and enjoying the music, Stanley's smile would often fade. Standing apart from the carousing, he would walk off to his bedroom on the other side of the house. It seemed as if he was terrified to let himself feel any pleasure at all.

I decided to draw him out. After I told him about my toxic upbringing and how the Woodstock concert set me free from the El Monaco, Stanley eventually told us about the years he had spent as a married man with four children. He had accomplished everything that mainstream society dictated he should do to be correct and successful. All that had done was to "drain fifteen years off my life, and gain fifty pounds around my belt line," as he put it.

He had found himself at an unavoidable impasse in his life only a few years earlier. "I was so utterly miserable that I often thought of killing myself," he confessed, the three of us high on weed late on a Saturday night, with an entire floor full of men having sex directly above our heads. "There I was," Stanley said in a distant monotone, "a grown man who had always been filled with an irrepressible lust for life. Then I suddenly wake up one day, and I'm a total stranger to myself. I could no longer stand being henpecked by my wife—a woman I had once considered as much a friend as a lover—while being ceaselessly devalued and despised by my kids. Those people didn't seem to have a clue that I existed as a fellow human being. I felt like nothing in their eyes, and in my own. It was as if I'd become a prop, some discarded and creaky chair left in the corner and only brought out when we had people over the house. It was a prison, and I wanted out.

"Luckily," he continued, "I had money and access to lots of photographers. Things had gone south in the bedroom between me and my wife, so I wondered if she might be having an affair. I hired a freelance photographer to follow her around during the days, while I was at work in the city. Sure enough, he got pictures of her meeting up with a younger man a few times a week at a nearby motel. The photos were compromising enough for me to go to a divorce lawyer. I was able to prove my wife's infidelity, and that was what I needed to get the hell out of there. She wound up marrying the guy, who works as manager of a local bank, a few months ago. I never see her or my children anymore. That part of my life is over."

"Stanley," I said, still taking in the immensity of his story, "I totally understand your need for personal freedom, maybe better than anyone. But I have to ask: Why did you bother to marry and have children if you were gay?"

"Well, that was another surprise," he laughed. "It turned out my trusty photographer was gay and he had the hots for me. I didn't realize that I felt the same way until—well, let's just say it came as unexpected."

"Did you fall in love with him, Stanley?" André asked. "Is he still in your life now?"

Stanley became very quiet, and his face filled with sadness. "I, uh, lost Brad this past January," he recalled as his voice began to falter. "We had been together just over a year, and I felt happier in my life than ever before. I dropped a bunch of pounds, watched what I ate, started to work out at the gym three days a week, and took up jogging. I felt great! I was free to be me, and could live like myself for the first time in years that I could remember. No apologies, you know?

"Anyway, we were out here on the beach last summer," he continued, "and I saw one morning that Brad had a large dark spot along the small of his back. I thought maybe it was a beauty mark that I hadn't noticed. But he told me it had appeared only a few weeks before, and he didn't know what it was. Within another week, another dark spot appeared on the front of his chest. Less than a month later, he had another on his forehead. He began losing weight, and we even had to leave a restaurant one night when he suffered an uncontrollable bout of diarrhea."

It was early morning by now, and Stanley's house had grown silent, as most of the guys upstairs had presumably either passed out or fallen asleep. Stanley continued his upsetting story about his lover.

"It got much worse over the next two days. Brad began to shiver intensely and he spiked a fever. By that Sunday afternoon, he was drenched with sweat and couldn't stand up. We were driving back to the city when he suddenly began to cough up blood. I drove him over immediately to St. Vincent's Hospital. It was the closest hospital I could get him to. They didn't know what it was at the hospital, either. The only thing they could tell me was that Brad seemed to have come down with a severe case of pneumonia. I saw, though, that there were other men on the floor where Brad was kept, and they—" Stanley had to stop; he sounded as if he might break down at any moment. "—they had the same sickness as Brad. It was so goddamn awful. Doctors and nurses wore surgical masks whenever they came in to see Brad. They tried everything they could, but Brad just got sicker. A month after he was admitted to the hospital, he died in my arms, saying he loved me."

Stanley looked ashen as he recalled the experience, and André and I felt sorry for him. "The doctors tell me I might have whatever the fuck Brad got. Y'know, I don't even know whether or not I'm really gay. All I know is that I loved Brad. Now he's gone." He looked right at me, and said, "I guess every freedom has its price, right?"

He tried to shrug it off, but it was clear that he was alone now and scared. Perhaps having us at the beach house that summer was a relief to him, but it only saddened and confused André and me—about everything. Looking at Stanley after he told us his story, I saw a man who was slowly being annihilated from within. The love of his life had died, leaving him with nothing. That night, Stanley Grier, that summer's troubled emperor of Fire Island, revealed to me and André that he knew damn well he wore no clothes at all. He was naked in his sorrow, immersed in his rage, and intent on reaching the frightening realm of death.

Stanley excused himself, and invited us to sleep in his bedroom just off the kitchen on the main floor. We thanked him, though he seemed not to hear us at all. He slid open the glass door to the deck, and walked off into the darkness of the sand and sea. Not wanting to go to sleep with Stanley wandering around the shoreline high and in such a morose state of mind, we decided to follow him. He stopped about twenty feet away from the water's edge and stood silently. We could only make out where he was thanks to the bright moonlight. After a time, he turned away from the water and made his way back slowly to the house, whispered a haunted "Good night" to us both, and went into the room that he had offered us earlier. We told each other that Stanley probably wouldn't remember what he had told us that night, even if we didn't believe it. Regardless, we agreed not to bring it up in the morning and settled down for the night on separate couches in the living room.

Troubled already by the story of Brad's death, I found it difficult to go to sleep. "It's so quiet," I whispered to André.

"Quiet like a graveyard," André whispered back.

"I love you, André," I said.

"I love you, too," he responded.

We finally fell asleep for a few hours. When we woke up around nine in the morning, we found Stanley seated out on the deck with a mug of hot coffee. He was still staring out at the ocean with a sorrowful frown upon his face, and seemed very much unlike the man we had gotten to know over the past few weeks. Feeling uncomfortable, we thanked Stanley for having us and headed back to Manhattan. When we got up to the apartment, Alyce asked if we had had a good time at Stanley's. "Yeah," I said sarcastically, "it was a real gay old time." André excused himself and went back to sleep in the bedroom. Unable to conceal anything from Alyce, I told her what Stanley had told us. She hadn't known too much about Stanley's private life, so she was as upset by his loss as we were.

That was to be our last visit to Stanley's beach house. I called Stanley a few days later at his apartment, but someone else picked up the phone. It turned out to be his neighbor, who explained that he was watching Stanley's place for him. I asked where Stanley had gone, but all that the neighbor knew was that Stanley had left the city for a long vacation in Europe before gearing up for the spring season fashion shows that September. I asked the neighbor to let Stanley know that I had called, and to give him our phone number so he could call us when he came back. September came and went, but we never did hear again from Stanley, and neither did Alyce. It was as if the man we saw that moonlit night on Fire Island had disappeared.

Stanley's boyfriend wasn't the only victim of the "gay plague," as the media had begun to call it. From back in 1979, when I first learned that my old Hollywood friend Jerry had died from a strange illness, I had already developed a small but growing awareness that something very worrisome was happening within the gay community. By 1983, it seemed like gay men in New York were dying in unprecedented numbers. André and I were shocked as we started to hear that more and more friends of ours—gay men we knew from the clubs and colleagues in the arts community—were suddenly being hospitalized. The pain and suffering they endured was horrible; it seemed that death was their only reprieve. It was the worst nightmare imaginable, a nightmare that didn't end. It almost felt as if we were being punished for letting down our guards a little. Just as things had started to get better for the gay community—just as we were beginning to gain some acceptance and have our rights acknowledged—this plague came and wiped out any sense of security we might have had. We realized that we and everyone we knew could very well get sick and die within a matter of weeks or even days.

This new disease was all any of us talked about in the bars and clubs, or at parties. Everyone was scared. There was no end to the speculation. Initially, I thought that the illness must have started at the Mineshaft, what with its anonymous sex and highly risky behavior. The local gay newspapers—the only papers in New York that were providing any coverage about the emerging health crisis—talked about the bathhouses as the places where the illness had first begun to spread. Some scientists thought that it had come from Africa, and had first been caught by gorillas. There was no way to know what was causing the disease or how it could be stopped. The only thing anybody knew was that the illness seemed to be transmitted through sexual contact between men. That was it. No rhyme, no reason, no cure, no end.

Everybody was afraid of contracting the disease. Even Renee put some distance between us at first. I did not begrudge her the parental instincts that caused her concern, and I eventually insisted that she and I only stay connected by phone until we knew more about what was happening.

Meanwhile, André became utterly frantic about our health. We had never discussed the details of his sex life after we stopped sleeping together, but his extreme nervousness led me to wonder if he might have contracted the illness. Apparently, he was worried, too. After he moved back in with me, he had spent many nights away from the apartment. Given our open relationship, I had had a pretty good idea what he was doing. As word of this new illness began to spread, however, André stopped going out at night. He spent much of his free time in the apartment, his mood swinging between apprehension and melancholy.

There were times, late at night, when I would hear water running in the bathroom sink. I would walk over from the living room and listen at the bathroom door. And then I would hear him weeping. It broke my heart to hear him suffering like that. Some nights, I would knock on the door to make sure that he was all right. He always said he was fine, and that he would be out in a minute. I would check on him not only in case he wanted to share his fears with me, but also to make sure that he wasn't doing something to hurt himself in there. In those early days, when we knew so little about the disease, it often seemed as if death was just around the corner—that it was not a matter of if, but rather *when* we, too, would get sick. It was hard not to buckle under the constant threat of death. We all felt so helpless.

We wound up going to see André's former lover, Bill. He was as afraid as everyone else, and he kindly gave us free physicals. He checked my blood pressure, looked in my throat, and did the usual things that doctors do.

When I asked if he knew whether I might have this gay disease, he said flatly, "I don't know. None of us know. There's no way to test for it yet. We don't even know what we're looking for at this point." He paused. "Tell me something, Elliot. Have you had sex with multiple partners over the past months, or even over the past few years?"

"No, I haven't been having sex with anyone. Not even with André since he moved back in with me."

There was an awkward moment between us, since Bill clearly thought that André and I had gotten back together after André had moved out of Bill's place. I ended the silence in the room with an embarrassing admission. "You see, Bill, André and I have a strictly platonic relationship. We're together, but we don't *get* together—not physically, not anymore."

He looked at me very seriously, and said. "That's good, Elliot. While we're talking about it, I would advise you to avoid sex with *anyone*. I've told André to do the same. At least at this point."

Sensing that we were going out of our minds, the good Dr. Bill gave us a few bottles of pills before we left the office "to keep the blues away, and to keep your minds calm." A few days later, Bill called us with the news that we both had relatively clean bills of health. But that did little to calm us. Within a few months, he was writing us both prescriptions for antidepressants as if he were giving away candy.

The leather bars and the bathhouses were the first to be closed by the department of health. Then, one after another, the sex clubs were shut down. The bars were nearly empty. Almost everyone we knew stopped having sex, terrified of catching the disease. One morning, I read in the newspapers about a wealthy real-estate developer from the Bible Belt named Stephen Strong, whose son was reported to have died suddenly of pneumonia. *Pneumonia,* I thought. *Yeah, right.* I was certain that this dead young man had in fact been the Stevie Strong whom I had met a few years earlier.

A few months later, Alyce called to tell André and me that Stanley Grier had committed suicide in his apartment on the Upper West Side. As she learned from one of Stanley's neighbors, Stanley was upset to have found a few lesions on his body—the same kind that Brad had had. One evening, Stanley came home early from work and promptly shot himself through the mouth with a handgun. It was a terribly sad end to the life of a lost, lonely man. The worst part of it was that we understood how Stanley must have felt. It was overwhelmingly frightening to think that we were being targeted by this gay cancer, and that we could die at any moment. At times, the threat of imminent death was almost unbearable.

For all the talk within the gay community, the public at large remained almost silent about the growing epidemic. At best, the situation was met with denial and resistance. At worst, gay people were shunned and blamed for bringing this new plague to the planet. And it wasn't just the mainstream media that did us wrong. Elected officials from Mayor Koch to President Reagan initially ignored our desperate pleas for action, refusing to even mention the gay cancer in public.

The gay community quickly began to mobilize in order to increase awareness of this devastating disease and to search for a cure. Larry Kramer, a novelist and playwright we had heard about, founded an organization called the Gay Men's Health Crisis, which aimed to educate the public, raise funds for research, influence policy, and provide care for the sick. In the process, Kramer helped extend the notion of gay rights and lead thousands to demand that the government find out what caused the disease that was wiping out so many of us. Gay activists emerged, and protests spread from coast to coast.

By April 1985, Kramer finished a play called *The Normal Heart*. Set between 1981 and 1984, *The Normal Heart* chronicled the first years of the crisis. Using his protagonist, Ned Weeks, as a surrogate, Kramer had written about his own agonizing personal experiences as an activist, fighting with doctors, politicians, friends, and lovers to establish formal recognition of what was eventually named Acquired Immune Deficiency Syndrome (AIDS).

Joseph Papp felt it was his duty as a human being to stage an off-Broadway production of the play at the Public Theater, and André and I went to one of the very first performances. Kramer's play so perfectly encapsulated what we were going through that it felt like watching the end of a universe take place in real time on a bare stage. We both left the show that night utterly numb, and spent the rest of the evening taking turns holding Shayna in beaten silence.

Then there were the hospital visits, and the funerals. It was all I could do to keep waking up every day—so many of our friends and colleagues were dying. There was Bobby, our favorite waiter at our favorite Italian restaurant. Wayne, who owned a hardware store in Chelsea, and his boyfriend Charlie, who was an accountant by day and an inspired jazz guitarist by night—they died within four months of each other. Angelo and David were Juilliard-trained dancers who tried one night back in 1981 to teach André and me how to tap-dance, with hilariously bad results. Angelo died from the illness on Christmas Eve 1984, and a broken-hearted David took a fatal overdose of sleeping pills the following Valentine's Day.

Not all of the men who died were from New York. Jackie had been born and raised in Texas during the Dust Bowl years. He had gone on to work as a stuntman on various Hollywood movies for two decades, before a back injury forced him to retire. Jackie had worked mostly in low-budget Westerns; his natural tan guaranteed him plentiful work as an "Indian." Jackie was one of the most captivating men I had ever met. He brought to the East Coast some fairly wild stories about his time in Hollywood. He once told us how legendary Western movie star John Wayne called him into his trailer during the making of a film. When Jackie got there, Wayne chased him around his dressing room wearing only a towel knotted at the hip, playfully shouting "Coochee coo-chee coo, yuh sweet-ass Injun!"

He also talked about how he was almost cast as a Mexican bandit in Marlon Brando's first and only directorial attempt, *One-Eyed Jacks*. Jackie told us that he was passed over for the part, though, because he wouldn't let Brando masturbate him at the end of the closed-door audition. After the film's release, Jackie would always refer to that movie as "The One-Eyed Jack-off."

I told him about my brief time trying to break into Hollywood as a production designer, and how I failed so miserably at it. Placing his big arm across my shoulders, he looked me right in the eyes and said in his easy Texan drawl, "Elliot, there ain't nothin' but a whole world of hurt out there in them goddamn Tinseltown hills. You ask me, I say you done a helluva sight better for yourself pullin' on out of there when you did. Set your sights on other horizons, baby. Take it from me, the last of the Hollywood Mohicans." Jackie had a sweet and gentle heart to him, and he forever changed my previously wary view of people from Texas. They weren't all like that mean-eyed, trigger-happy ranger who had pulled me over on that desolate Texas highway years before.

Jackie had been closeted during his early years, but came out in a big way after his injury forced him to quit doing stunt work. At forty-five, he moved to San Francisco and fell madly in love with Martin, a gifted poet twenty years younger. When André and I first met them, Jackie was driving a taxi cab and Martin was working as a creative writing teacher for the New School, while also finishing the third of three wonderful novels that were never fated to be published. It was Martin who got sick first. He was admitted to a hospital within a month of his first lesions and dead from the disease less than three weeks after that. Jackie sat and held Martin's slowly trembling hands during his final hours of painful suffering. When he was told by the head nurse that he was not entitled to be by Martin's side because he was not a family member, Jackie got up from the hospital room chair and headed for Texas, driving the taxi cab that still belonged to his employers. We never heard from Jackie again, but we did catch a rumor that he had been found dead at the wheel of his taxi after driving it into a ravine somewhere out in the lonely hills of Maryland. A fitting way for a stuntman to die.

Vincent, Michael, Joey, Sidney, Tommy, Alan—all of them wonderful guys, and all of them dead within weeks of getting sick. Whenever we found out a friend was sick and in the hospital, we would go to visit. The lifeless men we saw in those steel beds might as well have been strangers to us. We would say their names, tell them we were there with them, tell them we loved them. Sometimes, they would open their sunken eyes and smile weakly when we spoke. More often, they just lay there like gaunt zombies, their skin riddled with dark lesions, as the hospital nurses tended to them wearing gloves and surgical masks and hoping like everyone else that they wouldn't catch the disease. As time went on, we'd only hear about a friend's illness after he had already succumbed to it. Far from being cruel, this allowed the one who was dying a final dignity. Many wanted their friends and lovers to remember them as they were, not as they had become.

Over the next two and a half years, we must have attended over thirty funerals—nearly one each month. And with each funeral, attendance seemed to shrink. Once it was known that someone had died from this gay cancer, only a handful of family members, if any, would show up, and perhaps a few close gay friends. Straight people shunned these funerals, and many used the situation to fuel existing prejudices against gays. Terrible as it might seem, we felt almost a sense of relief once we began to get reports that heterosexual men and women were getting the disease as well. The involvement of straight men and women let us hope that there might finally be formal acknowledgment of the epidemic by the White House. But we also worried that we'd be blamed even more vehemently for the fact that straight folks were getting sick. It was starting to feel a little scary again, walking the streets of Manhattan as a gay man.

In early August 1985, we went to another funeral. This time, we were paying our respects to a twenty-one-year-old named Daniel, whom André had once directed in a play at Columbia University. André had turned forty-two in June, and it was upsetting for him to see a young man half his age lying there dead in a casket. We were all brought to tears when we realized that not one member of his entire family was there at the funeral home. Daniel's father had apparently paid for the arrangements, and flowers had been sent by aunts and uncles and cousins, but this young boy's relatives themselves were nowhere to be found. It was the saddest funeral that André and I were to witness in those terrible years.

As we left the funeral home, one of the other mourners, a friend of Daniel's from school, shared a story about how he and his friend were thrown out of a local bar by two drunk straight guys. They'd been told, "God is killing you faggots because it's what you deserve. You're all gonna die, you fuckin' queers! Go home and fuckin' die!"

This ugliness filled us with sorrow and rage. André looked at the man with tears in his eyes, and said, "Who are they to judge us? Who are they to say we should die?" We all nodded our heads in agreement, but there was nothing left to say.

As we made our way back home to our apartment, André stared straight ahead and didn't say a word. I knew that he had been upset by what we had heard, but he was keeping it inside. Once we got to the apartment, he opened a bottle of wine and proceeded to drink from it directly. About an hour later, with the silence standing like an invisible wall between us, I spoke up.

"What's wrong, André? Tell me what it is. Whatever it is, I'm here. Let it out."

He stood up from the couch, his eyes filled with tears. "Why do they hate us so much, Elliot?" he asked, still bothered by the people in the mourner's story. "I am not some horrible monster. I am a good person, a kind man. I have love in my heart, but my heart is being broken by all this death and hatred. It makes me—I am so sad because I—"

Unable to finish his remarks, he fell to his knees and broke down in front of me, his sobs growing louder and louder. I put Shayna down, knelt gently next to André, and draped my arms over him. Our embrace threw open the floodgates, as we began to weep together. André's voice grew hoarse from crying. "André, it's okay. It's okay, babe," I kept saying, trying to comfort and soothe him.

"I hear what people say about us. Maybe what they say is right, Elliot. Maybe this is some kind of a curse, some kind of plague meant to destroy us. Maybe there is something wrong with us. I do not understand. Why would God allow something like this to happen? Why allow so much misery and pain?

"Sometimes," André continued, "I hate myself so much because I know that I am different. These people, they do not understand. I never chose to be the way that I am. When my father suspected the way I was, he grew so distant; he shut me out of his life as if I were a stranger to him. I am his son, his *only* son. My mother and my sisters have always loved me, no matter what. But my father—in his eyes, it was as if I no longer truly existed. He never said a word, but I knew. I could never change who I am. But maybe that is why we are all dying now. I love my father. Why could he never love me?"

I could feel the depths of André's anguish. I took a few deep breaths and tried my best to calm him down, or at least ease the pain that he was going through.

"Listen," I said, "we have no idea why this thing is happening to us. You can blame a goddamn scientist who fucked up in a lab, or a sick sheep that passed it on to a horny herder, or the KKK. We don't have any real idea why this is happening. All we know is that we *don't* know.

"And hey," I continued, "so you've never had a good relationship with your father. What about me with *my* mother? Imagine if you had to live with my mother every day when you were a kid. As a matter of fact," I joked, "take my mother *now*—please!"

That got him laughing a bit, and he finally got a hold of himself. "So sorry. I am so sorry, Elliot," he said, as we held each other there near the foot of the couch. For the first time in a long time, there we were again—two lost souls, united in a world of madness and pain. I consoled him, telling him that everything would work out. I assured him that we would find a way through the terrible days ahead. I wanted to make sure he understood that I would be a source of strength and support for him no matter what.

But the real truth was that I was as scared as everyone else. I knew I was not going to be able to don my Super Elli cape and make everything right. All I could do was to try to ensure our survival. And that was why I decided that neither of us would attend any more funerals of those who died from AIDS. André and I simply had no strength left to handle the heavy burden of loss that weighed so relentlessly upon our community.

That night, after André passed out with Shayna sleeping next to him, I wrote down the name of the young man whose funeral we had attended that day. It was the thirty-fourth name on the list of people we knew who had died over the past two and a half years. I brought the list into the kitchen, and there I took a match and set fire to it. I dropped the flaming pieces of paper into the sink, and then slowly doused the burnt offerings with water from the faucet.

❁   ❁   ❁

"Elliot! André! Come over here, my angels!"

Spotting us from twenty feet away, our wonderful friend Colleen Dewhurst excused herself from the crowd of fans waiting for her autograph and moved toward us with arms opened wide and a smile as bright as the sun. She had just finished a program of readings from Eugene O'Neill's work as part of a centennial celebration of his plays held at the Ellington Room in our Manhattan Plaza apartment building. We were waiting our turn to congratulate her on the performance, but she had looked up and seen us. And when Colleen saw her friends, she went to them with hugs and warmth and love. We didn't get to see her as often as we liked, as she'd been busy not only with her career, but with a new project.

After she had been named the president of Actors' Equity Association in 1985, Colleen helped found the nonprofit organization Equity Fights AIDS, working closely with others to organize various performances and readings to benefit AIDS research. She dedicated herself to her mission with the fire and aggression of a mother tiger protecting her young. Everyone in the theater community loved Colleen for her strong leadership, and for her dedication to the cause.

We heard from colleagues about how she personally visited every theater to map out the most effective strategies for soliciting donations from audiences following performances, ironing out the specific language that the actors were to use when explaining what Equity Fights AIDS was all about. Colleen had also made certain that everyone refrained from referring to those with AIDS as "victims." People with AIDS wanted to be treated as *people*, not just statistics. "Call them victims," Colleen said, "and you deprive them of their dignity as human beings. Our goal is to help them, not to hide them."

We saw Colleen make her own passionate plea for the organization first-hand. In 1987, André had directed her in a well-received play called *My Gene* as part of the New York Shakespeare Festival. After the curtain call each night, Colleen stepped forward and appealed to the audience about the need to support AIDS research through donations to organizations like Equity Fights AIDS. Still mesmerized by Colleen's impassioned performance in the show, the audience probably would have jumped off the Brooklyn Bridge if she had suggested it. Suffice to say, she made her case for AIDS, and the audiences responded. Donations were made, minds were changed, and the public perception of AIDS began to shift. I like to think that part of that change came from Colleen's inspiring work both inside and outside the entertainment industry.

With Father Rodney Kirk, the director of our apartment complex, and his partner Richard Hunnings, Colleen had also helped put together the Manhattan Plaza AIDS Project. The Project was meant to ensure that people in our building who had AIDS would receive help, care, and compassion. André and I contributed any free time we had to the AIDS Project, which always needed volunteers. We helped get people to doctor's appointments, made sure that they had food to eat, and took the time to talk to them. After all, these were people like us—people who had families and friends and wishes and dreams, people who had stories to tell and few willing listeners. I did what I could to try to raise spirits and make people feel a little better, even if only for a few minutes. André, a better listener than I, would simply sit with people and let them talk about their own lives. The experience did much to teach us how to take better care of each other. It helped us feel human again.

"Now, how are you both feeling? Been to the doctor for your tests, I hope. We're still healthy, aren't we?"

Colleen was always stern but careful when it came to our own health. She teased me about being heavier than I'd been the last time she saw me, but immediately told André that he looked thinner than when they had worked together on *My Gene*. "Are you feeling all right, André? Are you taking care of yourself?"

"Yes, of course, Colleen," André grinned, looking a bit like a little boy. "I am thinner, but only because I have been afraid lately that maybe I am getting a bit fat."

"If *you're* fat, André," I quipped, "then they'll soon be assigning a zip code to my ass!"

Colleen and André both laughed, as I knew that they would. I didn't mind if the laughter was at my expense, because we now knew how precious it was to be able to enjoy any moment of any day. By the late 1980s, scientists had come up with a test that could confirm whether people had the virus—the human immunodeficiency virus, or HIV—that led to AIDS. If you had the virus, you were "HIV-positive." If you didn't, you were "HIV-negative."

We had gone back to our good friend doctor Bill to take the HIV test. We learned within a week that we were both negative. Bill, looking thinner than he had ever been in the nine years we had known him, was not so lucky. He told us that he had taken the test, and discovered that he was positive. We would lose Bill to AIDS two and a half years later.

Bill would eventually turn over his practice to a younger doctor—an Orthodox Jewish man named Menachem Gould. Dr. Gould was never late for *shul,* ate only kosher foods, and seemed to unwittingly embody all the other stereotypical Jewish-doctor traits. But he was also a mensch who continued to write us prescriptions for antidepressants, just as Bill had done. Even if we hadn't already needed those pills, Bill's death would have sent us tumbling back into the warmly placid world of Ritalin and Prozac anyway.

By the end of the 1980s, as people from the straight community like Colleen Dewhurst and so many others joined hands with gay activists to ease suffering and find a cure, many of us in the gay community began to get more involved. It had been one thing to march down a city street once a year to declare our pride in being gay, but now we began to make our presence known throughout the city and throughout the year, trying to get others to acknowledge our rights. United amidst the madness and chaos, we began to stage protests, and to wear red ribbons to show support for AIDS research and tolerance.

As awareness grew, the public began to admit that we had a serious crisis on our hands. The death of Hollywood star Rock Hudson represented a major turning point in the recognition of HIV/AIDS. His friend and former colleague President Reagan had no choice but to break his silence on the topic, finally mentioning the disease by name and calling it "a top priority" during a 1985 press conference. Slowly, advances were made, with the Food and Drug Administration approving the drug azidothymidine (AZT) for the treatment of HIV infection in 1987. There was still no cure, but at least there was some kind of progress, no matter how grudging.

"I'm just glad to know that you are both happy and healthy!" Colleen said. I sensed that being able to see the two of us standing there, still alive, gave Colleen a deep feeling of hope. "Will I see you both later this evening

over at Circle in the Square?" she asked, naming a landmark independent theater on Broadway. "I'll be doing more readings with some other actors. Perhaps we can have a late supper together afterward. Catch up a bit."

"We'll be there," I told Colleen.

"Yes," André added, "and it would be lovely to get us together again for
one of our dinners. Maybe even see about doing another show together."

"You bet we will," she said, pulling us into a three-way hug before being
ushered back to her adoring fans by a timid publicist.

Colleen didn't have much longer to raise awareness of the AIDS crisis, as
she succumbed to her own struggle with cervical cancer in 1991. But her
devotion to and support for AIDS patients was not forgotten by those in the
theater world. When Equity Fights AIDS merged a year later with a similar
group, Broadway Cares, they created the Colleen Dewhurst Society, which
recognized those who included the newly named Broadway Cares/Equity
Fights AIDS organization in their will or estate plans. We remained proud of
all Colleen had done in her life to help the fight against AIDS in the industry.
But it was the memory of that sweet, unexpected embrace at the O'Neill centennial that stayed with us as a treasured gift.

18

Woodstock Daddy vs. Riverdale Momma

"Guess what? I'm getting married!"

"Who is this?"

"Elliot! C'mon, you know who this is."

"But is this *really* you? What if this is some remarkable mimic, trying to trick me into thinking I'm listening to my sister?"

"Cut it out! You know it's me. And I'm getting married. Didn't you hear?"

"Wait a second, sis, now just wait," I said. "His name isn't Boris, is it?"

"No, it's Yuri. Yuri Brisker."

"What? *Who?* Yuri *Brisket?* So you're marrying into a family of Jewish pot roasts? He's kosher, at least?"

"Okay, fine, keep making fun. You're the first person I call with the news, and all you can do is to make jokes."

Although Renee had initially put some distance between us in the early days of the AIDS epidemic, she had quickly gotten over her concern about the disease once she realized that her HIV-negative brother and his boyfriend were not going to infect her or her child. Soon, we were back to our old habits, traveling to New Jersey at least a half-dozen times a year. We always visited during the holidays, when we could catch up with my niece, Alyse. After receiving a master's in biology, she had found a well-paying research position at some big biochemical firm. As a scientist, Alyse was very concerned about AIDS, and she always shared with us any information about the fight for a cure that she had learned from her colleagues. It gave me such joy to know that Alyse accepted and still loved me and André without any fear or judgment. And I saw how much it meant to André that Alyse thought of him as part of the family, as much her uncle as I was.

It was during the holidays that we first got to know Yuri. He was a bright yet soft-spoken artist who seemed to adore my sister. He was not very tall, but he projected solid strength. Yuri was my age, only two years older than Renee. He looked younger than his years, though, and I chalked much of that up to his boundless imagination. Yuri had been born in Leningrad, Russia, in 1935, and only came to the US in the late 1970s. He had graduated from the Leningrad Institute of Finance and Economy, which meant he was that rarest of artists—one who understood and could actually handle issues involving money.

Yuri had a small workshop in New Jersey, where he created and sold museum-quality sculptures. He created relief designs and beautiful sculptures in marble. He had great knowledge of Russian antiques, and would go on to create a line of musical Fabergé-style eggs, and later a series of 24-karat gold-plated musical jewel boxes.

The fates had presented my sister with Yuri at the right time in her life. It seemed clear to me that love had—at long last—finally found Renee. I didn't know whether or not Momma liked Yuri, or had even met him. As an artist, though, Yuri was going to have to wage an uphill battle to win over a woman who had inadvertently thrown away Mark Rothko line drawings worth a few million dollars in order to make more room for the vacuum cleaner.

As Renee and I talked, I tried to find out why she wanted to get married again. "So are you going to have a big wedding ceremony, or what?" I asked, remembering what Renee's first wedding had been like.

"No," she said, still sounding excited. "We're not doing any of that. Nothing crazy, and definitely no big gathering."

"What are you going to do, get married at City Hall?"

"Yes, actually."

"Really?" I said, surprised.

"Yes, we're going to go over to the Monmouth County Court House and get married in a civil ceremony by a judge."

"What, no guests?"

"No, you see, Elliot," she continued, speaking with conviction, "I've already had a big wedding. This is something different for me. This is something that Yuri and I just want to do, but without all the complications and the plans and—"

"And the family?" I interjected.

"Yeah," she sighed, "I suppose it's that, as well."

"How are Rachelle and Goldie, anyway?" I asked, the names of my older sisters sounding weirdly foreign to my ears. There had been an utter lack of communication between us since the early 1980s. I was convinced that my two older sisters and their families judged me harshly because I was a gay man who lived with my love and best friend. The AIDS crisis certainly hadn't helped things, either.

"I haven't heard much from them the past few years, Elli. Your guess is as good as mine. I suppose we have to assume no news is good news, right?"

"Well, I haven't heard a goddamn peep from either of them since after they came to the housewarming party at our apartment. I expect that they were more interested in seeing the big apartment than in seeing me. After all," I said, bitterly, "it's only been about eight years since I've heard from them."

Renee agreed, and I could tell from her voice that she probably felt as hurt by our older sisters as I did.

But then I asked the question I could no longer avoid saying out loud. "And what about Momma? Does she know you're marrying a kosher brisket?"

"No, no, Momma's getting too old for that kind of thing now, Elliot," Renee said. "She's really started to slow down quite a bit, Elliot. And whenever I go over to check in on her at the apartment, she always seems so scattered."

"So what?" I blurted out. "Scattered? You just described Momma's entire life!"

"Well, anyway," Renee said, sounding like she wanted to drop the subject of our mother, "I thought you might like to hear my happy news."

"No, you're right, I know, I'm sorry. I'm a putz. Believe me, sis, I'm thrilled for you. But tell me—and I have to ask, because I'm not only your big brother, but also Momma's rabbi savior. Are you doing this because you really love him?"

Without hesitation, Renee responded, "Yes, I love him, Elliot, I really do.

And he loves me." She sounded so happy, and happiness was all I ever wanted for her.

"Then you have my undying support and love. You deserve it, kid."

"Thanks, big brother," she said, still the little girl who had followed me around our Brooklyn neighborhood so many years ago.

Living in an expensive city like New York, we were always looking for work. We had been able to earn a nice chunk of change by licensing *The Music Keeper* to a Polish film company that produced a Polish-language version of our play for TV. The money had kept us afloat for about eight months, but then we were right back to where we started.

For about a year, I supplemented my salary at the New School with money from interior design jobs; I also did some mural work to keep up with the rent and bills. But then I got a good break from an associate of mine at the New School, a professor of comparative literature named Dorie Benning. Dorie also taught at the New York Institute of Technology, and she managed to talk the chairman of the humanities department into offering me a job teaching my "Absurd, Twisted Humor" course there. By 1991, I was earning a reasonable living, shuttling between the New School and at NYIT's Long Island campus.

Spending more time on Long Island, I forged relationships with other creative folk at the college. As a result of my new friendships, I managed to secure the use of the John Drew Theater out in East Hampton during the summer of 1988. The year before, André had worked on a play in Belgium and had connected with the widow and daughter of the beloved songwriter Jacques Brel. After asking their permission to create our own English-language musical revue, using several of Brel's French-language songs that were as yet unknown in the US, André and I wound up writing a new piece that we called *Jacques Brel Blues*.

Dorie was taking a long tour of Europe, so we stayed at her summer house in the Hamptons. The show premiered in August, and it went over well with the audience, but not with the local critics. André was angered by the jeering reviews, and heaped contempt on what he felt was the provincial ignorance of the Long Island theater scene. I wasn't bothered by it, though. By then, I cared more about how actual people responded to whatever we put on the stage. That was ultimately what mattered to me the most, and it certainly provided me with the validation I felt was necessary to continue putting pen to paper and pages on stages.

André felt differently. Despite his slow start, André's reputation had grown steadily since his return to the United States. By the early 1990s, he had firmly established himself as a sensitive and innovative director, doing sensational work at various regional theaters, including Goodspeed in Connecticut and the Ubu Repertory Theater and the Manhattan Theater Club in New York. He had cultivated an especially good relationship with the Vineyard Theatre, directing at least one play for them—and often more—each season. The Vineyard Theatre provided a comfortable creative environment that was very close to the one André had once enjoyed at the Théâtre National in Belgium. Just as he'd had access to some of the best actors in Europe, at the Vineyard André had the opportunity to direct many equally brilliant young American actors, including Christine Baranski and Griffin Dunne in their first New York theater performances. As work picked up in the States, he began to accept less work overseas, preferring to increase his presence in New York.

Still, even with his newfound success, André was frustrated with certain aspects of his career. Too often, he was overlooked or exploited by his employers or colleagues. Sometimes, he was flat-out abused. One time, an off-Broadway theater was putting together a production of a new work by an esteemed playwright. The playwright had specifically requested that André be engaged to direct the new work, and André had excitedly begun preproduction, developing his ideas for the play. Then the producer of the play was able to cast a certain Big-Name Actress for the lead. Shortly afterward, the producer told André that he was being let go from the production because Big-Name Actress felt that his approach "didn't quite work" for her. Another director had been hired—one who had worked with Big-Name Actress before, and was rumored to be sleeping with her. The writer was powerless to stop the personnel change, since her play needed the support of a producer, and the producer needed Big-Name Actress, and Big-Name Actress needed her lover.

André was very disappointed, but he accepted the situation like a gentleman. Curious to see how the play had turned out, he took me to see it a few weeks into its run. Only a few minutes into the performance, André went pale with rage and stormed out of the theater. Rushing after him, I asked what was wrong. "That show," he said, his face flushed with anger, "the entire direction, the lighting, the use of the scenery, the delivery of the actors' lines—all of it comes straight from the notes I worked out with the playwright. The director, he must have taken my notes on the show and used them. He stole my entire concept. That is *my* vision up there on the stage!"

He was furious, and yet there was nothing he could do. Instead, he had to watch as his version of the show became a hit and was taken to Broadway with the Big-Name Actress and her handpicked fraud of a director. Unfortunately, this was not an isolated occurrence. One night soon after we'd heard that the play had gone to Broadway, I came home and found André two bottles of wine in. I told him how sorry I was about the production. "Forget it," he slurred. "This is not the first time this has happened to me, you know. It is nothing new."

"What do you mean?" I asked, puzzled.

"Well," he said, nearly falling off the couch, "look at my hand. How many fingers am I holding up?"

"Five," I said.

"That is how many times this has happened to me in my career," he said, nodding his head dramatically and sounding almost amused.

I was shocked. He had never mentioned any of this to me before. "How come you never told me about it, André?"

"Because," he said, suddenly very sullen, "because, Elliot, there is nothing I can do about it. I want to keep working in this town, so I do not complain. I do what I need to do to make everybody happy. So everybody is happy— except me." His voice suddenly broke, as he choked back tears. "I am ashamed, Elliot. Goddamn it! I wanted to finally have my work on Broadway. I thought, after all this time, I had earned it. But they stole it from me, Elliot, the heart- less bastards." Then he got up from the couch, and shuffled off to bed.

He had always liked to drink, but as the years went on he became an even heavier drinker. In addition to the wine he drank by the bottle at night, he started to have a little bourbon, and to take uppers or downers according to his mood. It numbed him, I guess, and made it possible for him to carry on. Gradually, André seemed to accept his lot. "I do not think that I am meant to achieve more than this, Elliot," he told me. "I am a journeyman, one of those artists for whom the art itself has to be the final reward. And you know, I think I am at peace with that now."

He had also learned to keep a stiff upper lip when his vision was second-guessed or rejected, either by a star actor or by a producer. No matter how much these interventions hurt and humiliated him—and they did—he never complained in front of his colleagues. Perhaps if he had fought back a little more, he might have gotten himself closer to Broadway. It just wasn't André's style to be confrontational, though, and consequently he never quite managed to put himself over the top.

André might have convinced the rest of the world that he was resigned to his fate. But I lived with him, and I knew how sad and broken he often felt. He had a more successful career than I did at that point, but I knew he needed me to be there for him and to check on him and to stay strong for him—especially when I knew in my heart that he was very often ready to fall to pieces.

Preoccupied with the restrictions put on him, and busy with his own more high-profile work, André had little time for my offbeat projects. Our last attempt to work together—on a project called *Big Breaks,* which was to be a largely improvised movie about starving artists—didn't attract investors, and thus never made it off the ground. So, in between teaching gigs, I began to strike out on my own, developing my own crazy ideas and trying to get other people to help me run with them.

We were like caged mice, and the wheel that kept us running in a ceaseless spin, moving nowhere fast, was the entertainment industry. And yet I wasn't ready to get off the wheel. The art of storytelling, of making people laugh, remained irresistible to me. I knew I still had more to give.

⚙   ⚙   ⚙

Teaching year after year—and spending so much time sitting on my keister, either typing out ideas for short stories, novels, film scripts, or watching various TV programs—had made me gain weight. It also didn't help that none of my projects seemed to be moving forward, and that I had been using antidepressants and not really tending to my body in any kind of responsible way. About a year after we stopped attending the funerals of friends and colleagues who died of AIDS, I stepped on a scale in the bathroom and realized that I had put on nearly seventy pounds. I wasn't entirely concerned. With so many around us growing gaunt and emaciated from AIDS, it gave me a small measure of satisfaction and control to know that I was gaining weight. In some absurd way, it led me to believe that my ability to keep weight on my body meant I wasn't going to get sick and die. Totally self-deluded bullshit, of course, but it worked for me. I also recalled that after I'd gotten down to a svelte 175 pounds years before, André had told me that he actually preferred me as a heavier guy—as a *bear*, as the type was known in the gay community.

Saddled with my new weight, I half-hoped that André would want me sexually again. No such luck, though. Feeling increasingly lonesome and unloved, I had sought refuge in food, just as I had back in my youth in Brooklyn. My stomach felt tight like a medicine ball, but had in fact become flabby and distended. After my morning showers, I would walk slowly around the apartment with a towel draped around my fat midriff, the free end slung over my shoulder, looking like one of the Roman senators written about in ancient history books. Then I would go to the large bedroom mirror and see my low-slung and increasingly toneless and tubby gut staring back at me in mute accusation. My body was rapidly turning into a large planet of fat, a repository for all the disappointments and sadness that had invaded our lives in recent years.

With everything that was happening, it came as quite a blow when our beloved dog Shayna—the source of so much comfort—died in the spring of 1989. She had stopped eating, and was having trouble walking. After we brought her to the vet and had some x-rays done, Shayna was diagnosed with kidney cancer. Shayna had been like a child to us, and it was devastating to lose her. André had been especially traumatized when she passed away. We had purchased her a cushiony dog bed to make her more comfortable. In her final days, André would lie down on the floor next to her, petting her increasingly frail body with tender little strokes and kissing her lovingly on the top of her head. When the time came to put Shayna out of her misery, André had refused to come with me to the vet's office. I tried to convince him to come, believing in my heart that Shayna might wonder where André was in her final moments, just as my father had wondered about Momma when she never came to say goodbye. But André had told me he couldn't bear to go and see his beautiful Shayna suffer like that.

About a month after we lost Shayna, I missed her so much and I could see that her absence was still affecting André. He came home one day and was surprised to see me with a brand-new Yorkie that I had picked up a pet shop earlier that day. "Meet our new baby, Molly," I said. I'd named her after Molly Picon, a great star of the Yiddish theater scene in New York. Molly was barely six months old, according to the vet. André played with her a bit, but I could see his heart wasn't really in it. He still missed Shayna, and it was hard for him to accept this new dog and give her love and devotion as he had lavished on Shayna. Molly was much more my dog than *our* dog, at least for the first few years.

We found new ways to console ourselves in those troubled times. André began to focus intensely on the study of Zen Buddhism. In his quest for spiritual solace, and increasingly estranged from the Catholic faith, André had also explored Transcendental Meditation, where he picked up the notion of the mantra and incorporated it into his meditation regimen. "You need to empty your mind of all thought," he said, "and just pick a word to be your mantra. Say the word over and over to yourself with your eyes closed, and concentrate on your breathing. Let the world go and embrace the inner silence."

He often asked me to join him in meditating at the apartment each morning and each night. One evening, I tried it, sitting cross-legged across from him on the shag carpet in our living room. I wasn't wearing a shirt, so the added weight around my stomach was hard to miss. André looked at me sitting that way and said with a teasing chuckle, "It is uncanny, Elliot, how much you look like the Buddha."

Yeah, eat your heart out, you Buddhist Belgian bastard, I thought. "Gee, thanks!" I said.

We lit some candles, burnt some sandalwood-scented incense, and began our quest for inner silence. Unfortunately, Molly Picon had other ideas. Seeing us sitting completely still on the floor meant only one thing to Molly— playtime! We didn't get more than two minutes into the meditation before Molly was hopping back and forth between us, licking at the fronts of our crossed legs, and giving little "Hey, what about me?" barks while jumping into our laps.

"Listen, I don't think this is going to work," I said.

"I know," he said, ruefully. "Molly always makes so much noise. Shayna would not have interrupted us like this."

I ignored his hostility toward Molly, and put my shirt and jeans on so I could take her outside for a walk. That was more my speed, anyway, when it came to issues of the mind. Meditation seemed to encourage the abandonment of all thought, but I liked to keep my thoughts buzzing all around me—like bees drawn to honey.

"Did you at least pick out a mantra for yourself?" André asked.

"Yeah," I responded. "I picked 'egg cream.'"

He had waved his hands swiftly back and forth. "No, Elliot. But you are not supposed to share the word with *anybody.*"

"I'll not only share the word with you," I replied, "I'll share the egg cream with you if you like. I'm going to get one while I'm out. Want one?"

"No," he said, returning to his peaceful mood, "but please do me a favor, and don't come back to the apartment with Molly for at least a half-hour. Give me my time to meditate. Is that all right?"

"Yep," I said, "no worries, no interruptions, no disruptions, no eruptions, no problem."

No way, I thought as I scooped up Molly and we left the apartment. *I give him a week before he gives up on this meditation shit.* A week later, he was still meditating—and I was still eating too much.

We had always relied on pot, alcohol, and TV to help get us through tough times, but there were now a few advances in technology that offered new ways to numb the pains of life. I was immediately intrigued by MTV, a cable channel that turned the "music video" into the principal vehicle for pop music. The music video was a fun way to experience new music, and it changed how music was marketed. It was also a medium that attracted some of the top movie directors of the 1970s—Francis Ford Coppola, John Landis, Martin Scorsese, Brian De Palma, and even André's one-time colleague William Friedkin—who made what could only be described as mini-movies set to music.

And of all the artists MTV promoted, there was no one quite like Madonna. Though not a trained vocalist, Madonna did possess a great sense of style. She was one of the first to recognize MTV as a playhouse in which she could continually reinvent what it was to be a female pop star. We loved her in part because she helped bring gay and lesbian images into the main-stream, borrowing from our club culture to create some of her most iconic hits. Her music videos made every kind of human sexuality acceptable—or at least, with the help of MTV, *visible.* Madonna took sex itself back out of the closet through her videos—and most of America, gay and straight, real-ly liked what they saw. Most important, her slickly produced electronic dance music brought back the joy and freedom that the gay community had lost in the dark early years of the AIDS epidemic. André and I were definite-ly fans of her work.

André and I had always had a collection of vinyl records, but we also wound up buying ourselves a CD player. It was amazing how clear the sound was on these discs—no scratches or audible pops like you would hear on LPs after sev-eral listens. Some of the first CDs we bought were records by the Beatles, who were being reintroduced to the buying public again. After a few listens, I decid-ed my favorite Beatles song was "Help!," sung by John Lennon. André's favorite Beatles song was "Yesterday," sung by Paul McCartney. We enjoyed the novelty of the CDs, though we never did get rid of our many records.

The most important addition to our entertainment arsenal for me, how-ever, was the VCR. Cable had been exciting, but the VCR allowed everyone to turn their private residences into home movie theaters. We set up a mem-bership at the neighborhood video rental store, so it was easy to get all kinds of movies to watch. I was like a kid let loose in a candy store; I must have watched at least one movie on videotape a day. I watched everything, but mostly I revisited the films I had loved when I was younger. Marx Brothers movies, Barbara Streisand movies, *The Wizard of Oz,* and any other Judy Gar-land movies I could get my hands on. The VCR was my new drug. I loved the thrill of turning out the lights and losing myself in film after film, sitting on the couch with Molly on my lap.

While I went to the VCR to get my daily fix, André wasn't really that interested in it. He kept me company a few times when we first got the VCR, but fell asleep on the couch midway through each film. Afterwards, when I wanted to watch a video, André chose instead to retreat to the bedroom and read with a bottle of wine and a few antidepressant pills.

My near-constant need to disappear into our VCR reminded me a little of my own father. I recalled how, when I was a kid, the only thing that ever seemed to give my father any pleasure was his radio. He was clearly in his own world at those moments, but I remembered how sad he seemed to be, hunkered over that set, trying to lose himself in its transmissions. Maybe if I hadn't been so engrossed in my new obsession, I would have felt sad about myself as well. As it was, I kept my viewing schedule packed so I wouldn't have to think about it too much.

I was particularly excited to rent some of the Italian-made *Hercules* movies from the late 1950s, mostly because they featured a hunk named Steve Reeves. Sitting in the safe darkness of the apartment, I remembered how I had lusted after Reeves when I was a teenager. His thickly muscled chest, steely abs, massive pectorals, sublimely oiled biceps—he turned me on like crazy, and seeing his movies made me feel like a young man all over again.

I had unconsciously begun to use the videos as outlets for my sexual desire. One evening, I found myself made especially horny when watching Elia Kazan's *Splendor in the Grass,* which starred Natalie Wood and a drop-dead gorgeous young Warren Beatty in his feature film debut. It had been so long since I had acknowledged my own pent-up need for sexual release, and I decided to give in. I felt tingly with anticipation as I unzipped my pants and let my fingers do the walking. I yielded to my physical desire—surrendering myself to the frisson that shot through my body as I performed my furtive one-hand dance—when I sensed someone else there in the room. "Oh, sorry, Elliot," André whispered from the entryway to the kitchen, sounding more embarrassed for me than shocked by what he had walked in on. "I thought you were asleep. Sorry to disturb you. Go back to what you were doing. Good night," he said, and he walked back to the bedroom and closed the door.

Well, that's just great, I thought. The mood was broken; the moment, passed; the curtain, fallen. I put myself away in defeat, feeling ridiculous and unfulfilled. Sitting in the dark of the living room, I realized just how isolated and empty I had become. Rather than actually living my life, I was watching others play-act theirs through the prism of Hollywood. I felt unhappy, emotionally abandoned, and utterly bereft of any passion or pleasure in the act of living. The VCR was acting as a shock absorber for the pain of my domestic situation with André. I thought again of Pop, lost in the isolated enjoyment of his radio, and a terrible thought came to me. Was it possible that I had become just like Pop, and André had become just like Momma? Here I was, channeling my desire for affection into these movie viewings, and there was André, coldly oblivious to my needs and dismissive of my unending love for him. The thought was far too disturbing to consider for very long, so I tried to put it out of my mind by continuing to watch the movie. Soon I came to a scene in which Natalie Wood's teenage character is asked by her teacher to read aloud a passage from a William Wordsworth poem. I sat in silence and wondered if Wordsworth's words applied to my own life:

Though nothing can bring back the hour,
Of splendor in the grass, of glory in the flower;
We will grieve not, rather find
Strength in what remains behind.

I hated Wordsworth.

❁   ❁   ❁

"Hello, is this Elliott Landy?"

"Well," I said into the phone, "you got the first name right."

"Oh," the young woman said, sounding a little flustered. "I'm sorry, I was reading from the wrong place on the list here. I mean, um, hi, I am calling from ABC News. I'm looking to speak with a Mr. Elliot . . . *Tiger?* I think that's the name. Yes, is Mr. Elliot Tiger available to speak?"

Didn't I shake this problem in Belgium? I thought, as I recalled seeing my name misspelled on the sign all those years before by the student waiting for me at the train station.

"Actually, the last name is *Tiber,* with a 'b' for boy; not tiger, with a 'g' for girl."

"I'm sorry, sir, I'm nervous," said the voice.

"Not a problem," I said, "Now, what can I do for you? Have I won a trip to Honduras or something? What's this about?"

"My name is Brenda Siegel," she said, "and I'm calling on behalf of the ABC News program *Turning Point.* Our segment producer is putting together a special TV program on the twenty-fifth anniversary of the 1969 Woodstock Festival."

Huh? I thought. *Where did this come from?*

"Who told you to give me a call?"

"John Morris—the gentleman who was in charge of building the stage at the Woodstock concert site—suggested we reach out to you. He told us about you and said we should contact you about your involvement with the Woodstock festival. So we looked you up in the phonebook."

It turned out that John Morris had indeed told the folks at ABC about the family running a dilapidated hovel of a motel in White Lake, just a few miles from Max Yasgur's farm. The motel, and its significance to the festival, had not previously been on the network's radar.

She continued, "Our producers would love to talk with you, Mr. Tiber, about the role you played in the Woodstock scene back in 1969."

I heard what she said, but I wasn't sure how to respond. Ever since I had driven away from the El Monaco, I had always told people about how I'd helped make Woodstock happen. About a year earlier, I'd even made a semi-documentary film called *Ticket to Freedom* about it. The idea had been to intercut short dramatized scenes from my Woodstock experience with comic monologues (by me, of course), some of my original home movie footage of the festival, and reminiscences by other Woodstock participants. André hadn't been interested in directing, so I'd enlisted the help of a great New School film professor named Phil Katzman. I'd gotten the former talk show host Virginia Graham to play an indignant White Laker in one of the reenactments; and through André, we were able to get *Law & Order's* Michael Moriarty as well. And, perhaps most important, I'd been able to secure the participation of my idol, Richie Havens. Richie Havens, who had helped make Woodstock into the miracle it was; Richie Havens, whose song, "Freedom," had launched me on my journey to better things; Richie Havens, the living embodiment of the love-filled Woodstock spirit! He had agreed to appear in the film, doing a panel discussion about the festival with me and a few others in Central Park's Strawberry Fields—very near to where the vigil for John Lennon had been held a decade before. He'd even written some wonderful original music for the film.

With such big names attached, I had had high hopes for the project. I really thought that *Ticket to Freedom* would turn some heads. So I had been severely disappointed when the film was released straight to video. It had seemed as if nobody cared about Woodstock anymore.

And now here, out of the blue, was a woman looking for "Elliot somebody" to find out what he—I—had to do with the festival. I was finally being given the chance to share my story. While I didn't realize it at that moment, I was being given an opportunity to become part of Woodstock history.

After a few moments of awkward silence, the woman on the phone cleared her throat. "Mr. Tiber?"

I took a deep breath and said as casually as I could, "I'd be delighted to, but only on one condition."

"Uh, okay, and what would that be, sir?" she said, nervously.

"First, Brenda, you can start by calling me Elliot," I said. "I may be old enough to be your daddy, but you sure don't have to keep reminding me of it!"

"Okay, then, Elliot," she said, trying it out. "When can we call you back with more questions as a sort of pre-interview?"

"Tell them to call here anytime they want. Just be aware, though, that I never speak on Sundays, and that I'm a gay atheist Jew. Make sure your boss knows it before he or she calls, got me?"

Later that day, the executive producer called to find out more about the place where most of the Woodstock Ventures team had stayed while they had prepared the festival. We discussed how, as president of the Bethel Chamber of Commerce, I had been entitled to sign legal permits to myself for outdoor concert events—and how pivotal that was to Woodstock being able to work. The producer asked if I still had the permit. Luckily, I did. It was one of the valuable items I had given to Renee for safekeeping before I went to Belgium, and had kept in my security box at the bank when I returned. This news seemed to please the producer very much.

And then came the clincher: "Tell me, Elliot, would you be willing to travel back up to White Lake? We'd like to include some on-camera footage of you up there near the original festival site. We'd arrange for transportation, of course."

"Can you also get me a bulletproof vest?" I responded, certain that my return would probably incite a riot, with yours truly offered up as the town's sacrificial deli sandwich.

"Oh, I don't think there will be any need for that," he laughed.

"No, huh?" I asked. "Just wait. You don't know that place like I do. I don't think the years have changed the place all that much."

1993. Freedom revisited. Promoting my Woodstock film *Ticket to Freedom* with Richie Havens, tickets in hand.

❀   ❀   ❀

I told André about the phone call that night over dinner at our favorite Italian restaurant. "The producer said that my story is unique, one that they had yet to hear about in their research."

André just nodded at me, chewing his food slowly and jotting down notes in his dog-eared copy of Shakespeare's *King Lear,* which he was to direct for a repertory company up in Canada that fall. As with all his productions, he was completely immersed in his preparations. I could tell that he was only half-listening to me.

"So anyway," I continued, unfazed by André's apparent lack of interest, "I plan to meet with the segment producer tomorrow morning at the ABC offices."

Still nothing from André.

"I asked them if I could bring Molly with me, and they said that would be fine. And they have also offered to take me upstate in a limo to where my old motel used to be back in White Lake," I continued. "They want to interview me on camera."

"So?"

"So *what,* André? What do you *think?* This is exciting, no? Maybe you can even come with me so you can see what's left of the El Monaco and where Woodstock happened."

"You are *still* willing to put yourself through this Woodstock stuff again?" he asked, staring at me incredulously.

"Yes," I said, without a second's pause. "Damn it, André, I'm proud of what I was able to do that summer, and I'm eager as hell to revisit that crazy but beautiful time in my life."

André kept looking anywhere but at me. "I do not know why you want to do this, Elliot. I think it is a stupid and trivial charade. You have better things to do than to talk about some hippie music festival that people no longer know or care about."

"Bullshit!" I shouted at him, temporarily forgetting that we were in a restaurant. I looked up at the waiter and silently mouthed the word "sorry" before continuing in a somewhat more hushed tone. "You don't know what the fuck you're talking about, you know that? Besides, let's face it. Things haven't exactly been going my way these past few years. You at least have your work as a director. You're plugged into something that you value. Now I have a chance here to share the truth of my life, to bring back memories of something that was very special for me. And you know what? I'm proud of the part I played in helping Woodstock to become real, and I miss the joy and the freedom that experience gave me. Earlier today on the phone with that producer, reliving the memories of that incredible summer, I felt good about myself for the first time in ages. Don't you understand that?"

"Actually, no," André shot back in a bitter whisper, "I do not have a clue in heaven what it is to feel good about anything anymore. All I know is I have this production of *King Lear* that I need to have ready for rehearsal in three weeks. And I simply do not know how I am going to do it. If I make it too bold, the critics will call me an erratic lunatic. And if I make it too accessible, others will invariably take pieces of my own approach and appropriate it for their own artistic success elsewhere. So no, I do not understand this good feeling you have for Woodstock. I do not have that freedom and I probably never will. You will forgive me then, Monsieur Tiber, if I am less than excited about your phone call from ABC television today. I am not some Woodstock groupie, and frankly I think it is beneath you to do this interview."

I sat for a few minutes, as the silence at our table grew. It dawned upon me that, after all these years, André had about as much appreciation for what Woodstock signified to me as my mother did. "I can't believe it," I told André as he poured himself some wine, "but you're about as bad as my mother."

Picking up his copy of *King Lear,* he waved it slowly back and forth in front of my face. "Elliot, you know this play as well as I do. I think that you will be made to look just like the Fool who serves Lear if you carry through with this interview. Do you really want that?"

"Better to be a happy fool than a miserable king," I said, feeling more certain than ever that I was doing the right thing. "Listen, you direct your next play and I'm going to see about setting myself free again. Maybe you can't understand that, but this is as much about who I am as *how* I am."

"I would envy you if I believed that freedom was anything but an illusion."

"Then let's drink, André, to the power of illusions. May it set us free."

It was a strange ending to a strange night. But I was determined to make the most of the meeting at ABC the next day, and intended to follow the media trail wherever it might take me. I had been Eliyahu Teichberg, then Elliot Tiber, and then Super Elli in my most heroic moments. But now I had come back to my truest self, a person I liked, a person who wanted to reach out and touch the world. I was excited to see where this next chapter in my life might take me.

❀   ❀   ❀

"But can a cow actually have an orgasm?"

"Of course," I said, sitting in a wooden chair placed near the original concert site at the farm that had once belonged to my friend Max Yasgur. "I read about it in *National Geographic* when I was a kid. Didn't you read no magazines?" I teased. "Besides, I didn't say that cows had orgasms. I said that the *people* had orgasms as soon as they saw Max's field over here."

"Yes, uh," the twenty-something producer stammered, "it's just that we think it would be better if you didn't use the word 'orgasm.'"

"Okay," I said, playing along, "so what would you like me to say instead?"

"Maybe you could just say that the show organizers all leaped and danced for joy when they saw it."

Are you fuckin' kidding? I thought.

If someone had told me seven months earlier that I would be back in the upstate New York town of Bethel, being interviewed alongside a bunch of cows about the part I had played in saving the 1969 Woodstock festival, I would have thought that person was cuckoo. And yet, there I was.

The crew had already shot footage of me walking alongside the long-empty swimming pool next to what had once been our dilapidated El Monaco motel. Though my motel was still an Italian restaurant, it seemed that Gino Morino, who had bought the place all those years ago with his eight brothers and their families, was no longer around. Instead, ownership of the restaurant had fallen to a single man—and a grumpy one at that.

In fact, he had refused to allow the news crew to shoot near the pool unless he got paid. The producer had given the restaurant owner a hundred dollars in cash, after which he muttered, "You have one hour—and only over by that abandoned swimming pool, understand?" *He could have been Momma, the way he barked out the order,* I thought. *Some things never change.*

We were done in about thirty minutes, and then we headed over to the old Yasgur farm. Of course, my good friend Max had sold his land in Bethel back in 1971 and gone down to Florida, where he died of a heart attack at fifty-three. But the magic was still there. I got goose bumps. I couldn't believe that I was back after so many years. It felt fantastic to be in this place again, sharing the story of how my one phone call helped give birth to the Woodstock festival.

We did five more takes of me explaining the reaction of Mike Lang and his gang when they saw Yasgur's farm—and on each take, I said "orgasm." I didn't care, though. I was going to tell my Woodstock story exactly as I remembered it, and I wasn't going to hold anything back. As luck would have it, *Turning Point* did in fact air my interview intact, "orgasm" and all, right there on national TV. Go figure.

After that first appearance on the ABC special, I received several other media requests. Some came from viewers who had learned about me on the TV show, while others were hand-delivered to me by Alyce Finnell, who still had many New York media contacts. I also was hired by a bunch of colleges to give lectures on Woodstock. Given these new opportunities, I decided it was time to step away from my teaching jobs—they had become too routine, anyway—and spend more time sharing my Woodstock stories.

All the hoopla re-energized me and gave me a sharper presence of mind and sense of personal worth than I had possessed in years. The attention made me feel better about myself as well. I got myself back to the garden, as it were, and started to shed my excess pounds through a happy return to vegetarianism and a healthy embrace of portion control. I began to reinvent myself both physically and spiritually. Recalling during interviews that I had helped deliver a baby right there on the floor of the El Monaco front office during Woodstock, I decided to call myself "Woodstock Daddy." The name stuck, and became a consistent part of my shtick, which played to the best of my twisted, absurdist tendencies.

My interviews took me around the United States and into Europe as well. Along the way, I met up with some old friends. In the days leading up to the twenty-fifth anniversary that summer, I even had the pleasure of reconnecting with Mike Lang, Stan Goldstein, and many of the others from Woodstock Ventures at a reunion in Manhattan. I had asked André to attend the reunion with me, but to my deep disappointment, he had declined. I was particularly hurt, because I had been by his side a few months earlier when André won the Obie Award for Best Director for his work on Polly Pen's musical *Christina Alberta's Father*, staged at the Vineyard Theatre. I had supported him and now I wanted him to support me—and yet he refused to come. Instead, Alyce came with Molly and me. It was very sweet to see everyone again. There were still some very good vibes twenty-five years later. It was really wild to see that we had all aged a bit but were still happily fueled by some of that original Woodstock magic.

I kept telling my story even after the anniversary passed. And I began to make prominent mention of the fact that I was gay. For me, the freedom that I'd won in the summer of '69 owed as much to my coming out as a gay man as it did to the Woodstock festival. More often than not, however, this detail never found its way into any articles or appearances. At the time, the Woodstock story was still very much the property of long-haired heterosexual men. Nobody wanted to hear that a gay man had helped shape the event into the world-famous cultural phenomenon that it had become.

As a result, my sexuality was either edited out or ignored by less-than-enthusiastic producers and show hosts. I bided my time, though, and continued to make appearances and give talks about my various special Woodstock memories. In a direct reversal of First Lady Nancy Reagan's anti-drug "Just Say No" campaign from the 1980s, my own personal mantra during this time was to "Just Say Yes" to every request to share the story of my role in the crazy world of Woodstock. And that's precisely what I did.

❀ ❀ ❀

While all of this new Woodstock activity was going on, Momma was living at the Hebrew Home for the Aged at Riverdale. She had been staying there for the past three years, ever since Renee had realized Momma couldn't live by herself anymore. Of course, Renee and Yuri had suggested that she move in with them, but Momma wouldn't hear of it. She told Renee that she wanted to live alone and die alone, if necessary, with none of her children there.

Renee had come to see me, nearly in tears, and my heart melted. For so many years, I had willfully avoided taking any responsibility for my mother's well-being. I was done with her. I felt terribly guilty about everything that

Renee must have gone through, and so I promised that I would help find a good assisted-living facility for our mother. With the help of Alyce Finell, who knew everyone in the city, I got Momma past the mile-long waiting list at the Hebrew Home for the Aged, a home for elderly New York Jews. Once Momma heard she'd be fed a steady diet of kosher food and have access to a legion of wizened rabbis with God's home phone number memorized, she was willing—and even pleased—to move in. I didn't want Momma to know I had helped out, and Renee promised not to tell.

After years of absence, I began to see Momma again. The visits, of course, did not go very well. The first time, she looked up at me in the doorway and almost smiled before reverting to the same scowl she'd worn when I had left her in Israel. Very slowly and deliberately, she said, "So this is the way you treat a mother." She grumbled a few more indiscernible words under her breath and refused to say anything else. I tried to talk with her about her new home, about all the different things that I had been doing while teaching in Manhattan and on Long Island. Somehow, I thought that she might finally see that I had achieved a satisfying life for myself—even if I wasn't the sperm-donor rabbi of her Jewish-mother fantasy world. But no. She just sat and stewed in her rocking chair, ignoring me and looking out the window.

On my second visit, I tried to get her to venture out to the recreation room by giving one of my humorous talks to the old folks about what it was like to grow up as one of the wild and crazy Teichbergs in the Bensonhurst section of Brooklyn. Talk about a tough room. Most comedians worry that they might die onstage if their acts don't make the audience laugh. This was the opposite: I was afraid that my listeners might tumble forward out of their wheelchairs while I was doing one of my improvised routines. Nearly every old person in that room sat there motionless, staring at me like overmedicated zombies. I could have read a page from the phone book and gotten the same response. It made no difference anyway—Momma still refused to take one step into the recreation room.

When I showed up for the third visit, I told my mother about the ABC interview and the fact that a large number of radio and TV programs wanted to interview me. It was only when I mentioned that the topic of discussion would be the Woodstock festival that she broke her silence by blasting forth with her usual sharp-tongued anger and accusation. It was as if not more than a weekend had passed since we had lived together in White Lake.

"No! No more of your talk about that *verkakte* festival, with all the mud and the traffic. I won't have it!" Momma yelped at me. "So, what do you want I should say? That I'm happy you should tell your stupid stories?"

"It's not like that, Momma," I said, trying in vain to get her to understand me. "These people are interested in what I have to say. There are so many people out there who want to hear about what happened back then in 1969. I'm as surprised as you, but it's really happening."

"It should *never* have happened, you understand me?"

"But Momma," I said, again reasoning with my petulant child of a parent, "don't you understand that without Woodstock, we would never have been able to get out of debt?"

"You, now you talk about how you're Mr. Big Spender, huh? Well, what have you got to show for it now? Where's your money *now*, Eliyahu? Didn't I tell you you'd lose it all? I *told* you. Would it kill you to listen to your mother ever in your whole life?"

My mother stared at me with an expression that almost resembled regret.

"Eliyahu," she continued, "your father would never let this happen. He would try to stop you from opening your mouth to every stranger you meet. He'd use the belt on you!"

Enough, I thought, *I can't take this anymore.* I could no longer ignore the pent-up rage and frustration I'd suffered for decades as a result of this impossible and thoughtless woman. And I could not forget the way she'd slandered and abused my father, a good man who had asked so little of her. Hearing my mother mention my father, I snapped. For the first time in my life, I was ready to stand up to her. She was going to hear me, once and for all.

"There's no way in hell, Momma, that Pop would have done anything but support me on this," I said. "Pop wasn't just my father, you know. He was a *man,* Momma. A strong and beautiful man who did nearly everything he knew to do to make things work—and to make you happy."

"He never gave me one moment of happiness, that man!"

It took every ounce of my strength to keep from strangling her to death. The nerve she had to say such a thing about my father!

"And you! You never gave me any happiness in my life, either! You, the only son of the family, and what do you go and do with yourself? You waste time drawing pictures, writing stories, making the mischief with all those naked filthy hippies that came and nearly destroyed us at that dirty festival with the mud and the garbage in the fields. I have nothing but shame for you. Only a *meshuggeneh* like you would keep reminding the world of the damage you did back there. You be sure and make sure to not tell anyone that I was a part of what you did. To think you want to celebrate such a thing. It's a *shonda*—a disgrace!"

I sighed, looking down at the ground. No matter how much time had passed, she knew exactly how to push my buttons. She had brought me low yet again.

And then from somewhere deep inside myself, I summoned up a second burst of courage. I stood up from my chair, looked Momma right in the eyes, and told her, "You win, Momma. Everything you say about me is correct. You're right. I never did anything that made you happy, just as you never made me happy. When I was a kid, you called me fat and stupid. Well, here I am as a man. I'm still a little fat, but that's only because I escaped your vile clutches and got to find out what *real* food tastes like. And I must still be a little stupid, since I actually thought that coming to visit you here today was a good idea. Face it, Ma, I'm just your pointless loser of a son. I'm never going to be what you want me to be. But you know what? Even after everything you've put me through, I have to say that I'm feeling pretty good about my life at this point. Being a part of Woodstock made me happy, because I discovered that I had a life worth living. And that's why I got the hell away from the motel, and the hell away from you."

"Oy vey, will you listen to him?" my mother wailed at the ceiling, beyond which her invisible Hebrew god sat in judgment. "Hear how he talks—and to his *mother,* no less. You are a disappointment to me, Eliyahu!"

"And you are a disappointment to *me,*" I shot back. I was done with the battle and finished with the war. "Take care of yourself, Momma. It's time for me to go back out there to tell the world about Woodstock. And don't worry, I'll be sure to explain how excited you were to be a part of those three days of peace, love, and music. Oh, and I'll tell folks how you helped all those young people who stayed at our motel for the festival, too!"

"*Feh!* Lies, all lies! You keep me out of your crazy stories about that Woodstock!"

Over the years, I had always come back to this woman, looking for something I could never find—love, support, acceptance. Whatever I thought could happen to open up some type of dialogue between me and my mother was clearly not about to materialize. I got up, left Momma in her room, and never looked back. Finally, after nearly sixty years of trying to win my mother's love, I'd simply had enough.

In January 1995, less than six months after that last encounter with my mother, the phone rang. I picked it up, and could hear right away from Renee's voice that something was wrong.

"She's gone, Elliot," Renee said, her voice broken and raspy with fatigue. "I received a call from Riverdale only a few minutes ago. She passed away early this morning."

"What happened?" I asked. "How did it happen?"

"She went in her sleep. The last few times I visited her, she only sat in her room and looked out the window. I think she just didn't want to live anymore, Elliot."

I heard the words, but I couldn't process them. I felt like an actor in some second-rate movie, trying to indicate to some invisible camera in the room my feelings after hearing the news. The problem was, I didn't have any feelings at all. The sudden news left me bewildered. I was in shock—completely unable to externalize my emotions. I remember hearing Renee tell me that she would call Rachelle and Goldie, and that she would be in touch when plans had been finalized. I mumbled that I understood, but I was still thinking about what had happened. It was official. My mother had died. She was ninety-five years old when she went, and I was fifty-nine. This struck me as entirely appropriate to the oppositional nature of our troubled relationship. In death, as in life, we were total opposites.

I rented a black limousine to take André and me to the funeral on Long Island. Back in the 1940s, Momma had bought four cemetery plots out there for the family. My father either didn't know or didn't care—choosing instead to be buried upstate. In retrospect, I couldn't help seeing this as his ultimate rebellion against her. But once Momma's mind was made up, there was no changing it. With Pop or without him, she was going to be laid to rest in the spot she'd spent hard cash to get.

The entire funeral was a blur to me. I knew that my family—including my sisters Rachelle and Goldie—would be attending. I suspected that my older sisters would be irritated that I had brought André to the funeral, but I didn't really care. Still, there was no way I was going to be able to get through the day with my mind clear. So early that morning, after I'd showered and gotten into a suit, I grabbed a large pinch of marijuana and took about ten strong hits off my small glass bong. André, sensing the kind of day he was also going to have, joined me. By the time the car showed up at our apartment building, we were both safely cocooned inside our own respective pot bubbles.

I found myself totally numb as we walked into the temple, and I did little more than stare into space during the funeral service. My sisters, especially Renee, were tearful, holding onto their husbands. All I could hope was that we would get from the temple to the cemetery without any major incidents. The rabbi asked if I would say a few words about my mother, but I politely declined and left the eulogies to my sisters.

It felt as if I'd been put in some strange dream. Before I could even register what was happening, I found myself standing over Momma's grave with a shovel of dirt in my hands. I slowly dropped the dirt across the top of the casket, and walked away from my gathered family. I didn't open my mouth until André and I were in the limo, being driven back to Manhattan on the Long Island Expressway.

How many times in my life have I wished that woman dead? I thought to myself. Now that it had happened, though, I felt neither sadness nor joy. She was my mother, and yet I had no tears to shed for the woman who had given birth to me. As we rode in silence, André tried to hold my hand, but I pulled away from his touch.

"You know, André," I said finally, "I don't even know what that was today. Some funeral for some old Jewish woman who died in the middle of the night in a nursing home—and I don't even feel upset about it. I don't believe that she's gone. I keep thinking she's going to turn up somewhere along this road, trying to thumb a ride back to the city."

André tried again to hold my hand. This time, I let him.

After another minute, I blurted out the question I had been thinking about my mother for nearly all my life. "What in the hell was *wrong* with that woman?"

"Elliot," André said, after a long and thoughtful pause, "you have to understand something. You don't know what that woman went through in her life before you knew her—before she was your mother. Things happen in life, good and bad. Often bad. There is a part of every person that no one can ever know. It is only fair to realize this."

"Bullshit," I snapped, welling up with anger at his words.

"You know how I prepare my shows, Elliot. The notes I make for the characters?"

"You're going to talk about theater to me now?"

"Please, Elliot. Let me finish," André continued. "As a director, I always write out the lives of my characters, from before they first appear in the play and on the stage. I know where all their vulnerable spots are, all their joys, all the sadnesses. I share these stories with the actor so that we both have an idea of who the person was before the play—and who they will be *after* the play ends. Well, I think this is the same thing here. There was so much that must have happened to your mother that you will never know. That she could never tell you. You told me that she lost nearly her entire family in Russia when she was not even yet an adult.

"What does that do to a young person's mind? How does that affect how she views the world, and how she acts? And now, she is gone. Her story is over, and there cannot ever be a moment when you understand all of it. How can you expect to know? It is a mystery. And what you need to do is accept it. You have to accept that you will never know where that woman came from before she appeared on the stage of your own life as your mother. The only thing you can do is accept, and try to understand. You never know where things will go next in life."

"And us, André?" I asked, thinking about everything at once, "where do you think we're going next?"

He sat quietly for a few moments, and said simply, "Fuck if I know."

Our gentle laughter at his sudden profanity broke the tension a bit, but the reality was inescapable. My momma, Sonia Teichberg—the single hardest person to please in my life and a relentless obstacle to everything I had ever considered deep and true and free—was dead. I had spent my whole life in a titanic rebellion against this broken human being, the source of my rage. With my mother's passing, I had lost the very best excuse for all the setbacks and failures that I had had in the past and might still have in the future. My closest enemy was gone forever. In theory, I should have been elated. In truth, I was scared to death.

19

All the World's a Stage

"I loved the part where the chubby guy kept calling himself a fucking idiot."

That was only one of many enthusiastic observations I shared with André that night in October 1997 as we sat in a downtown Village café. We had just seen *Boogie Nights,* the incredible second film from director Paul Thomas Anderson. The film was a sudden hit, and we were enthralled that someone had actually created a near-epic Hollywood feature film about the pornography industry—especially since we had done our fair share of skin-flick dubbing jobs back in Belgium. All the actors in the film were absolutely first rate, but we were particularly excited to see Philip Seymour Hoffman.

In the movie, Hoffman played Scotty, an overweight schlub of a boom operator. At a New Year's Eve party, Scotty poignantly reveals his homosexuality when he attempts to make out with the film's main character, Dirk Diggler—played by Mark Wahlberg—and is left emotionally devastated after Dirk rejects him. I had met Philip back in 1991, when André directed him in one of his first New York theater performances at the Vineyard. It was clear even then that he was a very sensitive and observant actor. Hoffman's portrayal of a lonely closeted young man with a flabby belly really hit home for me, and the scene led me to reflect on my own life.

Being with André in the coffee shop after the screening that night reminded me of the first time we had met, whiling away the hours in the White Tower only a few blocks away from where we now sat. After nearly thirty years, we still had great conversations whenever we were together. As the years had passed, André and I had fallen into a comfortable relationship. We both led fairly independent lives. André's directing career continued to thrive, and I maintained a busy schedule lecturing about Woodstock around the country. But we still made time for each other, going out to shows or the museums together, or spending a quiet evening at home. We were like an old married couple—stable, comfortable, and sexless.

In the first weeks of 1999, André had been preparing for an English-language production of Molière's comedy *The Learned Ladies*, which he had been engaged to direct at Princeton University's McCarter Theatre. He made out his list of preferences based on the auditions to the casting director in his usual direct and detailed way. As was his method, he spent a good amount of time plotting out interior lives for each character and devising a general scheme for the production design. He was working just as he always had. And yet something was wrong. André hardly spoke to me, preferring instead to stay in the bedroom with the door closed. His skin seemed to be taking on a slight yellowish pallor. And he had little appetite, which I learned that Valentine's Day after bringing lots of fresh produce home to make a healthy celebratory meal.

I put together a big and delicious Waldorf salad with feta cheese omelets on the side.

"C'mon, babe," I said to André, standing in the doorway to the bedroom, "I made us a nice salad and some omelets. I didn't even burn anything this time."

He was sitting at his desk, holding his head in one hand and scribbling little notes in his notebook with the other. He seemed not to hear me. "André?" I asked, as nicely as I could.

"What?" he shouted at me, his eyes looking more scared than angry. He saw immediately that I was hurt, and he apologized for being so harsh. "What is it, Elliot?" he asked, trying to sound calm, even though he looked slightly irritated.

"Nothing," I said. "I made sort of a Valentine's Day dinner for us and thought you might be hungry."

"No. Sorry, I am not hungry."

"Well, you have to eat *something*," I said, feeling a little worried. "If you don't want what I made, don't worry. We can have it another time. Let's just order in, okay?"

"No, Elliot," he said, pushing himself up out of his chair with more difficulty than I had expected, "I will eat."

We sat down at our dining table, the classical music radio station playing quietly in the background. He picked up his fork and nibbled at his salad and omelet. Molly hopped up on André's lap. Normally, we reprimanded her if she climbed up to get closer to the food on the table. This time, though, neither of us said anything. André looked at Molly, who was excitedly licking his face. Then he dropped his fork down on the plate, told me he didn't feel well, and took Molly in his arms to go lie down in the bedroom.

I finished my meal alone, the classical music my only companion. "Happy Valentine's Day," I said quietly. I didn't understand what was wrong, but I knew something was definitely not right.

André had planned meetings for each day of the following week with his colleagues at the McCarter Theatre. On Wednesday afternoon, he came back early from the theater.

"Are you all right?" I asked.

"Yes," he said, looking away from me. "I must be getting the flu or something. Let me stay in here by myself. I do not want you to catch whatever this is." I didn't get a chance to ask more, because he went to the bedroom and closed the door.

I left him alone for an hour, but then I knocked on the door. There André was, sitting at his desk with his head back. He had a handful of tissues up around his nose, and I could see that he was having a nosebleed. Scattered amid his papers and notebook on the desk were a half-dozen crumpled bunches of tissue, all blotched with blood. "André, you're bleeding," I said, feeling helpless and scared.

"No, no, I am fine, Elliot," he said, "I must have sneezed too hard. It will stop. I need to finish my work on this show."

"But I'm worried about you, honey," I said, trying to get him to stop looking at his work so I could talk with him about it. I sat down on the bed. "Listen, I don't know if you've got the flu or what, but you look terrible," I continued. "I'm serious, André. Your skin's yellow, and you look like you've lost weight. Do you have a fever?" His forehead was beaded with perspiration, and he felt alarmingly warm. "Christ, you're burning up! You have to go a doctor, André," I said. "Seriously, we need to get you checked out."

"Our doctor left," he said, sounding a little spaced out. "Remember? Dr. Gould moved his practice out to Long Island. Bye, Dr. Gould."

His voice had a strange sing-song quality to it, and I thought he might be drunk or stoned. "Are you high on something?" I asked, feeling awkward and square to even ask such a question.

"No, no. Please, Elliot, I am fine," he said. "Need to work, to finish," he said, slurring his words in a way that had become all too familiar over the past drunken months. "Maybe take a rest." I checked on him about an hour later. Molly was nestled near his feet on the bed, looking up at him worriedly. I could see that even though he was still sweating, he had begun to shiver in his sleep. I brought a blanket and draped it over him.

I was about to turn off the desk light when I happened to look down at some of his work on the desk. Normally, his handwriting was precise and meticulous. What I saw written across those pages, though, was a disoriented mess. It was full of partial thoughts and sentences, none of which bore any relation to each other. A word that began in his usually elegant script slid down the page vertically as if he had fallen asleep or passed out while writing—which is probably what had happened. Next to a half-filled glass of water, I noticed that there was a clear plastic bag holding a bunch of white tablets. The tablets had the letter "D" imprinted onto them. *What in the hell is this stuff? Why is he taking these?* I thought to myself.

I heard him groaning a bit behind me, so I swiftly put the tablet into my pants pocket and turned around to see how he was doing. André was still half-asleep as he pulled himself slowly out of the bed and into the bathroom. His hand trembled as he opened the bathroom door. He left the door slightly ajar, and I could see he was seated on the bowl. I asked him again if he was all right, but he just groaned again groggily. I heard a weak stream of urine hitting the toilet water, and I wondered if perhaps he had taken too many of those tablets. I didn't know what to do. He got up off the toilet and staggered again out of the bathroom and back toward the bed, not even seeming to realize that I was standing right there in the room with him. In all the time I had known André, he had *never* left a toilet unflushed. I went into the bathroom, and I happened to look down at the bowl as I flushed. André's urine was a dark brown color. I was no doctor, but I knew enough to realize that that was not a good sign.

I decided to call my niece Alyse about what was going on. She thought André might be having an issue with his liver and suggested I take him to a hospital immediately. Ignoring his weak pleas, I got André into his shoes and pulled a warm jacket over him. He lay back down on the bed, groaning. I scanned the bedroom quickly to find his wallet and passport, in case I needed to provide the hospital with proof of his identity before he could receive any medical treatment.

He had great difficulty walking on his own, so I put his arm around my neck and my arm around his waist, and led him out of the apartment building and into a waiting taxi. I could see how hard it was for him to stand up, the sweat beading up and running down his forehead. "Get us to a hospital," I said to the cabbie, hearing the panic in my own voice. "Right away, it's an emergency!"

It was late on a brutally cold mid-February night, so there wasn't much traffic as we drove quickly uptown toward the hospital. As I sat in the back of the taxi, I held André's hand, and I could feel that it was swollen. *Why had I waited so long? Why hadn't I taken him to a doctor sooner?* I kept asking myself. I was nearly hysterical, but I tried my best to keep myself focused.

I knew I was going to have to keep my edge in order to stay by André's side. From the early years of the AIDS crisis, I remembered that gay partners were not recognized as legitimate family in the unblinking eyes of medical bureaucracy, and thus we had no legal right to be with patients. So I had already figured out what to say when I spoke to the admissions nurse.

"Please, help André," I said to the nurse. "I'm his brother."

"If you're his brother," the nurse replied, "then why is his last name 'Ernotte' while your last name is 'Tiber'?"

I quickly made up a story about how he was my younger half-brother, his Belgian father having married my widowed mother long ago. The nurse was satisfied, but she said it might be some time until André could be seen by a doctor. She then asked for André's insurance information, and I had to explain that he had none. Instead, I pulled out my credit card and gave it to her. "I'll pay for anything André needs—I just want my brother taken care of quickly. Can't you see he's in pain?"

Thinking fast, I put my hand in my pocket and felt for the white tablet that I had found on André's desk. I showed the tablet to the nurse, and told her I believed André had been taking them. She looked at the pill and said it was most likely a painkiller called Demerol. Fearing an overdose, she asked how many he had taken. When I said I didn't know, she said she'd get André in front of a doctor as soon as she could.

I sat down next to André, and we waited and waited. I kept my arm wrapped around André's body, so he wouldn't fall forward or tilt over to his side. After a while, though, André seemed a little more lucid than he had been. He looked around slowly as if emerging from a dream, and asked where we were.

"The hospital," I told him. "You're very sick, André. Don't you remember earlier?"

He shook his head.

"André," I asked in a hushed tone, "why have you been taking Demerol?"

"How do you know I—"

"I found them on your desk, André. The nurse told me what it was. What the hell's going on, André?"

"It has been helping me to work," he said. "It stops the pain inside me. Where is that tablet you found?"

"The nurse has it," I told him. "I showed it to her so she could tell me what it was. You had me so worried, and I wanted to make sure what you may have taken."

"So the nurse has it?" he asked.

"Yeah," I said, knowing that he probably wanted it.

"*Merde,*" he said. "I feel awful."

"They'll bring us in soon. Try to rest. I'm here for you."

It was about two in the morning by the time a nurse came out from the examination wing and called out André's name. An orderly was with her, pushing an empty wheelchair. She explained that the doctor was now able to see André.

"You'll have to stay in the waiting room until the doctor is finished with his examination," she said to me. André's nose started to bleed again as the orderly helped him onto the wheelchair. He still seemed disoriented. Once he realized he was being wheeled away from me, he looked terrified and tried to hold on to my hand.

"It's okay. André, it's okay," I said, trying not to burst into tears. "Listen,

I'm going to be right out here waiting for you. They're going to take a look at you so they can see what's wrong and get you healthy. Don't worry, okay? I'm not going anywhere. I'll be here."

He looked at me and nodded hesitantly as they carefully pushed him past the doors and into an examination room. I wanted so badly to go in with him, but all I could do was wait. So I stood among the few others who were also waiting, pacing back and forth—too worried to sit down, and terrified by everything that was happening.

Another hour passed. Finally, a young physician came out and asked to see a Mr. Elliot Tiber. "That's me," I said, worriedly. Dr. Henning, as he quickly introduced himself, was at least six inches shorter than I was, but he had a strong presence and a no-bullshit approach to the job at hand.

"The good news is that your brother wasn't overdosing on Demerol earlier. His blood pressure was very high, but that was because he was severely dehydrated. We've got him on an IV drip now, though, and that should stabilize him so we can find out a little more about what's happening."

"But what *is* happening? What can you tell me, doctor?" I said, urgently.

"Well," he responded in a flat voice, "we'll need to wait a few days for the blood tests, but the preliminary evidence leads me to believe that André is suffering from hepatitis. I don't know what type yet. Could be A, B, or C. Probably hepatitis B, though, from what I can see so far."

"What? How can that be? What would have caused *that?*" I asked, incredulous.

"Actually, it could have been anything." Dr. Henning said. "Hepatitis can be transmitted through blood transfusions, intercourse, or a needle, and in fact, it can be in a person's system for years."

Immediately, my mind turned to the many nights when André had stayed out and away from the apartment. I began to wonder if he had been with other men after we were both proved to be HIV-negative. The old feelings of anger and betrayal I once had now mixed with my far stronger feelings of unconditional care and concern for what André was going through.

"Is there a shot or something that he can take or something?"

"Do you know if he has ever had a vaccination for hepatitis B?" Dr. Henning asked.

"I don't know," I said. "I don't think he has, no."

"Well, do you know if he has been on any medication for any chronic illnesses?" the doctor asked.

"Uh," I said, feeling scared and foolish, "as far as I know, he has never been on any meds for any disease."

Frowning, he then asked, "Has your brother been a big drinker?"

"Uh, he drinks one or two bottles of wine most nights," I said, feeling powerless and dumbstruck.

"That certainly doesn't help things here. He could be suffering from cirrhosis of the liver," he said. "Okay, let's take things one at a time then. Right now in addition to the IV for the dehydration, we're also giving him liquid Demerol for his pain."

"Can I see him?"

"Sure, follow me," he said. "We have him in our post-examination room, and he's asking for you." As I followed him through the doors down a corridor, he continued. "Meanwhile, I'll make sure to share everything we're doing now for your brother with Dr. Schlottman. He's our top liver specialist here, and going forward, he will be the doctor treating André. Okay?" Before I had a chance to respond, he shook my hand and wished us both well.

By then, it was around four in the morning. André was lying on a gurney in a grim, dreary, and windowless room behind the smaller examination cubicles. There were four other patients there, each in their own space separated by long white plastic curtains. As his half-brother, I was allowed to stay with him as we waited for a hospital bed to become available. After a while, I walked over to the nurse sitting behind the desk and asked her about the possibility of getting a private room for André. The nurse advised me that a private room was just under six hundred dollars a day, and would most likely not be fully covered under most health insurance. I told her that I would be paying directly and that money was no object. She assured me that she would look into availability. I sat down next to André's bed; my heart was beating wildly. He looked very uncomfortable, and there was nothing I could do for him other than stay by his side.

After two hours, the nurse hadn't managed to come up with a private room. So I went down to the night admissions office. There, I encountered a surly creep who told me there were no more private rooms, but that for *eight* hundred dollars, André could have a "private suite." Without any thought other than André's comfort, I arranged right there and then for André to have the private luxury suite, the expense charged to my Amex credit card. Once the administrator assured me that Mr. Ernotte would be moved to the room immediately, I went back to the post-examination room. André was up. He looked at me, tears mixing with the sweat on his face, and he said, "I feel so terrible, Elliot. I feel so stupid. What is happening to me? Is it AIDS?"

"No," I said, unsure but ultimately convinced that André didn't have the illness. "They think it's your liver. The doctor thinks it may be hepatitis, but we won't know until they get the tests back. For now, try to relax. Try to sleep."

Finally, an orderly came in to move André to his "suite." What a difference from the room we had left! This room had the decor of an upscale hotel. It was cheerfully wallpapered, and had a big TV hanging from the ceiling. There was a bouquet of fresh flowers and a bathroom close to the bed. It also had two comfortable guest chairs, one of which seemed to be a recliner. Best of all, André was able to see Central Park through the window. He slowly held out his hand to grasp mine. "I'm so glad to be out of that other room," he said.

In spite of the Demerol, André seemed to be in pain. The nurses brought him meals, but André only spooned down some cherry-flavored gelatin and a few sliced carrots, feeling too uncomfortable to eat. Eventually, André put his head back and fell asleep.

Three days passed. Dr. Schlottman, a tall man with thick glasses and a neatly trimmed mustache, came by several times to see how André was doing. Waiting for the test results, the doctor wanted to make sure that André was as comfortable as possible. André understood that everyone was doing their best to help him, and he maintained his natural graciousness despite his discomfort. Because of the Demerol, André slept for hours at a time and would then be awake for two or three hours. I massaged his arms and legs, trying to make him feel better. It was difficult, though, because he was still in pain—and the pain was only getting worse.

On the fourth day after André arrived at the hospital, Dr. Schlottman came to see us. He asked me to step outside into the hallway to talk. The tests had come back, and Dr. Schlottman's suspicions had been confirmed: André had chronic hepatitis B, a condition that had been made worse over time by his drug and alcohol abuse. He explained that André's liver had been irreparably damaged and told me to prepare for the worst.

"We can keep him comfortable, as we are doing now," Dr. Schlottman said. "But I'm not going to lie to you, Mr. Tiber. I'd say that he has perhaps only a few weeks left at most."

Hearing the doctor's abrupt prognosis hit me like a ton of bricks.

"I can't believe that the disease could act this fast," I said.

"He was probably masking his symptoms with the alcohol and the Demerol," Dr. Schlottman pointed out. "If he'd seen a doctor sooner, it would have been easier to identify and treat the disease. And if he'd gotten the vaccine, all this might have been prevented. As it stands now, his liver is in very bad shape."

"I've spoken to some people here," I said, "and I've been told that you guys do liver transplants. If that's true, how can we get the process started? How soon can we get him the transplant? I can pay for it, no problem. Whatever it costs!" I said, almost pleading.

Dr. Schlottman could see that I was suffering greatly, and tried to reassure me. "There's a pretty long wait list for that procedure, but I'll check into it and get back to you. All I can tell you at this point is that we will do the best we can. In the meantime, do you pray?"

"No," I said, dismissively. "I don't believe in God."

"I don't, either. What about your brother, though? Does he pray?"

I was too shaken to answer. Dr. Schlottman patted me gently on the shoulder, and told me he would be back to see us the next day. I stood there, trembling with fear and fury.

Arrangements had to be made. I called Alyce to let her know what the situation was, and Alyce made sure our neighbor, Miriam, could take care of Molly while I was at the hospital with André. Alyce also promised to come to the hospital herself to help out. Then I called Emily Mann, the McCarter Theatre's artistic director, to explain that André wouldn't be able to go forward with the Molière play and to tell her where André's production notes were kept. Emily was quite upset; she and André had become very friendly in the two years since he'd begun to direct works for her.

The next morning, André felt worse. Once he learned from Dr. Schlottman that he had hepatitis B, André actually seemed relieved that there was at least a name for what was happening to him. Over the next four days, though, there was no improvement. In fact, André's kidneys were starting to shut down. Further x-rays revealed that fluid was filling up his lungs. Though he was almost skeletally thin, his stomach was distended and puffed out just under his ribcage. Nothing brought down this bloating.

Dr. Schlottman spoke to me in private again. "Listen, with the loss of liver function," he explained, "all other organs in André's body are also in danger. That's why he's getting worse. With time, even his brain function will start to decline, and he may suffer from bouts of delirium and even dementia. Then there's the heart."

"What about the heart?" I asked, feeling paralyzed by every word he was telling me. "You're saying he has a heart condition now?"

"Elliot," he calmly explained, "the heart is an organ, too. With his liver going out of commission, he faces the very real chance of losing his life even faster as his body continues to shut down. Tell me, does André still stand by his do-not-resuscitate order?"

I nodded, feeling like I was going to faint.

Dr. Schlottman looked me square in the eye. "Listen. You need to act, and fast. Contact André's friends and loved ones, family members, anyone who you think he would want to see—and who you think may want to see him before he goes. And you need to be with him now as much as you can. Make the most of the time you have left with him, because even with a transplant— if he lasts that long, and if I can make it happen—I think we're looking, at best, at another two years of life. You're in the best hospital in the country for a liver transplant. This is the first hospital to have successfully done it. But his quality of life is going to be compromised no matter what. You need to get the word out, Elliot. Your lover doesn't have much longer to go."

"What?" I said, looking at him incredulously. "He's not my lover, he's my—"

"Oh, yeah, that's right, Mr. Tiber," he said. "How silly of me, I meant your 'brother.' Just do what you need to do, okay? There's not much time."

André's pain kept getting worse, and his periods of lucidity were becoming increasingly brief. There were times when he spoke only in French, so I paid to have him attended by a French-speaking nurse, Janet Durand. Janet came in during the day, and I stayed with André through the night, sleeping in the recliner next to his bed. Alyce helped out, too, staying with André in the evenings so I could run back to the apartment to shower and change clothes. I was in agony whenever I left the hospital, worrying that André might pass away without me being there.

I was in such a state of agitation that I wanted to run through the hallways of the hospital screaming. I called Emily Mann back at the McCarter Theatre, and told her that André probably only had another week or two left. She said she would drive into the city to see him, and the news soon began to spread like wildfire throughout the theater community about André's condition.

Over the next few days, a small but sincerely concerned group of actors and designers visited André in the hospital. I was especially pleased to see Phil Katzman come by to visit. Phil was horrified to see the condition that André was in, and he asked me if there was anything he could do. I thanked him, but there really was nothing that any of us could do, other than to visit and spend some time with André.

By this point, André was only able to remain conscious for about an hour at a time. The pain was so intense that it hurt him to even breathe; his discomfort prevented him from being able to speak with the few people who visited. Perhaps word got around that he was already beyond saving. Soon enough, there were no more calls or visits. It made me angry that more people did not come. Where were all the people who had learned so much from André? Why hadn't his colleagues showed up to pay respect and offer support? Hadn't he given them so much of himself over the years?

But Alyce was always there for us. She came to the hospital as often as she could—practically every day and night. Alyce remained in André's room, reading to him, talking to him, and comforting him. Alyce was so generous with her emotional support, and never once cried or showed any weakness. One evening, I was in the hallway walking back toward the room while André was awake. As I approached the entryway into the room, I could hear André speaking with Alyce.

"I am sorry to tell you this, Alyce," André said, his voice made raspy from the pain inside. "I am sorry but for so long, I . . . I never really liked you, Alyce. I think I . . . I was . . . jealous, *jealous* of how you were close with Elliot. I felt left out. But I was wrong, Alyce," he said, his voice weakening a bit, "so wrong. You drop everything in your life and come and sit here with me, day and night—just like Elliot. And you look after my Elliot, and take care of Molly. You are such a wonderful person. I . . . I love you, Alyce, and I am sorry."

Alyce told André everything was good between them and that she loved him, too. Then, in the reflection of the darkened window, I saw Alyce lean over and give André a long and tender hug. I never told her or André what I had heard them say to each other, but my heart was filled with joy for the bond that they forged in those final days.

On the morning of Friday, February 26, less than a week and a half since André had first been admitted to the hospital, I called the Ernottes' home number in Liège. Fanny answered. I told her it was me and that I was calling about André, but then I asked Janet to get on the phone and explain the full situation to her in French. Because his disease was terminal, I had Janet tell Fanny that she and the rest of the family should fly over to New York to come see André as soon as possible. Fanny told Janet that she would take the next flight out of Belgium—unfortunately, the rest of the family lacked current passports, and wouldn't be able to get any on short notice.

When André was awake, I told him that Fanny and his family were coming in from Liège to see him. His eyes opened a little more brightly at the mention of the visit, and he was especially pleased that his mother was coming to be with him before his time was through. "*Maman,*" he whispered a few times before he fell back into sleep.

Fanny arrived the next day and went directly from the airport to the hospital. When she entered the room, Fanny and I looked at each other for the first time in more than fifteen years. Her hair was a little grayer and she had put on a little more weight, but she was still Fanny. We stood in the doorway, hugging each other very tightly as we both began to cry. I was so overcome with emotion that I couldn't think how to speak French to her. Thankfully, Janet explained that André was not dying from AIDS, but that he had hepatitis B and his liver was starting to fail.

Fanny sat by André's bedside and gently stroked his bearded cheeks as he slept. After only a few minutes, he began to stir a bit and open his eyes. It was then that he saw Fanny. He breathed in excitedly and was about to speak, but was overcome. Mother and child were reunited, and the love between them was almost too beautiful and tragic for me to witness. I felt as if I had invaded their private moment.

Later, Fanny left; she was to stay at Alyce's apartment for the duration of her visit. We were alone then, André and I, and he tried to say something to me in the hoarse whisper that was now his speaking voice. But then he was overwhelmed by a wave of pain so strong that he squeezed his eyes shut and bit his tongue so hard that it began to bleed. "Oh, God, Elliot," he whispered, as I wiped the blood from his lips and chin. "God, it hurts. Please. Please, Elliot, the morphine. I need more of it. Tell them, please. The pain is so bad. Help me, I cannot take . . ."

I ran for a nurse. "Please," I begged, with tears in my eyes, "please, he's in so much pain. Can't you give him more morphine? He's suffering. Help him, please."

The nurse saw the despair in my eyes, and immediately increased the morphine dosage, assuring André that he would feel better in a few minutes. He nodded, eyes closed in pain. I held his hand. "It's going to be okay, André," I whispered over and over again—even a good half-hour after the morphine had already knocked him out.

Fanny stayed another two days, taking over so that Janet could get a few days off. I called Renee while André was asleep and told her what was happening. "Oh, no," she said, and I could hear that she was close to tears. "I thought that he looked so happy and healthy when you were here for Hanukkah," she said. I told her that André probably wasn't going to last more than a week or two. Even saying those words into the phone nearly took my breath away—Renee and I both couldn't believe that he was already so sick. "Are you taking care of yourself, Elliot?" she asked, sounding more concerned for me than for him. "I just want to make sure that you keep yourself safe and healthy."

"I'm fine, sis," I assured her. "Do you think you and Yuri can come to see him?"

There was silence. "I'll try, but I don't know, Elliot," Renee said. "I adore

André, but I don't know if I can handle it. Especially now with Rachelle being so sick."

"Rachelle's sick?" I asked, surprised. "What's wrong with her?"

"It's cancer, Elliot," Renee said. "Honestly, I didn't know if I should tell you or not but in light of what's happening with André—well, I figure you have the right to know, even though it's been years since you've talked to her or seen her."

Now it was time for me to be silent. "Yeah, well," I said, unsure how I felt, "I'll have to think about this. I'm so overwhelmed with André right now."

Renee said she understood. We were both being beaten down pretty hard by life. We agreed that we would each do what we needed to do, and not judge each other for it. Renee would see to Rachelle and keep in touch with Goldie and her family, and I would see to André—and when it was all over, we'd get in touch.

Alyce was napping on the recliner on the final day of Fanny's visit. I sat on the edge of the bed, massaging André's arms and caressing his head. He was no longer able to eat any solid foods, so the IV provided his only sustenance. When he was lucid during those few days, he talked to me about his life and how disappointed he had been by much of it. "What did I ever really accomplish, Elliot?" he said, a sad and bitter look on his face. "Who will remember me or my work in ten or twenty years? Who remembers me even now? Why have so many of my friends not come here to see me? Do any of them know that I am sick? Maybe I have been fooling myself all these years. Maybe I am just one more director among thousands of other directors who tried to leave a mark but who missed the prize."

"Don't you dare think that way about yourself, you understand?" I said, suddenly feeling fiercely protective of him. "You're no failure. You are an amazing man, a remarkable artist. And don't you worry, André—there were a number of people who came by earlier when you were out of it. I'm sure that word is getting around and you will start to hear from more people before you know it."

He turned his head to the side and tried to rest. Later that Sunday, Fanny came to see her son for what we all knew would be the last time. As they held hands, I saw again what a real and lasting love between a mother and son looked like. I was so glad that André and Fanny had had those days together.

Before she left for the airport, Fanny pulled from her purse an old notebook. She brought it over to André and put it gently against his chest. He opened his eyes and looked at Fanny. As he thumbed through the notebook, a sad expression crossed his face. He looked up at me and said tearfully, "Elliot, look . . . one of my poetry books from when I was a boy." As he looked at his mother, he said to her, "You kept my poetry."

"I have kept almost everything you have ever done, my beautiful son," she said. To the world, he was a man of fifty-four, but to Fanny, André was still her child. *"Je t'aime, mon fils,"* she said, and then she began to sob, burying her face in the crook of his neck. I looked at Alyce, and we quietly excused ourselves from the room. Ten minutes later, Fanny emerged. Her eyes were red with tears, and it looked like she was almost ready to buckle under the weight of the moment. I was about to ask Fanny if she wanted me to take the taxi with her back to the airport, but Alyce piped in and made the same offer before I had the chance to suggest it. Perhaps she was reading my mind. As I hugged Fanny goodbye, she held my face in her hands just as she had when we left Belgium so many years before. And just as she had done then, she said to me, "You bring my André back home to me, my sweet Elliot."

"I promise, Momma."

She kissed my cheek tenderly, and then she left to return to Belgium. I looked in on André, who had laid the old notebook open across his chest. Who would visit him now, in his last days? I decided to take action.

❁   ❁   ❁

"Well, good afternoon, Mr. Ernotte," said one of the friendlier nurses. "Wow, it seems that you have received some very special deliveries today."

It was Tuesday, March 2—two days after Fanny had left. As André awoke slowly at the sound of the nurse's voice, I chimed in. "That's right, babe. They've been coming all day while you were sleeping. Let's take a look, shall we?" Scanning the room, André was treated to the glorious sight of a half-dozen beautiful flower arrangements—yellow roses, pink lilies, purple orchids, and large white daisies. It was a positively gorgeous sight to behold, and it made André smile.

"Well, what in the world can *these* be?" I asked.

"I do not know, *mon cheri*," André said, curious. "Who are these from? Are notes attached?"

"Let's check." I picked up the large bouquet of plump and full yellow roses over by the window, and looked around for a note. I found one addressed to "M. Ernotte" pinned to the front. "Look, it's for you," I said to André, "maybe it's from someone back in Belgium or perhaps in France. Why not open it and see?"

André looked a little confused, but I could tell he was as pleased and excited as his weakened state would allow. He pulled open the envelope and was delighted to see that he had received a "Get well" note from none other than Annie Cordy, our great Mimi from *Rue Haute*. "Well?" I said. "Go ahead and read the note."

"Yes, I will," said André, reaching slowly for his glasses. "Interesting," he said, "the note is typed in English. Perhaps she thinks I have forgotten my French by now," André supposed. I rubbed a sliver of ice from the hospital cup across his lips, since they were so dry and his voice was raspy. "It reads, 'My dearest André, I heard from our colleagues here in Belgium that you have taken ill. I am so very sorry to hear it, my good friend. I hope you will be better soon. I want you to know that I learned more from you about acting in our time on *Rue Haute* than from anyone else. You are a saint, and I will always adore you. From your loving 'Mimi,' always. Annie C.'"

We looked at the other floral arrangements, and André grew happier as he read each note. The senders were all European. "I guess with the distance, it still takes time for word to get around about certain things," I said. "Who's that card from?"

"This one is from Bert Struys," André said slowly. "He writes he is living in Austria and found out I was sick through Annie. I find it hard to read this one. He wrote it in script—and in English, too. How strange! But it looks like it reads, 'I owe my career to you, and I wish you a speedy recovery from your illness.' At least, I *think* that is what that last word is. I guess that is right, yes," André said. "Wow, it is remarkable that he remembers me."

"That's right," I said, moving on to the next bouquet. "Hey, who's this from?" I said, placing a bouquet of purple mountain lilies on the rolling table top next to André's bed.

He rested for a few moments, then smiled again and opened the note. "What? I cannot believe it!" he said.

"Huh? What? Who sent this one?" I asked, excited to see what he was so pleased about.

"This is amazing, Elliot. These special Queen Fabiola lilies have been sent here by Queen Fabiola of Belgium herself. I can understand why *this* note is typed. After all, she is the queen."

"Wow, look at that!" I said, duly impressed. "Well, you've been remembered by your country's queen. But when did you ever meet her?"

"I told you about that," André said, coughing a little. "Do you remember she was at the opening of our show *Attention: Fragile?*"

"Oh, yeah, that's right," I said. "Christ, I totally forgot about her."

André read the note carefully, and grew very quiet. "What a lovely note, but—"

"But *what?*" I said, unsure what he was thinking.

"Nothing, I guess," he said, sounding a bit puzzled. "I find it strange that she misspelled her own name in the note."

"Really? Show me. Where?"

"Look right here." He pointed to the spelling of the Queen's name on the note in the envelope. "Her name has only one 'b,' but this spelling here features two 'b's in the name."

"Huh," I said, shaking my head. "Well, you know what they say—two 'b's or not two 'b's."

"That *is* the question—yes, Elliot?"

"Uh-huh, yeah," I said, quickly turning around to the chair behind me and picking up the delicate vase of large white daisies. "Want to see who else cares enough to send you a card and flowers? What about *this* one?"

André looked at the envelope happily, slowly opened it, and began to read the note inside to himself.

"Who's it from?" I asked.

André looked at me from over his reading glasses. After a few long seconds, he sighed and began to smile a little. "Elliot," he said "I know."

"You know?"

"Yes, I know."

"Know what?" I said, getting a little fidgety. "Oh, you know who the note's from? Well, don't keep me in suspense. Tell me who it is."

"Elliot," he said again, shaking his head and laughing quietly. "I know this is you."

"Me? What?"

"You are the one who sent me all these beautiful bouquets and notes."

"Me? No, what are you kidding? Where do you get that idea from? I think that morphine's making you a little loopy. How silly!"

"Elliot," André said, speaking to me in that calm way that always gave him the upper hand. "This note is written from Mort Shuman."

"Mort? Good ol' Mort? Hey, that's great. I knew if anyone was going to reach out and wish you well, it would definitely be our good friend Mr. Shuman."

"El, honey," André said, smiling but too weak to laugh. "Mort Shuman died in 1991."

Oh, shit! I thought.

"Really, are you sure about that, André? I think you may be wrong."

I'm such a fucking idiot!

"No, I am correct," André said. "Sadly correct, but correct all the same."

"Wow, that's such a shock," I lied, trying desperately to cover up my ruse. "So you're saying that Mort is—"

"Yes, Mort is *mort,* as we say in French."

Well, he had found me out. The day before, I had made up notes from people who had been important to André. But running on a lack of sleep and trying to organize the six separate arrangements from the florist at the same time, I had messed up by including Mort.

"I'm sorry, babe," I told André, "I didn't mean to trick you. It's just that I wanted to make you—"

"Feel better, I know," André said, nodding his head gently. "But you have, Elliot, by going to all this trouble in order to make me feel happy, wanted, remembered. That is so beautiful, El. I know that you love me. And that is more important to me than anything from anyone else in the world. Thank you, my love. You are the best thing in my life, the best part of my life."

"I love you too, André," I said. "I always have, and I always will."

We kissed gently on the lips, surrounded by the floral arrangements I had summoned. Then I sat right next him and we held hands until André was safely asleep in the land of morphine.

It had only been about two and a half weeks since I had brought André to the hospital, but it felt like it had been months. André's health continued to go downhill. When he was conscious, he could barely talk above a whisper, and I could see he had resigned himself to his fate. I had fresh arrangements of roses brought to the room every day. After all, roses had always been his favorite. To further ease his mind and perhaps make him feel a little more like he was back with me and Molly at the apartment, I taped many of André's favorite songs from our records and CDs—the music of Jacques Brel, the torch songs of Billie Holiday, the beautiful song "Somewhere" from *West Side Story*—and brought these mix tapes to the hospital. Each day I played him songs that had been a strong part of the fabric that wove our private lives together, hoping that the music would somehow comfort him.

It was on the third weekend at the hospital that André, in great pain, asked to see Molly one last time. I knew there was no way the hospital would permit a pet to visit. So I got our neighbor Miriam to dress up like an old woman—the better to deflect attention—and sneak Molly into André's room. Her costume and makeup were so effective that a nurse personally escorted her to André's room, Molly hidden out of sight in a tote bag.

Once Miriam arrived, Alyce and I snapped into action. Alyce stood guard outside the door as I carefully brought Molly over to André. Molly was very excited to see André after all those days away from him. Molly's little tail went wild as André spoke to her and held her close to his chest. After only about ten minutes, depleted by the effort, he fell asleep with a sweet smile on his face. I thanked Miriam and told her what a wonderful thing she had done for André. Being able to grant André's small wish to see Molly that last time was a blessing.

Two days later, Dr. Schlottman came to see me. "I'm sorry, Elliot," he said, "but André is no longer a viable transplant candidate. His system is too far gone." Dr. Schlottman felt that with André's body in such a state of exhaustion, he might not make it through the night. "His vital signs show the end is near. Elliot," he said. "It's happening."

Alyce gave me a hug. "At least he won't be in pain anymore," she said. She went over to André, kissed his forehead, and left the room. My eyes filled with tears as I sat down next to the bed. André's eyes were closed, but it was obvious that he was in pain. He tried to say something. I put my ear close to his mouth to hear him.

André opened his eyes, looked at me calmly and whispered, "Elliot, please . . . ask . . . a priest . . . a priest before . . . before I . . ."

He was unable to continue. I went out into the hallway and told Alyce. Amazingly, she returned in fifteen minutes with a priest in tow. As the priest said the last rites in a low voice, I wept quietly to myself. His pain had been terrible, but it was coming to an end.

The priest and Alyce left, and I was alone with my love—my brother—my best friend of almost thirty years—for the last time. I held André's hand in mine. His eyes were closed. I reflected on all the years we had been together, most of them good. I started to talk to him, sharing my feelings in a way that I had never been able to before. "André, honey, it's been a hard road for us both. I know that neither of us have been perfect, and I know we've both caused each other pain over the years. But I want you to know that I wouldn't have walked away from *any* of it. I don't know where you're going, my love, but I will never forget you. In my heart, you'll always be alive. You'll always be my beautiful André. Always, always, always."

I laid my head down on his arm for several minutes as his breathing grew shallower and shallower. Then he stopped breathing entirely. I looked down at the love of my life, lying still and quiet in the bed. His unbearable pain was over at last. I looked around the room, saw the many bouquets of roses, and noticed the whiteness of the curtains that hung across the window. André Gilbert Ernotte was gone.

I walked out of the hospital room, and saw Alyce standing there. I looked at her, and before I could say anything, Alyce understood. Her bravery dissolved, and she broke down. I hugged Alyce, and we both cried, overcome by sorrow and exhaustion. Losing André had been the most painful experience I'd ever had, and I was so grateful I'd had Alyce there for support.

Once André's death certificate had been signed, the head nurse asked me to sit down and wait for the social worker, who would guide me through the next steps. Then came the preparations. I had promised to accompany André's body back to Liège for burial in accordance with Fanny's wishes. To do this, I had to sign a lot of paperwork and charge eight thousand dollars to my credit card to pay for the special steel-lined coffin that was required for legal transport. Alyce called the Vineyard Theatre, which agreed to have a prepared statement to share with the press. She also got in touch with Janet Durand, who called Fanny in Liège and told her that André had passed and that I was planning to fly him back home within the week. I don't know what I would've done if Alyce hadn't been there to help.

I got home from the hospital that night around eight o'clock and retrieved Molly from Miriam. Miriam told me how sorry she was, but I was too shocked to acknowledge what she had said. Once back in the apartment, I clutched Molly in my arms and tried to explain to her through my tears that André would never come home again.

I took in the silence of the apartment, the hugeness of his absence enveloping me. I went into the room where he had slept those past several years, and it was suddenly too much. Still in my long winter coat, I crawled into the bed and laid my head where his head had lain all those years. I still felt his presence in the room, and I held Molly close to my body as I cried myself into a much-needed sleep.

❀   ❀   ❀

André's death was major news in Belgium. André was only fifty-four years old, and the Belgian entertainment community was shocked and saddened. Five days after André died in New York, I was on a plane bound for Brussels. I had gotten myself a seat in first class—just as I had done the first time I flew to Belgium. And I took a night flight—just as I had on that first trip. I sat up the entire trip, staring out the window into the darkness of the night sky. Food and drinks were brought, but I wasn't hungry or thirsty. In truth, I wasn't there at all—I might as well have been sealed in the steel coffin along with André. Emotions only surfaced when I saw Fanny waiting for me in the airport lobby.

"Well, Fanny," I stammered, trying very hard not to break down, "I brought him home."

Fanny drove me back to the family home in Jupille. It seemed a far different place without André. Inside, everything had remained very much as it had been when I first saw it. André's father, Jules, looking older than I remembered, quietly greeted me with a handshake. He was still in his pajamas and robe, and one side of his face seemed to have sustained some paralysis from a recent stroke. I told him how sorry I was for André's death. Fanny repeated my sentiments in French, and I could see from the tears in his eyes that he understood. André's sisters Lilly and Claudette were there as well, and each gave me hugs of comfort that were more awkward than heartfelt. Fanny made me some coffee and prepared some poached eggs with slices of a baguette. I ate what I could, but my depression over André had left me with barely any appetite.

I was very jet-lagged, so I told Fanny that I was tired and needed some sleep. She led me to André's old room. I got out of my clothes, put on my pajamas, and crawled into the small twin bed in which André had slept and read and dreamed as a boy. I fell asleep, thoughts of André filling my mind.

Two days later, the memorial service was held. I travelled to the church with the Ernotte family, my suitcase already packed into the trunk of Fanny's car so that I could go straight to the airport after the service. Dozens of André's theater friends came from Brussels. A crowd of his college classmates also came to say a final farewell. I searched the faces of his friends and colleagues as the priest spoke in French. Everyone looked like they had suffered real loss—especially André's father, who hid his anguished sobs behind his handkerchief. We then proceeded to the cemetery, where André's coffin sat above the freshly dug gravesite, and the priest intoned various prayers. I had nothing to say, and desperately wanted to return home to Molly and to the apartment. I maintained the irrational hope that somehow I would find André there, waiting for me.

Before I left, I hugged each and every one of André's relatives—particularly Fanny, whom I knew I would miss the most. As I got into the cab, I looked back at André's heartbroken family. I waved gently at them. They waved back, and I think we all realized that we were never going to see each other again.

"You have quite a number of phone messages," Alyce said. She'd been house-sitting and taking care of Molly while I'd been gone. I was exhausted, but I told Alyce she could stay at the place since it was so late. I think she knew that I wanted to be alone. "Don't worry about me, Elliot," she said. "You take care of yourself. When you're ready to talk, I'm a phone call and a cab ride away."

All I could think of was André. I couldn't help thinking that he wasn't dead, that he was just out of town directing a play and would be back before I knew it. But André wasn't coming back—that was a fact, and one that I needed to get used to pretty quickly. I wandered into his bedroom and turned on the lights. It still felt like he was there. I could almost smell him. I opened the sliding wooden doors to our closet, and there they were—at least thirty of André's shirts, kept throughout the years like some kind of fashion scrapbook. I took out one shirt after another, removed them from their hangers, and placed them on the bed. I spent the entire night wrapped up in his shirts—still feeling him, smelling him, seeing him in my mind's eye.

The next morning, I got up and went into the living room. I looked through the various editions of the *New York Times* that had been delivered while I was gone. Alyce had pulled out the *Times'* half-page obituary, which featured a picture of André that must have been provided by the Vineyard Theatre. *Playbill* had a more in-depth obituary, listing a great many of André's accomplishments. In both pieces, I was listed as André's "companion." I suppose that was a correct description, since state laws still prevented gay and lesbian couples from being legally married. I knew that André saw me as a hell of a lot more than that—he and I were partners, equals, true loves. I sat there reading the obituaries, and then my sense of loss overwhelmed me all over again.

Bracing myself, I sat down to listen to the messages left on my answering machine. There were calls from various theater people saying how sorry they were to hear that André was sick, messages from people—including Renee—sending condolences after André died, and a message from the program director at the Vineyard Theatre, informing me that they wanted my assistance in organizing a memorial service for André. Finally, there was a message from the office of some lawyer, Bruce Dolan. I was in no state to talk to any of these people, so I ignored the messages and clicked on the television.

But a few hours later, I gritted my teeth and called the Vineyard Theatre to work out some of the details for the memorial service. They wanted to do it on the afternoon of May 10, a Monday, the better to ensure good attendance, since most theater people didn't have to do matinees on Mondays. The Vineyard asked me if I'd do a eulogy, and I promised I would. As I hung up the phone, I still felt unable to accept the reality that André was gone from my life forever.

In the month that followed, I only left the apartment to walk Molly or to buy basic groceries. I was despondent. I started to take the Demerols left over from André's desktop supply. The tablets helped me sleep, which was all I wanted to do anyway. I just existed in the apartment, taking mental stock of everything that was in it and dwelling on my memories of André. Everything reminded me of him—his books, his favorite albums, his shirts.

Whenever I came back to the building after walking Molly, I'd check the mailbox. One day, I found a thicker-than-usual statement from American Express. I opened the envelope and was shocked to see that I owed over thirty thousand dollars in hospital costs and other expenses that I had incurred while caring for André. Sitting on the couch in a stupor, I saw the light flashing on the answering machine. I pressed play, and out came another message from that lawyer, Bruce Dolan. For all I knew, his office was calling on behalf of the hospital because they had discovered that I was not actually André's brother and they wanted to sue me for fraud. Worried, I popped another Demerol and ignored the message again.

"Elliot? Elliot, are you in there? Come on, Elliot. Open up! It's me. Elliot! Elliot, let me in!"

Someone was yelling and banging on my front door. The noise filtered into my dreams of days gone by in Brooklyn, in Bethel, in Belgium. But as I rose from my nap on the couch, I realized that the voice shouting on the other side of it was my kid sister Renee. I opened the door.

"Well, look who's here?" I said.

"Can I come in and talk to you, Elliot?"

"Go ahead," I said, not caring how ragged I looked and how dirty and disorganized the apartment was.

"What's happening to you in here, Elliot?" she asked, looking around the apartment with alarm. "When's the last time you've had a shower?"

"Listen, did you come here to evaluate my grooming habits?" I snapped.

"No," Renee shot back, "I came here to tell you that Rachelle died yesterday."

My baby sister shouted me out of my trance state with news of our oldest sister's death. Silence hung in the air between us as I took in what Renee had told me.

"Listen," she continued, standing toe to toe with me for perhaps the first time in her life, "I know you've lost André and that you must be devastated. But this is our sister, Elliot. Rachelle has been suffering so badly for all these months, and now she's gone. I thought you might like to know that you have lost a sister."

"Renee, I'm sorry, but I can't fucking hear this now. I just can't, okay?"

I turned away from her, and looked out the window at the skyline, completely unable to process the news that Rachelle was gone.

"Will you come to the funeral with me and Yuri, Elliot? Goldie and her family will meet up with us there. But we'll take you with us, Elliot, if you like."

"No, no, Renee," I said, feeling dizzy. "I'm sorry, but I can't."

She looked at me sadly, and said, "Okay, Elliot. You do what you need to do. But before I leave, I want to ask you something. Do you really want to live like this? Don't you think that André would want you to take part in life? He would never want to see you like this—*I* don't want to see you like this. I love you, Elliot, but I can't watch you destroy yourself." She began to cry a bit, but then gathered herself and walked to the door. "When you need Yuri and me, Elliot, we will be there. Reach out to us. Don't bury yourself in the past. We all die, Elliot. After everything you've gone through over these difficult years in this city, you should know that better than anyone. It's up to you, Elliot. It's up to you."

She left, quietly closing the door behind her. Alone in the apartment again and feeling foolish, I wanted to scream at the entire world. There was too much hurt everywhere I looked, and it made me feel so hopeless that I wanted to die.

The phone rang. Out of sheer anger, I grabbed the phone and shouted, "What?"

"Yes, is this Mr. Tiber?"

"Yes, who is this?" I shouted again into the phone.

Seemingly unperturbed, the voice on the other end politely said, "This is Rita Johnson with the offices of Bruce Dolan. Will you hold to speak with Mr. Dolan, sir?"

I was too worked up to do anything but say, "Yeah, sure."

"Please hold then, Mr. Tiber."

Silence followed, and then a man with a low voice got on the line.

"Hello, Mr. Tiber?"

"Yes?" I answered, warily.

"This is Bruce Dolan. I am Mr. Ernotte's lawyer, and I wish to offer my condolences for your loss."

I was caught off guard by his words and thanked him.

"We've been trying to reach you for several weeks. Is everything all right?"

"Yes, I've been . . . sleeping," I responded, still unsure why he was calling me.

"I understand, sir. But it is important that you come to my office as soon as you can."

"What's this all about?" I asked.

"It has to do with Mr. Ernotte's will, in which you have been named. Can you be here by four o'clock this afternoon?"

❁   ❁   ❁

I had no idea what I was going to find out. I put on the most presentable clothes I could find and walked with Molly to the lawyer's office on Forty-seventh Street. If I was going to hear bad news, I wanted to have my dog with me.

In the waiting room, I introduced myself, but I didn't sit down. I just stood there by the front desk, holding Molly.

After a few minutes, a tall man with a shock of grey hair walked out and extended his hand. "Mr. Tiber? Bruce Dolan. It's good to finally meet you."

"*Finally* meet me? What, am I known for something?"

"Well, let's say that André was very fond of you."

"How do you know André? I don't know what any of this is about."

"I can see you don't. Please follow me. We can talk about this better in my office."

Mr. Dolan explained that he had worked as André's lawyer for the past nine years. "André had me draw up his will so that, upon his demise, you would be named as sole executor of his will and the sole beneficiary of a life insurance policy. In addition, he further stipulated that you would be the recipient of any and all bank accounts expressly in his name should he predecease you."

I had no clue what this man was talking about, and told him as much.

"What it means, Mr. Tiber, is that you have inherited approximately half a million dollars."

I took a few deep breaths and said, "Mr. Dolan, if this is some kind of sick joke, then I can assure you—I ain't laughing."

"No," he said matter-of-factly. "It's no joke. Here are the documents." He handed me a folder of documents. I looked through them and recognized André's signature throughout. It all seemed so unreal. But the more Mr. Dolan explained how everything led back to me, the more it started to sink in that this was really happening.

"I don't know what to say."

"Oh, that seems odd," Mr. Dolan said, with a gentle laugh. "From what André told me, you've always had something to say."

When I came home from Belgium, I had had no idea how I was going to handle all the expenses I had incurred over the last weeks. Within a week of my meeting with Mr. Dolan, I found myself able to pay down the entire American Express credit card bill with a single check. Through André's incredible generosity, I was totally debt free and sitting on a half-million dollars. I was financially secure, but my heart still ached over the loss of my eternal friend.

A little after three o'clock in the afternoon of May 10, I put on a black suit, tucked a purple rose into my lapel, and headed down to East Fifteenth Street for André's memorial service at the Vineyard. The lobby displayed photographs of André and posters of his productions. The theater was packed—all four hundred seats were occupied, and many more friends, former students, and colleagues stood in the back and in the aisles.

I had asked Emily Mann to let me be the last one to speak. For an hour before I went on, theater producers, agents, and actors spoke of their adoration of André and testified to his unique talent. As I listened, with Alyce seated beside me, it dawned on me that many of the people who were speaking so lovingly of André were the same people who had caused André so much misery in his career. I watched in growing disbelief as these hypocrites made their way up to the podium and spoke of André's great gifts and kind heart. There was the theater critic who had written an unfairly scathing review of one of André's first works in New York, now declaring him a gifted visionary. What a genius André had been! Then there was the producer, one of those self-important big spenders who had foisted his own unsolicited opinions onto André's direction of the show, never letting him forget for a second that it was only their money that mattered, and not his art. What a wonderfully sensitive and considerate colleague André had been! And there was the same Big-Name Actress who had denied André his shot on Broadway, wiping away false tears with a handkerchief and praising him for being a true craftsman, a talented and dedicated director. What an honor it had been to work with him!

I couldn't take any more of this bullshit. I looked at Alyce, who was trying to stay focused on the positive memories being shared about André. Yeah, it was true—he *had* been a talented director, a wonderful colleague, a visionary. But how would these assholes have truly known that? Where had they been when he needed them? What had they done to help this genius get the fame he deserved? Why hadn't any of these special, important people come to see him when he was sick?

I grew increasingly livid at the hypocrisy that was oozing throughout the theater in memory of my love. Suddenly, I knew what had to happen. I had to speak on behalf of André, who was no longer able to speak for himself, and who had always been too refined and too genteel to ever tell these "friends" of his the truth. I was going to tell these spineless sycophants what they'd done to André.

I stood at the podium, tilted the microphone closer to my mouth, and spilled forth my soul with all the subtlety and neatness of a carotid artery rupture.

"Well," I began, looking slowly to my left and right, "I want to thank everyone for coming today. I'm sure that André would be very touched to hear all the nice things that you have said about him." I stopped for a few seconds, listening to the low rumble of conversations going on in the audience. Having tired of listening to the speakers, people obviously thought it was fine to chat among themselves. I was unsure of what to say at first, but then the words just came.

"My beautiful André is gone from this life forever. He's gone from this theater, this town, this world—a world that took so much more out of him than he was allowed to give back, a world that left him feeling robbed and disappointed. You see," I continued, my voice growing louder the more I spoke, "there was a lot more to André than the man you knew. The man you worked with, and the man who tried so bravely and constantly to be understood, to be heard, and to be trusted! I don't know how many of you really understand, sitting here . . . sitting here with your crocodile tears and your kind words and your protected, pretty, perfect *fucking* cozy careers. Warm spotlights and secure projects were always assured for you. Always a 'green-light-go' wherever you walk. And always a quick escape hatch to dive down whenever a show doesn't work out." I believe it was right around the time that I loudly pronounced the word "fucking" that most of the chatter stopped.

"You don't understand," I said, pointing my finger out at them in angry accusation. "You don't have any kind of a clue what André went through. He spent so much of his life and his energy trying to be someone you would all approve of. Someone you would all recognize as a creative director worth your time, your money, and your precious investment. You knew the André that you saw on stages, in theaters, and at opening nights. But there was so much more to him. I knew the *real* André," I said, "and I'm going to tell you about him." At that point, utter silence blanketed the theater, as the initial confusion now shifted into a kind of collective group shock. My despair was equal to my rage. "André Gilbert Ernotte was a sweet and trusting son to his parents, and a loving brother to his sisters. The little boy in Belgium who listened to jazz records and wrote poems had all kinds of visions that he hoped he might someday be able to turn into reality. He tried to make his place as an *artist* in this vapid, empty, rotten, vicious cesspool we call 'show business.'

"I knew the André who came home night after night from rehearsals, broken and bent and hollow, but always trying to keep his creative heart beating and his mind alive while he worked on your wretched vanity productions. Trying to convince me that after more than twenty years as a fine and competent director, it didn't bother him that so many of you still felt you had the right to tell him how to direct a scene, where to place a spotlight, when to cue music, who to hire for a role.

"You ran my André around this city like some kind of warped puppet on a string—your very own Pinocchio, who might never have become a real boy under your care. Well, from where I have stood these past twenty-eight years, André Ernotte grew from a real boy into a real man. And he will always be the very best and kindest and most gracious director that I have ever known."

I shook my head and slammed both my hands hard against the top of the podium. "But of course, *you* never did know André. You never really looked and saw him, standing there right in front of you. And so, yes! Yes, my beloved André is dead. He is fucking dead! He will never come back. And since he ain't here to get any of this off his chest," I spat out at the paralyzed audience, "I came here to do it for him. In case there are any misunderstandings out there, let's get one thing straight: I despise each and every one of you for making every one of André's days here in this town that much harder and sadder."

I looked around the room at the rows of theater vampires. I then calmly removed the purple rose from the lapel of my jacket and placed it on the podium as I started to hear small bursts of whispers from those in their seats.

"Who *are* you people, anyway? What the hell are you doing here? Do you even know what I'm talking about?" I was starting to completely fall apart, but the words kept flying out of my mouth. "All of you are sitting here today in this theater that my precious André loved so much. You're here to pay your respects. But I don't think you understand what a horrid, hypocritical pile of shit you really are. You had a genius in your midst, okay? A beautiful guy! And you tortured and taxed his spirit so hard that he didn't stand a chance when his body got sick. So for that, I thank you. No, really. *Thank* you! Thanks a fucking lot!

"And so," I concluded, having poured every bit of poison out of my system and onto the stage, "to my lover André, I have this to say: 'Goodnight, sweet prince.' And to the rest of you here today, I say, 'Go fuck yourselves!'"

The boos and hisses increased, drowning out the sound of Alyce clapping in loyal if confused support. I took a step back from the podium, jumped over the edge of the stage, and walked straight out of the theater. I charged past the gallery of mascaraed ghouls and left the whole moronic world to which my love and I had already given too many fruitless years. *I set you free, my friend,* I said to André in my mind. *I hope you liked it.*

❀   ❀   ❀

My body was filled with adrenaline as I walked, and I had to keep fighting the urge to pick something up and hurl it through the storefronts I walked past. I must have walked dozens of blocks before I found myself in front of a Hertz car rental center. At that moment, I realized with certainty that I needed to leave, to get out of town. I gave the gentleman behind the counter some information, pulled out my American Express card, and was soon behind the wheel of a small economy car.

I didn't know where I was going, and I didn't care. *The more distance I put between myself and those people right now, the better,* I thought to myself. Before I realized it, I was heading north. I drove along the West Side Highway; and then onto the Major Deegan in the Bronx. I had taken this route hundreds of times—it was almost automatic. The next thing I knew, I was on the New York Thruway approaching the exit for Route 17B. The car and I were headed up to a place that was all too familiar. Next stop: White Lake, New York.

The last time I had been to White Lake was for the ABC interview in 1994, and that was only for a few hours in a limo driven by someone else. Now here I was, driving a two-door Ford Fiesta by myself into the darkness of the upstate New York night. I felt like I had slipped back in time. I approached the usual spot, and there it was—the ugly site where our motel had been located was almost exactly as I had left it five years ago. I pulled over to the side of the road, killed the headlights, and sat there in the car, looking around.

What had been the main building of the El Monaco remained an Italian restaurant, but it was a Monday night and the restaurant was closed. Meanwhile, the old Ritz Cinema across from the old motel was now a *glatt* kosher supermarket. The town had changed. Hasidic Jews had begun to move into the area and had taken over many of the local businesses—a clear sign that my old Nazi enemies from 1969 were dead, converted, or had left town. I got out of the car and lit a cigarette. How many cigarettes had I smoked here? How many evenings had I felt like this—tired, distressed, and alone?

Standing in the boneyard of my bad motel and thinking again about how great Woodstock was, I realized that it was oddly comforting to be back in this place. Whether I liked it or not, White Lake was sacred territory for me. And because this was only the second time in my life I had been in the place without Momma shrieking my name, I enjoyed the chance to just experience it for what it was.

But once I got back into the car, the incredible stress of the day caught up to me with a vengeance. I was completely wiped out, and there was no way I was going to be able to head back to the city that same night. I checked that the car was locked, in case Bigfoot came along and wanted to eat me. Then I pushed the driver's seat back and lowered it all the way. Soon I was fast asleep.

I awoke in the morning, and wondered for a few seconds whether I had dreamed the past thirty years of my life. Maybe it was only the day after the Woodstock festival finished, and I was just sleeping off the exhaustion. Looking around in the early light, so much seemed so familiar—the doors on the old motel buildings were still painted in different Miami Beach colors. But not everything was the same. The lawns I'd had to mow for ten years were gone, replaced by a big blacktop parking lot.

I lit a cigarette, blowing the smoke out into the fresh country air as I quietly made my way through a stretch of trees. And there it was: the same lake in which Pop and I had seen naked men and women—even children—splashing together happily in harmony. I looked down into the calm water rippling away from the grassy banks. In the early morning breeze, I thought I could hear the singular voice of Richie Havens singing "Freedom" from Yasgur's farm across the water. I thought about a lot of things. I remembered my time with Felix and Jerry out in Hollywood, fixing up Marie Dressler's old mansion while failing at making a new life. I remembered the crazy nights I spent looking for love in those leather clubs. I remembered the love that I finally found with André. I remembered my adventures in Belgium, faking my way in French and stumbling into a successful career as a TV show creator, a lecturer, a novelist, a playwright, and a screenwriter. I remembered the unchecked hedonism of New York City in the late 1970s, and how the wildness of that moment devolved far too soon into a world of pain and unimaginable loss. And I remembered the past few months, the sorrow and the exhaustion and the anger that had boiled over in that cathartic moment the day before.

It was all there before me like the smoothly flowing water in that lake—all the events that had occurred in my life up to that moment. Was there anything I would have changed or tried to do differently? The answer came to me, fast and certain: *No.*

White Lake had helped me get my bearings again. By going back to the place where my journey had started, I began to figure out what my journey had been, and where it might go next. Maybe that was the lesson I learned: you have to go home again if you ever really want to leave.

As I drove back to the city, I remembered what Renee had said when she came to see me at the apartment. How André would never have wanted to see me spend the rest of my life dwelling on the past. Suddenly, I knew in my heart that I had to keep moving forward, to always reach for the strange and new and wonderful in this life.

The early morning sun blazed in the May sky, shining like a single spotlight focused on the road ahead.

Epilogue

Soon after I returned from White Lake, I packed a suitcase, picked up Molly, and gave up our beautiful Manhattan Plaza apartment, which held too many memories. I rented a car and drove to New Jersey to make amends with Renee and Yuri. They received me with open arms—we had all been through a lot. They allowed me to stay with them to heal and find the spring in my step again, and so I spent a few weeks at their home. I probably overstayed my welcome, but they said nothing. Caught up in my deep despair over André's sudden passing, I found myself writing down all the events of my life up until then, and I noticed how Woodstock figured prominently. A few pages turned into nearly two spiral notebooks filled to the brim with thoughts, feelings, and remembrances. I still felt the heartache of losing my soul mate, but I found that the writing was giving me something I needed badly—perspective.

While I was recovering at Renee's, I got a call from Alyce Finell, who said that a bunch of reporters had expressed interest in talking with me for the thirtieth anniversary of the Woodstock festival. I knew it was about time to do something, so I returned some calls and agreed to do some new radio and TV interviews. One day in July, I got a call from a man named Roy Howard up in Bethel, New York. It turned out that Roy was the current owner of the farmhouse and surrounding land that had once been owned and lived in by my old friend Max Yasgur. Roy wanted to know if I would come up and be a part of the anniversary gathering that he and his companion, Jeryl Abramson, had planned. "Sounds like something I'd like to do," I said, "but where would I stay?"

"No worries, Elliot," Roy said. "You come up here, and you can stay with us at our place. It'll be a real homecoming." I liked the sound of that. Roy made me feel—maybe for the first time—that my contribution to the Woodstock miracle had earned me some love and respect from the same place that had only ever regarded me with anger and hatred in the past.

So off Molly and I went. Roy and Jeryl's anniversary event featured all kinds of local musical talent, and was attended by hundreds. It felt more like the original festival than any of the other commemorative events I'd gone to. I talked, I reminisced, I made friends. I enjoyed myself.

With the money that André had left to me, I spent the next five years wandering around the world like a gypsy. Thailand, Japan, Taiwan, France, Italy, Morocco, Mexico—I just kept moving, taking Molly and my growing Woodstock manuscript everywhere I went. Eventually, I got tired of traveling. Thirsting for a proper egg cream, I returned to New York.

In New York, I tried on my Super Elli costume again, trotting my new manuscript around to all the book publishers. Unfortunately, the costume didn't fit me so well anymore, and most of the publishers that I met didn't seem to see the story. Then, through Alyce, I met Joan and Lydia Wilen. The Wilen sisters were successful, bestselling authors and screenplay writers. As we got to know each other, I came to realize that Lydia and especially Joan were incredible networkers. They knew a lot about the book business, an area in which I'd lost reliable contacts over the years. I told Lydia and Joan about my life, and they seemed to appreciate my taste for the absurd. They also saw an opportunity to help me.

It turned out that they had just published a new book, *How to Sell Your Screenplay,* through a small firm on Long Island called Square One Publishers. Joan told me about the company's publisher, Rudy Shur, with whom she and Lydia had worked for years. He had a great track record of producing solid titles, and they actually *liked* him. Joan had a strong intuition that we'd get along—she felt we had a lot in common. She suggested I talk to Rudy about my Woodstock idea. I took her shrewd advice to heart, and gave him a call the next day.

After I explained the story, Rudy told me that while he liked the idea, he didn't publish memoirs. He said that I would be much better off finding a company that specialized in autobiographies, and gave me some names. At that very moment, Super Elli took over. I asked him, "Just tell me—where were you in August of 1969?"

Silence.

Uh-oh! I thought. *Maybe he hadn't even been born yet. Oy!*

Finally, he responded. "In August of 1969, I was a partner in a psychedelic shop located in Forest Hills, New York. It's a long story, but I can tell you from experience: never open a retail store located on a second floor." We both laughed. Then he spoke again. "Okay, send me the material and I will look at it—but do yourself a favor and call the other publishers."

I contacted the publishers he'd recommended, but the few who actually took my calls weren't interested in my book. Two weeks passed. I called Rudy back.

"So?" I asked. "What did you think?"

"I read through the material," he said, taking his time to answer. "It's certainly interesting, but it's too focused on the festival. There's not enough about you and your family."

"Not enough stuff about my family?" I asked, puzzled. "People want to know about Woodstock. Who cares that my mother was a crazy Russian she-devil?"

"Well," Shur replied, "people already know about Woodstock. It's in the history books. There's nothing new to really say about the festival itself, but that story about you and your parents and how Woodstock came along and saved you guys from ruin? *That* is the heart of the story."

"Great," I said, feeling sure that Rudy was on my side. "Let's do it!"

"No, you don't get it," Rudy continued, sounding a bit torn. "Let me explain something. This is a memoir. I don't publish memoirs. My house is not set up to produce and sell your kind of book the way it deserves to be produced and sold. It's not for us," he said. "At least, not the way you've got it written right now."

"Well, then," I said, "if it's okay with you, I'll rewrite the storyline a little and send it back to you to see if it is more in line with what you're thinking. No strings attached. Just let me try."

Ten phone calls and a number of rewrites later, we had become friends. We had both grown up in less-than-normal households—and we shared an odd connection. We discovered that his mother and mine were both European refugees named Sonia!

With our connection developing, and the upcoming fortieth anniversary of Woodstock promising good publicity for the book, I was able to convince Rudy to take me on and put out the first memoir under the Square One name. In turn, Rudy convinced me to work with a co-writer, bestselling author Tom Monte, to smooth out the rougher patches in my manuscript.

Taking Woodstock was published as a hardcover in June 2007, and earned critical praise from *Publishers Weekly, Library Journal, Booklist, Kirkus Reviews,* and *Midwest Book Review,* among others. In response to all the requests for appearances coming from California, Square One's marketing and publicity director Anthony Pomes set up a three-week book tour he called our "West Coast Invasion." So I packed up Molly and a dozen of my own copies of the book, and wearing a t-shirt I had made with the *Taking Woodstock* cover on the front, I headed off to California.

As part of my itinerary, I was scheduled to appear on a San Francisco morning talk show. The show taped segments on Friday mornings and aired them two days later. Molly and I showed up around 5:30 AM at the TV studio, and a producer's assistant groggily brought us to the green room. I sat down in a chair across from the only other person in the room, a young man who told me his name was David. David explained that he was the assistant to the show's first guest, who was already in the studio with the host. I looked at the green room's video monitor, which showed a live feed from the taping session. I did a double-take when I saw that the guest being interviewed was none other than celebrated film director Ang Lee.

I recognized Lee from the Academy Awards, where he'd won the Oscar for Best Director the year before for *Brokeback Mountain.* I was a huge fan of the movie, and spoke of it so often, in fact, that Anthony Pomes at Square One had begun to refer to my project as "Brokeback Woodstock." Now, here I was, appearing on the very same TV show as Ang Lee!

The show could have interviewed any other famous director that day. But no, it had to have been Ang Lee, an artist who had created the most successful movie about gay love ever made. If that wasn't serendipity, I don't know what was. Clearly, the universe was telling me to make my move. There was a stillness in the air as I watched Lee talk with the host. At one point, I heard the host ask Ang where he got his ideas for films. Grinning, he told the host that he got ideas for films from just about anything. In that single moment, I thought of all the pleasure, pain, success, failure, laughter, tears, joy, and disappointment I'd experienced in my life. I knew that I would be lucky if I got even two minutes with Lee back in the green room before he left—and I knew that I had been waiting for those two minutes for almost forty years.

So when Ang Lee got back to the green room, I did what I have always done: I opened my mouth and talked. I introduced myself and told Lee how much I enjoyed his films. I was impressed at how serene and humble he was. It turned out that he was appearing on the show to promote his new film, *Lust, Caution,* which had been slapped with a NC-17 rating due to its explicit sex scenes. I quickly told him why I was appearing on the show. And to further illustrate the point, I deftly pointed down at the book cover on the front of my T-shirt. Whaddya know? My chutzpah made Lee laugh.

And then, as the early-morning seconds ticked down, I went for it full-blast. I told Ang Lee my story—Pop and Momma and that soul-sucking motel and Max Yasgur and Mike Lang and the miracle of Woodstock. Lee listened, laughing again when I told him about how my Jewish mother nearly had a stroke when I made a huge white cross out of bed sheets on the motel lawn in preparation for the landing of Mike Lang's heaven-sent helicopter.

"Here," I said, pulling out the last of my copies of the book and sticking my business card inside it. "This is my story. If you think you might want to do a comedy next, maybe we can work together."

He nodded graciously and thanked me for the book. Then he casually passed it over to his assistant. I figured that was the universe's way of saying that my pitch had failed. But I shook hands with Lee and we wished each other luck.

I left Molly in the green room with a production assistant and headed into the studio to tape my own interview segment. I felt like my fingertips were pulsing with electricity from having talked with Ang Lee. I tried my best to keep cool during the interview, but all I could think about was my amazing chance encounter with that award-winning cinematic genius. It wasn't until I was in a taxi leaving the studio with Molly in my arms that I started to get depressed. I began to think that I might have come on too strong, or presented the book too quickly. Maybe my book promotion T-shirt prevent-

2008. With Ang Lee at Focus Features' New York office. I'm so grateful to Ang for turning my story into such a beautiful film.

ed me from being taken seriously. I was second-guessing everything. By the time I got back to the hotel, I was convinced that I would never hear from Ang Lee again.

Apparently, fate had other ideas. Two months later, my phone rang. The caller was none other than James Schamus, then the CEO at Focus Features and Ang Lee's friend and frequent collaborator. He told me that both Ang and he had read my book, loved it, and thought it had all the makings of a freshly funny and heartfelt look at the Woodstock Nation.

As he talked, I thought to myself, *This isn't happening. I must be hallucinating.* In fact, it wasn't until January 2008, when Focus Features sent out an official press release announcing the film adaptation, that I began to believe that my story was really going to be made into a movie. That shot at a bona fide big-budget motion picture had finally come my way.

The rest of the year felt like a dream. I liked that my book, brought out by an indie publisher, was also being made into a film by an indie production company. The film was shot from August to October 2008 in the town of New Lebanon, about two hours from White Lake. To help create the Woodstock moment, Ang got the locals to play hippie extras. I visited the set on the first day of shooting, and was able to have Renee and Yuri and Alyse's son do cameos as White Lake townsfolk shocked by the sudden frontal nudity of the Earthlight Players. I myself appeared as an older leather-clad S&M daddy in a gay bar sequence that was ultimately cut from the film.

The film's release was scheduled to coincide with the fortieth anniversary of Woodstock. In anticipation of the movie's success, twelve international firms bought the book's translation rights, along with book club and audio book rights. I was busy doing interviews either for the film or for the book for nearly eleven months. I was even invited to attend the Bologna Film Festival as a guest of honor, the visit tied in to the publication of my book in Italian.

In the midst of all this joy, though, sadness again came my way. Molly had not been feeling well and couldn't walk without falling over. When I took her to a vet, x-rays showed that she had an inoperable brain tumor. She was my last tie to the life I had had with André, and the decision to put her to sleep was very hard. It reminded me that even when everything is going well, tragedy can strike. Life is fragile.

Right around my seventy-fourth birthday, James and Ang invited me to a private screening of the finished film. As the movie unfolded, I saw my own twisted but ultimately redeeming life unfold. I marveled at the creative images that flickered across the screen. When I saw the British actors Imelda Staunton and Henry Goodman playing my Old World Jewish parents, I was amazed. They had done such remarkable work, Imelda perfectly capturing my mother's eccentricities and Henry channeling my father's soft and tender soul. After the film ended, I left the screening room. Ang and James were standing there, waiting to hear how I felt about the final cut. I walked over to them, tears running down my face, and gave them both a huge hug. I told them how superb their work turned out, and how deliriously happy I was with the film.

The film received its international premiere at the Cannes Film Festival, an honor that made me very proud. My life was being shared with filmgoers throughout the world—my story had become a part of history. Back at home about six weeks later, the film was given its national premiere in New York City. It was pouring rain the entire afternoon, and it kept on raining as everyone arrived to walk the red carpet into the theater. I told the many interviewers that the rain was being provided by Focus Features as an homage to the heavy rains that had produced all that mud at the original Woodstock festival.

As we walked in, I happened to see Mike Lang. He and I shook hands warmly—after all, the whole crazy scene might not have happened if he and I hadn't clicked. When the film ended and the lights came up, everyone applauded. I could tell that Mike was as touched by the film as I was, especially after seeing how miraculous our connection had been all those years ago. Onstage, he and I hugged, to the delight of the audience.

In an evening of wonderful moments, perhaps what stayed with me the most was my brief encounter with Meryl Streep. Her daughter, the actor Mamie Gummer, appeared in the picture as Mike Lang's assistant, and so Meryl had come to the premiere to support her. Meryl was very low key, letting her daughter have the spotlight that night, just as any truly loving mother would do. As I made my way over to Meryl, I offered my hand and complimented her on her daughter's performance. She thanked me, and congratulated me on having the story of my life made into a film.

I then told her that my partner for almost thirty years, André Ernotte, had directed her in a play when she studied at Yale—and that André had always spoken affectionately of her over the years. I could see that André's name resonated with her, and she laughed gently, remembering having worked with him. When I told her that the only thing I wished on my special night was that André could have been there with us to enjoy it, she hugged me and nodded her understanding of my loss. We posed together for a few photos, and parted. Having that brief connection with Meryl made me feel that André was looking down on everything that was happening—and smiling.

A small, intimate film about a big, boisterous cultural event, *Taking Woodstock* was not a huge moneymaker. Some liked the film, some didn't. Over the years, though, the movie has been recognized as one of the softer and more contemplative entries in Ang Lee's canon. And it continues to win new fans. Every other day I get emails from people who have seen the film or read my book or have done both, and it fills my heart with joy to see how the story of my life has affected others. I think the film stands up on its own. It may be my story, but it's Ang's vision—and I feel blessed to have gotten to work with him.

Eventually, I got myself a new Yorkie, a little boy named Woody Woodstock. I also wrote a "prequel" memoir called *Palm Trees on the Hudson: A True Story of the Mob, Judy Garland, and Interior Decorating*. I'm still lucky enough to make appearances and to lecture at universities both in the US and abroad, and I've done hundreds of interviews in the last decade. If, as André pointed out to me after my mother's funeral, we are reflections of our past experiences, then I hope the words in this book prove that no matter how wacky your life may be, dreams *can* come true. The key is to never give up. Never be afraid to be a superhero. Who knows what remarkable adventures may come your way? And yes, I still have my Super Elli costume. I'm ready to go wherever the road may lead me.

About the Author

Elliot Tiber is a gay rights pioneer who has written and produced numerous award-winning plays and musical comedies. As a professor of comedy writing and performance, he has taught at the New School and Hunter College in Manhattan. His first novel, *Rue Haute,* was a bestseller in Europe, and was published in the United States as *High Street.* The novel was made into a 1976 French-language feature film adapted and directed by coauthor and partner Andre Ernotte. As a humorist, Mr. Tiber has appeared on CNN, NBC, ABC, CBS, BBC, and CNBC, as well as on television shows in France, England, Tokyo, Moscow, Berlin, Belgium, and elsewhere throughout the world.

Mr. Tiber's memoir *Taking Woodstock,* which he wrote with Tom Monte, was first published in 2007 and was soon after turned into a feature film by director Ang Lee. He is also the author of another memoir that explored his life before Woodstock called *Palm Trees on the Hudson: A True Story of The Mob, Judy Garland, and Interior Decorating.* In addition to his work as a writer, Tiber is a highly sought-after lecturer who has appeared in many international venues. Mr. Tiber lives in the Miami Beach section of Florida, where he continues his work as a writer; a painter; and a humorist.

TAKING WOODSTOCK
A True Story of a Riot, a Concert, and a Life

Elliot Tiber with Tom Monte

Before there was a Woodstock Concert, there was Elliot Tiber working to make a go of his parents' upstate New York motel. The Jewish clientele who had frequented the Catskills had discovered Florida, and the upstate tourist business was dying. To save his family's livelihood, Elliot put on plays and local festivals. In the process, he became the area's issuer of event permits. He even used his own income from work as a Manhattan interior designer to support the family business.

In the summer of 1969, Elliot Tiber's life changed in a way he never could have foreseen. Working in Greenwich Village, a mecca for gays in America, Elliot socialized with the likes of Truman Capote, Tennessee Williams, and a young photographer named Robert Mapplethorpe, and yet managed to keep his gay life a secret from his family. Then on Friday, June 28, Elliot walked into the Stonewall Inn—and witnessed the riot that would galvanize the American gay movement. And on July 15, when Elliot read that the Woodstock Concert promoters were unable to stage the show in Wallkill, he offered them a new venue. Elliot soon found himself swept up in a vortex that would change his life forever.

Taking Woodstock is the funny, touching, and true story of the man who enabled Woodstock to take place. It is also the personal story of one man who took stock of his life, his lifestyle, and his future. In short, it is like no history of Woodstock you have ever read.

$24.95 US • 240 pages • 6 x 9-inch quality paperback • ISBN 978-0-7570-0293-9

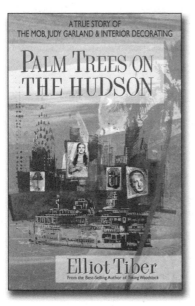

A TRUE STORY OF THE MOB, JUDY GARLAND & INTERIOR DECORATING

PALM TREES ON THE HUDSON

Elliot Tiber

From the Best-Selling Author of Taking Woodstock

PALM TREES ON THE HUDSON

A True Story of the Mob, Judy Garland & Interior Decorating

Elliot Tiber

Palm Trees on the Hudson is the hilarious prequel to Elliot Tiber's best-seller *Taking Woodstock*. Before Elliot found financial success by bringing Woodstock to his motel in upstate New York, before he took part in the historic Stonewall riots, he was one of Manhattan's leading interior designers. The story of how he got there is every bit as fascinating as his Woodstock concert adventure.

For ten years, Elliot worked hard to become one of New York's top interior decorators. Then, in the spring of 1968, Elliot was given the biggest opportunity of his career. He was hired to throw a lavish birthday party aboard a Hudson River dayliner. Included on the guest list were New York's rich and famous—politicians, financiers, entertainers, and even Elliot's icon, Judy Garland. For the big night, the ship was transformed into a floating Arabian fantasy, complete with exotic palm trees, sumptuous food, and gilded servers. Every detail was in place. But as the ship began its circle around Manhattan Island, things began to go awry, and what Elliot had hoped would be his entrée into the heady world of New York's elite turned into a very different kind of event—one that would change the course of Elliot's life.

By turns comic and tragic, *Palm Trees on the Hudson* is the take-no-prisoners memoir that gives readers a more intimate look at the man who went on to fight back at Stonewall and who helped give birth to the Woodstock Nation.

$24.95 US • 192 pages • 6 x 9-inch quality paperback • ISBN 978-0-7570-0351-6

MOMMA & ME -
GUNS WERE
BEING AIMED
AT US WHEN
WE POSED FOR
THIS PHOTO.!

RENEE & ME
THE LITTLE
TEICHBERGS

THERE'S MY ANDRÉ
ON THE LEFT,
TENNESSEE WILLIAMS ON
THE RIGHT, GREG
MOSHER IN THE
MIDDLE -

THE ROAD
TO HELL
STARTS
HERE

El Monaco
MOTEL